FEMINISM SEDUCED

FEMINISM SEDUCED

HOW GLOBAL ELITES USE WOMEN'S LABOR AND IDEAS TO EXPLOIT THE WORLD

Hester Eisenstein

Paradigm Publishers
Boulder • London

Copyright © 2009 Paradigm Publishers

Published in the United States by Paradigm Publishers, 3360 Mitchell Lane, Suite E, Boulder, CO 80301 USA.

Paradigm Publishers is the trade name of Birkenkamp & Company, LLC, Dean Birkenkamp, President and Publisher.

Library of Congress Cataloging-in-Publication Data

Eisenstein, Hester.
  Feminism seduced : how global elites use women's labor and ideas to exploit the world / Hester Eisenstein.
      p. cm.
  Includes bibliographical references and index.
  ISBN 978-1-59451-659-7 (hardcover : alk. paper)
  ISBN 978-1-59451-660-3 (paperback : alk. paper)
  1. Women—Employment. 2. Power (Social sciences) 3. Feminism. 4. Globalization. I. Title.
  HD6053.E35 2009
  331.4—dc22

                                                              2009000036

Printed and bound in the United States of America on acid-free paper that meets the standards of the American National Standard for Permanence of Paper for Printed Library Materials.

Designed and Typeset by Straight Creek Bookmakers.

14 13 12 11 10   2 3 4 5

Contents

❊

Preface and Acknowledgments

It has taken me a relatively short time to write this final version of the book, but a relatively long time to overcome my dread of publishing it. As a card-carrying member of the U.S. academic feminist community, I felt that the framework of analysis that I was developing would be anathema to many, if not most, of my colleagues. Very often in the early stages of this project, I would have the following prototypical conversation with one of my colleagues. Colleague: "What are you working on?" Me (hesitantly): "I am working on a critique of international feminism." Colleague, rising to her full height and looking displeased: "Well, *I'm* an international feminist!" Serve, volley, net, as the Australians are wont to say.

I may as well warn the reader, then, that this book is something of a polemic. Recent histories of the women's movement present the achievements of "second-wave" feminism in a celebratory fashion, as moving us (that is, the women of the world) rapidly and powerfully toward a better world. I want to challenge these optimistic accounts and to raise some troubling issues about how feminist energies, ideologies, and activism have been manipulated in the service of the dangerous forces of globalized corporate capitalism. Hence, "feminism seduced."

At its core this book is a critique of the process of economic globalization, with special emphasis on its implications for women. At this writing, the dangers of extreme globalization are on full display, with the world financial crisis that erupted in 2007–2008. Whatever the final outcome, it is already evident that this crisis threatens continued dramatic losses for banks, other financial institutions, and businesses in the "real" economy, not to mention the impact on individuals and families, whose tax dollars will help pay for the mounting cost of government "bailouts," and whose jobs, housing, and life savings are at risk.

I should also make clear at the outset that this is not an account of the international women's movement and its achievements worldwide. (For information on this topic, I refer interested readers to the many analyses of women's global activism; see, inter alia, Antrobus 2004; Basu 1995; and Ferree and Tripp 2006.) Rather, I look at attempts to use, and indeed to contain, feminist energies, attempts that would not be necessary (it goes without saying) if the women's movement were not a significant force in the world. In order to do this, I present a reinterpretation of the development and growth of the women's movement, principally in the United States but also around the world. I question the triumphalism of many accounts, which see only victories and breakthroughs for women. I want to paint a more nuanced picture, showing some of the relationships between changes in the structure of world capitalism and the (no doubt) revolutionary changes in gender relations over the past thirty plus years.

The point of view I am presenting in this book runs counter to much of the conventional wisdom about the status of feminism in the world today. If we imagine the political spectrum, drawn like a half moon, where liberals are on the left and conservatives are on the right, it is usual to consider that feminists are on the left or liberal side of politics. In the United States, the standard-bearer for feminist principles is the Democratic Party, whereas in recent years the Republicans have made political hay by embracing antifeminist ideas such as the right to life. Similarly, when the left-leaning government of Jose Luis Rodriguez Zapatero was reelected in 2008 in Spain, he appointed a majority of women to his cabinet.[1]

In this framework, liberal-left governments accept feminist ideas about a woman's right to self-determination and autonomy, whereas right-wing governments seek to revive an older idea of a woman's place as subordinated to her husband within the family. It is in this context that the 2008 presidential candidacy of Hillary Rodham Clinton made sense, along with that of the victorious Barack Hussein Obama. Both of these represented the legacy of the civil rights and the women's movement in conventional politics (although the nomination of Sarah Palin for vice president by the Republicans complicated the picture).

Following this logic, most writers would probably argue that in this period the major struggle, for feminists, is to counter the extreme antiwoman policies of the Republican Party, and the extreme antiwoman policies of fundamentalist Christian and Islamic establishments at home and abroad. Against a retrogressive view of women's role as subordinated to fathers and husbands, feminists would argue for the right of women to be considered fully autonomous human beings around the world. And I do not disagree with any of this.

But even though at one level this is an accurate picture of world events, at another level it leaves out the realities of economic globalization. I want to propose an alternative interpretation of the rise of contemporary feminism, within the context of global capitalism, and to introduce the idea of feminist complicity (witting or unwitting), or perhaps a better word would be congruence: in what ways do aspects of the contemporary feminist project aid and abet the strength and power of neoliberalism, or free-market capitalism? To make this argument, I want to show how the many and varied feminist struggles of the 1970s have been selectively filtered into what I call hegemonic, mainstream feminism, of a kind that can be readily used by people whose motives are anything but woman-friendly.

In recent years mainstream organizations have taken up the claims of feminists that women play a major role in economic life. Consider, for example, the following blurb for a Demos forum held in 2008 in New York City:

> In 2006, *The Economist* coined the word "womenomics" when it declared, "Forget China, India and the Internet, economic growth is driven by women." In a three-part series it cited studies suggesting that the rapid entry of women into the workforce has added more to GDP than new jobs for men—and more in productivity than the technology sector. The World Economic Forum now explicitly publishes an annual gender empowerment index as a critical component in each country's economic competitiveness. The World Bank has launched a major initiative, "Gender Equality as Smart Economics."[2]

As feminists, should we not rejoice? Does it not appear that, at long last, the powers that be have begun to recognize the economic and social contributions of women? Is this not what feminists have been pleading for? Not so fast! What I will argue is that this apparent acceptance of feminist principles is in fact an attempt to co-opt the energies of feminism into the project of corporate globalization, an enterprise that has been having disastrous effects on the lives of most women.

The idea that corporate capitalism has found feminism useful is not original with me. Some years ago Judith Stacey pointed to the "ironic role second-wave feminism has played as an unwitting midwife to the massive social transformations of work and family life that have occurred in the post–World War II era," and to how "feminist ideology helped legitimate the massive structural changes in American work and family that invisibly accompanied the transition to post-industrial society in the 1960s and 1970s" (Stacey 1987, 8). Internationally, Gayatri Chakravorty Spivak (1999) has pointed to the uses of Western feminism for the expansion of globalized capitalism.[3]

More recently, Johanna Brenner (2003) has argued that mainstream feminist goals are entirely compatible with the economic doctrines of corporate globalization. Zillah R. Eisenstein (2007) has pointed to the use of "sexual decoys" by the now openly imperial United States. And Kristin Bumiller (2008) has argued that the feminist movement against sexual violence has been "appropriated" by the neoliberal state. I want to elaborate on these insights in what follows.

The premise of this book is that we are living through what Ed Herman calls a "counterrevolution," "in which the governing classes of the West, taking advantage of the collapse of the Soviet Union, corporate globalization, increased media concentration and commercialization, the sharp attrition of labor organization and political influence, and hence the greater political power of the corporate elite, have been dismantling the welfare state and noncorporate rights and entitlements and moving the world toward a laissez-faire and dog-eat-dog—or rather tiger-eat-rabbit—world" (Herman 2006, 1).

My account of feminism is located in the context of the world in 2009, with the United States the major economic and political actor, economically weakened since the 1970s but still claiming global military and political hegemony. Arrayed against it are the European Union, Japan, and the newly industrialized countries (NICs); the rising economies of Brazil, India, and China; and Russia, wounded but aspiring to return to being a major power.[4] At the bottom of the world order are the impoverished countries of sub-Saharan Africa, South Asia, and Latin America, wracked by poverty, war, and disease. Interacting with all of these nation-states are the "multinational" corporations, by and large based in the developed countries, protected by their governments, and competing as part of an international struggle over market share and resources.

The fundamental goal of the developed countries is to make the world safe for the expansion of capitalism in its neoliberal form. This is a brutal, ruthless, and dangerous system, precisely because it is based on economic competition and military force. But the nature of the system is effectively disguised by its multiple engines of propaganda and cultural persuasion. Not least of these is the claim that the United States is primarily a force for good in the world, a country that seeks only the extension of democracy and free markets to the people now deprived of these essential benefits. In this welter of propaganda, one central claim is that the extension of capitalist democracy is the best hope for the world's women.

I disagree with this claim. Despite changes in my thinking since the heady days of second-wave feminism, I retain from that era a conviction that the international women's movement has a role to play in building a world where poverty and exploitation can be overcome. It is, of course, nonsense to think that a small minority of women can significantly modify the current international capitalist order. It is, however, imaginable that a majority of women—fundamentally united on their goals and the means to pursue them—could indeed challenge this system, given that it depends utterly on their labor, productive and reproductive.

Right now, however, there is considerable confusion as to where the interests of women lie. Is the extension of the capitalist system to untouched areas of the world in fact the best bet for women to achieve autonomy, as April Gordon argues (Gordon, 1996)? Or is there no such thing as a unified women's movement, or even a set of interests uniting all women, since women in all of their variety are so diverse and incommensurate in their needs, cultures, and consciousness as to no longer constitute a historical subject, as some transnational feminists argue (Grewal and Kaplan 2000)? Or do the majority of the world's women require an alternative to corporate capitalism for their liberation? I argue in this book for the latter view.

My approach in this book differs sharply from that of the school of "transnational feminism" as developed by Inderpal Grewal and Caren Kaplan. I share much common ground with these writers inasmuch as they critique international capitalism, as I do, as a "system founded on inequality and exploitation" (Grewal and Kaplan 2000, 2). But where I part ways with them is when they speak of the impossibility of transcending the differences between Third World and First World women to create a united international women's movement that can be a force for political and social change. Indeed, they explicitly reject such a project: "It would be impossible for us to advocate a transnational feminism as an improved or better or cleaned up kind of international or global feminism. Transnational feminism, for example, is not to be celebrated as free of these oppressive conditions. In fact, there *is no such thing* as a feminism free of asymmetrical power relations. Rather, transnational feminist practices, as we call them, involve forms of alliance, subversion, and complicity within which asymmetries and inequalities can be critiqued" (Grewal and Kaplan 2000, 2; emphasis in original). I cannot accept the pessimism of this point of view, since it leads to a politics of endless analysis and critique rather than to a place of unity and shared political struggle.

Capitalism as a system uses women's productive and reproductive labor, as socialist feminists have pointed out for at least two centuries. But in addition, the system is now making active use of women's ideological and political labor, taking the ideas of feminism and turning them to its own ends. I want to expose this exploitation of feminist ideas and of women's labor, and suggest that the road to women's liberation does not lie through the infinite extension of free-market capitalism through globalization. I also want to contest the idea that there is no alternative to globalization or global capitalism (more on these terms later on). Many writers (including feminists) have expressed the view that there is no alternative to capitalism. But I believe that one of the most important things we on the Left can do is to reiterate the notion that alternatives to the present system are possible. In the slogan of the World Social Forum, another world is possible, and another world is necessary.[5]

But one requirement for the creation of another world is the need to see the actually existing world clearly. How does corporate capitalism function today? More specifically, how have the captains of capitalism accommodated feminism, how have they made use of feminist ideology, and how have they facilitated changes in the condition of women that, for some, have created unimaginable freedom and luxury, while for others, unrelenting poverty, illness, and despair?[6]

This is a synthetic work, based not on primary research, but on the plethora of existing studies on gender and globalization. I therefore stand on the shoulders of a couple of generations of women's studies scholars whose writings made this book possible. This book is also a product of the antiglobalization, or social justice, movement that famously burst onto the U.S. scene in Seattle in 1999. This work draws simultaneously on the traditions of women's studies scholarship and of political economy. Although addressed to members of the international women's movement, it also seeks to persuade male colleagues on the academic and political Left of the central role of women and of gender in the operations of global capital.

This book is broad in scope, and many of the topics I am tackling belong to the domain of specialists. I am sure, therefore, that scholars and activists alike will want to take issue with my interpretation. But I very much welcome a debate about what I am saying here. A great strength of second-wave feminism has been the willingness to entertain a rich variety of viewpoints and to argue freely over them. It is in this spirit of open dialogue that I offer this book to the reader.

STRUCTURE OF THE BOOK

The structure of the book is as follows. In the Introduction, I will trace the autobiographical, intellectual, and political events that led me to write this book.

In Chapter 1 I will do an overview of the contemporary period of "globalization" and its impact on women. I will give a brief economic history of the transition from the Long Boom of the period after World War II to the restructured world economy that was created from the 1970s onward, showing how this restructuring depended on the use of women's labor, both in the United States and overseas.

In Chapter 2 I will trace the rise of the new feminism that emerged just prior to the current phase of globalization, placing it in the context of the history of women's workforce participation, the nineteenth- and twentieth-century debates over "protection" for women, the rise of labor feminism, and its replacement by mainstream feminism. I am primarily analyzing here an ideal type of feminism, in the Weberian sense, a hegemonic or mainstream feminism,[7] selectively shaped by corporate interests as the global world economy has been restructured.

In Chapter 3 I will trace some fault lines of race and class in the development of twentieth-century feminism. I will place these in the context of the campaign for suffrage, in which the interests of black women and white women fatefully diverged after the Civil War, and I will suggest that a similar tale can be told about the evolution of feminist struggle in the twentieth century. I will argue that the fault lines of race and class weakened feminism as a social force, given its consistent failure to challenge the assumption that the interests of all women were the same, regardless of race, ethnicity, or class. I will show how some of these issues got played out in the arenas of reproductive rights, violence against women, and the conflicts between First World and Third World feminists over the ideologically charged issue of female genital cutting.[8]

In Chapter 4 I will lay out what I see are the uses to which hegemonic feminism has been put by the globalizing powers that be. Here I will focus on the United States, painting a picture of its transformation into a low-wage economy with a severely weakened labor movement, and in this context looking at the decline of the family wage and the ending of the traditional welfare system.

In Chapter 5 I will look at the imposition of structural adjustment programs (SAPs) on governments in the Global South, and how these have put an end to the state-led development policies of the postwar era. I will look at the strategies used by women in the Global South and the "emerging economies" of eastern Europe, where SAPs have made life for most women and children a question of basic survival. In this context I will look at export-processing zones, microcredit, sexual trafficking, and migration. I will suggest that both international agencies and national governments have begun to promote the idea of the individual development of women in place of the autonomous economic development of Global South nations.

In Chapter 6 I will discuss Islamophobia and the war on terror, arguing that, in the construction of a post–cold war Islamic enemy, women have become an iconic category. I will interpret this as essentially a revival of colonial feminism in the service of U.S. empire. I will illustrate this point with a discussion of anti-Islamic politics in Europe, and of the civil wars in Yugoslavia. And I will suggest that the use of Islamophobia conceals a deeper agenda on the part of capitalist interests, namely, the drive to penetrate all parts of the world and link them to a market economy.

Finally, in the Conclusion I will turn to some ideas for the development of the more radical streams of contemporary feminism. My goal will be to suggest some ways in which feminists who consider themselves antiracist and anti-imperialist can contribute to the construction of another and very different world.

ACKNOWLEDGMENTS

For the overall framework of my analysis, I am indebted to the work of many inspired and courageous feminist writers and activists. These include Jacqui Alexander, Teresa Amott, Carol Barton, Johanna Brenner, Masani Alexis De Veaux, Silvia Federici, Maria Mies, Valentine M. Moghadam, Chandra Talpade Mohanty, Jean L. Pyle, Kathryn B. Ward, and Christa Wichterich. In addition, this work draws, as noted, on the prolific energy of the international antiglobalization or global justice movement, and its academic and journalistic interpreters, most especially the writings of Walden Bello, Michel Chossudovsky, David Harvey, Naomi Klein, William K. Tabb, and Ellen Meiskins Wood.

I was very much assisted in the birth of this book by a number of feminist academics who are also, luckily enough, good friends. These include (alphabetically) Renate Bridenthal, who invited me to write for *Science and Society* and who encouraged my critique of hegemonic feminism; Chilla S. Bulbeck, who read an early draft and was extremely helpful throughout the project; Patricia Ticineto Clough, who was deeply supportive of my work despite our philosophical differences; Masani Alexis De Veaux, whose invitation to give the International Women's Day lecture at the State University of New York at Buffalo (UB) in February 2005 was a vote of confidence, as well as a reminder of the wonderful teaching partnership we shared during my years at UB; Jennifer Leigh Disney, whose friendship and academic collaboration are precious to me; Marnia Lazreg, who validated my notion that feminism was being used to dissolve the bonds holding together traditional societies in the Muslim world; and especially Ida Susser, with whom I worked closely and collaboratively as we developed our two writing projects (see Susser 2009), and whose warm and steady support helped me gain the confidence to go public.

I appreciate the close readings of the near-final draft provided by Renate Bridenthal, Jesse Goldstein, Nancy K. Miller, Soniya Munshi, Victoria Rosner, and Ida Susser. Michael Menser made helpful suggestions about the Conclusion. I am grateful to Marcia Wood, who helped me turn anxiety into productivity. I want to pay special tribute to the late Sean Gervasi, a brilliant political analyst of U.S. empire. Thanks also to Hosu Kim, Kristin McDonough, and Spenser Sunshine for research assistance and to Ron Hayduk for his enthusiasm.

Many of my ideas were developed in the classroom, in the Sociology Ph.D. Program of the Graduate Center, and the Sociology Department of Queens College, at the City University of New York, where I teach courses on gender and globalization, international feminism, women and work, and the sociology of gender. Conversations and debates with several cohorts of students shaped many of the arguments in this book.

I thank the Queens College administration and the Department of Sociology for two years of relief from teaching duties, a Fellowship Leave of Absence in 2002, and a Scholarly Incentive Leave in 2006–2007.

The editorial collective of *Socialism and Democracy,* and especially its excellent editor Victor Wallis, were important in helping me develop my analysis. The invitation to edit a special section on gender and globalization was a great encouragement. (See Eisenstein 2004.)

I participated in a Marxist-feminist group comprising Mimi Abramovitz, Renate Bridenthal, Linda Gordon, Leith Mullings, and Lise Vogel, meeting in 2002; a Professional Staff Congress–CUNY study group organized by Anthony O'Brien, meeting from 2003 to 2005; and a seminar funded by the Rockefeller Foundation Humanities Fellowship Program, "Facing Global Capital, Finding Human Security: A Gendered Critique," at the Graduate Center of the City University of New York, meeting from 2002 to 2005. All were influential in the gestation of this book. For the "Facing Global Capital" seminar, many thanks to the coconveners, Patricia Ticineto Clough, then director of the Center for the Study of Women and Society and the Women's Studies Certificate Program at CUNY; and Linda Basch, director, and Kristen Timothy, research fellow, the National Council for Research on Women.

I appreciate the warm friendship of Frances Goldin, activist par excellence, and my agent since 1980, and her wonderful colleagues Ellen Geiger and Josie Schoel, who represented me at the Frances Goldin Literary Agency.

It has been a pleasure to work with Dean Birkenkamp, Melanie Stafford, and their colleagues at Paradigm Publishers. Many thanks to Jan Kristiansson for her meticulous copy-editing.

I am grateful for the loving support of my stepfamily: David, Sarah, Angela, and Katherine Tanzer; Kenneth J. Tanzer; and Charles E. Tanzer. My sister, Paula Eisenstein Baker, was a wonderful ally and supporter. My brother, Jethro Mark Eisenstein, also encouraged me.

Last but not least I thank my darling husband, Michael David Tanzer. An economic consultant who has thoroughly imbibed feminist principles, he provided inspired editing, assistance with statistics, generous intellectual and material resources, reassurance, and unconditional love. Words cannot really express what I owe him, but I want to record my gratitude for his loyalty and solidarity.

Needless to say, all errors and omissions are solely my responsibility.

Hester Eisenstein

Introduction
How I Came to Write This Book

❄

For most of my professional life, I felt certain that the women's movement was a force for progressive social change. I agreed with my namesake Zillah Eisenstein (1981), who argued that even the most liberal, middle-of-the-road women's organizing automatically pushed the agenda of politics toward a more fair and equal society. Unhappily, in recent years I have come to fear that this is not the case, and that feminism in its organized forms has become all too compatible with an increasingly unjust and dangerous corporate capitalist system.

Let me say at the outset that I criticize feminism from within. The revived women's movement of the 1960s and 1970s transformed me from a diffident and bored historian of nineteenth-century France into a committed feminist scholar and women's studies activist. I have been a professional feminist for more than thirty years, have written primarily about feminist theory and practice, and have introduced many generations of students to these issues.[1]

It is precisely because I have spent my professional career doing what I could to advance the cause of women's rights that I feel called upon to enter an international debate about the role of the women's movement. I am not writing from the perspective of those on the Right who see feminism and the women's movement as pernicious causes of social decay. This book is not part of the backlash, in Susan Faludi's sense of the word (see Faludi 1991). I speak as a progressive, a person of the Left, who seeks to realize the potential of women's movement activism to create a more just and a more ecologically sustainable social order.[2]

The context of this discussion is the relationship of feminism to capitalism. In the early years of the women's liberation movement, there was much debate over the relationships among feminism, capitalism, and Marxism. Had the Communist revolutions, from the USSR in 1917 to Cuba in 1959, succeeded in transforming women's lives? Was the liberation of women from patriarchal oppression possible under a capitalist system? Titles like *Capitalist Patriarchy* and *Women and Revolution* were required reading in the early women's studies courses. Among the new acolytes of women's liberation, many had emerged from experiences in the civil rights movement and in the male-dominated New Left. Stung by accusations that organizing autonomously as women was a way of dividing and subverting the movement, these writers spilled much ink in debates over what Heidi Hartmann dubbed the "unhappy marriage" of Marxism and feminism as they sought to understand the relationship between class oppression and gender oppression (Eisenstein 1979; Hartmann 1981; Holmstrom 2002, 4–7; Sargent 1981).

It was common at that time to hold these discussions in the context of a critical assessment of capitalism. It was agreed on the Left that it was our job to place on the table for discussion the economic system that controlled our lives. As the late James Weinstein wrote in 1976, "Capitalism is the unspoken reality of American politics." Both political parties sought "to keep corporate capitalism out of, 'above' politics." Now it was the responsibility of socialists to "bring capitalism into politics as the great issue of our time" (Weinstein 2002).

In the 1980s, with the decline of an active women's movement, or rather, with the entry of many feminists into mainstream institutions including universities, the focus of women's studies scholarship moved away from Marxism and toward an engagement with postmodernism and poststructuralism. In the U.S. academic scene, Michel Foucault, Jacques Derrida, and Jacques Lacan became the patriarchs of choice, as writers such as Alice Jardine sought to examine the ways in which feminism was or was not compatible with these new modes of analysis (Jardine 1985). The postmodern turn, with its emphasis on discourse and its distrust of grand narratives, undermined a systematic analysis of the capitalist system, and feminism itself was attacked as a totalizing concept. But in a curious dialectic, deconstruction and poststructuralism evolved in the direction of postcolonial studies, and by the 1990s Marxism and the critique of capitalism were once again on the agenda.

In this, the academic scene reflected the growth of an international movement that proudly called itself anticapitalist. The international debate over globalization began following the fall of the Soviet Union and the entire Eastern bloc in 1989–1991. These events were taken by the corporate press and mainstream commentators to mark the end of any serious challenge to capitalism as a system. The ideologies of neoliberalism and the free-market "Washington Consensus" were proclaimed to be dominant across the globe. (For more on these terms, see Chapter 1.)

The opposition to the Washington Consensus was most dramatically signaled in the North by the events of November 1999, when college students, trade unionists, environmentalists, educators, feminists, immigration activists, and other groups gathered to protest the meeting of the World Trade Organization in Seattle.[3] The international meetings of the World Economic Forum at Davos,

Switzerland, and the counter meetings of the World Social Forum in Porto Alegre, Brazil; Mumbai, India; and other world cities of the Global South beginning in 2001 posed the terms of the debate starkly. If the financial and political elites of the North stood for the unbridled growth of a neoliberal model throughout the world, then farmers, ecologists, Left politicians, indigenous activists, labor organizers, and women's groups (among many other constituencies) declared the need for an alternative to neoliberalism for the sake of sheer survival. Declaring globalization a recipe for impoverishment and ecological disaster, these activists stood for the creation of an alternative economic and social system.[4]

In contrast, advocates of globalization, such as Thomas Friedman, argued that this new world order was good for everyone. In *The Lexus and the Olive Tree,* Friedman recounted in glowing terms how the new global economy was governed by the Electronic Herd, the instantaneous registering of investor and speculator decisions about where to switch investments. He painted an optimistic portrait of a world in which the demands of international investors served as an invisible hand bringing wealth and the comforts of modernization to any country that complied with its requirements. If a country got with the program, its inhabitants would live happily ever after (Friedman 2000). (See Chapter 1 for further discussion of Friedman.)

Friedman's giddy optimism was echoed by some Western feminists. Accounts of the contemporary women's movement argued that we were living in the best time ever for women (see Evans 2003; Freedman 2002; Rosen 2000). The confidence expressed in these assessments was startling. For example, consider the words of Estelle Freedman:

> Feminists from around the world have challenged the hierarchy of male and female, public and private, citizen and mothers. Millions of women and their male allies now engage in the serious political task of transforming gender relations and gender conventions. They struggle as grassroots leaders in peasant villages, as candidates for national office, in international agencies that challenge discrimination. Wherever democratization occurs, women's groups seek to extend it to the fullest. Given the momentum that feminism has built thus far, combined with ongoing global economic and democratic movements, the quest for universal recognition of women's equal worth is not likely to be reversed. (Freedman 2002, 13)

These writers seemed to have abandoned the project of using feminist theory to critique capitalist assumptions. Thus Judith Stacey wrote:

> I would ... propose that feminists forsake nostalgic exhortations for "revolution" altogether and retire the category as an analytical concept or goal. In the wake of 20th-century horrors, we should have learned that actual revolutions invariably fail to accomplish their utopian goals, or to remain revolutionary.

Even at their best, they catalyze counter-revolutionary terrors, and at their worst, well.... The very concept of "revolution" now seems fundamentally ahistorical and flawed. And contra Frances Fukuyama, there is no "end of history." In these "sadder and wiser" years of my feminist "maturity," I have come to believe that the best we can hope and struggle for are radical reforms pursued through democratic means, which inevitably will prove inadequate and ephemeral. (Stacey 2001, 101)[5]

I will return at the end of this chapter to the relationship of feminist academics to the possibilities of change under capitalism.

I turn now to the account of my development as a critic of feminism in its relation to globalization. I am influenced in this debate by my own location. The overwhelming experience of my life has been the ease with which gender discrimination could be reversed. I have been able to make a living from feminism since 1975, when I offered my first course in feminist theory (see Eisenstein 1983; at the time the Barnard College Committee on Instruction declined me permission to title the course "Contemporary Feminist Theory" on the ground that no such field existed). Of course, this is due to the strength of the women's movement. But no matter how begrudgingly, state, academic, and corporate structures have been able to make way for the demands of gender. To my mind, then, gender has been a more malleable feature of public life than either race or class.

I was poised to take advantage of the new feminist wave, coming from an educated upper-middle-class Jewish family, proceeding to graduate school, earning my credentials as an intellectual, and then being picked up by the wave of activism that exploded in the 1960s and 1970s. Along with Betty Friedan, I can say that feminism changed my life. Despite the turbulence produced both by external events and my own intellectual, political, and personal changes—I moved to Sydney and then to Buffalo before landing on my feet in CUNY and New York—I now find myself earning a comfortable living as an academic, and having the luxury of writing this book.

In short, the gender revolution went far enough to replace my deep unhappiness and sense of isolation with a sense of participation and enjoyment of life. But this is from someone who, no matter what the vicissitudes, never once had to worry where my next meal was coming from. I was and am solidly placed in the professional middle class, legitimized by a movement that insisted on the right of women to a professional career alongside marriage.

Born in 1940, I was initially shaped by the 1950s. This was the McCarthy period, and a period of heightened domesticity: women were being hustled back into their kitchens, and the red scare had people spying on their neighbors and coworkers. My own household was silent on these issues, except when my parents discussed who was and who was not an "Elk." Even within our Upper West Side

New York apartment, they did not feel free to use the word *red* or *communist*. So the secrecy and fear of this period were experienced within my family.

For me, learning to be a girl meant coping with the appearance of breasts and menstruation, mastering household skills, dressing correctly, and being as pretty and respectable as possible. In my family, Judaism was a primary cultural stream, along with intellectual New York culture. My parents read the *New Yorker* religiously, and aspired to belong to the literary world. My mother was a respected book editor, working for McGraw-Hill and then the art book publisher Harry N. Abrams well past retirement age. My father was part of a real estate firm, but his intellectual and emotional life centered on being a pillar of our (fairly liberal Reconstructionist) synagogue and on reading. He steeped himself in Proust, Mann, books about science, biographies, and history. He read to us as children from Dickens, Trollope, and Conan Doyle/Sherlock Holmes. We were a highly literary family, and dinners were regularly interrupted when someone jumped up to look up the exact meaning of a word or the origin of a phrase.

We discussed current events at dinner, and I was conversant enough with some of the issues to be honored when I wrote a piece titled, "Why Did They Cry?" for my junior high school civics class. We had been asked to write an editorial for a newspaper on the death of Joseph Stalin in 1953. Although in our view a vicious dictator had bitten the dust, I was puzzled by the fact that the newspapers were reporting long lines of sobbing Russians waiting to see his embalmed body in the Kremlin. My other vivid memory from junior high school is of the wall maps we were shown of the (so-called) Far East, with China painted a vivid red, and the red/blood dripping down the Korean peninsula. I have no memory of any discussion of the execution of Julius and Ethel Rosenberg in 1953, although my parents, as active members of the New York Jewish community, must have been deeply aware of these events.

At Music and Art (now LaGuardia) High School, I was on the fringes of a Bohemian group of artists and musicians. I went through high school and college in a state of embarrassment, anxiety, and uncertainty. Although I performed at a high level, I nonetheless felt like an outsider. I sang Pete Seeger songs, but did not understand the context. The extent to which I had absorbed my parents' liberal democratic version of reality can be measured by the fact that in my early years in graduate school at Yale I had a boyfriend who served in the Green Berets. I adored John F. Kennedy, whom I worshipped uncritically as U.S. leader of the "free world." I remember huddling anxiously with Linda Gordon and the other members of our cohort in the lobby of the Sterling Memorial Library, wondering whether the Cuban missile crisis would bring us to atomic war with the Soviets. On the day we heard of Kennedy's death, I sobbed uncontrollably.

My first introduction to second-wave feminism was at a meeting held at Columbia University in 1969. I entered the hall feeling skeptical, saying to myself, This has nothing to do with me. But the speaker was a woman architect from

Yale who remarked that "there is no male chauvinism like Yale chauvinism." As a graduate student at Yale who had just joined the faculty there, I was galvanized by this statement. I had suffered since 1961 as one of a handful of women graduate students in a sea of mostly white male colleagues, the subject of endless baiting and smart-ass remarks. Until then I had had absolutely no vocabulary to describe this experience. This was my "click" moment (to use Jane O'Reilly's term) when I began to understand that all the discussion about feminism indeed had something to do with me (see O'Reilly 2002).

From that point on I read every single feminist text I could put my hands on: Kate Millett, Juliet Mitchell, Shulamith Firestone, Mary Daly, Susan Brownmiller, Robin Morgan. Everything that was being said about women as a suppressed class, a sex class, an oppressed group, seemed to speak to me directly. Looking back, I suppose that I embodied the prototypical middle-class feminist, although unlike Betty Friedan I had not succumbed to being a suburban housewife. Rather, I had become an intellectual woman, excluded from the secrets of European housekeeping. I was banished from the world of true womanhood because I had dared to train as a professor.

For me, feminism was an entrée into the world of women from which I had felt exiled. If my mother had sternly divided the world up between my sister and myself, so that my sister would become the housewife and mother, while I would become the intellectual, feminism as a movement welcomed me back. In some ways, then, the women's movement became for me the Good Mother that my own mother, for all her strengths, had been unable to be. A consciousness-raising (CR) group that I helped to found with Nancy K. Miller, Ellen Sweet, and others met for about ten years, from 1970 to 1980. Although the focus of our group was primarily on career issues, we tackled personal concerns—sexuality, motherhood, family conflicts—as well, and I experienced within it a profound healing process. Along with the help of some feminist therapy, the CR experience helped me to change being female from a traumatic and conflictual condition into a source of strength.

I discovered Marxism and feminism at about the same time. In 1964, I was in Paris doing the research for an extremely uninteresting dissertation in nineteenth-century French history. At a dinner party held by Nancy K. Miller (this predated our consciousness-raising group), I was trying out my French, and chatting happily about my enthusiasm for the war my country was pursuing in Vietnam. I was shocked at the barrage of angry criticism I received. "You Americans are making the same brutal, vicious mistakes that our government did in Indochina," I was told. Throughout my year in Paris, I received my first lessons in imperialism. I defended my original position fiercely. But by the time I returned to the United States, I was converted to opposing the war and to embracing a Marxist perspective.

Meanwhile in Paris, I was reading Simone de Beauvoir, and observing my female colleagues in the Bibliothèque Nationale. As I waited for my books to be delivered to my table, I surreptitiously watched other female scholars as they walked down the aisles. How did they manage to be so intellectual and so sexy at the same time? As an American woman, I had struggled with this dichotomy all my life. De Beauvoir's reflections on how one is not born, but becomes a woman created a framework for me to think about this and many other puzzles about sex, sexuality, and gender (see Eisenstein 1991a).

As the second wave of feminism hit the shores of the United States, in the following few years I was ready to be picked up and carried by it. The area of activism I found myself in was the newly invented field of women's studies. I was passionate about this work, because in my own education there had been nothing to indicate that women could possibly make a contribution to culture, politics, economics, or history. I was elated at the idea that curricula could be transformed to include women's history, and I was already sympathetic to the movement for black studies. Indeed, while I was at Yale I supported the activism of black students who successfully petitioned the administration to introduce black studies courses. Having moved to Barnard in 1970, I was focused on helping to establish the Barnard College women's studies program, and collaborating on the Scholar and the Feminist annual conference series (now extended into an online journal; see http://www.barnard.edu.sfonline). The women's studies movement, along with radical movements in disciplines such as history and anthropology, was part of an ongoing struggle to change the curriculum to encompass the experiences of the mass of people, rather than just elites. Not surprisingly, this debate is still very much alive today as a component of the culture wars.

For personal and professional reasons I moved to Australia in 1980. The feminists I met there eased my transition with their extraordinary blend of fierce activism and sardonic humor.[6] In Oz, they told me, the action was not in the academy, but in government. This was my introduction to the "femocrats" (feminist bureaucrats), who had leveraged an alliance with the Labor Party into extraordinary access and influence for feminist ideas.

The femocrats were able to lodge a claim on the state by means of an appeal to fundamental principles of Australian political culture (see Eisenstein 1996). Since the nineteenth century, the political economy of the country had been based on a protectionist system that gave industry, labor, farmers, and mining interests specific measures to ensure their survival. In an act of brilliant political maneuvering, the femocrats established a similar claim, basing their legitimacy on being representatives for women as a whole. The era of the femocrats saw extraordinary gains for women, from federal funding for child care and domestic violence programs to the ascent of feminist women (both working class and middle class) to senior positions in state and federal bureaucracies.

When the winds of change began to blow in the 1980s, and Bob Hawke's Labor Party decided to open the Australian economy to the world market, the femocrats' claim to legitimacy was swiftly undermined. From being what the Australians had approvingly called a *sectional interest,* they were transformed into the new category of a *special interest,* in the American sense. From being substantial citizens helping to set the agenda of the Labor Party, and indeed the conservative parties as well, women became "whingers," a group seeking unwarranted special treatment.

Neoliberalism and the free market were the watchwords of the new Australian economy. Egalitarianism, "a fair go," and a strong role for government intervention were now obsolete. It was not just femocrats who were no longer fashionable. The traditional claims of labor were also losing legitimacy. Trade union membership dropped dramatically, from 50 percent of all workers in the 1980s down to 19 percent currently (Australian Bureau of Statistics 2008; Leigh 2005). Meanwhile, the gap between rich and poor grew alarmingly. In short, I witnessed the globalizing of the Australian economy before I ever heard the term.

From my Australian experience I learned that political claims made by women were profoundly linked to larger political and economic structures. In Australia, as in the United States, a middle-class, white women's movement had limits. Both immigrant and Aboriginal women made it very clear that the demands of white women activists were not congruent with their needs. During the 1980s and early 1990s, a separate set of demands expressed by these groups of women was placed on the table, and a healthy dialogue had begun to emerge. But this whole debate and its powerful effects on the Australian political scene were rendered virtually irrelevant when the larger context changed so dramatically.

There was a further complication. The Labor Party was able to distract the electorate with its attention to the issues raised by women, immigrants, and Aborigines, while carrying out an economic agenda pleasing to international capital. The advancement of women's interests, via federally funded child care and domestic violence and rape prevention, was compatible with policies that simultaneously increased the gap between rich and poor and weakened the labor movement. Anna Yeatman suggested that the femocrats were being used as a smokescreen while the Labor government hacked away at the welfare state. At the time, I was frankly shocked by Yeatman's argument and argued with her in print (see Eisenstein 1996, 194–197; Yeatman 1990). I felt that she was accusing the femocrats of being careerist and of turning a blind eye to how they were being manipulated. Of course, in making this point I was also defending my own career choices, so I was hardly objective.

But Yeatman's accusation stayed with me. Was it possible that the energy of the women's movement was being co-opted? Shortly after returning to the United States in 1988, I gave some minor assistance to the production of a book that examined the rise of "state feminism" around the globe (see Stetson and Mazur

1995). In the wake of the UN international women's conferences, commencing with the International Year of the Woman in 1975, many governments around the world established ministries, cabinet positions, or a special government office dedicated to women's needs. These appeared to be victories for the women's cause. Yet the success of women in creating special agencies for women was not connected to any larger success in extending and strengthening welfare state provisions for the poorest part of the population. Indeed, the growth of women's agencies took place while debtor governments in the South came under savage attack via structural adjustment programs (SAPs) imposed by the international financial agencies based in Washington. The safety net around the world was being shredded simultaneously with the increasing visibility and activism of a global feminist movement. (On SAPs, see Chapter 5.)

As a result of my experiences in Australia, I began to watch for relationships between globalization and gender. From 1988 to 1996, I taught in the Women's Studies Program at the State University of New York at Buffalo (UB). There I offered a graduate course in feminist theory. I sketched out a history of post-1970s feminist theory, from the books covered in my *Contemporary Feminist Thought* (1983) through writers influenced by postmodernism and poststructuralism (see Nicholson 1990). The course made for lively debates, but I felt increasingly dissatisfied.

One of my colleagues at UB was a brilliant Guyanese economist named Monica Jardine, who held degrees from Columbia, and also from Binghamton, where she was a student of Immanuel Wallerstein, the noted world-systems theorist. Monica and I shared syllabi, and one day Monica invited me to her class, in which she was teaching a famous chapter from Karl Polanyi's *The Great Transformation* (1944) on the English Poor Laws. "You are teaching theory up in the air," was the essence of her comment to me. I began to rethink my course to make it more grounded in social and economic realities. The encounter with Jardine was another step in my quest to develop a political economy of gender and, indeed, of feminism.

Another formative experience at UB was the course that I team-taught with Masani Alexis De Veaux, poet, essayist, novelist, and biographer of Audre Lorde (see De Veaux 2005). Like me, Masani was from New York. But, as we often remarked, we came from different class backgrounds. While my mother hired "Negro" maids to help raise us, Masani's mother cleaned other (white) women's houses. Together, we taught a course that covered black and white feminisms. While I gave an account of the development of white feminism—from abolition and suffrage to the second wave of the 1960s and 1970s—Masani traced the history of black feminism from Maria Stewart to Audre Lorde. (For an introduction to this literature, see Guy-Sheftall 1995b.) As we intertwined our two narratives, we saw that the split between these two communities was a root cause of the continued weaknesses of organized feminism.

Before the U.S. Civil War, black and white women leaders had joined forces in a powerful coalition to end slavery. But after the Civil War, black activists felt betrayed by the white leaders of the suffrage movement, who pursued a policy of "expediency": they sought an alliance with Southern white elites, arguing that the votes of white women would counter the votes of blacks and new immigrants (see Giddings 1996). A similar splitting off took place in the 1960s and 1970s, when the "beloved community" of black and white solidarity evoked by Ella Baker and the Student Non-Violent Coordinating Committee (SNCC) gave way to a set of separate movements: black power for black men; white feminism for white women; anti-war and student movements for white men; and black women left— as Barbara Omolade ruefully noted—on their own (Omolade 1990). I began to wonder, Did the fault lines of race and class keep U.S. feminism from reaching its full radical potential? (On this history, see Chapter 3.)

A third experience at UB was witnessing the work of my colleague Isabel Marcus, professor of law, who became active in a group that traveled to the former Communist countries of eastern Europe to export the ideas of U.S. feminism. Under the auspices of the Network of East-West Women (www.neww.org/en/home/index/0.html), a fascinating debate ensued between Western feminists and Eastern bloc women activists. Although the collapse of communism had brought political freedom to these countries, it also opened the way for a particularly rapacious and lawless form of capitalism. The Western feminists were introducing important ideas about domestic violence. But the eastern European and Russian women were losing free day care, maternity leave, guaranteed employment, free education, and other legacies of the Communist regime. Ironically, they associated feminism, that is, women's rights, with the tired rhetoric of the bad old days. (On these issues, see Funk and Mueller 1993.) Were feminists from the United States emissaries of U.S. culture and values?

In this context I became aware of a new discussion about *civil society*. I was familiar with the term from debates about the concept in Karl Marx and Georg W. F. Hegel. But this seemed to be a new usage. The neoliberal economic paradigm suggested that the gaps left by a diminished public sector could be filled in by the renewal of civil society, defined as private nongovernmental organizations (NGOs). Many of the NGOs that were springing up were women's groups. Did powerful world leaders consider that taking up the work formerly carried out by the welfare state would be the job of women? (On civil society in its meanings after 1989, see Wickramasinghe 2005; for further discussion, see Chapter 5.)

In 1996 I was recruited to become the director of women's studies at Queens College, CUNY, in New York City. In this role, I participated in a conference on women and development, initiated by a group of feminist graduate students, and was thereby introduced to the growing literature on this topic.[7] Although there was a range from radical to more conservative positions, writers and activists found common ground in researching the gendered effects of development on women in the Global South. These advocates then sought to use the dire situation of women as a lever to affect official development policy by the international financial institutions and by governments.[8] I began to sense the presence of an unwritten script. Assuming no more radical political revolutions in the Global South, the task of creating social justice now fell on the shoulders of women. This was to be accomplished by incorporating the needs of women into the development process. Empowering women, it seemed, would make up for the end of state-sponsored economic development. (See Chapter 5 for my elaboration of this idea.)

Meanwhile, in women's studies literature, a dominant theme in the 1980s was the integration of feminist theory with poststructuralist and postmodern modes of thought. I was unable to conform to this academic mode. I carefully read many postmodern and poststructuralist feminist texts, but did not subscribe to their postulates. I did not believe that discourse was the shaping agency of politics and culture, nor did I accept the need to abandon "grand narratives" such as Marxism or feminism. Along with Susan Bordo and Nancy Hartsock, I read declarations of "the death of the subject" with considerable suspicion, given that women had only just begun to claim their right to subjectivity and agency (see Nicholson 1990).

The premise that these writings were more radical than Marxism did not convince me: I felt this revolution was located more in discourse than in politics. But I was struck by one tenet of postmodernism, namely, that something important had shifted in the 1970s, and that this change, a restructuring of the global economy, had consequences for politics, culture, and, most especially, the situation of women. The period of "Fordism," the expansive industrialization of the United States and other Western countries during the Golden Age of the Long Boom from 1945 to the 1970s, had been replaced by "post-Fordism": deindustrialization, and an end to the Keynesian welfare state. Some felt that this shift in the organization of international capitalism was matched by a cultural, and indeed epistemological, break of major proportions. (For a skeptical view of the latter claim, see Harvey 1989.)

As noted, I did not buy into the notion of an epistemological break, the death of the subject and of grand narratives, and the new reign of discourse. But I certainly accepted the need to analyze the major economic restructuring of the 1970s and 1980s. I began to incorporate this work into my teaching. Teresa Amott argued that the massive entry of women into the workforce in the 1970s coincided with the end of the Long Boom. In her memorable phrase "up the down escalator," she held that women had become serious economic actors at precisely the wrong time. Was it an unfortunate coincidence that women had been drawn into the economy in a productive capacity at precisely the historical moment when there was going to be such a dramatic slowdown? (Amott 1993, 81). Or was it, as she demonstrated, that the slowdown caused women to become the cheap workforce of choice? Amott's analysis started me thinking about the significance of the changes in the United States and the world economy, and the relation of these changes to women as workers, in production as well as reproduction.

At the turn of the century, a number of books began to appear, by Susan Brownmiller (1999), Ruth Rosen (2000), and others, on the history of the women's movement. Although they provided a lively and provocative history of the political actions of the women's movement of the 1970s, few directly addressed the political economy of feminism. Many writers pointed to the rapid rise in participation by women in higher education after World War II, and the steady increase in married women's workforce participation from the 1950s onward. But the emphasis in most of these texts was on the political organizations, the consciousness-raising, and the cultural impact of the second wave. There seemed to be insufficient attention to the link between the massive increase in women's workforce participation, as the U.S. economy shed manufacturing for service jobs, and the rise of feminist consciousness and activism.

Meanwhile, the events of 1989–1991, the fall of the Soviet Union and of the communist regimes in Eastern Europe, provoked a wave of commentary about the end of the cold war and the triumph of democracy. *Globalization,* the term introduced in the mainstream press, described a new era during which the benefits of capitalism could now be enjoyed throughout the world without opposition from regimes that claimed to provide an alternative economic system. As a feminist, I was most aware of the growth of what was starting to be called *global feminism.* This was celebrated as a result of the series of conferences organized by the United Nations, from the first conference in 1975 in Mexico City, followed by conferences in Copenhagen (1980), Nairobi (1985), and Beijing (1995). Was global feminism a product of globalization?

I developed a new course intended to introduce undergraduates to the issues raised by the process of globalization, because it seemed directly relevant to their lives. The Queens College student body comprises a high percentage of students from immigrant families, and our students are often the first members of their families to attend college.[9] My course was intended to introduce undergraduates to some of the issues raised by the process of globalization, because it seemed directly relevant to their lives. This course assumed no prior knowledge of feminism or feminist theory.

This was a very interesting teaching experience. From my point of view, I was teaching an oppositional or critical discourse, a way of unveiling an oppressive, racist, sexist power structure. After all, women's studies essentially contested the rest of the curriculum. Thus, in my mind, I was teaching the students to develop a critical perspective, not a set of mainstream ideas. But I began to observe that many students were using the material in a very different way. Many students, I realized, were making use of the course as a way to further their understanding of the United States and of how U.S. culture functioned.

For students from South Korea, India, or Ethiopia, what I was teaching them in women's studies courses was the stuff of daily life. It was their bridge to the United States. They needed to learn this material for their own survival, for a way to fit into this very different, hypermodern way of life. Over and over again, students reported that the immigrant experience included a shift in gender roles. Students from traditionally patriarchal cultures such as that of Iran, or indeed of Italy, saw the relationships between their parents shift when fathers had trouble finding suitable work and mothers were forced into the paid workforce. The greater equality of gender roles imposed by U.S. economic conditions created turmoil and conflict among parents. Their daughters eagerly absorbed the material in women's studies courses as a way of making sense of their own family's life history. In short, my lessons in feminism were, to them, not oppositional at all. They were a how-to course in being U.S. citizens. I was giving them a powerful means of acculturation. In watching how my students absorbed and reacted to the material I offered them, I was in effect observing how closely the ideas embodied in U.S. feminism represented a path to modernity. (See Chapter 6 for my elaboration of this idea.)

In the larger political arena, my years as the director of women's studies overlapped with the Clinton era. President Bill Clinton and his openly feminist and therefore emblematic First Lady, former New York senator, presidential candidate, and now Secretary of State Hillary Rodham Clinton, drew on the ideas of mainstream feminism as a political strength. It was Bill Clinton who appointed the first woman to be attorney general—Janet Reno—and Madeleine Albright as the first woman secretary of state. Then, of course, there was the appointment of Ruth Bader Ginsburg as the second (white) woman on the Supreme Court. Another appointment that drew my eye was that of Charlene Barshefsky to head the negotiations for world trade.

Madeleine Albright, in particular, seemed highly symbolic. She freely identified herself as a feminist and actively brought together women in the State Department for supportive meetings, braving the resentment and anger of some male employees. At the same time, her ironfisted prosecution of the bloody air war in Kosovo recalled the behavior of British prime minister Margaret Thatcher in the Falklands War. In the Clinton regime, women could be explicitly feminist as long as they practiced the tough love of the new Democrats. Another striking example was Clinton's secretary of health and human services, Donna Shalala, the feminist-identified former president of Hunter College and the University of Wisconsin (now president of the University of Florida). Shalala chose to remain in the cabinet when the draconian welfare law of 1996 passed through both houses of Congress, with the support of the majority of women members. (For a discussion of this, see Chapter 4.)

In response to these events, I began to develop the concept of "Madeleine Albright feminism." I discovered, some months later, that Jacqui Alexander and Chandra Talpade Mohanty had coined the term *free-market feminism* with much the same meaning (see Alexander and Mohanty 1997b, xv). The Clinton administration was using mainstream feminism to sell "free-market" capitalism to the world. In my course on gender and globalization at the CUNY Graduate Center, I used the writings of Michel Chossudovsky (2003) and William K. Tabb (2001) to walk my students through the mechanisms of structural adjustment. Global South countries were being induced to reorient their economies toward export production, and to cut social spending to the bone in order to repay their escalating debt. I used the work of Ellen Meiksins Wood (1999) to illustrate the fact that at its inception, the "free market" was the creation of powerful economic actors. One could see the same interactions occurring today: the enclosures of agricultural land in preindustrial Great Britain had their counterpart in the rapacious behavior of twenty-first-century agribusiness. We read Maria Mies (1998), who linked the rise of informal labor among women in the late twentieth century to the "housewife-ization" of women in the seventeenth and eighteenth centuries. We read Christa Wichterich (2000) on the "globalized woman," and Grace Chang (2000) on the "disposable domestics" created by globalization, women fleeing the poverty of their home countries under the impact of SAPs, only to find exploitation and insecurity in their newly adopted rich countries.

My students were shocked to see how international financial institutions and the governments under their sway were creating conditions of increasing misery and poverty in the Global South and the newly liberated post-Soviet countries, while claiming that these policies would eventually produce prosperity, after a suitable period of austerity. We debated whether it would be better for countries to withdraw from the international trading system and to return to some kind of self-sufficiency. As my student Ching-Ning Wang put it, with elegant simplicity, "Grow rice; eat rice!" As we developed our thinking on these issues, it seemed to me that with the advent of globalization, the women's movement had reached a crossroads. As a feminist, one could throw in one's lot with the Thomas Friedmans of this world and agree that the unbridled expansion of neoliberalism would eventually create the best of all possible worlds. Or one could use all the brilliant insights and knowledge developed by feminist writing, research, and activism to fundamentally contest this system.

With the advent of President George W. Bush and the events of September 11, 2001, a newly intensified role for the United States as a military aggressor began. With this came a revived debate over imperialism, with a spate of publications attacking the U.S. role from the left, and defending it from the center and the right. (On this literature, see Arrighi 2005.) As the United States justified its murderous new role in Afghanistan and Iraq, women's rights were once again front and center. How could one criticize the United States for ridding the world of the Taliban, a regime whose notorious cruelty to women had been the focus of a major campaign by the Feminist Majority? Laura Bush was enlisted as a spokesperson for women's rights, and was being sent to tour the Middle East on behalf of the worldwide democratization crusade championed by her husband.

By now many writers—most notably Arundhati Roy (2003) and Laura Flanders (2004)—were satirizing the Bush administration's hypocritical embrace of women's rights. A government that revived the global gag order on abortion, that passed a law outlawing partial-birth abortion, and that embraced the views of the Religious Right on women's place was clearly using feminism in a completely cynical way. Yet the conventional wisdom, placing feminism on the left with the Democrats, and antifeminism on the right with the Republicans and their Christian fundamentalist allies, did not adequately account for the broader picture. Globalization and its twin, the endless war on terrorism, had as their premise a "we" of modernity—read: formal electoral systems and incorporation into the digitalized world market—that transcended the left/right divisions of U.S. politics. Women's rights were being enlisted as emblematic of, indeed synonymous with, modernity. (See Chapter 6 for an elaboration of this idea.)

As I immersed myself in the new literature on globalization, I became aware that women were enmeshed in these developments at a number of levels. (For the growing literature on gender and globalization, see Beneria 2003.) It was women's labor, productive and reproductive, that was being relied on as corporations cut their male workforces, and national governments slashed their welfare budgets. Here in the United States, the safety net for poor women established under Franklin Delano Roosevelt in 1935 was ripped to shreds in the welfare "reform" of 1996. The feminization of poverty, first noted in the 1980s, was accelerating apace as former welfare recipients found themselves consigned to low-wage jobs, and at increased risk for battering and homelessness.

If the developments in the national and world economy were making it harder and harder for most women to survive, why were so many of my sisters in the women's movement so cheerfully optimistic? Part of the answer lay in the paradox outlined by Johanna Brenner in her assessment of the achievements of U.S. feminism since the 1970s. As she noted, quoting the famous line from Charles Dickens's *A Tale of Two Cities*, "It was the best of times, it was the worst of times" (see Brenner 2000a). For women like me, profiting from the hard work and commitment of feminist activists in cracking open the worlds of professional work previously reserved for white men, it was indeed the best of times. The media presented the achievements of women—such as Carly Fiorina, until 2005 the CEO of Hewlett-Packard; or senior government officials such as President Bush's Secretary of State Condoleezza Rice—as evidence that barriers to women's achievement had now fallen. Oprah Winfrey and other much publicized celebrities seemed to demonstrate that the way to fame and power was open for women, regardless of race.

But behind the glitter, for most women, especially but not exclusively women of color—African Americans, Latinas, and others—the economic changes of the years since the mid-1970s were devastating. Most women were traveling down the escalator, having entered the labor market in massive numbers just as the U.S economy was moving south. From the much-vaunted Clinton "boom" to the hesitant recovery following 9/11, the majority of U.S. women were struggling to make ends meet. As Barbara Ehrenreich (2002) vividly demonstrated, survival on a minimum wage was a heroic endeavor.

This differential treatment of women is the product of the way in which the demands of feminism have been absorbed and co-opted within the U.S. capitalist system. Most Americans assume that the economic system currently in place in the United States—aka the U.S. way of life—is the only possible way to live. They accept widespread unemployment and other dislocations for the sake of a chance at the American dream by winning the lottery or emulating Jennifer Lopez. But in recent years, widespread debates over the impact of globalization have forced the U.S. media to start using the word *capitalism* and to initiate a widespread defense of the system. The scandals concerning the bookkeeping practices of Enron, World.com, and other major corporations, not to mention the worldwide economic collapse of 2007–2008, put the corporate sector on the defensive. Of course, the "war" on terrorism since September 11, 2001, has also brought ideas about U.S. values into sharp focus. Hence, discussions about capitalism, socialism, and alternative economic systems in general have once again become, if not fashionable, at least part of a broad public consciousness.

In this context, I want to challenge the U.S. women's movement to put the issue of socialism back on the agenda. This is already the case for much feminist organizing in the Global South, where the ravaging effects of globalization are only too apparent (see Moghadam 2005, especially Chapter 5). As Nancy Holmstrom writes, the changes wrought by globalization have placed issues of class, race, and gender front and center on the world stage. Two recent publications signal a revival of the socialist-feminist project (see Gimenez and Vogel 2005; Holmstrom 2002). It is high time.

Serious challenges to the free market are developing, especially in Latin America. Hugo Chávez of Venezuela and Evo Morales of Bolivia, among other leaders, are joining Fidel Castro of Cuba in openly criticizing contemporary capitalist relations and calling for new socialist alternatives. Women's organizations such as the Women of Color Resource Center and MADRE are working on economic justice issues for women at home and around the world (see Moghadam 2005; www.madre.org; www.coloredgirls.org). This kind of work, to me, is the cutting edge of women's organizing. The utopian core of feminism—its vision of justice for women and for all of humanity—cannot be realized within the violent and dangerous machinery of corporate globalization. It is time for the women's movement as a whole to align itself with the struggle for alternatives to the current economic world order. I hope to convince my readers of this view in the pages that follow.

I

Globalization and Women's Labor

❃

In the burgeoning literature on globalization, only a limited number of studies focus on the centrality of women's labor. Yet this process has drawn millions of women, particularly women of color, into a new female proletariat.[1] As Delia Aguilar notes:

> To speak of globalization without center-staging women of color would be a grave mistake. In the era of globalized economics where a race to the bottom is crucial for superprofits, it is primarily the labor power of "Global South" women ... that is the cheapest of all. From the maquiladoras in Mexico ... to assembly plants and export processing zones [EPZs] in Central America, the Caribbean, and the Pacific Rim, to subcontractors and garment sweatshops in global cities and in nations of the periphery, it is women's labor that allows and guarantees maximum profitability for the corporate elite, a tiny minority of the world's inhabitants. (Aguilar 2004a, 16–17)

Globalization as the word is generally used refers to a complex series of events stretching over a time span of some four decades beginning in the early 1970s. It involves a range of actors, from government and corporate leaders and major investors to central bankers and heads of international financial institutions.[2] In this account I will emphasize those parts of the process that seem most relevant to my argument: the ways in which the managers of the global economy are making use, not just of women's labor, but also of feminist ideology.

For global managers and their cheering section in the corporate media, globalization is a process of integrating countries into the world market by dismantling the mechanisms, from tariff policy to capital flows, that gave countries control over international investment. The collapse of communism in the former Soviet Union and its allies after 1989 facilitated this process enormously. Using "free-trade" agreements such as the North American Free Trade Agreement (NAFTA) and structural adjustment programs (SAPs), the globalizers have transformed local economies across the world, allegedly "reforming" and modernizing them to get rid of archaic entities such as state-owned enterprises. To the globalizers this is an unmitigated good, and they have been assiduous in promoting this process as beneficent.

But from a more critical perspective, globalization has been a process of impoverishment and disfranchisement for many hundreds of millions of people. The macroeconomic changes adopted by Global South countries under the pressure of debt have in effect abrogated their economic sovereignty, opening their economies, with very few restrictions, to international corporations seeking a cheap and docile labor force and a high return on their investments (I will explain this process in detail in Chapter 5).[3]

In the developed world, meanwhile, the "social compact" extracted by labor unions and Left political parties from governments in the postwar era is under severe attack, symbolized by the attempt of President George W. Bush to demolish social security (thankfully unsuccessful) and to partially privatize the provision of Medicare (partially successful).[4] Highly paid manufacturing jobs have been cut dramatically, and a low-wage service economy has been constructed. The tax structure has been skewed to benefit the rich and the very rich, and a process of increasing inequalities has affected the United States along with the rest of the world. With the decline of unions, a "flexible" workforce of part-time, contract employees has emerged, producing an economy where some one-quarter of workers are earning poverty wages. All of these changes make up the process of globalization.

GLOBALIZATION DEFINED

What exactly does globalization mean? The word itself was introduced into the management literature in the early 1980s, and was rapidly taken up by the business and mainstream press.[5] The originator of the term was a much-acclaimed business writer, Theodore Levitt, who in 1983 pointed to the need for multinational corporations to make changes, both in their manufacturing techniques and in their sales strategies, calibrated to local social behaviors and cultural preferences, in order to be able to sell their products worldwide. Keep an eye on those social behaviors! This is the entering wedge for the uses being made of women, as workers and consumers, and the uses being made of feminist ideology, in the newly globalized world order.[6]

To grasp the process, it is useful to draw an analogy to the growth of the United States in the nineteenth century. One basis of the enormous wealth that was accumulated was the creation of a single market across the entire continent, so that goods could be shipped freely from state to state (see Tabb 2001). In the twenty-first century, the aspiration of the globalizers is similarly to create a single market out of the entire world. This means the destruction of all barriers to the free flow of capital, from tariffs to capital controls, so that nation-states in effect become like the states within the U.S. federal system: open for business without impediment.

New York Times columnist and writer Thomas Friedman is one of the major celebrants of globalization. According to Friedman, the relatively closed national economies of the pre-1970s cold war system controlled their own monetary and fiscal policies. But in the newly globalized economy, the main decisionmakers are no longer the political leaders of nation-states, but the Electronic Herd. Members of the Herd include institutional investors such as pension funds, corporations investing their profits, and, in recent years, "hedge funds" investing pools of capital around the world and betting on the rise and fall of commodities, companies, and national currencies. In this new era, the Electronic Herd roams freely across the globe. With the new diversity of financial instruments, everything can be bundled into tradable items, from mortgages to overseas bonds. The elimination of capital controls fosters a series of stampedes, with investors seeking the highest returns rushing in and out of national economies (Friedman 2000).

The removal of governmental regulations and other barriers to world investment was extremely profitable in periods of rapid economic growth. But this transformation also concealed major dangers should the world economy encounter a downturn. This was dramatically evident from 2007–2008, when a worldwide credit crisis ensued, linked to the issuance of housing mortgages in the United States to people who could ill afford them. The resulting foreclosures sent waves of panic throughout the world financial markets.[7] Particularly after the dramatic bankruptcy of Lehman Brothers, and the "rescues" orchestrated by the U.S. government of Bear Stearns, AIG Insurance, Fannie Mae (the Federal National Mortgage Association), and Freddie Mac (the Federal Home Mortgage Corporation), governments all over the world stepped in with multibillion-dollar bailouts of their own troubled financial institutions.

But to return to the optimistic narrative of Thomas Friedman: he calls the giant multinational corporations (MNCs)—companies such as Ford, Intel, Compaq, (the late)Enron, and Toyota—the Longhorn cattle, carrying out foreign direct investment, building factories, utilities, energy plants, and other long-term projects all across the globe. In the preglobalized era, when countries still maintained tariff walls, MNCs built factories abroad to jump over those walls and sell directly in foreign markets. But now, to compete in the global market, they can divide up their production chain geographically, producing and assembling their goods in the cheapest possible places.

Countries compete for the entry of MNCs because they need foreign capital, international standards and technologies, foreign partnerships, and market information. Governments now must heed the market, as political power no longer stems from holding office (Friedman 2000, 101ff.). Just as states in the United States compete with one another for corporate investment, with tax breaks and cheap land and utilities, so now all nations must compete for the favor of the Longhorns and the Electronic Herd.

This competitive vision is evident on the back pages of *The Economist,* where endless charts array the countries of the world according to their economic indicators, from gross domestic product (GDP) to trade balances to foreign reserves.[8] The overriding goal for each country is to attract investment, and to do this each must conform to the dictates of international economic orthodoxy, which means having to cut taxes, reduce public spending, privatize government enterprises, and eliminate capital controls, so that investors are no longer prevented from bringing their profits home.

The mainstream press celebrates this competition, and cheers on countries seen as conforming to the demands of the international investors. Thus, the former Soviet republic of Kazakhstan, and its capital Almaty, with skyscrapers sprouting in its newly created downtown, is featured in the *New York Times.* Dennis Price, general director of Bogatyr Access Komyr, the biggest Kazakh coal mining company, lets us know that "his" country is "well on the road to having one of the 50 most competitive economies in the world" (Greenberg 2006).

The "modernization" of women is considered an important indicator of a country's progress in the international economy. Thus, we learn from the editor of the Kazakh edition of *Cosmopolitan* magazine that "women are getting married later, they have their own apartments. Attitudes about sex are changing very fast" (Greenberg 2006). A similar phenomenon is taking place in India, where advertising campaigns have widely disseminated the image of a "modern" woman. In these ads "there is a sense of inevitability ... that India and Indian women have emerged out of decades of state control and finally have the opportunity to express themselves. There is a sense of having been 'behind' other countries for decades and having finally 'caught up.' The new liberal Indian women have finally joined a global league of modern female consumers" (Oza 2006, 25). I will return to this theme of women as an emblem of modernity in Chapter 2.

The Long Boom

The background to the current era of globalization is the worldwide economic boom that preceded it. The period from the end of World War II in 1945 to the mid-1970s is often called the Golden Age, or the Long Boom—the longest period of sustained economic growth in the history of the United States. Powered by the giant economy of the United States, most countries also experienced unprecedented economic growth, and some—such as Japan and South Korea—became powerful economic actors in their own right.

At home, the U.S. economy went into high gear. Consumer spending, pent up during the war years, sparked growth in cars and household appliances. Housing spending soared, meeting the needs of millions of returning soldiers and their families. Many (mostly white) families moved to the new suburbs like Levittown in Long Island, supported by the creation of Fannie Mae, which offered low-cost mortgages. Substantial public investments by the federal government included the G.I. Bill, which paid for college education for veterans; the national interstate highway system; schools; and utilities. Meanwhile, high levels of military spending resumed with the outbreak of the Korean "conflict" (1950–1953) and then the war in Vietnam (1965–1973) (Tanzer 1995).

Working families provided a ready market for consumer goods. Suburbanization meant the growth of shopping centers and drive-through restaurants, plus the automobile. "No single product—with its extensive linkages to other economic sectors, including highway construction and petroleum refining—has ever so dominated the imagination of the population, or the base of a national economy, as did the car. Perhaps one in six Americans owed his or her job to the car" (Bluestone and Harrison 1982, 114).

On the world stage, the United States emerged from World War II with more than half of all the usable productive capacity in the world, serving as banker to former allies and enemies alike. U.S. domination was cemented by the Bretton Woods Agreement of 1944, which effectively made the U.S. dollar the principal reserve currency. Under this agreement, the currencies of most other countries had fixed exchange rates pegged to the dollar. To participate in international trade, countries were required to acquire dollars, since they could not use their own currencies to pay for goods and services from abroad. The agreement also established the World Bank and the International Monetary Fund (IMF), the international financial institutions (IFIs) located in Washington, DC, that were designed to help rebuild countries after the devastation of World War II, and to regulate currency exchanges, so as to prevent a recurrence of the trade rivalries that had triggered the Great Depression of the 1930s.[9]

As the United States expanded with military bases and international security agreements, U.S. corporations with the necessary size and experience went with it. These companies made massive investments abroad in new plant and equipment, producing for foreign markets and later for the U.S. market. Direct investment by private U.S. capital abroad grew rapidly. The plants, mines, distribution centers, and offices of multinational corporations began to establish a global-scale production system. By 1978, one-third of overall profits for the 100 biggest corporations and banks came from overseas operations (Bluestone and Harrison 1982, 113).

Competing with the West were the Communist powers of the Soviet Union (after 1917) and of China (after 1949). Between the capitalist West and the Communist East were the countries of the Third World. The concept of a Third World

(*Tiers Monde*) was introduced by the French journalist Albert Sauvy in 1952. The First World was the West—the United States and its capitalist allies. The Second World was the Communist bloc of the USSR and Eastern Europe, Communist China, and North Korea, which "rejected market capitalism for socialist planning" (Prasad 2007, 11). Finally, the "ignored, exploited, scorned Third World" (Sauvy quoted in Prasad 2007, 10–11) was made up of the newly independent countries that, like the Third Estate of the French Revolution, sought to establish their own economic and political sovereignty.[10] The concept of an independent Third World was embodied in an important international conference at Bandung, Indonesia, in 1955, where leaders including Jawaharlal Nehru of India, Sukarno of Indonesia, and Gamal Abdel Nasser of Egypt founded the Non-Aligned Movement. Although divided ideologically, these nations all sought to make their own decisions about the path to development and modernity.

The ideological rivalries of the cold war gave Third World countries considerable room for maneuver, as the United States and the USSR competed to provide development assistance. Despite its free-market rhetoric, the United States supported state-led development for its allies: Japan, Taiwan, and South Korea. Even though there was great diversity among the developing countries in Asia, Africa, and Latin America, most pursued a common development strategy, which involved a significant role for the state in encouraging industrialization and economic growth. This was clearly the case for the Communist countries of the Soviet Union and China, whose revolutions had taken them out of the orbit of the capitalist system. But for other countries of the Third World, although still within the capitalist orbit, many governments sought to maintain sovereignty over their own economic development. Thus, in Latin America, Argentina and Brazil pursued a policy of "import substitution." Keeping tariff walls high, they encouraged local industry to grow, while seeking funds to build their infrastructure from such First World institutions as the World Bank.

The End of the Long Boom and the Restructuring of the World Economy

Much has been written about the transformation of the international economy since the end of the Long Boom, when, in the early 1970s, economic growth began to slow down worldwide. The challenge to U.S. economic hegemony had been building since the 1960s. The United States was threatened by the economic recovery of Europe and Japan, faced with a strengthened challenge from Third World nationalism abroad (symbolized by the Organization of Petroleum-Exporting Countries [OPEC] price revolution of 1973), and encountering rebellious social movements at home, from Black Power to the women's movement. Weakened by the prolonged war in Vietnam, the United States was losing its competitive advantage. High profit rates began to fall, and no major technological innovations had emerged to match the stimulus to growth represented by the cars, highway, and housing investments of the 1950s (Tanzer 1995).

In response to what both government and corporations perceived as a crisis of profitability, the 1970s saw the inauguration of a radical restructuring of the U.S. and world economy: the deindustrialization of the United States and the rise of the service economy, the ideological shift to neoliberalism, and the intensification of the U.S. role as an imperial power on the world stage. Initially, corporations moved some of their industrial production overseas to areas of cheap labor. Subsequently, they were able to use computerized technology to create just-in-time methods that lowered costs by eliminating big inventories. And reduced transport costs allowed them to streamline delivery by sea and by air.

In Third World countries, governments were induced or forced to open their borders to the free flow of foreign investment. This led them to restructure their economies to focus on currency-earning export industries such as electronics and textiles, drawing on the cheaper labor of women.

In developed economies, a struggle began to limit the role of the welfare state and to replace progressive taxation with tax cuts for the richest families. With globalization came an increasing gap between rich and poor, both within countries and among countries across the globe. Growth rates stagnated, but profits soared (see Amott 1993, 24–48; Pollin 2003, 17–18; Tabb 2001).

The Ideological Shift from Keynesianism to Neoliberalism

The structural changes produced by the search for higher profitability, described in greater detail in what follows, were accompanied by a sea change in political and economic ideology, usually characterized as a shift from Keynesianism to neo-liberalism: an all-out assault on the consensus symbolized by the New Deal.[11]

The Golden Age from 1945 to the mid-1970s had seen a kind of truce between capital and labor, with government accepting a major role in the preservation of high employment, and corporations grudgingly accepting a role for unions in collective bargaining over wages and conditions. The consensus was that government would intervene in the economy to stimulate growth and to preserve a minimal safety net for workers excluded from the workforce.[12]

Broadly, then, *Keynesianism* refers to the use of government monetary and fiscal policy to stimulate demand, to "prime the pump." That government had a major role to play in directing the market was widely accepted across the political spectrum in the United States, from the Eisenhower years through the presidency of Richard Nixon. It was agreed that smoothing out periods of recession and providing programs to sustain consumption through the elements of a "social wage" were normal functions of government. Hence, this period witnessed the introduction of health insurance programs such as Medicare and Medicaid; job creation programs such as the Comprehensive Employment and

Training Act; and community development programs directed toward inner-city enclaves such as those programs introduced after the urban uprisings of the 1960s. Even direct income support in the form of a guaranteed payment to all families was being considered by the Nixon administration in 1971 (see Fortunato 2007, 47). As Nixon is widely quoted as saying, "We are all Keynesians now."[13]

The shift to neoliberalism meant a turn toward deregulation of the economy. Neoliberalism preached a minimal role for government, but as many scholars have argued, what it really meant was that governments now became the engines of globalization. As the power of trade unions weakened, governments enhanced their capacities for control and repression, expanding incarceration and police powers, while whittling away the economic safety net.

Both a philosophy of limited government and a set of prescriptions for economic growth, neoliberalism was born in Chicago: "Starting from a tiny embryo at the University of Chicago with the philosopher-economist Friedrich von Hayek and followers like economist Milton Friedman at its nucleus, the neoliberals and their funders created a huge international network of foundations, institutes, research centers, publications, scholars, writers and public relations experts to develop, package, and push their doctrine" (George 2002, 4). As Alan Nasser points out, what is conventionally termed *neoliberalism* was really a return to the pre–New Deal consensus of permitting the business cycle to proceed untrammeled by government intervention. The ascendancy of this set of ideas is linked to the regimes of Margaret Thatcher in England (1979–1990) and Ronald Reagan in the United States (1981–1989), and received renewed vigor under the administration of George W. Bush. Its political effectiveness can be dated from the successful passage of Proposition 13 in California in 1978, which set limits on the growth of property taxes, and the firing of the striking Professional Air Traffic Controllers by President Reagan in 1981 (Amott 1993, 34; Nasser 2003).

The elements of the neoliberal offensive, driven by an increasingly effective coalition of right-wing and right-leaning politicians, were many. They included attacks on labor and the right to organize; delegitimization of the welfare state and the concept of progressive taxation; devaluing of the role of government in stimulating economic growth and full employment; privatizing or contracting out of public functions and organizations; and deregulation to remove the constraints on corporations imposed by government policies in such areas as environmental regulation, affirmative action, banking, utilities, and the media.

This process began with the New York City fiscal crisis of the 1970s. New York's municipal bankruptcy became the occasion for a counterattack on "bloated" unions and "out-of-control" welfare spending. Placing New York City in receivership under the control of the banks, the leadership of the city enforced what was in effect the first structural adjustment program (see Tabb 1982, 11; it was in the New York City fiscal crisis that "the liberal 1960s turned into the neoconservative 1970s." On structural adjustment, see "Counterrevolution in the Third World" later in this chapter).

The fiscal crisis of New York, Tabb notes, began the turn from "redistributive liberalism" to "neoconservative privatization" (Tabb 1982, 12). This ideological offensive represented a rollback of the social gains of the 1960s and early 1970s. Think tanks such as the Manhattan Institute and writers such as Charles Murray (1984) began to push this new ideology, which placed "personal responsibility" and an attack on dependency at the center of its worldview. The targets included not only the New Deal under Franklin D. Roosevelt, and the social programs of the 1960s in the United States, but also the "Evil Empire" of the Soviet Union. With the fall of the USSR in 1989–1991, the new ideologues expressed triumphalism over the end of the cold war, demonizing the remaining countries, Cuba for one, that made state economic planning and the elimination of poverty, disease, and illiteracy their main goals.

The rhetoric of neoliberalism condemned welfare and the welfare state as undermining individualized liberty and self-determination. As Nancy Fraser and Linda Gordon (2003) note, the ideological sleight of hand here was to conflate personal dependency (a feature of human life from birth as a helpless infant to old age) with dependency on the state, and to elevate autonomy and independence as the principal (and only) human virtues. The language was genderized: the expression, dripping with contempt, the *nanny state,* still used on a regular basis by the British weekly *The Economist* and even on occasion by the *New York Times,* evokes the idea that those who depend on the state for their sustenance are weak, that is, female, whereas those who successfully navigate the rough waters of the market are strong and virile, aka male (see Sawer 1996 for this point; see also Folbre 2001, 83–108, for a history and defense of the nanny state).

Deindustrialization and the New International Division of Labor

The U.S. economy had already begun a process of deindustrialization, or the growth of the rust belt. From the 1960s onward, manufacturers began replacing the postwar domestic strategy of moving industries such as textiles from the unionized North to the nonunion South with a new international strategy. They began to move some elements of production overseas, taking advantage of cheaper labor, anti-union policies, and the establishment of free-trade export-processing zones. The traditional U.S. industrial base was hollowed out, as great industrial cities such as Buffalo, Pittsburgh, and Cleveland lost their manufacturing base (see Freeman 2000, 24–30; Froebel, Heinrich, and Kreye 1980; Mies 1998, 112–120).

Scholars dubbed this change a "new international division of labor" (see Fernandez-Kelly 1989; Froebel et al. 1980; Mies 1998). What was the old international division of labor? From the rise of colonialism, colonized countries had provided raw materials to the governing powers such as the Netherlands and Great Britain, which turned those materials into manufactured goods to sell back to their colonies. Colonialism involved a brutal restructuring of indigenous economies, including the transport of peoples for slavery and indentured servitude from continent to continent, accompanied by the deliberate destruction of long-standing local industries, most famously the ancient and legendary indigenous muslin of Bengal, to provide a market for products from the colonial powers (see Kabeer 2000, 54–56; McMichael 2004).[14] In this period, core or developed countries sold two-thirds of their manufactured exports to the periphery and absorbed four-fifths of their primary production (Dicken 1998, 21).

In the postindependence era from the late 1950s on, the countries emerging from colonial rule in Asia, Africa, and Latin America sought to achieve economic independence through a process of industrialization. But the United States and the other industrial giants steadily tried to preserve the old colonial pattern. As the late Harry Magdoff noted, the goal of U.S. foreign policy after 1945 was to "make the world safe for mineral development." This meant integrating developing countries into world capitalist markets so that they never took a path toward self-reliance. They were to depend on exports of raw materials, adapting their industrial structure toward specialized exports at a price acceptable to the buyer. Thus, in Latin America, despite industrialization and the stimulus of two world wars, agriculture and minerals still made up 90 percent of exports (Magdoff 1969, 198).

In the new era of intensified international economic competition, this pattern was gradually replaced by a new industrial strategy of placing some elements of production in the former colonies to take advantage of the cheaper labor force. This was particularly widespread in the case of the electronics, toys, footwear, and textiles industries, where female labor was preferred. From Taiwan to Malaysia and Indonesia, from Mexico and the Caribbean to South America, women's "nimble [and cheap] fingers" made them the workforce of choice for these labor-intensive industries, which increased the profits of the multinational corporations, while they also brought in much-needed foreign currency to local governments (see Wichterich 2000, 1–33).

The growth of export-processing zones continues to this day, relying primarily on a young, cheap, fairly uneducated female labor force that is subject to extreme exploitation. EPZs grew from 79 in 25 countries in 1975 to more than 3,000 in 116 nations in 2002. Employment in the zones was estimated in 2004 at just under 42 million.[15] With labor organizing suppressed, and environmental regulations virtually nonexistent, these workers "endure unhealthy and unsafe working conditions," earning salaries that are inadequate to support them or their families. There is high turnover in these jobs, sometimes due to disabilities caused by the work, and sometimes due to the employers' preference for younger women: the average Mexican worker, for example, spends about three years in maquiladora employment (Cravey 1998, 6–7).

Simultaneously, other areas of production were retained within the continental United States through the use of automation and immigrant labor, primarily female, to reduce costs (see Fernandez-Kelly 1989). Despite this, a second wave of outsourcing took place, particularly in the white-collar service sector, from call centers in India to airline ticket centers in the Caribbean (see, for example, Glater 2004). Here, too, female labor was crucial, and companies went out of their way to make the work attractive to local women (see Freeman 2000 on "pink-collar" data entry processing in Barbados, for example).

Thus, one key element of globalization was the dispersion of manufacturing, and subsequently services, to cheap labor areas of the world, most notably China, via the establishment of a global assembly line. In some categories of production, the profitability of these areas is assured by the use of a low-paid female labor force. Here is the first use of women's labor as part of globalization. (For more on EPZs, see Chapter 5.)

The Growth of the Service Sector

Another major feature of globalization was the growth of the service sector. The traditional way of defining services was as a residual category, for things neither "dug out of the ground" nor manufactured (Dicken 1998, 388). Even though this definition is still essentially valid, modern service activities are a range of "lubricating" activities, that is, areas that "service" the entire range of production, as well as areas that represent human services in their own right. Service inputs are needed at every stage of production, from planning (feasibility studies) to actual production (quality control, accounting, and training) to "downstream" (advertising, repairs, maintenance, i.e., "service" itself!). But in addition, the service sector includes transportation and public utilities; wholesale and retail trade; finance, insurance, and real estate (FIRE); government; health; education; and business and personal services. This sector accounts for the largest share of GDP in all but the least-developed market economies (Dicken 1998, 387). (For a definition of GDP, see note 8 for this chapter.)

The expansion of the service sector was a worldwide phenomenon: "The field of services has been internationalized in response to the spread of multinational or transnational corporations (TNCs). As manufacturing TNCs have proliferated globally, so, too, have the major banks, advertising agencies, legal firms, property companies, insurance companies, freight corporations, travel and hotel chains, car rental firms and credit card enterprises" (Dicken 1998, 392). The growth of the service sector was well under way in the United States after World War II. But the process accelerated starting in the 1970s. From 1970 to 2000, service sector jobs more than doubled, from 49 million to 102 million, while employment in goods-producing industries increased by only 15 percent (from 26 million to 30 million).[16]

With the growth of the service sector came a rapid increase in women's employment. In the United States from 1970 to 2000, of the 57 million new jobs created, about 60 percent of these went to women. This trend was already visible by the mid-1980s. The shift reflected "both the increase in women's labor force participation and the disproportionate increase in service industries and in occupations where significant numbers of women [were] employed"(Kuhn and Bluestone 1987, 9). As economist Heidi Hartmann notes: "The process of drawing women into the service sector was an interactive process. The service sector grows because the availability of cheap female labor provides the supply and because the use of women in the labor market rather than at home also provides the demand for replacement services (fast food replacing home cooking, for example)... And the shift toward the commercialization of personal services is required by women's increased labor force participation" (Hartmann 1987, 55). As a result, the percentage of the adult U.S. female population employed outside the home rose from 35 percent in 1960 to over 60 percent today (Mather 2007).

Despite the attempts after World War II to return women to domesticity, married women increasingly stayed in paid employment from 1940 onward. In 1940, the labor force participation rate among married women was only 15.6 percent, whereas today it is well over 60 percent. (See Chapter 2 for further discussion.) For employers, this was crucial, since, particularly with the growth of the service sector, married women constituted a major untapped pool of labor. As we will see, the powerful taboo against married women in the workforce was overcome by a combination of the economic need for a dual-worker household and the ideology of 1970s feminism.

The Explosion of the Financial Sector

Underlying the rapid growth of the service sector was the enormous expansion of the financial sector. Increasingly, investors sought profits not through the process of manufacturing, but through finance. As the editors of *Monthly Review* note, the "enormous financial expansion of the system" has become "a primary means of utilizing economic surplus." Kevin Phillips argues that "in the last few decades, the United States economy has been transformed through what I call financialization. The processes of money management, securities management, corporate reorganization, securitization of assets, derivatives trading and other forms of securities packaging are steadily replacing the act of making, growing and transporting things" (cited in "Crises" 2002, 53). In Table 1.1, a comparison of goods-producing industries with those of finance, insurance, and real estate (FIRE), as a percent of GDP, shows the dramatic change. "In the absence of sufficient profit opportunities for the goods-producing industries, capital sought other means to make profits. That is where the explosion of debt came on stage" ("Crises" 2002, 53–54).

Table 1.1

	1947	1977	2000
Private goods-producing industries	41.9	32.9	22.5
Finance, insurance, and real estate	9.7	13.9	19.6

The 1970s and 1980s were marked by intensive growth in financial invest-ment and speculative transactions. The explosion in financial services is linked to another feature of globalization, namely, the deregulation of financial markets. Before the 1960s, countries exerted careful control over financial markets and institutions, so as to manage their economies and try to avoid periodic crises. But from the mid-1960s onward, these controls were dismantled.

Bank lending across national borders in the 1960s was only about 1 percent of the GDP of market economies. By the mid-1980s, it had reached 20 percent of much higher levels of GDP. Richard Barnet describes the global financial network as a maze of transactions, "a chain of gambling casinos ... [through which] trillions of dollars flow through the world's foreign exchange markets each day, of which no more than 10 percent is linked to trade in goods and ser-vices" (quoted in Tanzer 1995, 6). One measure of this growth of finance is that in 2006 the Bank of International Settlements, the Basel-based bank for central banks, calculated that the value of the total amount of financial "derivatives" outstanding was $415 trillion, or eight times the total value of world GDP for the year (Weiss 2007, 3).

The increase in the size of the service sector reflected a major shift in where investors were putting their money. From the end of World War II through the 1970s, goods production (mining, construction, and manufacturing) accounted for about 32 percent of all new private (nonresidential) investment, whereas in the 1980s and 1990s its share was only 18 percent. In contrast, in the FIRE sec-tor, the share of investment flows jumped from 16 percent in the first period to 30 percent in the second period.

Increased employment in this financial sector was required to handle the massive volumes of information being transferred in this industry. "Access to large pools of appropriate (often female) labor was a key requirement" (Dicken 1998, 418). Thus, the explosion in financial transactions directly impacted the employment of women. Again, the figures tell the story. In the 1960s and 1970s, the share of FIRE in GDP remained virtually constant, at between 13 and 14 percent. However, the percentage of employees in FIRE who were women in-creased sharply, from 46 percent in 1960 to 58 percent in 1980. Then, in the 1980s and 1990s, while the percentage of employees in FIRE who were women leveled off, the total FIRE sector grew rapidly, reaching 20 percent of GDP by 2000.[17] The two factors together, the increasing feminization of the FIRE sector and the increasing growth of the FIRE sector itself, were a major source of increased employment for women.

Suppression of Labor Unions and Shift to a Low-Wage Contingent Workforce

A closely linked development was the suppression of labor unions. In the business press, unions were blamed for the inflationary pressures that in reality stemmed largely from the combination of prosecuting the war in Vietnam and pursuing Lyndon Johnson's War on Poverty. The firing of the striking air traffic controllers under Reagan in 1981, as noted earlier, is often cited as a symbolic turning point. Unions were perceived by management as a drag on profitability, and the Reagan years inaugurated a period of severe attacks on labor organizing that has continued to the present day. (See further discussion of the continuing attacks on labor unions in Chapter 4.)

In addition, new models of employment were being developed that were to replace the traditional expectations of permanent well-paid employment with a workforce heavily based on contingent, low-wage labor. The pioneer in this area was the fast-food industry, where the ideal employee was young and replaceable, and where training was minimal, as was the expectation of promotion into management. These patterns were reproduced in "big box" retailing, with Wal-Mart the leading example. But low-wage jobs spread across the entire economy. More than 30 million workers, a majority female and a large percentage of them minority and immigrant, worked in areas ranging from poultry and fish processing, retail store work, hotels, janitors, and call-center workers, to child care workers (see Shulman 2005, 6–7).

A similar, if less visible, transformation took place in university hiring. Out of 1.1 million faculty members in the United States in 2003, only 28 percent were tenured and full-time and 12 percent were tenure track (that is, presumably on the way to receiving tenure); the remaining 60 percent of faculty members were part-time or non–tenure track (see Jacobe 2006, 46). At the City University of New York, where I teach, the majority of all classes are taught by adjunct professors with no job security, earning about $3,000 per semester for a three-credit course (Rajendra and Hogness 2008, 4). Inevitably, low-paid, part-time jobs such as adjuncting or working at Wal-Mart are largely women's jobs. (For more on this topic, see Chapter 4.)

Counterrevolution in the Third World

Meanwhile, for Third World countries, there were also drastic changes. The big jump in oil prices in 1973, under a revitalized OPEC, with the accompanying influx of petrodollars into First World banking institutions, had created conditions where banks and investors lent freely to the developing states of Latin America, Asia, and Africa.[18] But the decision of U.S. policymakers to dramatically increase interest rates as a weapon against inflation—the so-called Volcker shock of 1979–1982—sharply increased the cost of borrowing.[19]

> Two other shocks compounded the impact of U.S. policy on the Third World. The 1979–1980 oil price increase raised import costs for all the oil-poor LDCs [least-developed countries] while the recession in the West reduced demand for developing country exports. These three factors—interest rate increases, oil price hikes, and recession in the . . . [developed countries]—increased the need for foreign money even as it became less available. The debtors hung on by using new loans for the oil bill and for interest payments on previously borrowed money. In the last half of 1981 Latin America borrowed a billion dollars a week, mostly to pay off existing debt. (Frieden 2006, 374)

In the summer of 1982, Mexico declared bankruptcy, and this triggered an abrupt halt in private lending to the developing world: "The flow of funds shifted abruptly from southward to northward. In 1981 twenty billion more dollars had flowed into Latin America than flowed out; in 1983, as lending ended and governments scrambled to pay their debts, a net twenty billion dollars flowed out of Latin America" (Frieden 2006, 374). A debt crisis "of 1930s proportions" was the result (Frieden 2006, 374). This created an opening for the use of SAPs and a counterattack against state-led development in the Third World.

Creditors forced Third World countries to approach the International Monetary Fund "to plan a program of macroeconomic stabilization and economic adjustment," with targets for inflation, government spending, budget deficits, and other so-called conditionalities. Other investors regarded an agreement with the IMF as a "seal of approval," and would agree to resume their lending (Frieden 2006, 375). Thus, the debt crisis of the 1980s recapitulated the municipal crisis of New York City in the 1970s, but on a global scale. Just as major financial institutions were able to restructure the New York economy, so international banks could use the crisis to reshape the priorities of Third World governments.

The new neoliberal doctrine was first tried out under the dictatorship of Augusto Pinochet in Chile (1973–1990). It was subsequently imposed by the international financial institutions, particularly the Bretton Woods institutions (the International Monetary Fund and the World Bank), which used the debt crisis of the 1980s to restructure the economies of those countries that had come under their sway.[20] The new functions of the IFIs constituted, in effect, a counterrevolution against Third World countries, as SAPs, with their requirements of privatizing, cutting public spending, and reorienting economies toward acquiring foreign currency to repay their debt, effectively ended the era of state-led development.

Through the imposition of conditionalities, the IFIs virtually forced indebted governments to accede to a radical series of changes. In the name of what neoliberal economists termed *macroeconomic stabilization* and *structural reform,* governments were induced to devalue their currencies, cut public expenditures, end food and fuel subsidies to "realign" domestic prices to the world market, liberalize trade, privatize state enterprises, and regularize titles to land, often resulting in the forfeiture by peasant farmers of their customary land rights to large landlords (Chossudovsky 2003, 35–64).

A third international financial institution, the World Trade Organization (WTO), established in 1995, and based in Geneva, Switzerland, reinforced these policies with a set of rules about "free trade" that gave preference to the interests of corporations over national governments. The WTO, through its secret dispute mechanism, sought to ensure that national legislation on issues such as labor, health, and the environment did not interfere with "competitiveness" in the world marketplace. Establishing a series of protocols on agriculture, trade-related investment, intellectual property rights, and services, the WTO required member states to override national or even state and local regulations that barred the door to "free" (that is corporate) access to local markets (McMichael 2004, 172ff.).[21] These policies opened the door to the dramatic expansion of overseas operations by multinational corporations.[22]

Collectively, these draconian requirements were referred to in the mainstream economic press as the Washington Consensus.[23] The fall of the Soviet Union and of its satellite Eastern European regimes after 1989–1991 gave this set of policies new outlets, as formerly state-run enterprises were privatized, and national economies were forced to abandon state-led development. As Fred Rosen comments, with the sweeping adoption of the Washington Consensus, "the imperfect egalitarian instincts of Keynesian economics and social democratic policies were swept into the dustbin of ideas, left there to commingle with other antiquities like alchemy and astrology" (Rosen 2003).

We should note that the Washington Consensus, applied with such rigor to developing economies, was never required of the developed countries.

> Let's be clear right away that neoliberal theory is one thing and neoliberal practice is another thing entirely. Most members of the Organization for Economic Co-operation and Development (OECD)—including the U.S. federal government—have seen state intervention and state public expenditures increase during the last thirty years.... Even in the United States, President Reagan's neoliberalism did not translate into a decline of the federal public sector. Instead, federal public expenditures increased under his mandate, from 21.6 to 23 percent of GNP [gross national product], as a consequence of a

spectacular growth in military expenditures from 4.9 to 6.1 percent of GNP. (Navarro 2007, 21)[24]

In addition to the United States, some other countries were able to retain their state-led development policies and experienced rapid economic growth: the Tigers of Taiwan, Singapore, Hong Kong, and South Korea, and the newly industrializing countries such as Malaysia, not to mention China. But others in South Asia, Latin America, and sub-Saharan Africa, under the impact of SAPs over the period since the 1980s, suffered low growth and devastating increases in poverty, malnourishment, and disease. Widespread criticism of the impact of SAPs during the 1990s led the World Bank to modify its policies, acknowledging the burdens on "highly indebted" countries and placing a new emphasis on the need for "poverty reduction" (see Petchesky 2003, 142–151). Although this shift was a response to the intensified poverty produced by SAPs, particularly in Africa, governments were still required to follow the basic macroeconomic policies that had produced the intensified poverty in the first place: "The privatization of essential services, like water and electricity and the deterioration or privatization of public services, such as health and education, have never been in the interests of the poor. For instance, the imposition of user fees on health care or education has led to a sharp drop of hospital attendance and school enrolment from poor or low-income families and increased the gender gap, since girls and women are the main victims of those policies" (Dembele 2003). In extreme cases, SAPs helped to produce "failed states," where the fundamental elements of governance no longer functioned, and "ethnic" violence and civil war were the norm (see Federici 2000; for more on SAPs, see Chapter 5).

From the point of view of the U.S. elite, this ensemble of changes has been necessary to maintain the dominance of the United States, both as the premier economy in the world and as its overwhelmingly preeminent military power. Corporate globalization, then, has a military as well as an economic component. In a revealing policy document produced by the Office of Force Transformation in the Pentagon, Thomas Barnett and Henry Gaffney Jr. describe the world as divided into two parts: the globalizing countries and the countries in the "gap":

> As globalization deepens and spreads, two groups of states are essentially pitted against one another: countries seeking to align themselves internally to the emerging global rule (e.g., advanced Western democracies, Vladimir Putin's Russia, Asia's emerging economies) and countries that either refuse such internal realignment or cannot achieve it due to political/cultural rigidity or continuing abject poverty (most of Central Asia, the Middle East, Africa, and Central America). We dub the former countries the Functioning Core of globalization and the latter countries the Non-Integrating Gap. (Barnett and Gaffney 2003, 2)

In this analysis, the gap is where terrorism comes from, and it is the duty of the U.S. military to keep these new barbarians at bay. The authors argue that the United States pays in kind for its enormous balance-of-payments deficit by providing "security" to the rest of the world. Thus, the war on terror fits readily into a strategy of corporate globalization. At this writing, these policies have come together in the occupation of Iraq and the proposed privatization of much of its economy (see Klein 2004).

THE NET EFFECT OF THE CHANGES

What has been the net effect of the changes of the last four decades? In countries enjoying a massive influx of foreign investment, such as China, India, and South Africa, an increasing number of people have joined the middle class, and elites in particular are profiting, as individuals and as a class (see Oza 2006, for example, on India). But the enrichment of middle and upper classes is matched by the impoverishment of working and poor people. The effects of globalization include a decline in public health across the globe; an increase in desperate migration, from agricultural areas to the cities, and from poor countries to rich ones; and a growth of urban slums, not, as in the nineteenth century, because of industrialization, but rather because of its absence. As formal economy jobs shrink, the informal economy grows apace (see Beneria 2003; Davis 2006).[25]

The claims by globalizers of economic progress are belied by the statistics. Vincent Navarro argues that "neoliberal policies have been remarkably unsuccessful at achieving their declared aims: economic efficiency and social well-being." When we compare rates of economic growth in 1960–1980 with 1980–2000 for developing countries (excluding China), for annual economic growth the figures are 5.5 percent versus 2.6 percent. For annual economic growth per capita, they are 3.2 percent versus 0.7 percent.[26] In addition, "Mark Weisbrot, Dean Baker, and David Rosnick have documented that the improvement in quality-of-life and well-being indicators (infant mortality, rate of school enrollment, life expectancy, and others) increased faster during 1960–1980 than 1980–2000" (Navarro 2007, 23).

Even though developed countries also experienced lower growth in the neoliberal period, their much higher starting point means that income inequalities between the developing and developed countries have increased dramatically. In addition, inequalities have grown within countries. "If we consider these two types of inequalities together—that is, within countries and across countries, as Branco Milanovic has documented, the top 1 percent of the world population receives 57 percent of the world income, and the income difference between those at the top and those at the bottom has increased from 78 to 144 times" (Navarro 2007, 24).

Similarly, in the United States, Mark Weisbrot argues that the major impact of globalization for people is a "dramatically worse" income distribution:

> The central issue for Americans facing the global economy is income distribution. Whether it's international trade or investment, or immigration, the main impact on most Americans' lives has been on the distribution of income. And that distribution has gotten dramatically worse over the last 30 years: the rich have gotten a lot richer, the poor have languished, and the middle class has shrunk. From 1972 to 2001, the bottom 20 percent of wage and salary earners got only 1.6 percent of the increase in this income over the three decades. The majority got less than 11 percent. But the richest one percent received 18.4 percent of the increased income—vastly more than went to the majority of Americans. (Weisbrot 2006, 1)

All of the policies brought in under the aegis of neoliberal ideologies, including deregulation, reduction of public expenditure, and privatization of services, have benefited the richest part of the population at the expense of the poor and the working class (Navarro 2007, 25). In fact, we have witnessed the creation of a global class divide, where the elites from transnational corporations—those whom Jeff Faux has called "the Party of Davos"—feel solidarity with one another across national borders, while the poor of all nations are essentially abandoned to their fate (see Faux 2006; Davos is the town in Switzerland where the World Economic Forum usually meets). Thus, even though globalization is described as a process of improving people's lives across the world, in fact we have been witnessing a globalization of poverty (see Chossudovsky 2003; Davis 2006).

It is important to counter the glossy tales in the mainstream press about the benefits of globalization with the lived realities of the current system. These include the brutal deaths among those who seek to migrate illegally from the poor to the rich countries, and the daily dehumanizing life of the poor, living in favelas under the regime of drug lords and complicitous police forces (not to mention the urban planners and administrators who maintain the boundaries).

The same situation prevails in the inner cities of the United States, where racially isolated dead zones provide the revolving population for ever-growing numbers of prisons. As policymakers convince the public that poverty, homelessness, and the other corrosive effects of neoliberal capitalism are no longer the responsibility of government, there is increasing acceptance by the middle class of a permanent zone of hell to which the "underclass" is consigned, without hope of redemption. It is the job of the police to maintain this zone as separate as possible from the lives of the middle class. This is the meaning of debates over the level of crime and whether or not future mayors will keep the crime rate down (see Schwarz 2001; Stevens 2001).

THE NEW ENCLOSURES

Many writers see the modern process of globalization as a renewal of the enclo-sure movement that occurred during the early phase of agricultural capitalism in Great Britain. Karl Marx interpreted the enclosure movement of the early modern period in England as a necessary precondition for the rise of industrial capitalism. "Improving" landlords eliminated the rights and privileges of peasant tenants—their access to the commons, their claim on particular pieces of farmland over the harvest cycle—using law and force to repeal the last vestiges of feudalism and turn agriculture into a market-driven process of production. The thousands of peasants thus driven off the land became vagabonds who were first housed in poorhouses and then served as the reserve army of labor as industrialization took off (Wood 1999).

In the same way, contemporary globalization has as its goal the integration of all remaining parts of the world into one market economy. George Caffentzis, Iain Boal, Silvia Federici, and others have introduced the idea that the contem-porary capitalist project of globalization is a continuation of the English enclo-sure movement. This is a global elimination of the commons, a new enclosure movement, whose goal is to bring the still traditional areas of the world into the global marketplace (Boal 2007; Federici 2001).[27] David Harvey (2003) names this process "accumulation by dispossession." Older cultures are to be trans-formed, and their traditions of collective and tribal connections eliminated, so that self-sufficient, subsistence economies are replaced with societies made up of individuals and consumers.

If we accept this interpretation of globalization, we are witnessing a renewed phenomenon of "enclosure" in country after country across the globe. The pattern of privatization, a key feature of neoliberalism, has been extended from public health, education, and housing to water, with devastating effects. For example, in South Africa communities that cannot afford the fees imposed by private water companies have experienced serious outbreaks of cholera from people drinking unsanitary water.[28]

The process of industrialization in England was accompanied by intense displacement and disruption as a traditional rural way of life was broken up to make way for the factory system of the industrial era. A similar process is under way now, with many Third World countries experiencing what we might call a process of partial industrialization—the establishment of export enclaves (always subject to removal to even lower wage countries)—while their agricultural system is subject to a process of conversion to agribusiness.

In China, the massive migration of peasants from agricultural land, as they are uprooted by developers and drawn into factory work, has displaced 150 mil-lion peasants, who live in shantytowns under conditions of extreme exploitation (Kwong 2006). Some estimate that this is the largest internal migration in world history: "An estimated 20 million children have been left behind to fend for themselves, and rural authorities have noted a marked increase in robbery, petty crime, suicide and rape involving these unsupervised children. In cases where only the husbands depart for the cities the wives are left to care for children and in-laws and to till the family farm. Many are so overburdened that they choose to end their lives, most commonly by swallowing pesticides. China has the highest rate of female suicide in the world, and its rural rate is three times that of the cities" (Kwong 2006, 20). In India, competition from agribusiness, and from cheap agricultural imports, has begun to devastate farmers, who for some years now have been committing suicide in very large numbers (Pollin 2003, 138–142).

I have often tried to evoke the enormity of the change from feudalism to an industrialized society with my undergraduates at Queens College. Imagine, I tell them, that you are a family of serfs living under the feudal system. The bad news is that you have to stay there, and so do your children, for the foreseeable future. The good news is that you will probably not starve to death. When I present them with the idea that, in contrast, unless they have inherited wealth they will all have to sell their labor, women and men alike, for most of their lives, they are totally blasé. This is not news to them, nor does it appear horrific. When I suggest to them that their view of themselves as a commodity is the product of a long historical development, going back centuries, they usually roll their eyes in disbelief (although one or two people in each class appear to grasp how momentous a change this is in human subjectivity). In other words, most of my students, like most Americans, have internalized the requirement of competing in the marketplace for their subsistence as the most normal of situations, barely worthy of comment.

But this acceptance of the harsh requirements of the market, which my students share with most people in the industrialized world, is by no means a fait accompli in the places to which globalized capital is now spreading. Resistance to neoliberalism is showing signs of growth. The antiglobalization movement was gaining traction in the years before September 11, 2001, with its challenges to the international financial institutions in campaigns such as "Fifty Years Is Enough!" and its documentation of the increasing immiseration and growing inequalities around the world, both within countries and from country to country. Particularly in Latin America, strong, organized social movements, in some cases with a major presence of indigenous actors, have rolled back privatization—as in the famous case of the water system in Cochabamba, Bolivia—and have brought to power antineoliberal leaders such as Hugo Chávez in Venezuela, Evo Morales in Bolivia, and other left-leaning politicians (Danaher 1994; Grandin 2006).

Women have been major actors in the resistance to globalization. Some of the most well-known are intellectuals and activists such as the novelist and essayist Arundhati Roy and the ecological scientist Vandana Shiva, both of India, and 2004 Nobel Prize winner Wangaria Muta Maathai of Kenya, founder of the women's Green Belt movement, which has planted millions of trees in her home country and elsewhere in Africa. But masses of indigenous, peasant, and working-class women have also been in the forefront of many of these struggles. In India, women have been major participants in the Save the Narmada anti–big dams movement, and have led the Chipko movement (the original "tree huggers") that protects crucial forests against logging in Uttar Pradesh and elsewhere. Recently in Nigeria, women have become major actors in the struggle against the environmental and social impact of the operations of the big oil companies in the Niger Delta of that country. Most famous, perhaps, is the activism of the highly visible indigenous women of Chiapas, Mexico, in the Zapatista movement, whose uprising in 1994 in response to NAFTA was widely considered to be the beginning of the visible antiglobalization movement. Similarly, in the developed world, women have been leaders in movements to contest the destruction of the union movement, to resist the dumping of toxic waste, and to fight for public education, housing, and the rights of immigrants (see Ezeilo 2007; Maathai 2006; Marcos 2005; Naples 1998; Rowbotham and Linkogle 1994b; Roy 1999; Shiva 1989, 67ff.).

In response to the claims of the worldwide social justice movement, leaders of the G-8 and other members of the international elite have been forced to give at least lip service to the idea of ending poverty and debt.[29] (See Chapter 5 for further discussion of this point.) Former President Bill Clinton is enjoying a new career as an advocate of worldwide AIDS prevention and treatment, in collaboration with Bill and Melinda Gates. Given the widespread political and cultural resistance to globalization, it is an ever more urgent task for the elites of Davos to promote the virtues of neoliberal capitalism to the people being subjected to it. It is in this context, I want to argue, that the "freedom" experienced by women in the developed world becomes a selling point across the globe.

2

Women, Work, and the Mainstreaming of Feminism

✦

In this chapter I will argue that the ideology of twenty-first-century feminism lends itself to the principles behind globalization. Despite the backlash against feminism that began with the rise of the New Right in the early 1970s, a hegemonic version of mainstream feminism became widely accepted in U.S. life.[1] The entry of both working-class and middle-class married women into the paid workforce was accompanied by a "bourgeois revolution" for women. Liberated from the feudal aspects of the marriage contract, they emerged as economic actors in their own right.

As deindustrialization and the expansion of the service sector increasingly drew on women's labor, women successfully redefined themselves primarily as workers rather than as homemakers. Hegemonic U.S. feminism preached work as liberation, with individualism and self-development the major goals. The domesticity of the 1950s was trashed, and a new mythology was forged: the Horatio Alger protagonist as a woman.[2]

Women's studies scholarship contributed to what I call "the abolition of gender," that is, the notion that no essential differences between men and women could stand in the way of women's access to all areas of public life, from the cockpit to the corner office, and from the professoriate to the Pentagon. A show launched in 2005 on ABC television, *Commander in Chief,* encapsulated this view of women's liberation, although the series did not survive into a second season.[3] But the presidential candidacy of Hillary Rodham Clinton in the Democratic primary races of 2008 took the idea of the first woman president from a media fantasy to a real possibility, as did the nomination of Alaska governor Sarah Palin for vice president by the Republicans.[4]

PRELUDE: FROM THE COLONIAL PERIOD
TO WORLD WAR II

Where did hegemonic feminism come from? My contention, throughout the book, is that the rise of hegemonic feminism in the current era is deeply tied to the political economy of women's paid and unpaid labor. I see the unprecedented shift in women's workforce participation in the last four decades as the fundamental underpinning of the rise of contemporary feminism. In order to make this argument, I will turn first to a short summary of women's economic and work history in the United States. Even though this overview addresses the experience of the majority of women, I am aware that I am not doing justice to the complex interaction of race, ethnicity, and gender during these years.[5]

In the period from white "settlement" to the onset of the Industrial Revolution, virtually all necessities were derived from the farm economy.[6] In this respect the work of enslaved women in the plantation economy of the South was parallel to the work of white farming women in the Northeast. Agricultural tasks and household tasks, production of clothing, food, and other goods, were all women's work, and women's contribution to the family economy was crucial. Obviously, the conditions of slavery can in no way be compared to the conditions for women who were not enslaved, although this comparison was common among the white abolitionist and suffrage community in the pre–Civil War era. But no family, slave or free, could manage without the goods produced by women's labor.

In the colonial era, marriage was a vocation for white women. Being part of a husband and wife team was the chief means of survival. In the agrarian setting women's roles were multiple: they were midwives, psychologists, educators, and producers of cloth, cheese, butter, and a range of other foodstuffs. Wives were not necessarily limited to household production; they could also assume male roles such as innkeeper, lawyer, or, even, entrepreneur. Some women from major landowning and slave-owning families became important economic players: for example, Eliza Lucas Pinckney of South Carolina first developed indigo as a crop and Martha Smith helped found the whaling industry.

At this time, most unmarried women were impoverished and were considered by local elites to be a serious moral problem for society. They were often forced into workhouses, where their labor was used in the "putting-out system" (the predecessor of factory work) to spin, sew, and weave. Ruling groups expressed great concern over female poverty, and especially over a woman being unmarried, since marriage was perceived as a primary means of keeping women properly under control. In the Puritan Northeast, control of women was enforced with particular harshness. The famous case of Anne Hutchinson, expelled by the Massachusetts Bay Colony in 1637 for preaching to men, was only one of many cases of women being persecuted for a failure to adhere to the rules of wifely submission (Kessler-Harris 1982, 15–16).

To the political leaders of the new Republic, the "idleness" of women was seen as sinful. Thus, when Alexander Hamilton and his Federalist allies began to conceive of the need to defend the U.S. economy against cheap British imports by establishing indigenous U.S. factories, they considered unmarried women the ideal workforce. The initial factories producing textiles in Lowell, Massachusetts, famously drew on the daughters of white farmers. In part the factory owners shared a conscious desire to avoid reproducing the notorious "satanic" mills of England, and in part they sought to convince farm families that their daughters would make a suitable workforce. Thus, to reassure families that their daughters' factory work was respectable and would not injure their chances for marriage, factory owners built dormitories where religious services were offered and nighttime curfews were imposed. By most accounts the early mill workers were delighted with their economic independence, but not with their working conditions: they began to develop the first women's trade union organizations.[7] The era of the mill girls lasted until the severe depression of 1837, when massive immigration from Ireland allowed mill owners to switch to a largely immigrant workforce, and to speed up production while providing many fewer amenities.

With the growing reach of manufacturing, there was a steady decline of home production. As the highly religious "moral community" of the seventeenth and eighteenth centuries gave way to the culture of competitive individualism in the early nineteenth century, the ethos for both male and female workers began to change. Under Jacksonian democracy, men were expected to make their way in the harsh climate of the new industrialism, either as entrepreneurs or as deskilled former artisans, now streaming into the new factories. In contrast, the idea of the home as a compensatory "haven in a heartless world" became a mainstream ideology for white women.[8]

The Victorian ideology of separate spheres did not put an end to women working for wages. But it served to stigmatize those women who did seek work for wages, which included formerly enslaved African American women and immigrant women, thus sharpening class differences. The overall effect of the domestic code during this period was to keep women's wages so depressed that being a working girl was seen as a social problem (Kessler-Harris 1982, 49ff.). After the Civil War, the minority of unmarried women who had to work were now impoverished. The jobs available—teacher, domestic servant, textile work in factories or at home—did not pay enough to keep body and soul together. Some women workers sought to organize into cooperatives or unions—with some men supporting them while others opposed them as undercutting male wages. But middle-class women saw their role as protecting poor women, creating clubs to provide them with the proper attitudes and prepare them for marriage.

With the advent of the Progressive Era (1890s to 1920s), and with labor struggles increasingly bitter and violent, women reformers began to take on the problems of immigrant women workers. The organizers of the Women's Trade

Union League (WTUL), founded in 1903, established an effective cross-class alliance with women factory workers. With the assistance of the WTUL, the young Jewish and Italian women garment workers of New York's Lower East Side sought to unionize under the auspices of the American Federation of Labor (AFL), whose leaders tended to ignore or dismiss women workers. Middle-class and socialist allies volunteered for the picket lines, posted bail, and in 1909 organized a major parade in which women of all classes, including notoriously the banker J. P. Morgan's daughter Anne, showed their support for the strikers.

After a series of dramatic strikes from 1909 to 1913, the garment workers were able to win increased wages, a fifty-hour week, and the right to union recognition. The centrality of women for union organizing was proved dramatically by these events, but the deadly fire in March 1911 at the Triangle Shirtwaist factory in New York persuaded the WTUL that protective legislation by the state would be the best tool to aid working women. Overall, then, women reformers, dubbed "social feminists" by historians, shared a maternalist vision: poor women needed help, not to gain an independent income, but to be able to maintain their role as wives and mothers.[9]

The struggle for protective legislation in this period remained within this framework. Unions and Progressives came together in the campaign to create protective legislation, which was accepted by most states. Measures included limiting the number of hours women could work in a day, prohibiting night work, limiting the amount of weight women workers could lift, and excluding women from categories of work considered unsuitable for them, such as mining or selling alcoholic beverages. This movement received legal blessing in the *Muller v. Oregon* Supreme Court decision of 1908, which held that it was legitimate for the state to protect women, whose delicate constitutions and whose responsibility for childrearing justified this otherwise unconstitutional intervention into the market (Kessler-Harris 1982, 185ff.).[10]

The ideology surrounding women's work was further cemented with the introduction of what were called mothers' pensions, a small stipend for "deserving" widows and deserted mothers, also legislated by most states. Women were supposed to be married and raising children. Women who had to work deserved state protection. And worthy widows and other single mothers had the right to a government-provided income, so that they would not be driven into the workforce. (On mothers' pensions, see Skocpol 1992 and Gordon 1994; African American women were excluded de facto by the Jim Crow Southern states.)

The establishment of mothers' pensions and of protective legislation set the stage for the acceptance of the family wage, which was formally sought by the AFL from 1907 on as the way to permit working husbands to support their wives and children. The family wage (or living wage) assumed that all wage-earning women were single (and therefore should receive a lower wage than men) and that they would leave the formal workforce once married. Men, even while still single, deserved the higher wages necessary to support the family they would found, sooner or later.

For its time, the idea of the family wage embodied an important challenge to the capitalist system:

> In the lexicon of their day, unionists and their progressive allies wanted "a living wage" sufficient to sustain a working-class family in dignity and comfort. The living wage idea was itself often shot through with patriarchal and racist assumptions, but it nevertheless generated a radical critique of the capitalist marketplace. The labor movement's critique of "wage slavery" therefore embodied not just a derogatory comparison between white and black labor, but the promise that good wages would generate the conditions necessary for industrial freedom itself. As the eight-hour crusader Ira Steward put it in 1879, "when the working classes are denied everything but the barest necessities of life, they have no decent use for liberty." (Lichtenstein 2002, 5)

The claim from union leaders was echoed by middle-class reformers. Progressive Era activists saw a stable family with a working husband and a full-time housewife and mother as a key to social stability. This was the vision of many social feminists, such as Florence Kelley and Jane Addams, even though these women were themselves generally unmarried. (See Sklar, 1997.) But this was congruent with the ideology they were committed to, since married women were not supposed to be in the workforce or in public life. The flurry of social science research in this period on household budgets and the cost of living calculated the nutritional needs of families based on a male family wage.

In some cases, manufacturers pioneered the family wage themselves. Henry Ford of the Ford Motor Co. introduced in 1914 the (at that time) generous wage of $5 a day for workers who were married and therefore seen as stable. The Ford family wage proved to be a dramatic success, cutting down the high turnover previously common in the industry. This innovation contributed to a steady rise in Ford's profits, thereby allowing the company to beat out the competition. [11]

By World War I, the federal government had accepted the concept. Thus, the National War Labor Board used family-wage-based budget studies to adjust government-pegged wages. "Once the family-wage ideology became part of a cross-class ideology, it had the status of a truism, an easily accepted statement on the best organization of life" (May 1985, 11). The family wage had ideological resonance, even though the union movement was never powerful enough to win this level of pay for the majority of male workers.

From the 1880s onward, with the transformation of U.S. capitalism from the small businesses of the pre–Civil War era to the first giant monopoly corporations in oil and steel, the structure of business began to require massive infusions of clerical labor. With the introduction of the typewriter to industry by the Remington and Sons company, the reconfiguration of clerical work as a woman's arena took place over a remarkably short period of time, as manufacturers drew on the substantial pool of educated white women who were largely excluded from other professions. In 1880, only 4 percent of the clerical labor force were women. By 1890, the figure had jumped to 21 percent. And by 1920, women made up 50 percent of the clerical workers as well as 50 percent of all low-level office workers (Baxandall and Gordon 1995, 207, citing Davies 1984). From male clerks wearing green eye shades and sitting on high stools to write down columns of figures, the typical clerical worker became a white, educated, unmarried woman, the Gibson girl wearing the ready-to-wear shirtwaists being sewn in sweatshops in the New York garment industry by her immigrant sisters. The telephone industry similarly hired young white women.

During and then after World War I, employers in an increasing range of industries began to hire women workers. Women's increasing workforce participation during the war acquired "unprecedented public prominence," and after the second military draft of 1918, "women workers became a precious resource." But as women workers responded by switching workplaces to seek better wages and conditions, male workers objected strenuously: "Male unionists reacted with hostility when employers hired women to dilute skilled labor, break strikes, lower wages, or introduce new technology. Acrimony between men and women workers flared especially in metalworking plants, foundries, offices, coal mines, and on streetcar lines. Men rejected women workers' introduction into new fields most vehemently when they perceived a threat from women's economic competition" (Greenwald 1989, 125).

The situation was complicated with the emergence of early-twentieth-century feminism, defined as the idea that women can and should have independent incomes (see Cott 1987). An intense debate broke out among labor activists over the role of working women. Thus, for example, in Seattle married women who embraced the new feminist ideal, and considered that they had a right to work for wages, came up against the strongly held views of labor:

> Working-class feminists in Seattle clashed head on with opponents of married women's employment who subscribed to the ideals of the family wage and the moral economy, two of the most revered precepts of the Seattle labor movement. Wage work by married women violated both ideals; both condemned it as improper and unfair. The family wage ideal, in which the male breadwinner earned enough to support his wife and children, constituted a class aspiration shared by men and women. The idea of the moral economy postulated that financial need alone should determine who had a legitimate claim to wage work. From both perspectives, married women had no right to work except in cases of absolute economic necessity. Proponents of the family wage and the moral economy believed that their ideas represented the fairest arrangement possible in a highly competitive labor market with chronic unemployment. (Greenwald 1989, 121)

The whole discussion took place within the context of great labor ferment in Seattle, where radical views included the idea that workers should take over production altogether. But the labor movement in Seattle was fatally weakened after a general strike in 1919 was defeated, and employers launched an open shop campaign that diminished labor's power in the city. As a result, in the 1920s the labor movement was unable to stem the rising tide of married women's entry into the labor market. (Greenwald 1989, 149)

After World War I, white women's occupations included teaching, nursing, clerical work, factory work, and, for upper-class women, the beginnings of entry into law, medicine, and social work. Black women remained the majority of domestic workers and, in the South, continued to be agricultural workers, although the Great Migration to northern cities through the 1930s reduced their numbers.

The first wave of feminism had culminated in the passage of the Nineteenth Amendment, giving women the vote in 1920. In practice, this was a voting right primarily for white women, since voting for African Americans in the Jim Crow South was severely restricted or completely blocked. Now some white feminists turned their attention to issues of women in the workforce, developing an ideology of women's rights that challenged the protectionist consensus that lay behind the family wage concept. The debate over protective legislation, which was to rage among different groups of feminists from the 1920s until the 1960s, encapsulated two opposing concepts of the role of working women.

On the one hand, the new feminists argued that women should be as free as men to compete for work in an open market. On the other hand, other feminists—usually union activists—bitterly opposed this idea, arguing that women in the workforce required a range of protections, given their unique role as wives and mothers. From the perspective of the early twenty-first century, this famous debate over protective legislation has echoes in the contemporary debate between neoliberal advocates of the so-called free, deregulated market and their opponents who seek an active role for government in the operations of the economy.

An equal rights amendment (ERA) was introduced into Congress in 1923 by the National Women's Party (NWP) headed by Alice Paul. The amendment sought to abolish restrictive job protections so that women could compete equally in the workplace. In this move, Paul and her associates had the active support of manufacturers' organizations, which opposed protective legislation as they did most other forms of restrictive government regulation of business. But union women fought the Equal Rights Amendment bitterly, and were successful in preventing its passage by Congress until the 1960s. What was the basis of this split among working women? It was directly related to class differences. As Sue Cobble explains:

> The intensity of the battle over the ERA can not be understood without putting it in the larger context of clashing class interests, fundamentally opposing

philosophies of economic and political reform, and deeply held but divergent views on gender and women. As historian Carl Brauer observed, from the 1920s to the 1960s "the debate over the ERA had distinctly class, interest group and ideological overtones, putting affluent, business-oriented, and politically conservative women against poor, union-oriented and politically liberal women." Amy Butler's recent study of the clashes over the ERA in the 1920s makes a similar point. Both sides wanted "full citizenship for women," she concludes, but each had "competing political philosophies and class allegiances that prevented them from finding common ground." (Cobble 2004, 61)

On the one hand, educated women seeking to enter the male-dominated professions of law, medicine, architecture, and the like wanted to see themselves as competing on an equal playing field with their male counterparts. They chafed under the restrictions that kept women locked into only certain categories of paid work, and considered that they should be free to compete with their male brethren. But working-class women wanted the protection of a union and/or of state and federal legislation. They did recognize that some elements of "protective" legislation had discriminatory effects, but they also saw clearly that women in the lowest paid jobs had no capacity as individuals to "compete" against the power of bosses.

Women's work lives tended to be broken up by childbearing and childrearing. Given the additional responsibilities that women carried at home, formal equality at work would have a disparate impact on overall pay, pensions, and job opportunities, since women would lose years of service during the time they were out of the workforce raising their children. In addition, working-class women mostly worked in the low-wage, nonunionized industries such as textiles, laundries, and retail trade. Hence, to strip away the protections afforded by protective labor legislation would leave them even more vulnerable in the workplace.

The ideology of labor feminism meant that most of its leaders were deeply opposed to the Equal Rights Amendment. From the 1920s to the 1960s, an ongoing battle over the ERA pitted union feminists against business and professional women. The NWP had the support of the Chamber of Commerce and the National Association of Manufacturers, which opposed all government-established standards for labor (and, indeed, in that era the legitimacy of labor unions altogether). For NWP members, women did not need legislation to protect worker rights or labor standards: "Women, like men, they insisted, should be allowed to traverse the market without hindrances or protections. Theirs was a free-market rhetoric, touting 'liberty of contract' and a mythic kind of individualism" (Cobble 2004, 61). But women union leaders such as Evelyn Dubrow of the International Ladies Garment Workers Union saw the ERA as "a class piece of legislation" (cited in Cobble 2004, 61). Trade unions and social feminists, including Eleanor Roosevelt and Frances Perkins, opposed the ERA:

The ERA mandated formal equality for women, but in doing so would eliminate much of the "protective" labor legislation passed on behalf of women workers during the Progressive Era. Such protective legislation had often been based on a patriarchal definition of a woman's moral and physical capacity, but it nevertheless rested on an accurate understanding that for most working women, simple civil equality masked de facto discrimination and exploitation at the workplace. Thus, the Republican Party and most employer groups endorsed the ERA during the 1940s and 1950s, just as organized labor, Northern Democrats, and almost all union women denounced it. (Lichtenstein 2002, 94)

Labor feminists believed that working-class women needed the protection both of strong unions and of government legislation, since otherwise they would be left to the mercy of much stronger forces, namely, the power of employers (see Cobble 2004, 60–68, on the ongoing battles over the ERA during the period from the 1920s to the 1960s).

In the 1920s, then, a split emerged in the postsuffrage women's movement, with Alice Paul's NWP arguing impatiently that women did not need protection; they needed equal pay and equal access to professional employment. Union feminists disagreed vociferously. The cross-class alliance between middle-class reformers and union organizers concerning women's working conditions that had emerged from the successful unionization of female garment workers in the 1910s began to dissolve. Feminist ideas now traveled along class lines, with working-class women still wedded to the idea of the family wage and protective legislation, while professional women sought to compete on a level playing field with men.

During the Depression, married women were legally banned from some areas of work, with married teachers having to quit, although some managed to conceal their marriages and even their pregnancies successfully. After the enormous upsurge in labor organizing in the 1930s, Franklin Roosevelt's administration passed the 1935 Social Security Act, with a provision that brought state pensions for mothers to the national level. The tradition of the maternalists in the social feminism movement prevailed. Unemployment compensation was designed for men, while Aid to Dependent Children was intended to keep mothers out of the labor market. Thus, the New Deal legislation looked backward rather than forward for women, seeing them as primarily dependent on marriage, or alternatively, on state assistance, rather than as independent wage earners (see Gordon 1994; for more on women and welfare, see Chapter 4).

World War II was a watershed, with the government using intensive propaganda (most famously, "Rosie the Riveter") to encourage women to fill the jobs in war production vacated by the millions of U.S. soldiers fighting overseas. "Between 1940 and 1945, the female labor force grew by more than 50 percent, as the number of women at work outside the home jumped from 11,970,000 ... in 1940 to 18,610,000 ... in 1945. The proportion of all women who were employed increased from 27.6 to 37 percent, and by 1945 they formed 36.1 of the civilian labor force. Three-fourths of the new female workers were married; by the end of the war one of every four wives was employed" (Hartmann 1982, 21).

But this substantial entry of women into traditionally male jobs was seen as an aberration, and when the surviving soldiers returned from the war, women were encouraged to go back into the home. Despite the intensified culture of domesticity that accompanied the right-wing ideology of the cold war and the rise of McCarthyism (see May 1990), the entry of married women into the workforce resumed. This was the result of the postwar economic boom, which saw intensive growth in both the manufacturing and the service sectors. Corporations displayed a massive appetite for female labor, especially for married women, as "the growing shortage of young women in the 1940–1960 period" meant that employers turned to "the increased utilization of married women with husbands present" (Oppenheimer 1970, 186–187).

Within unions, the debate over married women working continued during the post–World War II period, as union feminists argued vociferously for the right of women to work alongside men in well-paid union jobs, and as the more radical unions fought hard for equal pay for black as well as white women. The increasingly rationalized wage system put in place by the postwar union contracts also acted to increase the wages of married women, black and white (see Cobble 2004). "Under these conditions, the family-wage ideology no longer served the interests of unionized men. World War II also brought married women into the labor force in much larger numbers than ever before, a development which became permanent after the war. This change in the composition of the female labor force gradually made the family-wage ideology anachronistic" (May 1985, 14).

From Labor Feminism to Mainstream Feminism

With the widespread entry of married women into the workforce, the gender order that had prevailed since the turn of the century was being tested. But labor feminists sought to protect the rights of women workers, including married women, without fundamentally challenging the overall gender arrangements. In strong contrast, the mainstream feminism that followed did not hesitate to sweep these arrangements away, creating essentially a new world for women in which paid work, rather than marriage, was their primary means of support. In this sense, the feminist "revolution" of the 1960s and 1970s was undergirded by the demands of the capitalist economy for women's labor.

To make this argument, I want to place the second wave in the context of two broad eras. The first is from 1940 to 1960, which is the era of "labor feminism." The second is from 1960 onward, which marks the emergence of "mainstream feminism."[12] These eras correspond to the entry of (predominantly) white married women into the paid workforce, with working-class women entering first in the 1940s, and middle-class women following in their footsteps in the 1960s (see Cobble 2004; Rosen 2000).

In referring to mainstream feminism, I am drawing on the original statement of purpose of the National Organization for Women (NOW), adopted at its organizing conference on October 29, 1966. "The purpose of NOW is to take action to bring women into full participation in the mainstream of U.S. society now, exercising all the privileges and responsibilities thereof in truly equal partnership with men" (reproduced in Carabillo, Meuli, and Csida 1993, 159).

As we saw, a broad consensus about the place of white women in the workforce had been established, building on the Victorian cult of true womanhood: it was both undignified and unrespectable for a married (white) woman to go out to work. This consensus about married women was part of a larger "culture of exclusion" that characterized the U.S. workplace in the early 1950s: "The culture of exclusion organized life in the United States in the early 1950s so thoroughly that it appeared natural and unremarkable to nearly all white Americans. 'You don't have to look for it to see it,' recalled one black paper mill worker. 'It was all right in front of you'" (MacLean 2006, 13). That culture was built on three pillars: the family wage, the racially segregated workforce (with its roots in the sharecropping system of the South), and racially exclusive immigration laws:

> Although that culture's operations were most visible in the South, where segregation was enforced by law, by custom, and ultimately by violence, it defined all regions of the country.... The family wage shored up the place of white men as household breadwinners and the citizens at the center of public life, as it consigned to secondary status not only white female wage earners but also most men and women of color. Sharecropping undergirded the entire system of segregation and disfranchisement that kept black Americans veritable outsiders in a land in which they had deeper roots than most white Americans. The system of racially driven immigration restriction limited Mexican Americans' and Asian American's access to good jobs and, in different ways, undermined their standing as citizens. (MacLean 2006, 13)

Although the dominant tone of the postwar period was geared to a return to family life, many of the married women who left their wartime male jobs remained in the workforce, albeit in traditionally female job categories. The majority of the "Rosies" who took nontraditional jobs during the war were low-income women who had left jobs in waitressing, domestic service, or other traditionally women's jobs. They could not keep the "plum jobs" when the war ended: "The postwar experience for most was not a return to full-time domesticity, but a return to the blue- and pink-collar ghetto of women's work.... The majority of Rosies may have lost their place at the welder's bench at the war's end, but their sense of what was possible and what they deserved had been forever altered" (Cobble 2004, 13).

Even though the total number of women in the labor force increased sharply during the war and then declined in the postwar period, overall between 1940 and 1950 that number increased by 4.18 million. Of this increase in women in the labor force in 1940–1950, 1.2 million were working in manufacturing and 1.3 million in retail trade. Since both of these sectors essentially involved unskilled and/or low-paying jobs, it seems evident that at least 60 percent of the increased female employment in this decade went to working-class women.[13]

Further support for this conclusion can be found in an examination of the increase in total female employment in terms of occupation. Of the 4.18 million increase between 1940 and 1950, 3.32 million women can be readily identified by class, with working-class jobs accounting for 2.54 million, or 77 percent (operatives and craft workers, clerical and sales workers, laborers and domestic servants); only 0.78 million of the increase in identifiable jobs, or 23 percent, were non-working-class: proprietors, managers and officials, and professionals.

Between 1950 and 1960, the total number of women in the labor force increased by 5.1 million. Of this increase, 3.29 can be readily identified by class, with the same working-class jobs accounting for 2.45 million, or 74 percent. Only 0.84 million of the increase in identifiable jobs, or 26 percent, were non-working-class.[14]

Overall, the most dramatic change from the prewar to the postwar period occurred in the employment of married women, which saw a sharp increase. This development was noted by the National Manpower Council in a special report on women's employment published in 1957 after a series of national and regional conferences. It is worth noting that this consciousness of the changing workforce profile was being expressed by representatives of management, educational institutions, and government officials *prior to* the visible beginnings of mainstream feminism in the 1960s (Kessler-Harris 1982, 300): "The most spectacular development of recent years ... has been the rise in the employment of women over 30, most of whom are wives and mothers. Among married women aged 35 to 44 and living with their husbands, the proportion in the labor force more than doubled between 1940 and 1955, from 16 percent to 34 percent. Among wives between the ages of 45 and 64, the proportion nearly tripled in the same period, from 10 percent to 29 percent" (National Manpower Council 1957, 132). Employment was increasingly significantly for all categories of women. But "older married women ... were in a much better position than any other group to respond to the steady high demand for workers and the weakening of cultural attitudes opposing women's employment" (National Manpower Council 1957, 132). Younger women were either still in school or married and caring for young children. Declining birthrates in previous decades had reduced the availability of younger workers, both male and female: "In the face of a growing demand for workers and the limited availability of other groups, many employers found it convenient to fill their needs by hiring older married women" (National Manpower Council 1957, 133).

As regards the massive entry of married women into the labor force during the long postwar boom, this can be seen from these figures. In 1947, about half of all single women were participating in the labor force, compared to only about one-fifth of married women and one-third of the widowed or divorced. Thus, it was almost inevitable that when employers turned increasingly to female labor, they would have to draw on the ranks of married women. From 1947 to 1965, the number of women in the labor force increased by about 10 million. All of the increase was among married women, while the total number of single women working actually declined slightly.[15]

The new consciousness of women workers expressed itself through the labor movement, newly powerful after World War II. Conventional histories of the women's movement have spoken of the "trough" or the "doldrums" between the two waves, the first rising in the 1830s and 1840s in conjunction with the Abolition movement, reviving after the Civil War and culminating in the winning of female suffrage in 1920, and the second arising in the 1960s (see, for example, Rupp and Taylor 1990). But there has been a process of "rewaving" going on among historians, with a new focus on labor feminism in the 1940s to the 1960s demonstrating that activism for women's rights did not disappear, but rather moved into the orbit of the union movement (see Cobble 2004, 236n29). The labor feminists of the 1940s inherited the mantle of the social feminism of the Progressive Era, but they developed a new framework for the defense of working women's rights.[16]

The campaign for the rights of working women began among blue-collar factory workers, who were "the first to challenge restrictions on women's rights and the first to experience some success" (Cobble 2004, 70). These blue-collar women workers were able to take advantage of the strength of their unions and, more particularly, of the ideology of industrial unionism:

> Blue-collar manufacturing women had powerful and progressive institutional vehicles through which to express their concerns: the large industrial unions that were firmly established by the 1940s. They had a mechanism through which individual and collective grievances could be advanced. Despite the paternalistic and hostile attitudes sometimes directed toward blue-collar women by their male coworkers and fellow unionists, the reigning ideology of industrial unionism was one that emphasized fairness through securing policies that treated all workers alike. The inexorable logic of bureaucratic, industrial-style unionism pushed for an end to differential treatment based on gender, race, and other personal or sociological characteristics. Unions sought to replace managerial prerogative and favoritism with impersonal, jointly established rules—the legitimacy of which depended on allowing few exceptions and insisting on the interchangeability of all workers. (Cobble 2004, 70)

As "combining marriage and wage earning for women became the norm, and minority and older women moved into a range of jobs that heretofore had been the preserve of younger, single white women" (Cobble 2004, 92), the labor feminists of the 1940s and 1950s worked within the labor movement for a series of issues—equal pay, maternity leave, access to seniority, and child care—that would make it easier for women to combine work and family life. For labor feminists, working women's rights were to be balanced against the needs of women as wives and mothers. They

> rooted their class politics in the realities of women's lives. They pushed for unions, employers, and the state to recognize the particular needs of women and the particular discriminations suffered by women as a sex. Women's problems will never be solved, Mary Anderson once asserted, by "conforming to men's ways." The world of work and the policies governing it needed to be transformed. Labor feminists wanted government and employer policies that would help women combine wage work and family life and would not penalize women for childbearing and child rearing. They wanted a sufficient standard of living for workers and a world in which care giving was as important as wage earning. (Cobble 2004, 144)[17]

Activism among union women in the 1940s was one of the founding streams of the revived feminist movement that emerged in the 1960s, although the red scare buried these voices (see Weigand 2001). The 1960s saw the decline of labor feminism and the development of mainstream feminism. Again, we look first to the figures on women's workforce participation. The period after 1960 clearly shows a relative shift toward increasing female employment in middle-class, rather than working-class, jobs. Thus, from 1960 to 1990 total female employment increased by 32 million. But unlike in the 1940–1960 period when middle-class jobs accounted for only one-fourth of the increase, now they accounted for one-half of the increase. Most strikingly, the number of female managers, officials, and professionals jumped more than fivefold, from over 3.3 million in 1960 to 17 million in 1990.[18]

The economy that drew in primarily working-class married women in the 1940s and 1950s was now, in the 1960s, beginning to draw in middle-class married women as well. This shift in employment patterns was a primary underlying cause of the rise of mainstream feminism. Indeed, a symbolic icon of this change is Betty Friedan herself. In the 1940s, she was an activist in the United Electrical Workers, producing one of the first pamphlets on sexual harassment. In 1963, Friedan published her instant bestseller, *The Feminine Mystique,* which introduced the idea of "the problem with no name," namely, the boredom, frustration, and impatience of her graduating class from Smith College, who were educated but isolated in suburban ghettoes. From a spokeswoman for working-class women in the 1940s, seeking to improve the lives of women workers on the shop floor, Friedan had now become the voice of the middle-class suburban housewife, who saw professional work as an escape (Horowitz 1998).

By the 1960s, the consensus among union women began to erode, as women workers gained further rights through federal legislation. The new feminism that emerged around the Commission on the Status of Women, convened under the leadership of Esther Peterson, director of the Women's Bureau under President John F. Kennedy, and the concomitant emergence in 1966 of the National Organization for Women, saw the arrival of new attitudes toward women in the workforce.[19] Protective legislation now seemed an anachronism, with women increasingly willing to compete without limits on how much weight they could lift, or how many hours in the day they could work.

The state laws melted away in a brief period of five years (Kessler-Harris 2001, 267). The new feminists rejected protection, and indeed sought (and won) affirmative action that would remove the barriers to the most lucrative jobs in all areas of work, including those previously seen as strictly men's jobs. And at a symbolic level, the newly organized women's movement, most notably NOW, poured resources into the long-standing campaign for an equal rights amendment to the Constitution, which gained traction in the 1970s, only to be defeated by the rise of right-wing organizing led by Phyllis Schlafly and her colleagues.[20] The embrace of the ERA meant that mainstream feminism no longer sought the protections for women's labor that had been enshrined in government legislation and in union restrictions. Whereas labor feminists had sought to pick and choose among these restrictions, trying to keep those that genuinely protected women, the new mainstream women's movement was eager to sweep away all "protection" and let women compete on an open playing field.

I dwell on this history of class differences and differences in attitudes toward protection and maternalism because the debates between labor feminists, on the one hand, and professional women, on the other, reflected a class divide among women that has only intensified in the era of globalization. The opponents of the Equal Rights Amendment in the 1960s, drawn from the ranks of labor and from the remaining activists for social feminism, argued that women in the workforce should not be thrown into open competition with men because of their special needs as wives and mothers. The Supreme Court opinion in *Muller v. Oregon* (1908), which agreed to protection for women in the industrial scene, but not for men, reflected what we now see as an archaic idea of women's frailty (Vogel 1993). In a 180-degree turn from such outdated notions of women's frailty, the Court held in 1991 that to bar women from working in the proximity of dangerous amounts of lead, on the grounds of "fetal protection," was a form of sex discrimination (see *Automobile Workers v. Johnson Controls, Inc.*).

This change in the attitude of the Court reflects the transformation in attitudes toward women working that is one of the basic achievements of twentieth-century feminist activism. But critics of the *Johnson Controls* decision have pointed out that the case should have been argued not on the basis of sex discrimination, but on the basis of the rights of *all* workers to be safe from dangerous working conditions, which can affect the integrity of reproductive genetic material in both men and women. It was the hope of some activists for protective legislation in the early twentieth century that establishing protections for women workers would be an opening wedge to the extension of protections to men. But instead the trajectory has been toward fewer and fewer protections for both men and women, as the union movement has lost power and as corporations have pushed for deregulation and against any restraints on their freedom to operate in the marketplace.

I am arguing broadly that labor feminism sought to gain rights for women while still holding on to some of the protections for women's special needs afforded by both unions and the state. In contrast, mainstream feminism vociferously sought to abolish these protections, seen as archaic. Here I am emphasizing one stream of activism, namely, the successful abolition of protective legislation. There is, of course, another stream of activism, namely, the use of state power through legislation and court cases. This activism ranged from using the Equal Employment Opportunity Commission to overcome discrimination to establishing affirmative action to open doors for women. But even though these areas of activism required intervention from the state, they nonetheless went in the same direction: rejecting the special exclusions and protections for women workers that had characterized the previous era.

In this sense, the mainstream feminism of the 1970s fiercely rejected the maternalism of 1920s social feminism, and what we might call the partial maternalism of union feminism. The right of women to compete in the market on equal terms with men was a cherished principle of mainstream feminism, as we will see in the next section. In the Conclusion of the book, I will return to this issue of maternalism and argue—against the dominant U.S. academic model that condemns special treatment for women as a form of essentialism—for a revived maternalism on the Finnish and Swedish models (see Pietila 2006).

The Second Wave: Feminist Interventions

As most readers know, the women's movement is one of the most lasting and influential of the "new social movements" arising from the stormy decade of the 1960s. In the U.S. context, conventional histories present two strands of the movement: the radical women's liberation activists, who saw themselves as social revolutionaries; and the liberal activists, who merely sought a piece of the pie for women. These two categories were first identified by Jo Freeman (1975), and are still used by most historians, although recent research has shown, ironically, that the "liberal" wing of U.S. feminism had its roots in trade union and Communist Party activism during the 1940s and 1950s (Cobble 2004; MacLean 2002; Weigand 2001).

While other activist movements—against the Vietnam War, for student rights, and for black nationalism (notably, the Black Panthers)—either faded or were crushed during the late 1960s and early 1970s, the U.S. women's movement continued to grow and to influence U.S. society profoundly. Recent histories celebrate this widespread influence, using expressions such as "tidal wave" (Evans 2003), "the world split open" (Rosen 2000), and "no turning back" (Freedman 2002) to indicate the breadth, depth, and permanency of the changes wrought by feminist activism over the four decades since 1970.

The explosion of activism marking the second wave of the women's movement has been chronicled many times (most notably by Davis 1999; Evans 2003; and Rosen 2000). Here I want to point to the range of feminist interventions from the 1960s onward. By feminist interventions, I mean the variety of ways in which activists sought to intervene in the "normal" fabric of U.S. life to bring about improvements for women. As the two streams of the movement flowed together—the radical women's liberation activists separating themselves angrily from the New Left, and the older generation of liberal activists stemming from the union and civil rights organizing of the 1950s, who formed the core of NOW—a wide range of agenda items was taken up by feminist activists.

Broadly speaking, the NOW wing of the movement turned its attention to the elimination of legal barriers to women's full participation in public life. The Equal Pay Act of 1963; Title VII of the Civil Rights Act of 1964, which established the Equal Employment Opportunity Commission; the addition of women to presidential executive orders barring federal contracts to discriminating companies in 1967; and a range of measures including the Equal Credit Opportunity Act (married women could obtain credit in their own names) and the Educational Equity Act, all carried the message that legal barriers were swiftly coming down. By the mid-1970s, the women's movement challenge, "waged by attorneys and activists through commissions, class action suits, hearings, and protests, had achieved a stunning series of successes" (Rosen 2000, 88), including "equal treatment for women in education and credit, eliminating criminal penalties for abortion, changing prejudicial rape laws, banning discrimination against pregnant women, equalizing property distribution at divorce, and offering tax credits for childcare" (Rosen 2000, 88, quoting Cynthia Harrison).

Feminist organizations such as the Women's Equity Action League filed sex discrimination complaints against more than three hundred colleges and universities, including all medical schools. NOW sued thirteen hundred corporations receiving federal funds, forcing back pay for many women workers. In 1971, the National Women's Political Caucus, with Bella Abzug, Shirley Chisholm, and others, began its project of running female candidates for political office. Title IX of the Education Amendment Act of 1972 forced schools to provide equal funding for girls' and women's sports activities. That same year also saw the passage by Congress of the Equal Rights Amendment, which was expected to be ratified rapidly by the states:

> *Ms.* magazine made its debut; women for the first time became floor reporters at political conventions; the Equal Pay Act was extended to cover administrative, executive, and professional personnel; NOW and the Urban League filed a class action suit against General Mills for sex and race discrimination; NOW initiated action against sexism in elementary school textbooks with *Dick and Jane as Victims*....
>
> One year later, in 1973, the Supreme Court ruled in *Roe v. Wade* that abortion was constitutionally protected by a woman's right to privacy; Billie Jean King beat Bobby Riggs in a much-hyped "Battle of the Sexes" tennis game; AT&T signed the largest sex discrimination settlement—$38 million—in the nation's history; ... a New Jersey court ruled that the state Little League must admit girls; and Helen Reddy won a Grammy Award for the hit record "I Am Woman," an explicitly feminist song that became the unofficial anthem of the women's movement. (Rosen 2000, 89–90)

Meanwhile, the former Left activists who became the founding members of women's liberation opened up the range of issues that historian Ruth Rosen summarizes under the heading "The Hidden Injuries of Sex" (Rosen 2002, 432).[21] This was perhaps the most distinctive contribution of U.S. second-wave feminism: the exposure of issues of bodily integrity. All of the unspoken grievances that welled up in the wake of the sexual revolution of the 1960s, which had produced an angry backlash among women revolutionaries whose own sexual autonomy had been violated by their brothers in the New Left, now found a voice. Using the process of consciousness-raising, a mode borrowed from the 1949 Chinese Revolution's method of "speaking bitterness" (see Eisenstein 1983), holding intimate discussions in small groups of five to ten, women began to open the door to public scrutiny of rape, of wife-battering, of incest, of marital and date rape, not to mention of sexual harassment in the workplace.

Like the first wave of the women's movement, the second wave set out to contest every aspect of culture and social norms that circumscribed the lives of women. But in contrast to Emma Goldman, or even Simone de Beauvoir, these activists found themselves in circumstances where achieving control of one's own destiny had the necessary material underpinnings. Contraception was legal and available. The changing U.S. economy, with increased automation and the growth of the service sector, made access by women to previously male-dominated jobs possible as never before.

The feminist interventions of the second wave ranged from the personal and bodily to the social, economic, and political. Think of a woman at the center of a circle, asking to be freed from subordination to her reproductive functions, and gaining freedom to control her own decisions about giving birth; about having sex; about not being raped, inside or outside of marriage; of not being subjected to incest. These are the changes that would permit an individual woman to exercise her bodily autonomy fully.

The circle then moves out beyond the individual to the social conditions required to ensure this autonomy. This meant the right to economic autonomy through access to a wide range of employment options, and the right to physical autonomy through the abolition of the controls exerted over women by men, individually and institutionally. Among other measures, women created rape crisis centers and women's shelters, sought to change the laws on abortion, sought greater control over health care, and sought assistance with child care. The latter goal was thwarted in one of the few major defeats of feminist activism in the 1970s, when so many barriers fell. President Richard Nixon in 1971 vetoed the Comprehensive Child Development Act, which would have provided child care to all women. Nixon felt that it would "lead to the Sovietization of American children" (quoted in Rosen 2000, 91–92). In this systematic demolition of obstacles, one was already breached: American women had long since won the right to choose their husbands. But in all other ways this was a movement to eliminate quasi-feudal controls on women through the control of their bodies and their work lives.

Many organizers focused on education, with activists such as Bernice Sandler bringing effective lawsuits against sex discrimination within universities. Women's studies programs, introduced around 1966 and 1967 in public universities such as the State University of New York at Buffalo, increased from a few dozen in the 1970s to the hundreds, with many universities including women's studies offerings as a required or at least an optional choice for undergraduate majors. Graduate programs in women's studies were also introduced, from the State University of New York at Buffalo to Emory University to the University of California at Berkeley, among others.

Within women's studies, and then across the disciplines, feminist theory flourished and subdivided: from socialist, liberal, and radical or cultural feminism to black feminism, multicultural feminism, lesbian feminism, ecofeminism, Third World feminism, and beyond. Originally, studies of feminist theory categorized it under three headings: socialist, liberal, and radical. At the risk of boring my sophisticated feminist readers, let me recapitulate these classic categories. Very briefly, socialist feminism sees women's liberation as dependent upon the abolition of capitalism and its replacement with a Marxist-inspired alternative economic system, variously named socialist or communist, but in any case departing radically from the contemporary corporate system. Most crucially, such a system would move decisionmaking about the economy from private hands into some form of collective choice.

Liberal feminists are those who believe that women's liberation can be accomplished through the current system, with sufficient reforms to allow women access to all areas of economic and public life. It is this version of feminism that

I am referring to as hegemonic, since it is congruent with the dominant U.S. ideology of economics and politics. Basically, liberal feminism accepts the modern capitalist system, but seeks to have women placed in decisionmaking positions in sufficient numbers to alter the priorities of government, so that so-called women's concerns, for education, child care, public health, and the like, will receive sufficient attention and funding to change the landscape significantly. Finally, radical feminism holds that women's liberation lies in the abolition of patriarchy, and in the creation of a world of women's culture and women's values. In the writings of founding mothers such as Mary Daly this biophiliac world would be based on the bonding of women with one another, rather than with men.[22]

More recently, women's studies texts have departed from this earlier framework and have sought to include the wide range of ideas produced by the proliferation of women's activism and cultural production, from black and Third World feminisms, lesbian feminism, and ecofeminism, to feminist varieties of postmodernism, poststructuralism, and queer theory. Many writers now refer to "feminisms" (rather than feminism) to capture the idea that the women's movement is now a series of movements, national and international, not all branches of which agree with one another. The hegemony of women's studies itself was challenged by the rise of postmodern philosophy, with its suspicion of "master narratives," and its querying of "woman" as a category, as well as by Third World feminism, which critiqued women's studies practitioners for homogenizing all women instead of recognizing the particularities of women as members of differing races, ethnicities, religions, not to mention sexualities and levels of ability or disability. (On the range of contemporary feminisms, see Tong 2008; on fault lines of race and class, see Chapter 3.)

Meanwhile, the women's health movement, most famously encapsulated in the Boston Women's Health Book Collective production of *Our Bodies, Ourselves,* became a national movement, taking on the issue of doctors' attitudes toward women patients, challenging the medical profession by introducing techniques for women to suction out menstrual blood and self-examine the cervix, and forcing drug companies to adopt notices of side effects for the pill and other prescription drugs. The right to safe and affordable abortions, the right to end forced sterilization, and the right of women to bear children when and if they wanted to were raised by the Committee to End Sterilization Abuse in New York and similar groups across the country. Overly medicalized birthing practices in hospitals were challenged, and the practice of midwifery, which had dwindled after the professionalization of medicine in the nineteenth century, was revitalized (see Boston Women's Health Book Collective 1992; Morgen 2002; Silliman et al. 2004, 225ff.).

Some women's organizations focused on the expansion of women's economic rights. Activists campaigned for comparable worth, seeking to increase women's wages by establishing systems of job evaluation that compared levels of skill between typical women's work, such as clerical tasks, and typical men's work, such as truck driving. (On comparable worth, see Remick and Steinberg 1984.) Others campaigned for affirmative action, opening many areas of formerly all-men's work to women. The numbers of women in professions such as law, medicine, and architecture rose sharply, and access was opened for women to compete for jobs such as police, firefighters, and railroad engineers, and in construction and mining, although these macho male-dominated work areas remained the most resistant to women's entry. (See the section "Work" for further details on affirmative action.) Activists sought to gain influence for women and women's issues inside the trade union movement, with the creation of the Coalition of Labor Union Women in 1973, and the founding of groups such as Nine to Five, which focused on women in clerical work (Milkman 1985).

Sexuality became a focus for extensive intellectual and personal exploration. The requirements of heterosexuality were subjected to intense scrutiny, and a strong lesbian and gay movement emerged as a social force in its own right. Conflicts over the suppression of lesbian influence within NOW and other organizations eventually faded, and the right of lesbians to sexual self-determination became part of the accepted canon of feminist beliefs. Adrienne Rich coined the expression *compulsory heterosexuality,* and the exploration of gender and its social construction eventually gave rise to the academic field of queer theory (see Rich 1980; on queer theory, see Duberman and Solomon 2003).

All of the issues concerning sexual violence gave rise to separate movements. Antirape activists sought, with some success, to change the attitudes and the legal framework surrounding rape and its legal proof. Kathleen Barry and others campaigned to make public the widespread incidence of incest and other forms of "female sexual slavery." Similarly, a movement against the battering of wives, spearheaded first in England, eventually created the legally recognized framework of ending domestic violence. Other groups worked to abolish pornography, even seeking legislation to establish that the sale of pornography violated women's civil rights. This campaign, organized by Andrea Dworkin and Catharine MacKinnon, actually eventuated in several city ordinances, although they were struck down by the courts.[23] The differences among feminists on issues such as pornography, prostitution, and sadomasochistic sex gave rise to major splits, as highlighted in the Barnard College Scholar and Feminist sex conference of 1982 in New York, with feminists divided between those focusing on the horrors of male sexual violence, and those seeking greater sexual self-determination for women, the so-called pro-sex versus the antipornography wings (see Barry 1984; Schechter 1983; Vance 1984).

Meanwhile, an explosive growth of women's cultural production, often sparked by lesbian activists, gave rise to feminist presses, women's bookstores, women's music festivals (like the widely known annual festival in Michigan), women singers and groups, and women's writing. The publishing acceptance of women's writing was notable from the 1970s onward, especially for African American writers such as Toni Morrison and Alice Walker, who became household names.

Women's intervention into law deserves special mention, as feminist lawyers sought out areas of discrimination that required change. They challenged the existing law on rape, which notoriously required witnesses to the act for the charge to be credible, and which excluded a married woman from rape protection when the attacker was her husband. Feminist lawyers reexamined the law surrounding domestic violence, and established new legal standards such as the self-defense doctrine in common law. Elizabeth Schneider was a pioneer in introducing the concept that for a battered woman, the battered woman's syndrome plus the generally lesser strength of women made it plausible for women who killed their drunken or sleeping husbands to argue that they were, in effect, defending themselves (see Schneider 2000).

Meanwhile, women sought and entered higher public office. Starting with the most visible campaigns—that of Shirley Chisholm for president in 1972, and the vice presidential campaign of Geraldine Ferraro with Walter Mondale in 1984—prominent women politicians such as Bella Abzug wielded significant influence, and paved the way for a marked increase in the number of women running for office in local, state, and national elections. The United States even acquired its first female Speaker of the House of Representatives in 2007 with the accession of Nancy Pelosi and its first serious candidate for president with Hillary Rodham Clinton's primary campaign in 2008, although the United States still lagged behind many countries in the percentage of women in government leadership positions.

The feminism of the 1970s reverberated across the globe, with feminist movements emerging in such industrialized countries as Great Britain, Germany, and Japan, as well as across the Third World. Some countries, Turkey, Egypt, and India among them, had preexisting women's movements dating from their nationalist struggles during the colonial period (see Jayawardena 1986). Across the world, women were able to establish historic footholds in public life with the growth of "state feminism." Following the 1975 UN international conference on women, country after country established ministries for women's affairs, or comparable institutions such as the Office for the Status of Women in Australia. (On the international growth of "state feminism," see Stetson and Mazur 1995.) The increasing acceptance of women as national leaders was an international phenomenon, evident in the election of Angela Merkel as chancellor of Germany and Ellen Johnson-Sirleaf as president of Liberia in 2005, and Michelle Bachelet as president of Chile in 2006. The influence of feminist ideas was apparent in the establishment of special police stations in Brazil and at least ten other nations in Latin America and Asia, staffed by women, to receive complaints of domestic violence, as well as in the creation of the first all-woman peacekeeping force by the United Nations, comprised of fighters from India, and deployed in Liberia (see "All-Female Peacekeeper Squad" 2007; Downie 2005).

Feminist influence, finally, was visible in the creation in 1975 of the International Year of the Woman by the United Nations. The year was extended to a decade, and then further extended to encompass a twentieth anniversary conference in Beijing in 1995, with follow-up conferences, "Beijing Plus Five," held in 2000. Feminist activism at the United Nations dates from the post–World War II era, predating the contemporary women's movement by a couple of decades. Among the bodies created by the United Nations were the United Nations Development Fund for Women (UNIFEM) and the Commission on the Status of Women, which oversees the implementation of the Convention on the Elimination of Discrimination Against Women (CEDAW). In addition, the proliferation of women's nongovernmental organizations received official recognition at the United Nations. (On the history of the United Nations and its involvement with international feminism, see Snyder 2006.) The attendance of feminist activists at these women's conferences, and at the series of UN conferences held on the environment (Rio de Janeiro, 1992), human rights (Vienna, 1993), population (Cairo, 1994), poverty (Copenhagen, 1995), habitat (Istanbul, 1996), and food (Rome, 1997), saw the emergence of international, or global, feminism: "If the Decade for Women generated the activities and commitment that nurtured local women's movements and gave birth to an international women's movement, and the 1980s enabled women to understand the links between their reality and the larger political, economic, social and cultural structures that framed that experience, the decade of the 1990s provided the stage on which this international movement announced itself as a global political constituency, a global women's movement" (Antrobus 2004, 80).

In this context, the campaign for women's rights as human rights was launched and developed into an international force that was able to affect international debates. Thus, the Yugoslav war crimes tribunal in The Hague, presided over by Florence Mumba of Zambia in February 2001, accepted the argument of feminist lawyers that rape and sexual enslavement in time of war are crimes against humanity.[24] (In Chapter 6, using the case of Yugoslavia, I will examine the uses of general feminist principles for the pursuit of particular U.S. foreign policy goals.)

Work

Although the women's movement raised many issues, the energy of the organized movement was focused overwhelmingly on campaigns for women in paid employment: equal pay; sexual harassment at work; access to training and promotion; access to traditionally male jobs through affirmative action; and achievement of "comparable worth," which means the alignment of the salaries of female workers in traditionally women's jobs such as nursing to those of men in traditionally male jobs such as truck driving. In these efforts, women activists followed the example of the black civil rights movement in seeking government support for equity in the workplace.[25]

The dramatic story of how white, black, and Hispanic women broke down barriers to women's employment, using an "insider-outsider" strategy, is told by Nancy MacLean (2006, 117ff. and 265ff). Members of the Equal Employment Opportunity Commission (EEOC) worked from within the government, while activists from NOW, women lawyers, and individuals willing to fight within their workplaces for more equitable treatment pushed from outside.

The moral authority of the black civil rights movement, and the skillful activism that black organizations such as the National Association for the Advancement of Colored People brought to bear to make use of the new machinery of the EEOC, gave political strength to women activists, who took advantage of the inclusion of the category of "sex" within Title VII of the Civil Rights Act of 1964. Black women leaders such as Pauli Murray, a graduate of Howard Law School, were pioneers in recognizing the double jeopardy experienced by black women. Murray, in fact, coined the phrase "Jane Crow" in the 1940s, after she herself was denied admission to the University of North Carolina in 1938 because she was black, and then refused admission by Harvard Law School in 1944 because she was a woman (MacLean 2006, 120).

Similarly, Phyllis Wallace, a black economist who earned a Ph.D. at Yale in 1948, arranged the EEOC hearings in 1967 that helped to desegregate the Southern textile industry, and created teams of scholars to investigate how testing of employees was used to segregate job categories. This research shaped the successful *Griggs v. Duke Power* Supreme Court case decided in 1971, which established the principle that where testing and other job requirements disproportionately excluded minority workers, and could not be shown to be requirements for the job, they were illegal (MacLean 2006, 132). Eleanor Holmes Norton, who joined Pauli Murray at the American Civil Liberties Union in establishing the Women's Rights Project there, became the most effective head of the EEOC in 1977 (MacLean 2006, 133).

Using individual complaints as their initial instrument, and then expanding their vision to create class action lawsuits such as the landmark case against AT&T in 1971, feminist activists won important cases against discrimination in a wide range of workplaces, from the airlines to U.S. Steel. Legal muscle was provided by such women lawyers as Ruth Bader Ginsburg, later appointed to the Supreme Court, and Judith P. Vladeck.

Vladeck was a pioneer in winning sweeping class action lawsuits, such as her successful case against Chase Manhattan Bank in 1979, which led to a $1.3 million recruitment and executive training program for women. She also won a case against Western Electric (now part of Alcatel-Lucent) in 1980, a $7 million settlement that was "one of the first payouts in an equal-pay class action on behalf of women" (see Koppel 2007). And in 1985, "construction firms at Manhattan's Battery Park City agreed to take on low-income women as apprentices and jour-neymen. The new headquarters of Non-Traditional Employment for Women, which she represented in that case, is named 'The Judith P. Vladeck Center for Women'" (Koppel 2007). The work of lawyers was backed by a broad movement of grassroots activism:

> The strength of the effort was due to a network of activists around the country. These activists were scattered everywhere, it seemed, not only in big coastal cities but also in places such as Tulsa, Oklahoma; Kalamazoo, Michigan; Columbia, South Carolina; and Pensacola, Florida. They picketed local newspapers over sex-segregated want ads, filed complaints against companies, distributed infor-mation at employment agencies, ran how-to workshops, pressured the EEOC on cases, worked with churches in stockholder campaigns against companies, organized demonstrations, and ran advice hot lines for women facing job discrimination.... "The more work I do, the more shit I uncover," wrote one tired but jubilant Toledo, Ohio, activist. (MacLean 2006, 139)

The sweep of change affected a wide variety of workplaces, and opened job opportunities to women across class lines, from working-class women in low-paying retail jobs at Sears and poverty-stricken Puerto Rican women gaining jobs in the building trades to women in management at Chase Manhattan (now part of J. P. Morgan Chase). In this sense the campaign to open all job categories to women and minorities was a genuine cross-class alliance, reminiscent of the days of the Women's Trade Union League in the Progressive Era.

At the ideological level, the U.S. women's movement set its sights on the dismantling of the gender rules that had governed the 1950s. Both radical and liberal feminists were united in their vociferous rebellion against the rigid sex roles of the white suburbs, with father as breadwinner and mother as housewife, which in the postwar era undergirded the expansion of consumption for the home.

The attack on sex roles was linked to the desire of feminists to overcome the traditional notion that married women should not be in the paid workforce. As we saw, even though such a stigma never prevented some married women—especially working class and immigrant—from working, it did radically restrict them to jobs that were seen as suitable for women. (Of course, African American women, from slavery onward, never had the luxury of such protections, being subjected to the harshest and most punitive labor conditions alongside their menfolk; see Davis 1983.) Now, women fought for and won the right to enter the most stereotypically male occupations, from firefighting to policing, and from mining and working construction to piloting airplanes (MacLean 2002).

The insistence on a changed language—firefighter instead of fireman—reflected this push to eliminate the barriers that had kept women out of the most highly paid jobs. Unions that had fought in the nineteenth century for protective legislation for women now shifted their views under pressure from women activists, and agreed that laws and regulations restricting the amount of weight women could lift, or the access of women to night shifts, were discriminatory. As we saw earlier, there was a swift erosion of protective legislation: "In five short years [1964–1969] the capacity of the law to treat women primarily as family members, valuable for their reproductive roles, had been transformed. Formally, at least, women of all races had become individuals under employment law" (Kessler-Harris 2001, 267).

Although the push to open jobs to women was most successful in the areas of professional work such as medicine, law, architecture, and the academy, most job categories were at least officially opened to women, although the struggle to make these legal openings real involved many lawsuits and much emotional staying power (MacLean 2002). The women's movement was equally successful in establishing the idea, if not the reality, that women were full citizens, with rights equal to those of their male counterparts.

Obviously, many struggles of the women's movement were incomplete. The backlash against feminism and black civil rights orchestrated by the newly powerful Evangelical-cum-corporate right wing accelerated in the 1980s (Faludi 1991). But most analysts nonetheless agree that the women's movement succeeded in changing the attitudes of most Americans toward the role of women. The (predominantly white) wives and mothers of public understanding in the 1950s had become workers, wives, and mothers.

In short, the women's movement created a successful "bourgeois revolution" for women in the United States. Whereas the English, French, and American revolutions of the seventeenth and eighteenth centuries replaced feudal relations with the rule of the white bourgeoisie, these revolutions notoriously did not extend to the rights of women, people of color, and those without property. Whereas bourgeois men freed themselves from the rule of kings, and freed working men from feudal relations of servitude, both bourgeois and working-class women remained subject to the rule of men within the family. It took the nineteenth- and twentieth-century women's movements to claim the rights of women as full citizens (Brenner 2000a, 222ff.; Pateman 1988). This unfinished revolution now seemed complete: women, especially women in the middle class, could escape from the category of "only" wife and mother into the world of the competitive, individualistic market. Although the U.S. women's movement produced myriad strands of thought and activism, including a strong tradition of socialist feminism and many varieties of Third World and women-of-color feminisms (see Holmstrom 2002; Mohanty, Torres, and Russo 1991), the dominant, mainstream version emphasized women as self-sufficient individuals.

Indeed, capitalism in its twenty-first-century version within the United States was profoundly welcoming to women. Ideologically, as we have noted, the Horatio Alger myth as applied to women dovetailed easily with the bourgeois individualism of hegemonic capitalism à la *Ms.* magazine. The heroic young woman business owner, making her own way by selling Mary Kay or designing her own website—all of these roles were featured by *Fortune,* the *Wall Street Journal,* and *BusinessWeek* in their regular stories on the most promising women in business.

The media both absorbed and shaped the ideas of the feminist movement in the 1970s, adapting it to the needs of consumer capitalism (see Rosen 2000, 294–330). They created the idea of the "first woman," virtually encouraging the women interviewed as pioneers in male-dominated areas of work to renounce the influence of the energies and the political achievements of the women's movement in catapulting them into these new positions. Typically, such a woman pioneer was expected to say, in response to interview questions, "No, I'm not a feminist, I don't burn my bra, I just want to do a good job." This pattern of journalism encouraged the transformation of feminism from a collective movement into an expression of an individual's personal ambition.

This feminism came to be identified with liberation from patriarchal constraints. The right to earn a living so as not to be dependent financially on a husband, the right to develop one's skills and abilities to the fullest, the right to control fertility so as not to be shackled by endless years of childbearing: in short, feminism, U.S. style, came to mean individualism and the right to participate in the market economy as a worker or entrepreneur in one's own name, separated from one's role as a wife and/or mother.

The changed social expectations made traditional homemakers into a dwindling class of women, who apologetically introduced themselves as "only a housewife." (Married women with children under age six, who were not working for wages outside the home, dropped from 12 percent of all adult women in 1970 to 4 percent in 2000.)[26] From a powerful taboo on having married women in the workforce, the idea that women, married or single, would spend most of their life-time working outside the home had become normative. Attitudes toward working women had changed profoundly. Thus, during the Depression, although women and men were not interchangeable workers, it was common practice to blame working women for high rates of unemployment. But when President Ronald Reagan tried to scapegoat women in the 1980s, this idea did not fly, and he was rebuked publicly by the American Federation of Labor–Congress of Industrial Organizations (AFL-CIO). "The ideological assault on female employment [lacked] the popular legitimacy it enjoyed in the earlier period" (Milkman 1987, 112).

The Abolition of Gender

The net effect of these changes was a profound and lasting challenge to the older gender ideology. As noted, I am calling this the abolition of gender. What I mean by this is that the 1950s ideology of sex roles was effectively replaced with a new ideology that downplayed gender differences and stressed the areas of commonality between men and women.

Feminist readers may bristle at this. Is it not the case that, far from abolishing gender, the women's movement put gender on the map? Did not the women's studies community, in particular, make it impossible for the scholarly world to continue ignoring gender as a category of analysis? Yes, indeed, they did, and this is one of the singular achievements of the contemporary women's movement. But while the *category* of gender was being established as crucial to all academic disciplines, from literature to politics and from history to the sciences, the *meaning* of gender was simultaneously being transformed.

I am pointing, in this analysis, to one pole of feminist debate; the other pole continued to stress difference. Much ink has been spilled on this argument among feminists, illuminated perhaps most succinctly in Ann Snitow's (1990) essay on sameness versus difference and discussed exhaustively by Carol Bacchi (1990) and Lise Vogel (1993). What path did women need to follow to overcome the discrimination against them on the basis of sex? To achieve equality, did women have to become exactly like men? Or did they require measures ensuring special access—such as maternity leave and affirmative action—to make their equality in the workforce a reality? This debate is unresolved at this writing. But while feminists were debating among themselves, a dominant or hegemonic stream that sought the abolition of differences is what entered mainstream thinking in the United States.

The rhetoric of the new mainstream feminism stressed equality and critiqued sex roles, assuming (correctly) that access to the entire range of workforce opportunities required women to downplay their differences from men, and instead to claim that anything men could do, women could do as well or better. The increased mechanization of many jobs made plausible the argument that brute strength was no longer an absolute requirement for many jobs. At the same time, women set out to prove that even where strength was required, women could demonstrate their capacity to compete with men. Thus, the first women recruits at the male military academies were encouraged to build up muscle as they trained, and it emerged that, even though on average women's upper body strength did not match that of men, their lower body strength and their endurance often beat those of their male counterparts. The passage of Title IX, and the explosion of women's sports participation, from kindergarten to college, took women in the same direction.[27] The idea of the woman athlete took hold in the public imagination, and sports heroines such as Mia Hamm in soccer emerged to reinforce the idea that women were much less different from men than had been assumed, although women's basketball and tennis continued to have rules that made the competition less strenuous.

One major camp within academic feminism gave its full support to the struggle of women for access to all job categories by demolishing the preexisting ideology of sex roles. The groundwork for this project was laid down by Kate

Millett (1970), with her devastating critique of the work of 1950s sociologists—with their Freudian underpinnings—to show that the well-established sex differences of the 1950s were the product of sexual politics, rather than of science. For Millett, and in this she was joined by Elizabeth Janeway (1971), and other bestselling feminist writers of the 1970s, the acceptance of radically different sex roles for men and for women was what underlay the exclusion of women from public life (see Eisenstein 1983).

All of this was a far cry from the social feminism of the 1920s, which, as noted, drew on maternalism as the basis of its claims for women. The maternalist conception of women, which was enshrined in protective legislation and in the Aid to Families with Dependent Children (AFDC) provisions of the 1935 Social Security Act, argued that women needed special treatment because of their unique role as mothers and rearers of children. The renewed cult of domesticity that characterized the United States during the McCarthyite 1950s essentially revived this view by encouraging the women who had entered the workforce during the war to return to their former roles as exclusively wives and mothers (see May 1990).

This, then, was the background to the analysis by Millett et al., which echoed and supported the arguments of mainstream feminists such as Betty Friedan, who sought to overthrow this antiquated gender regime. At least for middle-class feminists, the arguments of psychologists that women seeking careers were unnatural and needed therapy were part of an archaic way of thinking. To overcome this tradition, mainstream feminism emphasized all of the ways in which women were not different from men, but fundamentally their equals.

Academic feminist writing reinforced the arguments of activists that it was no longer appropriate to exclude women from any area of public life. In all areas of the social and even the natural sciences, feminist academics sought to show that the fundamental sex differences assumed by social science in the 1950s were exaggerated.

Women's studies programs across the country taught students to distinguish between sex and gender, with sex referring to biological characteristics and gender describing the social, cultural, and political expectations surrounding sex difference. The point of this distinction was to demonstrate the malleability of the sex-gender system, in Gayle Rubin's phrase (1975). That this was actually the case appeared more and more self-evident, as some women steadily made their way into previously male-dominated categories of work.

The academics influenced by 1970s feminism did their best to support these arguments with scientific data. Feminist writers such as the late Carolyn Heilbrun (1973) embraced the idea of androgyny. The successful campaign to eliminate "male" and "female" categories in job ads had its counterpart in the work of feminist psychologists such as Sandra Bem, who attacked the old categories of masculinity and femininity as belittling to women. Bem established a new psychological scale to measure androgyny, in which male + female characteristics meant healthy (Eisenstein 1983). In biology, Mary Brown Parlee examined cycles in men and women, showing that the emotional fluctuations experienced by women during menstruation were comparable to fluctuations experienced by men, diurnally, weekly, and monthly (Fausto-Sterling 1992, 102ff.). Indeed, when feminist sociologist Alice Rossi published an article gently expressing her doubts about this rush by women academics to downplay sex differences and to dismiss or minimize the importance of biological differences, she was in effect shouted down by indignant colleagues (see Gross et al. 1979; Rossi 1977).

Influenced by poststructuralist and postmodernist ideas, some academic feminists carried this idea even further. We should note that the undifferentiated category of "woman" had been contested by feminists of color from the outset, as this pushed aside all of the significant differences of race, class, and ethnicity that divided women in society (see Chapter 3). But from the 1980s onward, some of the dominant voices in academic feminism pushed the concept of the social construction of gender to the limit, querying altogether the category of "woman," so that claims on behalf of women were dismissed as "essentialism." Thus, for example, Judith Butler (1999) claimed, in very strong terms, that gender was simply a performance. Judith Lorber (2000, 2005), from a more conventional mainstream sociological perspective, proposed the abolition of gender altogether, although she mentioned in passing that this might not work for Third World women.

In this context of contesting gender categories as antiquated and oppressive, ecofeminists and other feminists who appealed to a more ancient notion of women's role were disrespected. Anyone laying claim to nurturance and maternal feelings for women was liable to be labeled *essentialist,* that is, someone who was conflating women with their biological bodies. In an era where everything about gender was seen to be socially constructed and therefore subject to transformation, even women making such appeals for political purposes, such as Sara Ruddick, were liable to this charge of essentialism (Ruddick 1995). Gayatri Spivak did concede that it might be acceptable for particular political purposes to appeal to what she called "strategic essentialism" (Spivak 1990, 10ff.).

What was the source of this flight from the body and from women's biological role? I believe that it was in part related to the politics of the U.S. welfare state. Whereas in European welfare states the needs of women as mothers were recognized in pronatalist policies such as family allowances, maternity leave, child care, and a range of other benefits, the only concessions made by the United States to women's role as mothers were through the AFDC system, under constant attack since its inception in 1935, and effectively gutted as an entitlement in 1996 (see Chapter 4). The debate among feminist lawyers over whether to seek maternity leave as a benefit for pregnant women, or whether to locate maternity leave within disability leave, available to men and women, illustrates this difficulty (see Vogel 1993). In the absence of a more broad-based welfare state, feminist activism was in a way forced down the path of minimizing difference as a way of ensuring access for women. (On the different path followed by welfare states in the Scandinavian countries, see, for example, Pietila 2006.)

Mainstream feminism, then, meant a wholesale rejection of the sex role ideology of the 1950s. As women brought lawsuits to contest their exclusion from male-dominated occupations such as mining, construction, and manufacturing jobs, and as law, medical, and other professional schools opened their doors to women, it became a kind of feminist orthodoxy that women were primarily to be identified by their work, rather than by their role as wife and mother. This, for example, was the meaning of the title *Ms.,* as opposed to *Mrs.*[28]

And, indeed, demographic changes seemed to reinforce this new identity. Census figures for 2005 indicated that 51 percent of women were living without a spouse, up from 35 percent in 1950.[29] Commenting on the figures, Stephanie Coontz notes that marriage was no longer the "main institution that organizes people's lives"; "it is simply delusional to construct social policy or make personal life decisions on the basis that you can count on people spending most of their adult lives in marriage" (cited in Roberts 2007).[30]

A striking indication of the power of this set of ideas among feminists of a presumably Left persuasion was evident in a seminar at the Socialist Scholars Conference in 2002.[31] At this seminar, Professor Mojubaolu Oufunke Okome (political science, Brooklyn College) gave a presentation about the power exerted by women in precolonial Nigeria in their kinship-defined roles within the family. Okome documented the many ways in which the power of mothers was honored and granted legitimacy within the kinship-based polity of traditional Ibo culture. She suggested that such a claim of power, and therefore of political legitimacy, could be reexerted by Nigerian women as mothers in the age of globalization. In other words, women could draw upon the preexisting powerful and socially accepted tradition of respecting motherhood as a way to gain political strength within the framework of contemporary politics, both local and international.

The audience of about thirty, presumably all self-defined feminists and socialists, was visibly unreceptive to this idea. In their responses to Okome's paper, they were virtually unanimous in their visceral rejection of such a concept. To this group, the idea of claiming power for women as mothers seemed anathema, an outdated concept from a more unsophisticated world.

FEMINISM AS AN ELEMENT OF MODERNIZATION

An intense political backlash against civil rights and feminist activism began in the mid-1970s, with the concerted attacks on affirmative action represented by the *Defunis v. Odegaard* case in 1974 and the *Regents of the University of California v. Bakke* case in 1978, challenging so-called quotas for minority applicants in law and medicine.[32] The Reagan era from 1981 to 1988 intensified the neoconservative reaction against the gains of the 1960s, with attacks on affirmative action for both blacks and women, a demonization of welfare mothers, and a generalized assault on the claims to equal citizenship and government assistance that had characterized the successful movements of the 1960s. (For more on the political sea change of this period, see Chapter 4.)

The right-wing assault against feminist ideas was at its most ferocious on the issue of abortion. Antiabortion activism became a serious social movement, winning victory after victory in state legislatures, where the right to abortion was whittled away with a series of legal restrictions such as requiring parental consent and instituting unconscionable waiting periods. At the federal level, Supreme Court decisions gradually restricted the precedent of *Roe v. Wade* by legitimizing the restrictions imposed by state legislatures. The appointment of John G. Roberts and Samuel Alito to the Supreme Court signaled strong momentum for this movement, as the "partial-birth abortion" decision of 2007 demonstrated.[33] In 2005, most of the more than three thousand counties of the United States lacked abortion services.[34]

Yet despite this all-out assault on abortion, which symbolizes the right of women to control their own reproductive decisions and thus the entire direction of their lives, most of the ideas of mainstream feminism became hegemonic in U.S. culture. Even though the rise of right-wing Christian fundamentalism, and its fateful alliance with the Republican Party, produced wave upon wave of backlash against feminist interventions and cognate ideas such as black civil rights and lesbian and gay liberation, this did not stem the tide. As Ruth Rosen concludes, "By the end of the twentieth century, feminist ideas had burrowed too deeply into our culture for any resistance or politics to root them out" (Rosen 2000, xv).

One measure of "the success of feminism in penetrating all the major institutions of American life" was the failure of the Reagan administration to undo Executive Order 11246, the long-standing measure that required affirmative action by all federal contractors (MacLean 2007, 308). Issued by Lyndon Johnson in 1965, this order had been reaffirmed by every president after him. The plans by the Reagan administration in 1985–1986 to repeal the order received unexpected opposition from the business community. The Business Roundtable and the National Association of Manufacturers, key players in the rise of the conservative Right (see Chapter 4), assured the White House that they wished to preserve the current system. Affirmative action had become "deeply entrenched in American institutional life" (MacLean 2006, 311).[35]

Considering the extraordinary reach of the women's movement in the United States, historians Rosalyn Baxandall and Linda Gordon speak about feminism as a modernizing force, removing the barriers to women's full citizenship:

Women's liberation was a movement long overdue. By the mid-1950s a majority of American women found themselves expected to function as full economic, social, and political participants in the nation while still burdened with handicaps. As wage-earners, as parents, as students, as citizens, women were denied equal opportunity and, often, even minimal rights and respect. Many women experienced sharp conflict among the expectations placed on them—education, employment, wife- and motherhood. Looking back at the beginning of the twenty-first century, we can see feminism as a necessary modernizing force and, not surprisingly, one which rapidly became global. Within the U.S., the movement gained widespread support so quickly because it met real needs, because the great majority of women stood to benefit from reducing discrimination, harassment, and prejudice against them. (Baxandall and Gordon 2000, 3)

Above all, then, U.S. feminism came to be associated with modernization. In effect, the development of capitalism in the twentieth century had modernized every aspect of life. Marriage in its 1950s form was an ancient social formation. With the entry of the majority of married women into the paid workforce, and with the concomitant growth in economic independence for women, the last relic of feudal relations was presumed to be banished from society.[36]

Lourdes Beneria has described the transition in very personal terms, as she traveled in her own lifetime from the warm, safe, but restrictive patriarchal world of a comfortable Spanish farming family to the exuberant feminist consciousness-raising world of 1970s New York. She grew up in Boi, a village in the central Pyrenees mountains with a five-hour horse ride to the nearest town, in "homes close together as fortresses, built with thick, gray stone walls and blueish slate roofs, homes still shaped by the needs of a nineteenth-century subsistence economy in the process of disappearing. To me, that medieval cradle had been deeply patriarchal, protective, loving, and nurturing while also authoritarian and oppressive" (Beneria 1998, 250).

But her complicated experiences with the feminist world developing in New York gradually changed her self-concept, as she moved from the silent strength of her traditional mother and sisters to a liberated and articulate scholar of feminist economics. U.S. feminist academics such as Adrienne Rich might claim that patriarchy was still present everywhere, from "the clay walls of a Berber village" to "an academic procession" (cited in Eisenstein 1983, 5). But someone like Beneria, who made the journey personally, could see the difference.

3

Fault Lines of Race
and Class

In this chapter I will explore some of the fault lines of race and class that have weakened the women's movement. In geology, a fault line is the dividing line between tectonic plates deep under the surface of the earth. Earthquakes are caused when the shifting of these plates creates a massive disruption and release of energy, producing powerful tremors on the surface. Within the contemporary women's movement, there have been a series of such earthquakes, as women of color and working-class women have challenged the dominant paradigms of white feminism.

One residue of these upheavals, taking place within arenas of activism and of scholarship, are the contemporary mantras of "race, class, and gender," and/ or "intersectionality," now ubiquitous in women's studies texts. Ideologically, these formulations acknowledge that the category of gender, taken on its own, invariably represents a white perspective.[1] But acknowledging the fissures of race and class in women's studies textbooks, although an important step forward, does not erase the fundamental social divisions that run through not only U.S. society but also the entire globe.

Contemporary feminisms have expressed themselves through the written word—manifestoes and position papers, articles, reports, books, not to mention media coverage—as much as through various kinds of political activism, from demonstrations to sit-ins to marches as well as more conventional activities in the political arena. In all of these arenas, feminists of color have developed an extraordinarily rich range of historical, political, and cultural analyses challenging the assumptions and the conceptualizations of the dominant feminist ideas of the 1970s as being primarily based in the experiences of white middle-class women.

A word here about vocabulary. The term *woman (women) of color* is controversial in that it places into the same category women from a wide variety of backgrounds, "colors," and ethnicities. Hence, some writers reject the use of the term, preferring a categorical denomination such as Native American, or preferably, to be more specific, say, Lakota. I am taking the liberty of using the expression in this book because I see the "color line" as fundamental to the politics of feminism, nationally and internationally. If, indeed, we are living in a world of "global apartheid," as Manning Marable (2004) suggests, in which the rich and developed countries continue their policy of neocolonial control of the poor and least-developed countries, then indeed there is a worldwide color line replicating the history of colonialism.

Similarly, within the United States the legacy of slavery and Jim Crow, and the continuing practices of structural discrimination within institutions ranging from education to criminal justice to the housing and job markets, characterize our social reality to this day.[2] The debates within feminism over race, class, and gender take place within this national and international context. It is in this sense that feminists of color, or Third World feminists, have taken issue with the principles and practices of hegemonic white feminism, insisting on the struggle against racism and class privilege at home, and against neo-imperialism abroad.

The dialogue among white feminists and feminists of color has been extraordinarily fruitful. In part, this is a result of an international discussion that has placed the concerns of Third World women at the very center of feminist debates (see the Conclusion). Acknowledging the progress of the international feminist debate over these issues, Nigerian academic Amina Mama notes that African feminists no longer need to contest the use of the word *feminist*: "The constant tirades against 'white feminists' do not have the same strategic relevance as they might have had 20 years ago when we first subjected feminism to antiracist scrutiny. Since then many Westerners have not only listened to the critique of African and other so-called third world feminists—they have also reconsidered their early simplistic paradigms and come up with more complex theories.... Western feminists have agreed with much of what we have told them about different women being oppressed differently, and the importance of class and race and culture in configuring gender relations" (Mama 2001, 3).

Yet one can still point to the failures of mainstream Western feminism to incorporate, or even to acknowledge, the concerns of Third World feminist writers and organizers. As Mama notes, "Changing the terminology [from feminism to womanism] doesn't solve the problem of global domination.... This does not get away from the main problem, namely white domination of global politics and northern-based white women's relative power to define" (Mama 2001, 3).

Revisionist historians have pointed to the errors of many histories of 1960s and 1970s feminism, which portrayed the women's movement as a predominantly white phenomenon, challenged by women-of-color feminists only from the 1980s onward. As Sherna Berger Gluck and her colleagues argue:

> For the most part, the early history of feminist activism among women of color and/or working-class and poor women remains, at best, particular and separate, and does not challenge the accepted paradigm of "second wave" feminism. It is only when autonomous groups like the National Black Feminist Organization (1973) and the Combahee River Collective (1977) come out with statements that explicitly ally them with "the women's movement," that at least some women of color become incorporated into the master narrative.
> This veil of silence, particularly with respect to working-class and poor women activists who remained anchored in their local communities, was lifted only after these women became more visible to the larger movement at and following the 1977 National Women's Conference at Houston. By 1982, on the heels of difficult political struggles waged by activist scholars of color, groundbreaking essays and anthologies by and about women of color opened a new chapter in U.S. feminism.... The future of the women's movement in the U.S. was reshaped irrevocably by the introduction of the expansive notion of "feminismS." Nevertheless this new perspective has not been seriously applied retroactively to revision of the earlier history. (Gluck et al. 1998, 32)

In a period of national and indeed international upheaval, working-class women organized their own struggles, from welfare rights to union organizing. Black, Chicana, Asian American, and Native American women, to name only some activist groupings, were well aware of the mainstream white women's movement from the 1960s onward. These women both absorbed and generated broadly feminist ideas in that they were organizing around the needs and aspirations of women in their communities. But even though they often challenged male dominance within their activist organizations, they chose to "tread lightly" when it came to speaking of male oppression toward women. As members of revolutionary organizations fighting for the rights of their ethnic communities, they perceived the white women's movement as having "a single-minded focus on gender" (Gluck et al. 1998, 50) and ignoring the survival issues that faced poorer women. These activists also wanted to remain firmly rooted in their own communities.

From the beginning of the second wave, the issue of race was contentious. The renewed women's movement of the late 1960s was widely perceived as white, even though the ideas of women's liberation were by no means limited to the white middle class. Indeed, the early writings of the second wave included important works by women of color, and the U.S. women's movement had deep roots in the activism of African American women from the early nineteenth century onward (see Giddings 1996; Guy-Sheftall 1995b). With the development of women's studies, feminism was redefined and reclaimed by a wide range of writers, including Native American, African American, Asian American, Hispanic, and other Third World voices. But the issues and the leaders that were given prominence in the media gave the impression that feminism was about the advancement primarily of white women.

In addition, despite the activism of black women in areas such as sexual harassment, the divide between white and black women that had grown up around the struggle for suffrage was partially replicated in the development of feminist activism. In a case of U.S. history repeating itself, the radical wing of second-wave feminism arose out of the civil rights movement, just as first-wave feminism had been born out of the Abolitionist movement (see Evans 1979). Because feminist ideas spread mainly via a process of consciousness-raising in small groups, inevitably the agenda items that became the focus of activism were related to the life experience of (mostly white and middle-class) participants. As noted, women's groups emerged simultaneously in many of the social movement organizations of the 1970s, including the civil rights, Native American, Chicano, Puerto Rican, and Asian rights movements. But as the civil rights movement turned toward black nationalism, accompanied by a strong ideology validating male authority (as epitomized by the Black Panthers), some black feminists felt there was no place for them either in that black movement or the white women's movement (see Omolade 1990).

At a more profound level, the continual struggle of women within the African American community from slavery days onward for dignity and respect was not perceived by white feminists to be part of mainstream feminism, although scholars such as Beverly Guy-Sheftall claimed Maria Stewart and Anna Julia Cooper as feminist forerunners. Certainly, white feminist leaders such as Gloria Steinem showed an awareness of race issues and when they spoke in public took care to include black women, such as the dynamic lawyer Flo Kennedy, at the podium. The early texts of the new women's liberation movement included articles by black women and other women of color (see, for example, Morgan 1970). But despite these important gestures toward inclusion, both class and race divided African American women, along with other women of color, from the predominantly white women's movement.

The very term *feminist* itself was perceived as "white," and Alice Walker coined the term *womanist* to convey the meaning of a different kind of feminism, one that encompassed the concerns of the black community (Walker 1983). What lay at the root of this persistent divide? In part, it was a matter of life experience. Whereas white middle-class women generally saw feminism as being about ending the oppression of marriage, gaining access to professional jobs, securing the right to abortion, and gaining freedom from sexual harassment, black women and other women of color often argued that their main issues were the struggle against racism, against high infant mortality rates, and for decent education, housing, and health care. If many white women were eager to get out of their kitchens into the paid workforce, many black women wanted nothing more than the opportunity to leave the workforce and raise their own children, rather than the children of white mothers (see hooks 1981). In a vivid review of the history of black women's activism, from the days of Abolitionism to the controversy over the Supreme Court nomination of Clarence Thomas and the testimony of Anita Hill, Beverly Guy-Sheftall notes that "an analysis of the feminist activism of black women ... suggests the necessity of reconceptualizing women's issues to include poverty, racism, imperialism, lynching, welfare, economic exploitation, sterilization abuse, decent housing, and a host of other concerns that generations of black women foregrounded" (Guy-Sheftall 1995a, 2).

Although some black women saw feminism as irrelevant to their lives, others saw the necessity of delineating and documenting the kinds of issues that would characterize an alternative tradition, that of black or Third World feminism. As a result, there was a flowering of publications by black feminists and other feminists of color during the 1980s, including the publication of the famous anthology *This Bridge Called My Back* (Moraga and Anzaldúa 1983). This literature gave rise to a very angry, bitter, but ultimately productive dialogue between white feminists and feminists of color.[3] As women's studies expanded within the academic disciplines, and as the women's movement grew to become an international network, the definition and the implications of "Third World feminism" became an important arena of debate and struggle.

With the growth of global feminism, the issues of race and class so hotly debated in the U.S. context reverberated in a myriad of venues, from the UN international women's conferences to the work of nongovernmental organizations (NGOs).[4] As mentioned in Chapter 2, the United Nations convened a series of conferences, initially to mark The Decade of Women in 1975 at Mexico City, and then in 1980 in Copenhagen, 1985 at Nairobi, and 1995 in Beijing. It was at Nairobi that U.S. feminists encountered African feminists, who instructed them in the gulf that separated First World feminists and those from the least-developed (most exploited) Third World nations.

For the African and other Third World women who attended the Nairobi conference, issues such as clean drinking water, the availability of sanitary napkins, infant mortality, and health problems such as fistulas were at the top of the agenda. These were problems that had long since been solved for the majority of women in countries with a developed infrastructure of sanitation and health care (Desai 2002, 29). The Nairobi debate echoed in many ways the debate that was under way within women's studies in the United States. In short, the U.S. movement that had focused on gender differences as the chief source of women's oppression came up against the realities of race and class, both at home and abroad.

A RACIAL STATE

The background to the contentious issues between white and women-of-color feminists in the 1970s is the racial history of the United States itself.[5] In her account of the relations between black and white feminists, Winifred Breines expresses a sense of grief and personal disappointment. She recalls how, as a white woman, she imagined feminism as a social movement that could inherit the beautiful vision of the civil rights movement, the "beloved community," as developed by the great civil rights leader Ella Baker in her work with the Student Non-Violent Coordinating Committee (SNCC).[6] Breines writes of the harsh discovery that the universalism of her white middle-class humanist vision could not be sustained in the face of the splits between black and white that emerged with the rise of the Black Power movement (Breines 2006). But was it naïveté or ignorance that led the ideologists of the new feminist movement to evoke a movement that would liberate "all women," ignoring the racial history of the United States from its inception?

The claims of the United States to be a beacon of democracy are belied by the history of fundamental racial events that are part of its foundation as a nation.[7] The origins of the racial state lie with the bloody and brutal "encounter" between the explorers, merchants, traders, missionaries, soldiers, and farmers from the European nations of Portugal, Spain, France, and Britain, and the "native" peoples of the American continent. As a white settler society, the United States was essentially founded upon the near-annihilation of the indigenous peoples that inhabited the continent. That annihilation was accomplished partially by warfare, partially by the introduction (accidental and sometimes deliberate) of deadly diseases such as smallpox to which the indigenous people had no immunity, and partially by a deliberate state policy of removal and dispersal of the already-established population. The expansion of settlement in the United States, which laid the basis for its overwhelming economic growth, depended on the dismantling of the way of life of the indigenous peoples, whose modes of production and whose mythologies and worldviews did not admit of the concept or the practice of private ownership of land.

Most of us were taught to read the writings of John Locke as an expression of the ideology of individual liberty. But in his *Second Treatise on Government*, Locke linked the idea of individual liberty to the ownership of property, and, more specifically, to the right of the landowner to make improvements in the productivity of his land. Representing the point of view of improving landlords such as Lord Shaftesbury, his sponsor, Locke held that it was not just the ownership of property that gave a man the right to the land, but also the work of improving it, developing methods of intensified cultivation, and producing crops for export. "If the unimproved lands of the Americas represented nothing but 'waste,' it was a divinely ordained duty for Europeans to enclose and improve them, just as 'industrious' and 'rational' men had done in the state of nature. 'In the beginning all the World was *America* . . . ,' with no money, no commerce, no improvement" (Wood 1999, citing John Locke; emphasis in original).

This was the worldview of the English colonizers who worked the land, not only in the United States but also everywhere they settled. To these settlers, unimproved collective land, as in Australia, was *terra nullius,* land belonging to no one. The presence of Native American, Australian, and other hunter-gatherers and nomadic peoples stood in the way of the establishment of a system based on private ownership of the land.[8] The profound racism of the settlers enabled them to justify both the enslavement of Africans and the subjugation of native peoples. Indeed, in the mercantile period a serious international debate arose over whether these non-European peoples were merely animals, or did they have souls? (The missionary Bartolomé de Las Casas famously argued for the position that they had souls. But this view, unfortunately, only lent fuel to the fire—pun intended—since it became ever more urgent to save their souls, if necessary by the most brutal means.)

By the eighteenth century, with the rise of the Enlightenment, antifeudal ideologies sustained the revolutions of 1776 in the United States, 1789 in France, and 1804 in Haiti. At this point, the institution of slavery was now in such blatant contradiction to the "rights of man" that a new justification had to be developed, based on allegedly essential, biological differences. Science was now enlisted to demonstrate the existence of "inferior races," a point of view demolished only with the discrediting of eugenics after World War II and the rise of an antiracist anthropology, pioneered by Franz Boas.

The rise of the civil rights movement, sparked by the activism of black soldiers returning after World War II from segregated service in defense of democracy and against fascism, fundamentally changed the racial landscape. The 1960s, and the Great Society programs inaugurated by President Lyndon Baines Johnson, were an era of profound challenge to the racial state, as state interventions included affirmative action and the funding of community organizations in response to the urban rebellions of the 1960s. The victories of the civil rights movement—the Civil Rights Act of 1964 and the Voting Rights Act of 1965, along with the contract compliance requirements imposed on corporations—helped to create an extensive black middle class.

But this expansive era soon came to a close with the economic crisis of the 1970s. After the "fiscal crisis of the state," conservatives targeted excessive government as the cause. Charles Murray (1984) and other ideologues of the New Right blamed the state for creating dependency, arguing that government programs caused, rather than alleviated, poverty. The right-wing rhetoric of this period argued that it was government social programs (rather than corporate restructuring) that caused the downturn of the 1970s. Hence, the debate was not just about fiscal policy (how government spending was not a stimulus to the economy, but a drag on it), but also implicitly about racial policy. In short, the attack on the welfare state in the United States had a racial as well as a gendered agenda (Omi and Winant 1986; for more on these developments, see Chapter 4).

History Repeating Itself

As the radical 1960s and early 1970s gave way to the reactionary late 1970s and 1980s, some of the fault lines of race and class had serious political consequences. For feminism, these fault lines were exacerbated by a series of historical experiences that continue to reverberate through U.S. society to the present day.

It is worth recalling the history of the relations between black and white women leadership in the struggles for the abolition of slavery and for women's suffrage. Black women such as religious writer and activist Maria Stewart were visible and active in the abolition movement; they were soon joined by white women, including the Quaker sisters Sarah and Angelina Grimké, in the 1830s and 1840s. This created a strong black-white alliance around this issue, backed by the great black leader Frederick Douglass, who had the ear of Abraham Lincoln, and who supported both abolition and women's rights. The major white suffragist leaders, Susan B. Anthony and Elizabeth Cady Stanton, poured their energies into circulating petitions to pass the Thirteenth Amendment, which abolished slavery in 1865.

But when the Radical Republicans in 1866 proposed the Fourteenth Amendment, covering citizenship, equal protection of the law, and due process, and the Fifteenth Amendment, covering suffrage for U.S. citizens, they added the category "male" in each case. Anthony and Stanton were outraged by this, having submerged their demands for women's rights in their campaign for the Thirteenth Amendment.

The conflict over who should be covered by these new amendments came to a head in 1869 at the annual meeting of the American Equal Rights Association. Lucy Stone, a leading white suffragist, and Frederick Douglass offered a resolution to support the two new amendments. They argued, let's give this right to black men as a stepping stone on the way to universal suffrage. But Stanton and Anthony opposed the new amendments, and held out for female suffrage. When the Douglass-Stone resolution passed, Stanton and Anthony defected into a new organization, the National Woman Suffrage Association (NWSA). (Lucy Stone founded the American Woman Suffrage Association as a separate organization with those who stayed behind; the two organizations merged again in 1890.)

In the following decades, Stanton and Anthony waged a fierce campaign for women's suffrage, during which they increasingly allied their cause to that of white supremacy. Henceforth, they were guided by political expediency, pandering to the institutionalization of U.S. apartheid after the crushing of Reconstruction. The period after 1877 saw the rise of the Ku Klux Klan and widespread lynching; the establishment of Jim Crow laws in the South through the "black codes," including poll taxes and literacy tests; and the spread of the phony science of eugenics to justify the creation of Southern apartheid and Northern segregation. The new racial regime was codified in 1896 with the *Plessy v. Ferguson* Supreme Court decision, which sanctioned the hypocritical doctrine of "separate but equal."

With a rising tide of institutionalized racism, conventions of the NWSA in the 1890s and 1900s repeatedly refused to reject Jim Crow laws and to condemn lynching. In 1903 a delegate from Mississippi argued that Anglo-Saxon women had the political clout to keep white supremacy going. Meanwhile, middle-class black women in the South sought to pursue a policy of "uplift" for their less fortunate black sisters. But their appeal to white women's organizations for assistance was usually rebuffed. From 1900 to 1920, when the Nineteenth Amendment was adopted, thereby ensuring the right of women to vote, the women's suffrage campaign regularly excluded black women. Alice Paul, founder of the National Women's Party, for example, was a notorious racist.

From the end of Reconstruction onward, major black women leaders and intellectuals called out the white women's movement for its exclusionist and racist policies. A founder of the antilynching movement, the fiery journalist Ida B. Wells, who was personally close to Susan B. Anthony, reproached her for being racist in public when she was clearly not in private. Similarly, the prominent educator and lecturer Anna Julia Cooper challenged white suffragists, calling them petulant Southern belles, and supporters of U.S. imperialism, who endorsed the crushing of Native Americans as well as blacks. Clearly, mainstream white feminism had become a racist, conservative force, very far from the radical views about marriage, sexuality, and religion espoused by a young Elizabeth Cady Stanton (see Caraway 1991, 117–167; Carby 1987, 95–115; Giddings 1996).

Thus, in the nineteenth and early twentieth centuries, the leadership of the movement for suffrage, one of the mainstream women's movement's major political goals, turned its back on the political and social efforts of black women. Suffragist leaders were part of the tide of white supremacy and anti-immigrant feeling governing mainstream U.S. politics, as the South regained its powerful position within the Democratic Party.

Just as in the nineteenth century women's suffrage grew out of the struggle for the abolition of slavery, so, too, in the twentieth century the struggle for women's liberation grew, in part, out of the movement for black civil rights.[9] Moreover, during the founding years of the various streams of feminist activism in the 1960s and early 1970s, the turbulent political and social context everywhere meant that white feminist activists, whether they called themselves socialist feminists, radical (cultural) feminists, or liberal feminists, could not help but be aware of issues of race, class, ethnicity, and national liberation: "Popular struggles around the globe were seriously disrupting what had seemed to be a stable social order. . . . For the United States, a list of 1960s social movements comes quickly to mind: civil rights, women's rights, the counterculture, black liberation, antiwar, women's liberation, gay liberation, Native American rights, Puerto Rican independence, and others. Joined by a variety of smaller racial/ethnic groups as well as by newly mobilizing movements of the elderly and disabled, these movements were still actively placing their demands on the public agenda in the 1970s" (Vogel 1995, 105).

The turmoil within the United States reflected upheavals in the rest of the world: "National liberation struggles reverberated throughout the Third World, the Chinese Cultural Revolution proffered a model of constant challenge to authority, democratic aspirations swept through Eastern Europe, and movements for self-determination ignited the countries of Western Europe" (Vogel 1995, 105). In this context it was impossible for women activists to ignore issues of difference, and they did not. Activist campaigns carried out by women's liberation groups such as Cell 16 and Bread and Roses in Boston addressed a wide range of class and race issues, from support for welfare mothers to demands for free child care (see Davis 1999, 81ff.).

Nonetheless, the largely white socialist feminist movement failed to attract large numbers of minority women, and black and Chicana feminists developed their own organizations instead. It was not that the ideas of women's liberation did not reverberate within the black and Latina communities. Indeed, as we saw, feminisms emerged simultaneously within the social movements of both these communities, as well as later on among Asian Americans and Native Americans, among other groups. But the thinking of women of color reflected their different location within their own struggling communities.

Inevitably, the thinking and theorizing of white feminists, whether socialist-feminist or liberal, grew out of their chosen methodology of consciousness-raising among their friendship networks. Not surprisingly, as noted earlier, in an essentially segregated society, most of these friends were white women, who addressed the issues of concern to them: work; sexuality (including sexual violence—rape and incest); reproduction, especially the right to abortion; and men/families as "oppressive" to their aspirations for economic and emotional independence.

Black feminists and other women of color had a complex reaction to this set of issues. They reacted, rejected, critiqued, but above all reframed the ideas of white feminists. Some issues—work, sexuality, family, reproduction—were seen as relevant, but needing reconceptualization. Other issues, crucial within communities of color, were virtually ignored by white feminist thinking: infant mortality, for example, or police brutality. And as black feminist thought developed, black writers revealed the long history of activism and theorizing that had characterized black women's traditions of struggle from the period of slavery down to the present.

The Critique by Women of Color

The rise of women-of-color feminisms is directly linked, as I have been suggesting, to the ideological positions laid out primarily by white feminist activists and theorists. In this section, I will outline the themes that grew out of the white feminist ideology of the 1970s, and the implications of these analytical positions for political strategy.

As we saw in Chapter 2, the women's movement drew on two strands of activism, the liberal and the radical wings, or the bureaucratic versus the collective (see Ferree and Hess 1994). The first strand grew out of social and labor feminism, uncomfortably allied to the professional and business women's organizations that supported the National Women's Party. In the early 1960s, the government-sponsored Commission on the Status of Women gave birth to the National Organization for Women and other national groupings, which eventually became part of a lobbying community in Washington. This is the strand that gave us equal credit, Title IX, affirmative action, and other government-led initiatives that began to break down traditional areas of sex discrimination.

The second strand comprised the group of younger women, mainly college educated, who had been activists within the New Left: the civil rights, the antiwar, and the student movements. Each of these "parent" movements, as a result of their male chauvinism, begat within themselves a countervailing feminist movement: SNCC gave rise to black feminism; Students for a Democratic Society (SDS) and other white Left groups gave birth to white radical feminism; and the Chicano movement gave birth to Chicana feminism (Roth 2004). Of these, it was the white radical feminists—setting up consciousness-raising groups across the country; campaigning for abortion rights and against rape and domestic violence; developing the women's health movement—whose ideological positions filtered into the mainstream, setting the stage for divisions within women's movement activism that have had lasting effects.

In what follows I will give a very schematic outline of these themes, and their political consequences for alliances across the lines of race and class. There is insufficient space in the compass of one chapter to track the many lines of ideology and policy that characterize the field of force of feminist activism over a period that now encompasses more than four decades. Indeed, there is now an enormous international literature tracing the critique by women of color of the fundamental ideas of mainstream, or hegemonic, feminism, as these were developed in the 1970s and then made their way into institutional life in the United States and elsewhere.[10] Here I will provide an outline of the broad categories of issues within which these conflicts have arisen.

First, what dominant voices in the women's movement said about major feminist issues did not correspond to the experience of people of color and working-class people. Second, some issues that were crucial to women of color/working-class women were not on the agenda of mainstream feminists. And third, some issues raised by mainstream feminists corresponded to the economic/political interests of the ruling elite, and hence helped to constitute a form of "imperial feminism." (I will return to the discussion of imperial feminism in Chapter 6.)

To make this argument, I will examine a (highly selective) series of issues. These are (a) gender universalism; (b) the definition of community; (c) work, paid and unpaid; and (d) families.

Gender Universalism. The first major fault line was the claim concerning the oppression of "all women," a concept that I call "false universalism" (Eisenstein 1983, 132ff.) and that Benita Roth calls "gender universalism" (Roth 2004, 188ff.). In this view, all women were oppressed as a group by all men: "A feminist perspective assumed that all women in the world, whatever their race, religion, class, or sexual preference, had something fundamentally in common. Some versions of feminism took this assumption a step further: they insisted that what women had in common, by virtue of their membership in the group of women, outweighed all of their other differences, or (to put this another way) that the similarity of their situation as female was more fundamental than their economic and cultural differences. The second step in this argument is what I term "'false' universalism" (Eisenstein 1983, 132).

The analysis developed by white women in the New Left was geared initially to defending the idea that women were actually oppressed, against the views of New Left men, whose ideology emphasized the twin oppressions of race and class and who ridiculed the idea that women as a whole fit into this category. Indeed, New Left women who were developing their feminist ideas initially seized on the notion that the condition of women as a group was analogous to the condition of black people (see Roth 2004, 188). The "woman as black" analogy survived for some time and segued into "the idea of the universal oppression of women as women and the consequent need for universal sisterhood. This argument by white women's liberationists countered New Left claims that women's liberation was narrow and individualistic" (Roth 2004, 192). Writers such as the late Ellen Willis and the authors of the Redstockings Manifesto developed the claim that the oppression of women was "primordial" (Roth 2004, 193), predating all other forms of oppression, including the oppressions of race and class. As Redstockings proclaimed: "We identify the agents of our oppression as men. Male supremacy is the oldest, most basic form of domination. All other forms of exploitation and oppression (racism, capitalism, imperialism, etc.) are extensions of male supremacy" (Redstockings 1970, cited in Roth 2004, 193).

From the beginning, this claim of universal gender oppression was rejected by black feminists. If "all women" were in an analogous position to "blacks," then where did this leave black women? More profoundly, it was impossible for radical black women to see their oppression as women separately from their oppressions due to race, class, and sexual identity. This point of difference was most powerfully expressed in the Combahee River Collective statement, published in 1977 by Barbara Smith, Beverly Smith, and Demita Frazier (see Breines 2006, 128ff.; "Combahee River Collective" 1995; the Combahee River in South Carolina was the locale of a military campaign during the Civil War, led by Harriet Tubman, that freed 750 slaves).

This document, arguably the first to use the term *identity politics,* sought to show that "the major systems of oppression are interlocking" and that "the synthesis of these oppressions creates the conditions of our lives" (quoted in Breines 2006, 128). The Combahee collective statement laid out a clear critique of capitalism, imperialism, and patriarchy: "We realize that the liberation of all oppressed peoples necessitates the destruction of the political-economic systems of capitalism and imperialism as well as patriarchy. We are socialists because we believe that work must be organized for the collective benefit of those who do the work and create the products and not for the benefit of the bosses" (quoted in Breines 2006, 129).

The Combahee writers thus committed themselves to combating sexism, racism, heterosexism, and class oppression and, toward this end, to developing an "integrated analysis and practice." The Combahee statement expressed "solidarity" with progressive black men; it rejected "the fractionalization that white women who are separatists demand." And the authors of the Combahee River statement were "critical of and deeply disappointed by white women's lack of effort to understand and struggle against racism in the feminist movement" (Breines 2006, 129).

Even though the development of gender universalism was a powerful intellectual and political tool, laying the basis for establishing gender as a category of social analysis, the claim that "all women" were more oppressed by their gender than by their social location within class, race, nationality, or ethnicity was by definition exclusionary. It thus set up an angry dialectic between white feminist claims and those of women of color that continues at this writing.

The Definition of Community. A second fault line lay in the definition of community. For many Left women, the New Left and the civil rights movement constituted an alternative community, replacing and improving on their communities of origin. This ideal was encapsulated in the widely used term *the beloved community,* which (as discussed earlier) spoke to the aspirations of these young idealists to create an alternative to contemporary society that would prefigure the world they hoped to create. With the painful decision to leave the Left, and in rebellion against male authority and privilege, the founders of women's liberation dreamed of an alternative community: a sisterhood of all women (see Roth 2004). "Sisterhood" became a common aspiration among second-wave feminist writers and activists, as exemplified by the title of Robin Morgan's anthology *Sisterhood Is Powerful* (1970). Such a model, for example, characterized the stated goals of the women's health movement, as well as its practice: women's health centers sought to build collectives within which women's personal lives and their professional commitments could be merged (see Morgen 2002).

In contrast, for black, Chicana, and other women of color, their community was their own particular racial and ethnic group. Although drawn to the ideas of the women's liberation movement, many were extremely reluctant to create a separatist subset that would threaten the cohesion of what were already beleaguered groups. What Benita Roth calls an "audience shift" on the part of white Left feminists—from addressing their political community in the New Left to addressing the oppression of all women—did not take place for feminists of color: "Seen from a feminist intersectional perspective, emerging white feminists' reorientation of political effort and shift in audience resulted at least in part from their privileged position in the race/ethnicity and class hierarchy. Although ... black and Chicana feminists debated the ramifications of autonomous feminist organizing for their politics and their communities, community as such was conceptualized as the entire racial/ethnic community in battle against white America's domination" (Roth 2004, 70). These two conceptions of community were obviously incompatible. A constant theme in the feminist writings of women of color was a sense of conflict between joining the "sisterhood" of all women and fearing that this choice entailed a betrayal of their communities of origin (see, for example, King 1988).

Paid and Unpaid Work. A third fault line was the issue of paid work. The mainstream expression of the centrality of work was Betty Friedan's 1963 manifesto, *The Feminine Mystique.* In this bestselling book, Friedan used the results of a survey of her classmates at Smith College to argue that educated suburban housewives across the country were suffering from "the problem that had no name." These presumably affluent middle-class women were wasting away in their suburban kitchens, devoting themselves to domesticity, when their intellectual capacities would be better served by meaningful paid professional work. Friedan was a major organizer of the National Organization for Women, founded in 1966, and one of the prime movers in the effort to get the newly formed Equal Employment Opportunities Commission to pay attention to sex discrimination as well as racial discrimination (see Friedan 1963).

As we saw in Chapter 2, the struggle to open all areas of work to women was a fundamental and lasting theme of the second wave. There is no doubt that the effort of the women's movement to open the doors that had been closed by generations of discriminatory practices was one of its historic achievements. In this, the women's movement joined forces with the black civil rights movement, which had achieved significant changes in patterns of black employment during the 1960s (see MacLean 2006, 76ff.). For black women in particular, access to clerical, professional, and managerial jobs in the 1970s permitted escape from the drudgery of domestic service that had been the fate of previous generations stretching back into the time of slavery. Therefore, I am in no way arguing that the organized feminist movement was irrelevant to the employment situation of most black women. What I am pointing to here, however, is the assumption by the 1963 Betty Friedan and her suburban readers that work would constitute a form of liberation for the housebound and bored domestic wife.

For most black women and other women of color, the issue of whether or not to join the paid workforce was not a choice that was generally open to them. Given the discrimination against black men, black women expected to stay in the workforce and in some cases to be self-supporting, whether or not they were married and had children. Thus, the perception that paid work was a form of liberation could seem alien, and indeed insulting. Even though the affirmative action movement assisted women of color as well as white women, the appeal to the suburban housewife for a chance to get out of her kitchen was an affront to black women, much of whose experience of work was historically to be located in that very kitchen looking after the domestic needs of white women and their children. Obviously, the meaning of work for black women, with the still vivid historical experience of slavery, was very different from that of middle-class white women. Mainstream feminist ideology of the 1970s preached that work—that is, paid work—constituted "liberation" for women. But for women of color, as well as working-class women, the option not to work was not on the table, nor had it been since before the founding of the republic (see Mullings 1997, 32ff.).

Families. A fourth fault line was the issue of family. The analysis developed by white radical feminists was implicitly antifamily, since they pointed to the prevailing patriarchal and male-dominated nuclear family as a major source of female oppression. In contrast, for black, Chicana, and other minority women, the family, nuclear or extended, was central to their survival strategies.

At the same time the radical wing of the women's movement was developing its ideology, the presumed crisis of the black family was receiving massive media attention. The continuing deindustrialization of urban areas as a result of the decline of U.S. manufacturing was already producing widespread unemployment and the rapid degeneration of inner-city communities. These were subject to increasing rates of crime, deterioration of housing stock, and the growth of drug trafficking, among other outcomes of disinvestment, discrimination, and neglect. The despair of these urban communities would soon erupt into violent rebellions, from New York and Newark to Chicago to Los Angeles in the period following the assassinations of Martin Luther King Jr. and Malcolm X in 1968.

In a 1965 report issued by the Department of Labor, *The Negro Family: The Case for National Action,* Daniel Patrick Moynihan, the politician and sociologist who served as an assistant secretary of labor under the Kennedy and Johnson administrations (and was elected in 1976 to the Senate from New York), set forth a program for the redress of black urban poverty. While acknowledging the impact of economic discrimination, the Moynihan report pointed to the fundamental problem in the black community as one of family structure. Although some middle-class blacks escaped unscathed, the family located in the urban ghettoes was disintegrating, according to the report; it was this condition that ensured the continuation of the cycle of poverty (U.S. Department of Labor 1965).

In effect, as Leith Mullings notes, the Moynihan report was trying to show that the reasons for black poverty lay not "with racism or the inegalitarian economic system, but rather with the culture of the poor." Concerned with what he saw as the dependency of black families on welfare, Moynihan pointed to the black family as the "focus of cultural deficiency." Even though discrimination and unemployment might play a significant role, "he concluded that African American society was a tangle of pathology and at its center was the 'pathological' and 'matriarchal' African American family" (Mullings 1997, 78–79).

The training and jobs programs constituting the War on Poverty launched by President Lyndon Johnson in 1964 were influenced by this ideological background. Some of the programs therefore sought to remedy the culture of the poor, rather than to eliminate poverty by, for example, creating full employment. The Head Start program, for example, was designed to compensate for "what were deemed to be inadequate home environments. While these programs did provide helpful early enrichment activities for some children," they were not a substitute for creating sufficient jobs for the unemployed. In this context, the media's continual trumpeting of the Moynihan report was a cynical attempt to blame the disintegration of previously cohesive black communities on an intrinsic failure within the black family, rather than on economic restructuring. As a result, when the War on Poverty was essentially abandoned under President Richard Nixon in 1973, the blame fell not on a political failure to remedy unemployment, but on the pathological, deviant family structure of African Americans, with its so-called matriarchal arrangements (Mullings 1997, 79).[11]

In this context of full-scale ideological warfare against the black family, black feminists were not inclined to join in an attack on families as patriarchal. The contradictions were intense. White middle-class feminist women, expressing their desire for independence and paid work, were portraying their dependence within the nuclear family as a source of oppression. But black women were being blamed for the entire "pathology" of the black community because of their allegedly deviant, matriarchal role of working outside the home in greater proportions than Euro-American women (Mullings 1997, 163).

Within the radical black community, the Moynihan report contributed to a rise in "masculinism," a desire to show that men indeed were the leaders of the community. Some black women, against their better judgment, went along with this mythology, consenting to take secondary roles by way of supporting men's leadership. Others were critical, such as Michelle Wallace (1979) in her controversial book *Black Macho and the Myth of the Superwoman,* which created enormous anger among some black male leaders. But overall, with the black family under siege both culturally and economically, the white feminist position of locating oppression within the nuclear family was a nonstarter for women of color.

CONTESTED GROUND

How did these fault lines play themselves out within U.S. politics? I want to look at three areas of contention: first, reproductive rights; second, violence against women and racialized incarceration; third, the emotionally charged issue of female genital cutting (FGC).

Reproductive Rights

A first area of contention was the reproductive rights of women. How did the control of reproduction, and most specifically, the right to abortion, become such a political football? The story begins with the activism of feminists, who joined hands with radical doctors, all of whom were seeking to legalize abortion in the 1960s. As Rosalind Petchesky convincingly shows, the right to reproductive autonomy was a central theme of second-wave feminism (Petchesky 1990). For women seeking to control the course of their personal and working lives, control over fertility was a fundamental building block. As with so many other issues raised by the second wave, women's aspirations and their social and economic rights were out of synch. One has only to recall the struggle to make contraception available to poor women waged by Margaret Sanger in the slums of New York City in the period preceding and following World War I (Chesler 1992, 150ff.). Abortion had been made illegal during the period when medicine was professionalized and closed to women in the post–Civil War era, and was practiced surreptitiously and illegally for the ensuing decades, while the sale of contraceptives was made legal only in the 1960s.

After a concerted campaign by feminists, in alliance with sympathetic doctors, restrictions on abortion across the country began to be dismantled. The capstone of this campaign was the *Roe v. Wade* decision by the Supreme Court in 1973, which declared that abortion was an issue between a woman, her husband, and her doctor, and that there was no "state interest" at stake in the first trimester of pregnancy. With the promulgation of the *Roe v. Wade* Supreme Court decision, the Religious Right immediately seized on the issue of abortion as a central organizing principle.

Antiabortion forces were galvanized to set up a national movement, led by the Roman Catholic Church via the National Conference of Catholic Bishops, the National Right to Life Committee (organizing state-level groups), and Christian Evangelicals, who had previously "resisted political engagement." Soon after *Roe v. Wade,* right-wing forces mobilized around the idea of denying funding through tax dollars to women availing themselves of their newly won right to end an unwanted pregnancy. In 1975 the Catholic Church issued the Pastoral Plan for Pro-Life Activities, seeking a human life amendment to the Constitution and restriction of access to abortion through a return to criminalization (Fried 2006, 1–2).

This organized reaction by both the Catholic and the Evangelical hierarchies represented an opening for the leaders of what would be called the New Right, then gaining political traction, as they "saw the opportunity to expand [their] ranks by joining traditional conservative constituencies with the growing antiabortion movement. Opposition to abortion became the centerpiece of a broad 'pro–traditional patriarchal family, anti–big government and antiwelfare' agenda" (Fried 2006, 2).

A major vehicle for this ideological assault was provided by the Hyde Amendment. Representative Henry Hyde, a Republican from Illinois, successfully attached a provision to the 1977 appropriations bill for the Departments of Labor and Health, Education, and Welfare (now Health and Human Services) prohibiting Medicaid funding for abortions.[12] As Marlene Fried notes: "Attacking Medicaid payments for abortion was a perfect way to bring the two groups together concretely. Eliminating government funding appealed both to those who opposed abortion and those who opposed taxes and the welfare state" (Fried 2006, 2).

Meanwhile, the campaign against abortion took off at the state level, with state legislatures vying with one another to whittle away at the *Roe v. Wade* decision, introducing parental consent, waiting periods, and a whole series of other ingenious (and cruel) obstacles to immediate abortion. The right to life movement galvanized religious voters with gruesome pictures of aborted fetuses, and with theological arguments about the sanctity of life from the moment of conception. The Roman Catholic Church and the Evangelical denominations took up the battle cry, and the Religious Right succeeded in creating an energized social movement that rivaled the women's movement in its reach.

Although the Supreme Court did not reverse *Roe v. Wade* (abortion is still constitutional at this writing), the Court handed down a series of decisions, in response to court cases brought by abortion opponents, that allowed individual states to continue instituting limitations. Meanwhile, attacks on abortion providers, constituting a little acknowledged form of domestic terrorism, including several murders of doctors and abortion clinic staff, succeeded in intimidating many doctors and medical schools. The availability of medical abortions in most counties diminished drastically. South Dakota, for example, as of 2006, had only one clinic for its 775,000 residents (Clarren 2006, 34).[13]

Thus, abortion in the United States became a profoundly divisive issue, manipulated by the right wing as an attack on family values, and drawing in large numbers of activists on both sides. Everything in U.S. politics, it seemed, came back to abortion, from the selection of Supreme Court justices to the "global gag" rule, which prevented overseas organizations from even mentioning the possibility of abortion if they were in receipt of U.S. government funding (Finlay 2006, 91–99). The gag rule was introduced by President Ronald Reagan in 1984, reversed by President William Clinton in 1993, reinstated by President George W. Bush in 2001, and most recently lifted again by President Barack Obama in early 2009 (Stein and Shear, 2009).

Nevertheless, the legalization of abortion was a boon to all women. Once it was legalized, women of all races made use of this right, with women of color and poor women using the procedure in numbers well above their incidence in the population.[14] But Left critics of the mainstream abortion rights movement pointed out from the 1970s onward that abortion, by itself, did not solve all reproductive problems for most poor women. Socialist feminists active in the struggle for reproductive rights in the 1970s saw clearly that a campaign for abortion by itself would not meet the needs of poor and working-class women. They were aware that women of color, Native American women, and women in Puerto Rico had been subjected to sweeping campaigns of sterilization over the years. They also saw that in the black community women on public assistance were subjected to vilification for having children altogether, and were subjected to sterilization by some doctors, often without consent, or with consent that was coerced during labor. In addition, the inadequate health care available in inner-city communities gave rise to high rates of stillbirths and infant mortality.

Spurred by the widespread use of sterilizations of Puerto Rican women in New York hospitals as well as in Puerto Rico itself, Latina leaders emerging from the Puerto Rican Socialist Party, and the Puerto Rican independence movement, along with the Center for Constitutional Rights, founded the Committee to End Sterilization Abuse in 1974, led by the late Helen Rodriguez-Trias, MD, the distinguished Puerto Rican physician, and others. In coalition with other groups, they founded the Committee for Abortion Rights and Against Sterilization Abuse network, and argued that a feminist position on reproduction needed to include not only the right to abortion, but also the right to bear healthy children (Silliman et al. 2004, 226). Their activism led to the establishment of sterilization guidelines for the state of New York, which became the model for other state and federal regulations. Framing the debate as simply the right to terminate a pregnancy did not allow for public discussion of the rights of poor women to bear children, to protect them with adequate pre- and postnatal care, and to time their pregnancies through access to affordable and safe contraception.

In fact, the successful attempt by feminists to secure the right of abortion was a continuation of the work of the pioneers of contraception at the turn of the century. Margaret Sanger was the most famous activist for contraception when it was illegal in the United States. But the history of this struggle over contraception, abortion, and family planning must be placed in the context of U.S. racial history. The career of Margaret Sanger herself illustrates some of the ways in which struggles over reproductive rights have been continually entangled with issues of white supremacy. Sanger, who started out as a socialist seeking to protect poor women in the slums of New York from excessive numbers of pregnancies, ended up allying her birth control campaign with eugenicists, who preached the need to lower the birthrate for undesirable members of the population such as immigrants and African Americans (Chesler 1992, 196, 216–217).

From the time of slavery, the reproduction of black women was a focus of control, both by slave owners and by the state. Dorothy Roberts points out that in the contemporary antiabortion campaign, right-wing opponents of abortion have made powerful use of the sonogram, which shows the unborn fetus in graphic detail (Roberts 1997). This has become a tool of propaganda in the campaigns to "protect" the fetus against its own mother, thus pitting mother against unborn child. Antiabortion campaigners often use pictures of the fetus to evoke horror and revulsion in the hearts and minds of antiabortion voters. Indeed, some white feminist legal scholars date the beginning of the contemporary struggle, pitting pregnant woman against fetus, to the creation of the technology of sonograms. But this opposition between a mother and her unborn child was built into the economics of slavery way before the modern era, as masters calculated the value of unborn slave children, and compared this to the value of their mothers sans issue.

As slaves were intrinsically productive of wealth to the slaveholder, slave children while still unborn were counted as property that could be deeded or willed to slave owners' family members. The unborn slave, in other words, was considered an item of value, which could be sold, traded, or deeded before birth. Under slavery, masters sought to increase the black population for reasons of profit, especially after the slave trade was officially abolished in 1808. The incentive to slave owners to rape their female slaves, or to encourage rape by male slaves, for the purpose of an increase in the number of enslaved children was a notorious abuse under slavery (Roberts 1997, 22ff.).

With the abolition of slavery, this form of direct control by slave masters over the reproduction of black women came to an end. But the attempt to control the black population continued, buttressed by the ideological framework of eugenics, which emerged as a dominant pseudoscience in the early twentieth century. To improve the "race" (white), one needed to increase the white birthrate while decreasing the rate of increase among southern European immigrants and U.S. blacks. This became a powerful argument against social services. Why support the weaker races with social programs when they should be heading for extinction? U.S. elites pulled back from eugenics and its attendant social policies, such as sterilization, only when these ideas came into disrepute in the late 1930s after Nazi Germany's widespread adoption of such policies (originally modeled on California legislation; Roberts 1997, 56ff.).

Attempts to control the fertility of black women continued into the twentieth century. For example, in addition to the use of forced sterilizations, as noted earlier, many states, allegedly alarmed by the birthrate among unwed black teenagers, embraced the insertion of Norplant as a way to guarantee a lowered birthrate among black teenagers. This procedure involves the implantation of a series of rods into a woman's arm, under the skin. States were willing to fund the implantation of Norplant, despite evidence of its contraindications for many women, but refused to pay for its removal, despite symptoms of health damage to some of the teenaged women (see Roberts 1997, 113ff.).

This history of racial division played itself out in the struggle over the Hyde Amendment. Essentially, this tactic by the right wing divided women into those who could pay for a legal abortion and those who required state aid to pay for theirs. By denying Medicaid assistance to poor women, this legislation limited the newly won right of abortion to women with sufficient income to obtain one. By failing to fight effectively against the Hyde Amendment, mainstream feminist groups were acquiescing in this decision to link reproductive self-determination to those with a middle-class income or higher.

The struggle over the Hyde Amendment, which was introduced and passed every year after its initial passage in 1977, was fateful for the women's health movement: "There was no large visible mobilization against the Hyde Amendment. The reproductive rights movement focused on preserving legality rather than access. In this context, the Hyde Amendment became a cause and symbol of fractures among abortion rights advocates. It divided those who prioritized race and class issues from those who did not. Women of color reproductive rights advocates and their allies criticized the mainstream prochoice movement for not putting the needs of low-income women and women of color at the center of the prochoice agenda" (Fried 2006, 6).

Divisions over the Hyde Amendment reflected broader divisions within the women's health movement. Even as white and black women attempted to form coalitions around these issues, it was evident that white activists had trouble taking the issues of poor black women seriously. One African American activist, Julia Scott, speaking of her experience in a community-based organization in Newark, New Jersey, where she was charged with developing coalitions between black and white women around reproductive rights, points out the difficulties: "A group of people such as African American and Hispanic women and native Americans who have been subjected to sterilization abuse, you know, the guinea pig kind of thing, and with the birth control pill and the excessive use of hysterectomies in our communities. We very seldom have the luxury of coming together and organizing on just one simple piece, that being the right to abortion, but we see that within the broader women's reproductive health agenda." Scott notes that "there's been a real reluctance on the part of the white women's health movement and the reproductive health movement to be as concerned about some of those other things as they are about abortion rights. And indeed, when we lost the right for Medicaid funding for abortion, it was a clear signal for most women of color in this country that the white women's movement is not concerned about issues of women of color" (cited in Morgen 2002, 48).

Tracing a century of women of color activism around reproductive health issues,

> Loretta Ross [argues] that black women made significant contributions to the reproductive freedom movement even as they fought against racism within it.... In the middle and later 1970s, where predominantly white organizations failed to prioritize, and sometimes even to support, the efforts of women of color to address issues such as sterilization abuse and the effective denial of abortion rights to poor women by Congress (through the Hyde Amendment, which prohibits the use of federal funds to defray the cost of the procedure), racism diluted the effectiveness of the reproductive rights/women's health movements. (Morgen 2002, 51)

As Julia Scott notes:

> You know at some point you've got to have white women understanding the issues so that we're not always the one to bring it [our issue] up. And I believe that until the white women's health movement or the white women's movement period deals with their poor white sisters and really understands what it is like to be poor and without money, I think they'll get it a lot quicker. I think the divisions between the races are such that it is always going to be like an effort to put yourself in somebody else's place.... I think if white women look at their poor white sisters and the lives they have to live, they'll get the connections across racial lines. (cited in Morgen 2002, 53)

Analysis of the centrality of abortion to U.S. politics has focused on the manipulation of class interests by the Christian Right and the Republican Party. Thomas Frank's *What's the Matter with Kansas?* (2005) credits the Republicans with profiting from the emotional reactions of working-class abortion opponents to take their attention away from the economic restructuring that essentially impoverished the working class.[15] Although moderate Republicans in the middle and upper middle class were as accepting of the *Roe v. Wade* decision as their Democratic counterparts, among working-class voters the anger against legalized abortion was widespread. Frank's argument is that a clever Republican leadership seized hold of the working-class movement against abortion to win electoral power and to defeat the older, more moderate Republicans of the Kansas political class.

According to Frank, the attack on "liberals" and the eastern elite served as an all-purpose catchword to win over working-class voters, who were beguiled by social issues and who therefore ignored their own economic interests. They were caught up emotionally with the Christian Right, and they voted to ban homosexual marriage, while their anger was continually fueled by a barrage of clever rhetoric that blamed the eastern elite (John Kerry included) for sexual permissiveness, Godlessness, lack of patriotism, and opposition to guns. The Republicans attacked the Democrats as elitists, while themselves posing as Christian believers and defenders of the little people:

> Let us pause for a moment to ponder this all-American dysfunction. A state is spectacularly ill served by the Reagan-Bush stampede of deregulation, privatization, and laissez-faire. It sees its countryside depopulated, its towns disintegrate, its cities stagnate—and its wealthy enclaves sparkle, behind their remote-controlled security gates. The state erupts in revolt, making headlines around the world with its bold defiance of convention. But what do the rebels demand? More of the very measures that have brought ruination on them and their neighbors in the first place. This is not just the mystery of Kansas; this is the mystery of America, the historical shift that has made it all possible. In Kansas the shift is more staggering than elsewhere, simply because it has been so decisive, so extreme. The people who were once radical are now reactionary. Though they speak today in the same aggrieved language of victimization, and though they face the same array of economic forces as their hard-bitten ancestors, today's populists make demands that are precisely the opposite. Tear down the federal farm programs, they cry. Privatize the utilities. Repeal the progressive taxes. All that Kansas asks today is a little help nailing itself to that cross of gold. (Frank 2005, 76–77)[16]

Frank's analysis should be supplemented by the work of Kristin Luker, who investigated the background and the attitudes of proabortion and antiabortion women. It is important not to minimize the role of religious belief among the antiabortion forces, although the sincerity of these activists is being profoundly exploited by the leadership of the so-called prolife movement. But Luker's research showed that for the women who accepted abortion, the choice to have children was part of a larger worldview that one should choose children as part of a range of choices in life, including marriage, careers, and travel. For the women who opposed abortion, their attitude toward childbearing was part of a larger picture that involved much more sacrifice and acceptance, and much less individual choice, where the arrival of children was seen as part of God's will, and part of one's duty as a wife and mother. Not surprisingly, these attitudes divided along class lines, with the proabortion women anticipating successful economic careers for themselves, and the antiabortion women seeing themselves as part of a more traditional couple, with the husband as the main breadwinner. (See Luker 1984.)

Both of these analysts overlook the issue of divisions among women along racial lines as well. My account here may seem harsh. How could the women's movement not make the right to abortion a central issue for feminism? Yet if we place the abortion struggle in a broader context, it is clear that over time abortion became a single issue for groups such as the National Abortion Rights Action

League, later NARAL Pro-Choice America, while to women of color abortion was only one piece of a larger puzzle of gaining the right to reproductive self-determination.

This divergence of interests served to weaken the national women's movement, in a context where large numbers of women were being mobilized (against their own interests) to oppose abortion altogether. More broadly, as noted earlier, in the United States, the only industrialized country without tax-funded universal health care, the right to abortion hung on a Supreme Court decision, rather than on universal health care access, and thus became vulnerable to a clever and ruthless right-wing attack in which abortion stood in for the entire panoply of women's rights.

Violence Against Women and Racialized Incarceration

A second area of contention was the issues surrounding violence against women. The revelation of the degree of violence against women, from verbal abuse to rape, and from incest to battering, has been one of the signal achievements of the contemporary women's movement. The brutality that often takes place within the private walls of the home was named, described, analyzed, and made public by the activism and analysis of feminists from the 1970s onward. There has been widespread acceptance of the goal of eliminating violence against women, and indeed in 2008 a worldwide campaign on this issue was launched by the United Nations Development Fund for Women (UNIFEM).[17]

In the attempt to end private violence against women, feminist activists sought the help of the public sector. Like the civil rights movement, the women's movement—at least in some of its elements—turned to the government for redress. Thus, for example, the movement against battering of women sought and eventually gained funding for shelters (although, as is often pointed out, the United States still has many more shelters for abused animals than it does for wives fleeing abusive husbands). Similarly, rape crisis centers over time began to apply for and receive government funding.

Inevitably, the turn toward obtaining government funding drew feminist organizations into compromises. From freestanding groups with democratic structures, they became hierarchical and rule-bound in response to the wide range of government regulations required to become eligible for funding (Matthews 1994). But more fateful than this process of bureaucratization was the political outcome: an implicit alliance of these feminist activists with U.S. government agencies in a period when public policies were taking a reactionary turn. As Kristin Bumiller writes:

> Mainstream feminist demands for more certain and severe punishment for crimes against women fed into these reactionary forces. This resulted in a direct

alliance between feminist activists and legislators, prosecutors, and other elected officials promoting the crime control business. Although the feminist's "gender war" did not have the same impact on incarceration rates as the "war on drugs," it still contributed to the symbolic message.... Like other issues on the crime control agenda, the link to an actual rise in the crime rate was less significant than how violence against women shaped a generalized fear of disorder and the image of habitual and recalcitrant criminals. (Bumiller 2008, 7)

Funds for the prosecution of the crime of rape began to flow from the Law Enforcement Assistance Administration. Specialized sex crime units were established in urban police and prosecutors' offices. The high-profile case prosecuting the young black men who were falsely convicted of brutally raping a white jogger in New York City's Central Park in 1989 was accompanied by highly emotive press coverage of so-called wilding by young black men.[18] To the extent that the campaign against rape and domestic violence sought the intervention of the state, the consequences were severe for women of color. While white women organizers sought government funds and enlisted the assistance of prosecutors, some black women found themselves reluctant to work with a criminal justice system they viewed as fundamentally geared to controlling the African American population.

This conflict over using state power to protect women has a long and fateful history. In her landmark book on rape, Susan Brownmiller made the sweeping claim that men raped women simply because they had the physical power (and, she said, the correctly shaped genitalia) to do so. Her book is rightly credited with helping to put rape on the map as a crime against women's humanity. But she was also accused of failing to understand the historical significance of rape accusations against black men (Brownmiller 1975; Eisenstein 1983, 27ff.).

As Reconstruction was crushed after 1877, the myths of the sexually voracious black woman and the sexually predatory black man were weapons in the counterattack by Southern elites against the economic and social gains of the newly freed slaves and their families. The wave of lynching directed against black men (and some black women) was in part an attempt to discourage the rise of a viable black economic base in the South. But the press, both in the South and the North, defended lynching as necessary to protect the virtue of Southern white womanhood. The antilynching campaign of Ida B. Wells-Barnett, which raised the issue both nationally and internationally, clearly pointed to the real motives for these attacks, which were tolerated and often sponsored by local authorities (Carby 1987, 108ff.; Giddings 2008).

The issue of false rape claims echoed over the years through the cases of the Scottsboro boys in the 1930s in Georgia, taken up by the U.S. Communist Party, and the brutal murder of Emmett Till for allegedly whistling at a white woman in the 1950s in Mississippi—a case that galvanized the black community and was a key forerunner of the 1960s black civil rights movement. Hence, the eager embrace of feminist activists with U.S. government authorities, and specifically with prosecutors, left black women in an untenable position.

With the economic restructuring of the mid-1970s, state and federal policies targeted crime as the primary cause of social insecurity, rather than the economic changes that took manufacturing overseas and emptied the inner cities of industrial employment. Taking the focus off massive unemployment, government policies essentially criminalized the black poor, especially men but increasingly women, channeling them into the armed forces or into prison. With the punitive incarceration policies inaugurated by the Rockefeller drug laws in New York State and similar legislation across the country, black and Latino youth were being imprisoned at unprecedented rates. In 2008, the United States had 2.3 million people incarcerated, leading the world in both the number and percentage of residents behind bars (China was a "distant second"), with black and Hispanic prisoners far above their proportion in the general population.[19]

Strengthening the hand of the police and the courts against black men in the inner cities created a crisis for black women. Julia Sudbury argued that cooperating with white antiviolence feminists, whose work was institutionalized in state-funded agencies, meant a failure to contest the worldwide relationship of this intimate violence with state violence: against women of color in general; against immigrants from South Asia and the Caribbean in England; against Native American women in the United States. She called for a policy of fighting on two fronts. On the one hand, black women needed to combat the undeniable violence toward women that took place within their own communities; women had to "call out" black male leadership for their failure to address this issue. On the other hand, it was equally necessary to combat the official violence stemming from incarceration and police brutality within black communities.

Sudbury in particular made the connection between the successes of white feminist activism in the 1970s and the rise of globalization policies:

> The antiviolence movement has in many ways been complicit in the "law and order" agenda that has emerged as a response to globalization in Britain, Canada, the United States and elsewhere. White feminist activists generally think of the 1970s as a triumphant period in which second wave feminism brought the personal into the political arena, raising awareness about domestic violence, incest, and rape. Yet the 1970s also marked immense shifts in global capital that were enabled by developments in new technology. As corporations began to relocate their production operations in the Global South, unemployment hit urban communities of color in the Global North, and steady union jobs were replaced by irregular, "feminized," minimum-wage jobs. (Sudbury 2006, 19)

The response of governments to these changes was increasingly to shift resources away from social welfare programs and toward prisons, while simultaneously blaming the residents of inner cities for their deteriorating economic and social conditions:

> Governments responded to the creation of increasingly unstable urban "ghettos" by deploying punitive victim-blaming rhetoric that justified a shift from welfare and social services to policing and incarceration. This was facilitated by the growth of a transnational prison industry, first in the United States and then in Britain, Canada, and Australia. Corporations such as Wackenhut and Corrections Corporation of America developed sophisticated lobbying techniques to promote the use of incarceration as a "panacea" for social problems. Racialized practices of punishment became central to the political economy and social order of Western nations. (Sudbury 2006, 19)

To add insult to injury, the prison-building boom to incarcerate young men of color used funds that were freed up by reducing welfare payments, turning women of color into "welfare bums." In Sudbury's view, some black women's groups made the mistake of following white feminists into arguing for more law and order, rather than conducting an analysis of the use of state power against communities of color.[20]

I am not arguing here that black women, and women of color more generally, did not need protection against rape, physical abuse, and incest. But here, as elsewhere, the naive liberalism of mainstream U.S. feminism, its belief in the expressed values of U.S. democratic ideology, ran up against the realities of U.S. racial politics.

Female Genital Cutting

Finally, the last area of contention that I will point to is female genital cutting, a subject that I will use here as an illustration of the fault lines between what have come to be called First World and Third World feminism. A core feature of white feminist ideology that created difficulties for women of color was the tendency to adopt a stance of First World superiority. In her now famous articles "Cartographies of Struggle: Third World Women and the Politics of Feminism" and "Under Western Eyes: Feminist Scholarship and Colonial Discourses," Chandra Talpade Mohanty, a leading theorist of Third World feminism, challenged the tendency of Western feminist scholars to reduce the experience and the consciousness of non-Western women to a generic "Third World Woman" whose benighted conditions of life consigned her to a life of misery and hopelessness (Mohanty 1991a, 1991b).

In addition to being inaccurate, such a point of view made it impossible for Third World women and First World women to arrive at any kind of understanding of one another's local situation or particular issues (see also Mohanty 2003b). The debate over this issue is now worldwide and voluminous. What is the relationship between feminists located in the First World, and those in the Third World or Global South? Is it one of sisterhood and alliance? Is it one of mutual incomprehension? Or does it replicate the colonialism of the past? (For one view of the debate, see Kaplan, Alarcon, and Moallem 1999.)

To illustrate this point, I will take perhaps the most sensationalized and extreme case, namely, the critique of the practices of clitoridectomy and infibulation in Africa, Asia, and elsewhere, which became a staple of many feminist texts. I choose this example in part precisely because it is so emotionally fraught and seemingly (from a Western point of view) such an obvious atrocity. The issue of female circumcision, female genital cutting, or female genital mutilation, with all of its emotive connotations, can serve as a stand-in for all of the issues where the perspectives of white feminists and feminists of color can diverge fundamentally. To anticipate my readers' perhaps horrified reactions, I am not writing a defense of these practices. Rather, I am using this topic to illustrate some of the complexities of the First World–Third World feminist dialogue. I will use the expression *female genital cutting* to represent as neutral a position as possible.[21]

A focus on female sexual satisfaction was a central theme of some early women's liberation texts, most notably the essay by Anne Koedt on "The Myth of the Vaginal Orgasm" (1973). Reclaiming the right of women to enjoy orgasms—within a heterosexual couple, or a lesbian relationship, or as a solitary pleasure—was part of the ideological attack on patriarchy or male supremacy. Sexual satisfaction was being claimed as a right by U.S. women. How horrific, then, for U.S. and European feminists to realize that so many millions of women in Africa were seemingly deprived of this right with a procedure that excised the clitoris physically (not to mention the more extreme practice of infibulation—excising the vulva, sewing up the vaginal lips, and reducing the vaginal opening to a tiny hole). This procedure, often carried out under unsanitary conditions by traditional female practitioners, gave rise in many cases to serious infections or death. In this context, writers such as the late Fran Hosken took up the cause of ending female genital cutting in Africa and Asia (Hosken 1993).

This effort was echoed in the work of Mary Daly (1978), who pointed to FGC, Chinese foot-binding, and plastic surgery in the United States as a series of "sado-rituals" that illustrated the operations of patriarchy around the globe. Audre Lorde challenged Mary Daly on this point in a famous open letter in which she asked why Daly focused on FGC as the symbolic representation for the suffering of African women, rather than depicting the matriarchal strength of African women within their own culture (Lorde 1983). Nevertheless, in publications, international conferences, and legislation, an international campaign against FGC received widespread international publicity.

The famous African American novelist and poet Alice Walker took up the issue of FGC in a novel, movie, and book about the making of the movie. It is arguable that Walker's work had the effect of repeating the pattern of selectively reducing the experience of all African women to this one primitive sexual practice. The United States passed legislation criminalizing the practice of FGC in 1996 as part of the Illegal Immigration Reform and Immigrant Responsibility

Act. In a much publicized case, Fauziya Kasinga was granted political asylum from Togo on the ground that her fear of genital cutting constituted a legally valid claim of persecution (see Center for Reproductive Rights 2004; Coffman 2007; Eisenstein 1983, 109ff., 134; Walker 1992; Walker and Parmar 1993; and *Warrior Marks* 1993).

Meanwhile, Third World feminists tried to show why the single-minded focus on FGC was harmful. The isolation of this issue produced a distorted focus, making it seem as though this one practice was more horrific and damaging to women than the myriad other forms of violence and oppression suffered by women throughout the world, including in Western countries. As the Egyptian feminist Nawal El Sadaawi writes:

> I am against female circumcision and other retrograde and cruel practices. I was the first Arab woman to denounce it publicly and to write about it in my book, "Women and Sex." I linked it to other aspects of female oppression. But I disagree with those women in America and Europe who concentrate on issues such as female circumcision and depict them as proof of the unusual and barbaric oppression to which women are exposed only in Africa or Arabic countries. I oppose all efforts to deal with such problems in isolation, or to sever links with the general economic and social pressures to which women everywhere are exposed, and with the oppression which is the daily bread fed to the female sex in developed and developing countries, in both of which a patriarchal system still prevails. (quoted in Akale 1999, 4)

For one thing, to label female genital cutting, the ritual and practice of it, as a form of violence against women, as part of a growing catalog of such abuses from wife-beating to rape in Western feminist analysis, is to ignore the cultural role of such practices within the traditions of the peoples, and especially the women, who practice them. It is only with a cultural understanding of how genital cutting is part of long-standing and ancient customs that surround the growing up of young women and their preparation for marriage and entry into adult society that it is possible to create interventions that are likely to change these traditions.

For women like those interviewed by Rogaia Mustafa Abusharaf in the Douroshab township of northern Sudan, the ritual of genital cutting is linked to a system of deeply held beliefs about purity, morality, cleanliness, and virtue, as well as about female sexual and family power. Those seeking to end the ritual—and there is a long tradition of this by prominent Muslim leaders, predating the colonial conquest of the Sudan—have had to engage in dialogue with those who practice the custom. To condemn it as barbaric or as antiwoman is clearly counterproductive in this context (Abusharaf 2001).

More broadly, the focus on FGC in Africa encapsulated a politically damaging attitude toward that entire continent:

> Popular Western perceptions reduce Africa and African women in three distinct
> ways that could be called the "three Rs." First, they reduce Africa's fifty-four
> countries and hundreds of cultures to one uncivilized, "traditional" place out-
> side of history to be compared with the "modern" "West." Second, they reduce
> Africans, and African women in particular, to the status of their genitals, to
> being malicious torturers or hapless victims. Finally, uniform depictions reduce
> all cutting of female genitals to the most severe practice—infibulation. The
> cumulative effect of these reductions is that all African women are represented
> as having been infibulated due to unreasoned adherence to tradition and/or
> malicious ignorance. (James and Robertson 2005, 6)

As African women activists pointed out, this focus on FGC by U.S. and
European feminists placed them in a direct line of descent from the European
colonizers of Africa, including, most notably, Great Britain. The colonizers had
sought out and publicized those practices of African and Asian cultures that most
displayed a tendency to subordinate women as part of a propaganda effort to
show the superiority of the colonists. This attack on traditional practices created
a need to defend them as part of an attempt to preserve the identity of the colonized. Indeed, there were instances where a defense of FGC became part of the
anticolonial struggle. Thus, in the Sudan a law banning FGC during the colonial
period in 1946 and the arrest of a local midwife for carrying out this forbidden
operation led to riots and a retraction of the law by the colonial government (see
Akale 1999, 12).

Thus, the focus on FGC as an atrocity against women embodied a form
of neocolonialism on the part of U.S. and European feminists, continuing the
ideological work of colonial powers in "demonstrating" the primitive nature of
African cultures, which was one of the justifications for the European landgrab
of Africa during the eighteenth and nineteenth centuries. Not only did this
obscure the work of African activists who had been fighting FGC for decades
within their own countries. It also completely overlooked the role of European
and U.S. powers in the ravaging of African nations from the period of the slave
trade in the fifteenth century through the period of structural adjustment in the
twentieth and twenty-first centuries. Western feminists had chosen a focus on
African women's sexuality to the exclusion of the entire political economy and
colonial history of this vast continent of fifty-four different nations. A whole
continent had been "underdeveloped," in Walter Rodney's language, yet Western
feminists chose to focus on FGC (see Rodney 1972).

In this debate, African feminists did not defend the practice of FGC. But
they questioned the choice of Western feminists to focus on this practice without
placing it in the context of the horrific history of colonialism and its aftermath.
As the Association of African Women for Research and Development (Dakar,
Senegal) wrote in 1980, fighting genital mutilation "without questioning the
structures and social relations which perpetuate this situation, is like 'refusing to

see the sun in the middle of the day,' especially since Westerners necessarily profit from the exploitation of the peoples and women of Africa, whether directly or indirectly." Instead of "maternalism, ethnocentrism, and misuse of power," they wrote, Western feminists needed to see that the issue of FGC could be resolved only "with the conscious participation" of African women themselves (quoted in Eisenstein 1983, 142).

African women's organizations showed that the strongest indicators of whether campaigns against FGC will succeed are accessible health care, health promotion, and the education of girls. Yet "centuries of appropriation of Africa's peoples and natural resources have prevented the establishment of an adequate health and educational infrastructure. Foreign debt, another legacy of colonialism, and cuts in public expenditure imposed by the International Monetary Fund have also contributed to underdevelopment" (Sudbury 2000). In addition, the political and economic power of women was decisively eroded by colonialism: "To bemoan the oppression of Third World women without acknowledging the role of racism, colonialism and economic exploitation is to engage in what black British filmmaker Pratibha Parmar calls 'imperial feminism,' a standpoint which claims solidarity with Third World Women and women of color, but in actuality contributes to the stereotyping of Third World cultures as 'barbaric' and 'uncivilized'" (Sudbury 2000).

I have used the international debate over female genital cutting to illustrate the fact that the rise of international feminism created sharp debates between Western and Third World policymakers and practitioners. In the process, some of the blind spots of Western feminist analysis have been challenged by writers and activists from the Global South. In the course of the development of the international, or global, women's movement, from the first UN conference for women in 1975 through the pivotal conferences in the 1990s on the environment and population, many white Western feminists have been made aware of the need to understand the issues of women whose countries emerged from colonialism, only to encounter the neocolonialism and neoimperialism of the globalization era.

In this process of international encounters, shared research, inquiries, and data collection, the women of the Global South have developed a leadership position that has transformed the ideological basis of international feminism. The feminism developed by these leaders created an alternative and much broader agenda for women's human rights, ranging from access to a healthy infrastructure with clean water, adequate land for food self-sufficiency, and access to affordable health care. Third World feminist theorists writing in the North, such as Chandra Talpade Mohanty and Jacqui Alexander, joined feminist theorists such as Peggy Antrobus and the other members of the Development Alternatives with Women for a New Era network based in the Global South, to develop a program of women's issues that went far beyond the initial concerns of mainstream Northern feminist organizations such as the National Organization for Women. In the 1990s, international women's organizing around the series of international conferences succeeded in linking women's issues to a challenge to the macroeconomic policies of the Washington Consensus (Antrobus 2004).

It was women scholars and activists from the Global South who initially developed the analysis of structural adjustment as a program that depended on the unpaid labor and reproductive services of poor women. The agenda was further expanded with environmental issues as exposed by writers such as the Indian scientist Vandana Shiva: the struggle over the right to retain ancestral seed stores, the struggle against water privatization, the struggle to make a living from the worst and most depleted areas of land. It included the issue of nuclear testing, threatening the existence of island populations in the South Pacific, to which we could now add the threat of rising sea levels due to global warming (see Shiva 1989, among many other publications). I will return in the Conclusion of this book to the possibilities for a feminism that is shaped by the concerns of Third World women, both in the United States and in the rest of the globe.

CONCLUSION

As the juggernaut of right-wing organizing began in the early 1970s to bear down on U.S. politics, the women's movement was one of its prime targets. As we saw, the 1973 *Roe v. Wade* decision of the Supreme Court became an organizing key for right-wing leaders such as Richard Viguerie, since this decision—with all of its flaws—represented an emblem of female emancipation.

As we will see in Chapter 4, the right-wing coalition that was forming had a broad range of policies in its sights: for business, a halt to the increasing regulation of business by government, a rollback of taxation, and the crushing of union power; for the Christian Right, a return to "family values," meaning a restoration of patriarchal power in families and society; for supporters of smaller government, a reduction in personal and capital gains taxes. Even though the interests of this coalition were divergent, attacks on the rights of women, blacks, and gays were a uniting force, bringing millions of evangelically minded voters under the banner of the New Right.

In the context of such a powerful political shift to the right, it is questionable whether even a united women's movement would have had sufficient political power to reverse the tide. But as we saw in the case of the Hyde Amendment, divergent interests among women's movement activists served to undermine its power. As abortion increasingly became a political football, mainstream feminists focused on the legal issues, but did not sufficiently mobilize around the economic issue of affordability. A similar set of events surrounded the abolition of "welfare as we know it" in 1996 (see Chapter 4). Thus, the fault lines of race and class within the broader women's movement weakened it as a social force, just at the historical moment when a broadly based backlash against all of the gains of the social movements of the 1960s, from affirmative action to gay and lesbian rights, was becoming the governing principle of U.S. politics. I will turn to this period of backlash in the following chapter.

4

In the United States

A Political and Economic Sea Change

❈

In this chapter, I will argue that the willingness of women to enter the workforce in massive numbers, drawn by the rapid growth of the service sector, served the interest of capital in holding wages down. The income of wives supplemented that of their husbands, as unions weakened and corporations were able to resist the pressure for wage increases. Thus, historian Nancy MacLean argues that the most significant feature of the period since the 1970s for women was not so much the rise of feminism as it was the abolition of the family wage, something the working class had fought fiercely to obtain throughout the nineteenth and early twentieth centuries (MacLean 2002).

Similarly, the argument that all women should work played right into the hands of those seeking welfare reform. The idea that women ought to be working for wages reinforced the argument against paying for "welfare queens." Thus, a pillar of the New Deal was toppled with the aid of the ideology of feminism.

The net effects of the changes to the workforce were an erosion in the availability of high paying working-class jobs and a rise of service McJobs with low wages and few or no benefits. As women with education and access climbed the corporate ladder, reaching near parity with male middle managers, uneducated, poor women crowded into the jobs offered by retail organizations such as Wal-Mart, where much of the workforce was able to subsist only with the aid of food stamps, Medicaid, and section 8 housing. As poverty steadily increased under the George W. Bush administration, a new class divide opened up between the women for whom feminism was a ticket to advancement, and those left behind in the growing pool of the working poor—including new immigrants and those cut off from welfare.

POLITICAL BACKGROUND: HOW CONSERVATIVES
TRIUMPHED OVER LIBERALS

In this section, I will describe the political sea change that occurred between the still affluent 1960s and the recession years of the early 1980s. I have already described (in Chapter 1) the shift toward neoliberalism that most observers consider a centerpiece of globalization. But what were the developments within U.S. politics that made this shift possible? A variety of changes, from the splits that weakened the Democratic Party to the new glue that brought together a strengthened Republican Party, effected a transformation of U.S. politics.

The liberal coalition that emerged from World War II and presided over an expanding welfare state was shattered. The new ruling coalition, symbolized by the electoral victory of Ronald Reagan in 1980, was undergirded by a series of shifts in the balance of electoral power, with a severely weakened labor movement no longer able to sustain either the electoral majority of the Democrats or the legislation that had kept tax policy relatively progressive.[1]

A first element in this sea change was the decline of the labor movement. The percentage of workers in trade unions declined steadily from the high-water mark of 35.5 percent after World War II, falling to 31.4 percent in 1960, 27.3 percent in 1970, and 25.5 percent in 1975. (In 2008, unionized workers made up 7.5 percent of private sector workers and 35.9 percent of public sector workers, for an overall 12.1 percent share of the workforce [Greenhouse 2008].) Corporate leadership began an effort to weaken the labor movement, abandoning the "co-operative tenor" that had dominated much of labor-management relations with the biggest unions and replacing it with "a tough, adversarial stance" (Edsall 1984, 151). It is worth noting that the "entente cordiale" of big labor with big business did not preclude steady attacks on the power of labor throughout the post–World War II period, beginning with the Taft-Hartley Act of 1947. Whereas monopolistic and highly profitable industries such as auto and steel could live in harmony with their unions, firms in other, more competitive, and less profitable industries such as textiles were under constant pressure to reduce labor costs. After World War II, textiles led the way by moving out of the highly unionized North to the right-to-work South.[2]

Companies demonstrated an increasing willingness to defy the National Labor Relations Act and fire workers attempting to organize. Intensified management opposition to labor organizing "sharply reduced" labor's capacity to organize new workers. By dividing "the number of persons fired for union activity in 1980 by the number of persons who voted for a union in elections to obtain an indication of the risk faced by workers desiring a union, one gets a remarkable result: one in twenty workers who favored the union got fired" (Richard B. Freeman quoted in Edsall 1984, 152).

Even though there was a steady rate of victories in collective bargaining elections during the 1960s (around 60 percent), from the early 1970s onward unions began to lose. Management further escalated the attack by running decertification elections, seeking to persuade workers to vote out their existing union representation. Throughout the 1960s, the number of these remained relatively constant, averaging around 240 per year, but the numbers jumped tremendously in the 1970s, to an average of 419 in 1970–1975 and 712 in 1976–1980. In 1980 there were 902, and in 1981 there were 856 (Edsall 1984, 153–154).

Meanwhile, some firms began exploring a tactic that has since become very familiar, namely, the use of bankruptcy as a way to abrogate union contracts, a tactic that in 1984 the Supreme Court signaled it would uphold (Edsall 1984, 155). The attitude of many labor leaders in this period was one of resignation; they sought to protect the remaining members against the loss of their pensions, rather than seeking to expand into other areas. But more to the point, labor's leadership appeared to have counted on the continuation of the easy consensus relationship with management that was achieved, at least for the major unions, during the period of economic expansion of the 1950s and 1960s. "Labor did not recognize the adversarial posture of business until 1978, when its supposed allies in big business, particularly the members of the Business Roundtable, turned on the union movement in the congressional battle over the Labor Law Reform bill," defeating this attempt to expand labor protections (Edsall 1984, 156). "What galled labor beyond measure . . . was the defection to the anti-union camp of a raft of chief executives from the Fortune 500—men whom the unions had come to think of almost as allies. As many labor leaders see it, that crucial battle marked the end of a thirty-year entente cordiale. During this era of good feelings, many big companies had come to depend on the unions as a primary force for stabilization, both in equalizing basic labor costs within each major industry and in maintaining uninterrupted production for the life of the contract" (A. H. Raskin quoted in Edsall 1984, 156).

In 1981, President Reagan moved to break an apparently impregnable union, the Professional Air Traffic Controllers (PATCO), comprising 14,500 members with relatively high average annual incomes (over $30,000). By replacing the striking air controllers with military personnel, he was able to destroy the union. Reagan's hard-line stand against the air traffic controllers was seen by both labor and management as a watershed decision, triggering the resurgence of strikebreaking during the Reagan administration and leading to far tougher negotiating positions on the part of corporate executives and far more aggressive corporate techniques in riding out strikes (Edsall 1984, 161). The take-no-prisoners approach by corporate leadership toward union organizing, using increasingly sophisticated techniques to track and punish union organizers, has continued to this day.[3]

A second element in the sea change was a series of changes to the structure of the Democratic Party. The alliance of the labor movement with the Democratic

Party had been the backbone of the liberal legislation and tax policy of the 1950s and the 1960s. The bitter political feuding between labor's pro–Vietnam War leadership and antiwar members of the Democratic Party, culminating in the nomination of George McGovern as an antiwar candidate in 1972, essentially broke up a coalition of interests: "The Democratic-liberal agenda of the 1950s and 1960s—civil rights, housing, programs to alleviate hunger and malnutrition, federal aid to education, health coverage for the elderly and the poor, welfare assistance, job programs to counter recessions—was initiated by a wide range of forces. The one consistent element in all of these legislative battles, however, was labor's active presence in each of the lobbying coalitions" (Edsall 1984, 162).

Meanwhile, new Democrats elected after Watergate by the reform wing of the party in 1974 and 1976 came largely from suburban districts with few union voters. The traditional base of the Democratic Party in urban machines sensitive to ethnic voter blocs was giving way to a more middle- and upper-class constituency. New rules for the Democratic presidential nomination process limited the influence of labor within the conventions. In the three presidential elections of 1972 (McGovern), 1976 (Carter), and 1980 (Carter), organized labor was no longer a "key force" in selecting Democratic Party leadership (Edsall 1984, 163).

Ironically, the counterattack from the business community forced an about-face among the leadership of the American Federation of Labor–Congress of Industrial Organizations (AFL-CIO) in its negative relationship to the organized feminist community. At the time of the 1972 nominating convention, George Meany, the AFL-CIO president, had been quoted as saying, "We heard from the abortionists, and we heard from people who look like Jacks, acted like Jills, and had the odor of johns about them." Alexander E. Barkan, then political director of the AFL-CIO Committee on Political Education, called the Democratic National Committee a group of "kooks, crazies, queers and feminists" (both quoted in Edsall 1984, 160–161). But when the AFL-CIO, now on the defensive, organized a solidarity day protest on September 19, 1981, in Washington, drawing some 250,000 union members and supporters to express opposition to Reagan policies, "[AFL-CIO president] Lane Kirkland would lead the Solidarity Day march down Constitution Avenue with Eleanor Smeal, president of the nation's largest feminist organization, the National Organization for Women, to his right" (Edsall 1984, 161).

A third element in the sea change was the forging of a new alliance within the Republican Party, with the creation of a new coalition among business, the conservative ideological right wing, and religious fundamentalists. The groundwork for this new coalition was laid by Richard Nixon. Using the Southern Strategy devised by the then Republican strategist Kevin Phillips, and taking advantage of the identification of the Democrats with the interests of the black community and the civil rights movement, Nixon moved to detach white Southern Democrats from their party allegiance with a set of ideological appeals to the interests of white voters. Nixon, although outflanked on states' rights and racism by the governor of Alabama, George Wallace, was still able to win on a platform of states' rights and law and order, after the uprisings in the inner cities following the assassination of Martin Luther King.[4]

For business leaders, the reverses of the Vietnam War, which had brought military-industrial corporate interests such as Dow Chemical, Raytheon, and DuPont into severe disrepute, and the surge of liberal reforms produced just before and then during the "Watergate" Congresses of 1974 and 1976, required a regrouping of forces.[5] As Bryce Harlow, a veteran lobbyist for Procter and Gamble, remarked, "The danger had suddenly escalated.... We had to prevent business from being rolled up and put in the trash can" (cited in Edsall 1984, 114–115).

Business strategies included more sophisticated lobbying efforts, with the creation of "Astroturf grassroots" organizing among employees and stockholders, and the creation of new institutions such as the Business Roundtable, founded in 1972. With business leaders from major companies—General Electric, Alcoa, Campbell Soup, and U.S. Steel, among others—the Roundtable "became in effect the political arm of big business." Expanding its concern from labor-management issues, this group now focused on "the entire spectrum of public policy issues in Washington," including taxation, antitrust regulation, banking, and employment (Edsall 1984, 121). Similarly, a newly revitalized Chamber of Commerce became the basis for elaborate machinery to mobilize grassroots lobbying operations, recommend probusiness candidates to the business community, and provide resources for ad hoc coalitions on specific issues (Edsall 1984, 123–128).

The new strategies also included expending major sums on corporate advertising and the large-scale financing of right-wing think tanks such as the American Enterprise Institute and the Heritage Foundation.[6] Corporate backers included Joseph Coors of the Adolph Coors Company; Richard Mellon Scaife, Mellon heir; the John M. Olin Fund, established by Olin Matheison Chemical Corporation; Mobil Oil; Dow Chemical; Gulf Oil; and Sears Roebuck (see Edsall 1984, 117–120): "The financial backing for these institutions reflects the astute use of philanthropy by the corporate and conservative foundation community to finance credible intellectual arguments produced by highly respected and independent but conservative economists and social scientists" (Edsall 1984, 120).

But, above all, the strength of the Republican Party stemmed from its newly established "big tent" philosophy. The old split between business, accustomed to compromising with the Democrats, and the formerly fringe ideological right wing, as represented by the supporters of Barry Goldwater, was overcome, so that business interests, increasingly strong in the South and West, found a new partnership with the ideological Right. The Republican coalition now included both the business community, newly united in its determination to roll back liberal gains, and members of the Religious Right under the leadership of Richard Viguerie, cofounder of the Moral Majority, and Jerry Falwell, the television evangelist:

The defeat of Gerald Ford in 1976, the steady decline of the moderate wing of the GOP in the Northeast and Midwest, the success of highly conservative Republican candidates in the South, the steady movement of the financial center of gravity of the GOP toward the sunbelt, the expansion of the GOP's right wing in Congress from a dissident faction into a strong voting block, and the increasing convergence of conservative ideologues and the business community behind the same set of candidates have all functioned to ameliorate tensions within the Republican party. The result has been a far greater coherence of shared ideological and economic interests within the GOP than within the Democratic Party. (Edsall 1984, 103)

The newly retooled Republicans were able to use the resentment of those who lost ground during the economic slowdown of the 1970s to bring into office a regime that would fundamentally alter the tax structure. The Reagan forces were able to manipulate the discontent of the working class toward its former Democratic leaders, because of the stagflation of the 1970s, to bring to power a coalition that would fundamentally end the tradition of using government to bring greater equity through taxation. In this way, the party's supporters among the working class would pay the economic price, with a major redistribution upward toward the rich and powerful.

The political form that the economic turbulence of the 1970s took was a major power shift to the right. Once stagflation during the presidency of Jimmy Carter (1976–1980) exposed the Democratic Party's inability to manage the economy, white Reagan Democrats started voting Republican because of their resentment about how their improved economic situation (in the 1960s) and then their stagnating wages (1970s) subjected them to unfair taxation. Republicans used this resentment to build a coalition that then brought in the most drastic redistributive tax program, taking money from the poor and middle class and handing it to the rich. At the same time, they cut social programs for the poor. So in electoral terms the country moved right, rather than left.

For all its redistributive rhetoric, the Democratic Party had not fundamentally changed the profile of income distribution during its reign. But it had expanded social spending in the 1960s, especially for minorities and the poor, and it was this that infuriated the Reagan Democrats, who were already agitated about antiwar demonstrations, taxpayer support for abortions, and the perceived unfairness of affirmative action measures. A progressive tax system in the 1950s began to bite when people's income rose during the 1960s and they moved into higher tax brackets. This so-called bracket creep made taxation a volatile political issue in the 1970s. Democrats were blamed as taxpayers, encouraged by right-wing attacks on excessive taxation, got more and more fed up with those receiving benefits.

Into this fertile territory came the publications of the right-wing think tanks. Thus, the Center for the Study of American Business, founded in 1975 by Murray

L. Weidenbaum (chair of Reagan's Council of Economic Advisers from 1981 to 1982), produced papers on the high costs of government regulation in measures such as the Clean Air Act and agencies such as the Federal Trade Commission. Their overall finding was that by 1979 the cost of government regulation of business had reached over $100 billion.

The think tanks were producing so-called evidence that "the sharp expansion of the regulatory role of the federal government in the 1970s had contributed significantly to the decline over that decade in productivity, forcing companies to spend money to reduce pollution and to increase safety measures to meet federally mandated consumer standards, diverting capital resources from productive investments" (Edsall 1984, 217). This kind of work provided the intellectual justification for the Reagan administration's drive toward deregulation, through budget cuts, antiregulation appointments, and the giving of authority to the Office of Management and Budget to delay, revise, or kill regulatory initiatives.

Similarly, the American Enterprise Institute, a base of operations and a forum for conservative intellectuals such as the late Jeanne J. Kirkpatrick, David R. Gergen, Seymour Martin Lipset, and Nathan Glazer, emphasized deregulation and the need to increase our military capacity. Meanwhile, the Hoover Institution at Stanford housed the black conservative Thomas Sowell, who was laying out the argument that the network of social programs, including affirmative action, had weakened the ability of blacks to compete. And the National Bureau of Economic Research's Martin Feldstein launched an attack on capital gains taxes, seeking to show that the high rate of taxation on income from capital had lowered investments in plant and equipment in the previous two decades.

The new coalition of forces put together by the Republican Party, then, comprised big business, small businesses, religious conservatives, fiscal conservatives claiming to abhor excessive government spending (such as the notorious Grover Nyquist, who promised to shrink government to the size where he could drown it in a bathtub), and supporters of a vastly expanded military budget. At the ideological level, they developed themes that appealed to what would become the Reagan Democrats. Cut taxes above all! Using the highly dubious economic theory of "supply-side economics," they espoused drastic tax cuts and the elimination of wasteful, unnecessary government programs, usually equated with Aid to Families with Dependent Children (AFDC), food stamps, rent subsidies, and other safety net measures.

The ideologues of the new Republican coalition—Irving Kristol of *The Public Interest,* Congressman Jack Kemp, Jude Wanniski of the *Wall Street Journal*—were conscious of the need to develop an economic strategy that would appeal both to Wall Street and to the voters. The solution was produced by Arthur Laffer, sketching his new idea on a now legendary napkin in a Washington restaurant. Laffer drew a simple graph that showed a theoretical curve plotting government revenues as a function of tax rates. Up to a certain point, increased tax rates produced increased revenues for government. But beyond that point—this is where the curve turned down—increased tax rates produced decreased government revenues, as they became a disincentive for businesses and individuals to work hard to produce further income. If raising tax rates could actually reduce revenue, the logical corollary was that cutting tax rates would perforce increase revenues. The argument was that the money released by the lowered taxes would be channeled into investments and therefore eventually into growing efforts by businesses and individuals, who would then ultimately pay increased taxes.

This Laffer curve was "dubious economics, but brilliant politics" (Alperowitz and Faux 1984, 41). Rather than increasing demand in the economy, as was the point of Keynesian pump priming, this measure would increase the supply of money in the private sector, and therefore increase economic growth (hence "supply-side economics" or "monetarism"). Neoconservative writers working out of business-supported think tanks and media outlets such as *Public Interest, Commentary, Harpers,* and *Readers Digest,* began pumping out stories to build support for this new economic theory: "Freed from ... the traditional conservative demand for austerity as the answer to inflation, the neoconservatives could offer Republicans a magic weapon to cut into the heart of the Democratic electorate. Supply-side economics was a painless way to prosperity. Cut taxes, create jobs, and eventually have even more revenue for public spending" (Alperowitz and Faux 1984, 42). In California, landlords were able to get Proposition 13 passed, which cut tax rates on many categories of properties down to 1 percent of their assessed value, and capped rates of increase on taxes until the property was sold.[7] Across the country, local business groups and politicians organized tax limitation efforts, and thirty-six states enacted tax cuts in 1978. Reagan was elected on a wave of tax revolt in 1980, with those voting for him convinced that they were the hardworking Americans, whereas others were parasites on welfare (Alperowitz and Faux 1984, 43ff.).

Meanwhile, the actual outcome of the Reagan years was a steep rise in the federal deficit and in unemployment. Almost immediately after cutting taxes in 1981, Reagan in 1982 had to ask for the biggest tax increase in U.S. history. Reagan's own budget adviser acknowledged that supply-side theory was a hoax: "Stockman himself, as he admitted in an embarrassing interview published in the *Atlantic Monthly,* had abandoned the supply-side theory even before he submitted Reagan's first budget to Congress. Reagan's tax bill, he said, was a 'Trojan Horse' for the giveaways to big business, which was all they were interested in from the start. And when the legislation got to Congress, 'The hogs were really feeding,' he said glumly. In the space of a few months Laffer's theory was a piece of intellectual junk" (Alperowitz and Faux 1984, 46).

It is worth noting that Republicans seeking to end the decades-long Democratic "lock" on economic issues tried out several different electoral themes before hitting on the antitax rhetoric that became their "open sesame" to electoral success.

Richard Viguerie and Howard Phillips, the cofounders of the Moral Majority, had tried social issues such as busing and abortion, but were unable in the 1960s and 1970s to detach blue- and pink-collar workers from their Democratic allegiances. Once the two men hit on the theme that Americans pay too much in taxes, with the overwhelming success of Proposition 13 in California, they never looked back (Alperowitz and Faux 1984, 29ff.).

Above all, this new coalition skillfully used the political gains of the Left in the 1960s, including affirmative action for blacks and women, the right to abortion under the *Roe vs. Wade* decision of 1973, and the steady expansion of the AFDC rolls, as their wedge issues. As the economic restructuring of the late 1970s and early 1980s proceeded, creating rust-belt regions and devastated inner cities in the Northeast and Midwest, a vast machinery of distraction was put into place. "Family values," allegedly under attack from blacks, feminists, gays, and liberals in general, became the mantra of the New Right, with hot-button issues such as abortion bringing millions of genuinely concerned Christian voters into the Republican fold.

Meanwhile, the "war on drugs" was the pretext for a scare campaign about rising crime rates. In New York State, the Rockefeller drug laws (similar legislation was passed in California and elsewhere) made petty drug violations the basis of serious felonies. Prisons in rural upstate New York were then expanded to incarcerate city dwellers. Thus, the coalition simultaneously benefited from providing jobs for generally conservative rural prison guards, while increasing its rural political power—a power multiplied by the state legislature counting disfranchised urban prisoners as rural residents to inflate the population for redistricting purposes.[8]

The coalition with the Religious Right could blame feminists for rising divorce rates because they had fought for abortion rights and because they insisted on going out to work. The coalition could blame gays and lesbians for the decline of traditional marriage. And they could blame blacks for the allegedly dangerous rate of crime, despite the fact that crime rates continued to fall steadily. The family values rhetoric, and the escalated fear of crime, both carefully orchestrated and echoed in the media, were means of deflecting attention away from the transformation of the postwar U.S. economy.[9]

THE CREATION OF A LOW-WAGE ECONOMY

The new economy created in the 1970s was a low-wage economy, drawing heavily on female labor. As economist Teresa Amott notes: "Hiring women was a central part of the corporate strategy to restore profitability because women were not only cheaper than men, but were also less likely to be organized into unions and more willing to accept temporary work and no benefits.... This led to what has been called the 'feminization' of the labor force, as women moved into jobs that had previously been held only by men and as jobs that were already predominantly female became even more so" (Amott 1993, 50).

The widespread use of women's labor was accompanied by a major restructuring in which the proportion of traditional "smokestack" jobs for men was reduced: "The increase of eleven million jobs between 1973 and 1979 was concentrated in the nonmanufacturing sector of the economy, primarily services and retail trade.... *Increases* in employment in eating and drinking places over that period were greater than the *total* employment in the auto and steel industries combined in 1979. For the most part, restaurants and similar services generate low-wage, often part-time jobs. A large percentage of such jobs go to women who need them to maintain family living standards or to support themselves and their children" (Alperowitz and Faux 1984, 62).

Historically, the older industries (auto, steel, petrochemicals, tires, household appliances) were characterized by a small high-wage segment at one end, a small low-wage segment at the other, and a large "semi-skilled and skilled blue-collar and white-collar [segment in the] 'middle'" (Kuhn and Bluestone 1987, 11). But the newly expanding industries—high tech, business and personal services, and retail—have a "dual" market structure, with a small pool of well-paid managers and professionals at the top and a very large pool of poorly paid workers at the bottom. Thus, there is no equivalent to the old "middle-wage" blue-collar jobs.

Dramatic evidence of this change comes from the transformation of the department store industry. Traditional department stores benefited from a consumer boom, peaking in the 1960s and 1970s, but discount stores began to undersell them by lowering costs with reduced levels of service and automated checkout counters. The discount stores doubled the size of their (mainly male) managerial hierarchy, but also multiplied the number of "low-wage, high turnover, part-time jobs"—which went primarily to women (Kuhn and Bluestone 1987, 17).

This pattern was accelerated by the dramatic growth of Wal-Mart, the largest U.S. company in terms of revenue and employment, with annual sales of over $300 billion and 1.5 million employees around the world, over 70 percent of them women (Lichtenstein 2006, 3). Wal-Mart became the target of the largest ever class action sex discrimination lawsuit (see Featherstone 2004). The "Wal-Martization of America" is documented in a *BusinessWeek* article on the decline of social mobility in the United States: "For years, even during the 1990s boom, much of Corporate America had already embraced Wal-Mart-like stratagems to control labor costs, such as hiring temps and part-timers, fighting unions, dismantling internal career ladders, and outsourcing to lower-paying contractors at home and abroad. While these tactics have the admirable outcome of holding down consumer prices, they're costly in other ways. More than a quarter of the labor force, about 34 million workers, is trapped in low-wage, often dead-end jobs" (Bernstein 2003, 54). In an illustration of the lack of generational mobility,

BusinessWeek cites the case of Michael A. McLimans, who works as a delivery driver for Domino's and Pizza Hut. His wife is a hotel receptionist. Together they "pull down about $40,000 a year—far from the $60,000 Michael's father, David I. McLimans, earns as a veteran steelworker" (Bernstein 2003, 58).

There is no doubt that on one level the legitimization of paid work for women represented a major advance. Economist Heidi Hartmann argues that the rise of the service economy was a boon for women, despite the fact that it was accompanied by an influx of low-paying jobs. She cites the rising divorce rate and the rise of single parenthood as evidence that women were voting with their feet for economic independence (Hartmann 1987).

This was particularly true for black women, for whom the changes of the 1970s meant an end to the neoenslavement of domestic service: "Immediately after World War II, black women's earnings were about half those of white women. By 1981, black women's wages had risen to 92–95 percent of those of white women, ... largely due to the fact that black women workers are today no longer confined chiefly to domestic service jobs, but have moved into a wider range of occupations" (Kuhn and Bluestone 1987, 23).[10]

Despite these undeniable gains, the inclusion of married women in the workforce, including the mothers of young children, was of assistance to capital in keeping wages stagnant, and in abandoning the concept of a wage that would cover the expenses of wife and children, a goal for which patriarchal unions had struggled during the nineteenth century. Feminists in the 1970s were vociferous in their demand for women's economic independence, and indeed many feminist scholars and activists attacked the family wage of the nineteenth century as a trap for women. But Johanna Brenner argues that this was a misreading of the historical evidence. The family wage, for those workers who achieved it, represented a victory for the working class (Brenner 2000b, 11–58).

Although I am obviously not arguing for a return to dependence on men and marriage as the only options for women, I think it necessary to acknowledge that the independence won in the 1970s and 1980s came at a high price: the abolition of the family wage, both as a reigning ideology and as a reality at least for high-paid male workers, and an extended period of wage stagnation for all workers. (On this point, see MacLean 2002.) Even though the family wage concept may have been patriarchal, it was a wage norm that acknowledged the need to support "dependents." In the low-wage economy that replaced it, no such concept remained.

Comparing 1988 to 1973, Sam Gindin and Leo Panitch argue that working families responded to the changed structure of the workforce by incorporating the work of "more family members" (discreetly ungendered in their account). "In addition to the increase in debt ... working class families have restructured their own lives to maintain and increase their consumption by having more family members work (spouses, students) and by increasing the average hours worked per person" (Gindin and Panitch 2002, 38). In other words, the stagnation of wages was compensated for by the growth of dual-income-earner families.

What were the changes that ushered in the so-called service economy? These included the introduction of new technology to reduce the workforce size and increase productivity in the manufacturing sector. The star example here is the steel industry: whereas steel employed 500,000 American workers in 1970, roughly the same amount of steel is now produced by 155,000 workers (Weisman 2007). Additionally, as we saw in Chapter 1, there was the shift of investment to the FIRE industries—finance, insurance, and real estate—in a period where finance came to include the widest possible range of speculative instruments.

Corporations also moved their production to cheap labor areas, in electronics and computers, appliances, textiles, children's toys. In retail, they created the fast-food industry and the big box stores, of which Wal-Mart is the ideal type. And to accommodate the system of worldwide production, they created just-in-time systems of distribution, based heavily on computer technology, that enabled the garment industry to flash new designs around the world in a matter of seconds.

Meanwhile, corporations were able, with government allies, to dismantle the system of regulation that was limiting the flow of capital, both internally in the United States and externally across the globe. The Depression era Glass-Steagall Act of 1933 had kept banks, brokerages, and insurance companies separated, and placed a wall between commercial banks (handling individual and company deposit accounts and insured by the Federal Deposit Insurance Corporation) and investment banks (raising capital for companies by matching sellers and buyers of stocks and bonds). These barriers were repealed by the Financial Services Modernization Act of 1999, which opened the door to a wave of mergers and acquisitions and ultimately to the speculative frenzy that led to the financial meltdown of 2007–2008.[11] Legislation that governed utilities was also dismantled, so that companies such as Enron could speculate in electricity supplies without being governed by state rules about utility ownership. Municipalities began selling the upkeep of roads and bridges to private companies, while the privatization of prisons and the spread of "charter" schools continued apace. Thus, for example, the devastation of the city of New Orleans under the crushing power of Hurricane Katrina in 2005 was taken by city authorities as the occasion to replace much of the public education system with charter schools.[12]

A full-court press against union organizing continued throughout the period of the 1970s and 1980s (and remains in place at this writing), so that a climate of fear and harassment surrounded union-organizing efforts across all economic sectors. And last but not least, businesses substituted female for male labor wherever possible to cut labor costs. What I want to argue here is that these techniques by management to minimize costs and maximize profits were instituted during a period in which the rules governing female labor were being revolutionized.

THE FALL OF THE FAMILY WAGE

As we saw in Chapter 2, the family wage ideology of the nineteenth and early twentieth centuries had begun to erode as married women entered the workforce in large numbers after World War II. Even though union feminism offered some protection for women, the period of the late 1950s and 1960s saw an eclipse of union prestige and power. The McClellan Committee hearings of 1957 and 1958 helped to discredit unions, establishing an image of corruption and bureaucratic stagnation (Lichtenstein 2002, 162–164). Civil rights and women's movement organizers sought protection for their workplace rights, not through union organizing, but through government intervention: "From the early 1960s onward, the most legitimate, though not necessarily the most potent defense of American job rights would be found not through collective initiative, as codified in the Wagner Act [of 1935] and advanced by the trade unions, but through an individual's claim to his or her civil rights based on race, gender, age, or other attributes. If a new set of work rights was to be won, the decisive battle would take place, not in the union hall or across the bargaining table, but in the courts and the legislative chambers" (Lichtenstein 2002, 192).

From Title VII of the Civil Rights Act through affirmative action and comparable worth, activists used race and sex discrimination lawsuits to break up the barriers to employment for blacks and women. Meanwhile, feminists, as we saw, were able to dismantle protective legislation in a matter of five years as they sought and won the end of sex-linked job ads. In this climate the Equal Rights Amendment nearly won adoption, and the unions no longer fought against it.

Above all, the family wage idea was no longer on the agenda. As Ruth Milkman notes, the idea of the family wage had begun to erode "after the expansion of the female labor force had exhausted the supply of single, divorced, and widowed women, so that married women and even mothers were incorporated into the labor force in large numbers.... In the inflationary 1960s and 1970s ... the expanded demand 'pulling' women into the labor market came to be supplemented by a new family economics 'pushing women out of the home.'" The resurgence of feminism in the 1960s and its increasing popularity in the 1970s created "a new egalitarian ideology ... proclaiming women's right to equal treatment in the labor market" (Milkman 1987, 121).

Now both wife and husband were in the labor force, protective labor legislation was no longer in force, and corporations were still pursuing their intensive campaign against union power:

> Management efforts to avoid or eliminate trade unionism hardly weakened as the Republican 1980s gave way to a new decade and a new administration. Long, bitter disputes at the Detroit Free Press, Caterpillar, Staley,

Avondale Shipyards, Bridgestone-Firestone, Yale University, and the Port of Charleston testified to management self-confidence and the weakness of the contemporary labor movement. Even the notable 1997 Teamster victory at United Parcel Service (UPS) did little to reverse the anti-union tide.... The Teamster success at UPS generated no sea change in management thinking and relatively few organizing ripples in the economy's vast service sector. (Lichtenstein 2002, 17)

Corporations were now free to substitute female for male labor wherever they saw fit. The national press in the 1980s celebrated the unprecedented entrance of women into a range of formerly male-dominated jobs, from executive and lawyer to pharmacist, bartender, bus driver, and baker (Reskin and Roos 1990, 3). But a careful examination of these changes showed that in nearly every case of such "breakthroughs," the switch from male to female labor was a decision by management responding to pressures to become more competitive.

The 1970s saw the "birth of more than 20 million new jobs." In a situation where there was substantial growth in demand for labor, the jobs where male workers were plentiful stayed male dominated. Thus, carpentry and heavy-truck driving each added about 370,000 workers in the 1970s, while women "claimed only 2.7 and 5.6 percent," respectively, of these new jobs. But job growth "supports feminization when it creates a shortfall of male workers" (Reskin and Roos 1990, 40).

Using their template of "job queues and gender queues," Reskin and Roos show that in the eight categories of work their case studies examined, there were a series of factors that opened these jobs to an influx of women workers. (The job categories were pharmacy, book editing, public relations, bank management, systems analysts, insurance sales, real estate, insurance adjusters, bartending, baking, and typesetting for newspapers.) In each of these areas, the proportion of women workers grew dramatically. For example, in pharmacy in 1950 and 1960 women represented about 8 percent of all pharmacists. But by 1980, in a growing occupation, they "constituted 32 percent of all pharmacists" (Reskin and Roos 1990, 111).

What factors created these changes? They were pressure from antidiscrimination suits and affirmative action, women's greater willingness to compete for these jobs, and employers' willingness to consider women. But above all, these areas of work—from typesetting to banking to real estate—had undergone significant structural changes in response to competitive economic pressures. In these circumstances, a female labor force became more profitable.

Thus, the transformation of the pharmaceutical profession, with the advent of retail chain stores such as CVS selling drugs, made pharmacy a less attractive profession to males, while it opened these jobs to women. Similarly, the introduction of computerization to the insurance industry to cut costs decreased the role of independent decisionmaking among insurance adjusters, making these jobs less attractive to men; women eagerly filled this gap.

In other words, these professions opened their doors to women in a combination of increased supply of women workers and demand for them in a situation where employers were ready to abandon their usual preferred lineup or queue, which had put white men first. The willingness of women to compete provided a willing labor force. The expansion and restructuring of the industries created new openings. The restructuring made the jobs less interesting and prestigious, so that men went elsewhere (Reskin and Roos 1990, 29–68).

Women filled over 60 percent of the more than 65 million jobs created from 1964 to 1997 (Thistle 2006, 108–109 and n27). More than half the growth in jobs in the 1980s and 1990s were professional, managerial, and technical positions: women supplied the majority of these new workers. But women also supplied a far greater proportion of new workers at the low end of the employment sector. "Half of all women ... are still in low-wage service jobs or in sales and clerical work. ... Women have been instrumental in the rapid expansion of the low-wage lower tier of the service sector, providing the bulk of workers in both the fastest and largest areas of such low-wage growth. Nine-tenths or more of child care workers, private household cleaners, and nursing aides and orderlies are women" (Thistle 2006, 110).

We can compare the voracious appetite for female labor on the part of corporations to the conquering of a new region of the earth under globalization:

> Economists have long recognized that the development of new regions and the conversion of nonwage workers into wage workers can create great profits, leading corporations to set up factories overseas. To understand the gains of the past forty years, we must realize that a similar lucrative process was happening within the United States itself, in the very center of American homes. As the market reached into kitchens and bedrooms, turning many household tasks into work for pay, and as women themselves applied labor freed from domestic chores in research labs, hospitals, factories, and fast food restaurants, productivity rose greatly and a large new pool of income was created. (Thistle 2006, 112)

The good news for women was their access to all areas of work, no longer limited by sexist ideas of appropriateness. The stigma against married women working was abolished. Affirmative action opened up professional areas of work for Black women. Corporations now accepted and even sought out women at senior levels of management. The bad news was that the restructuring of the economy succeeded in freezing wage levels: adjusting for inflation, from the early 1970s until the upswing of the Clinton years (1992–2000), real wages stagnated or fell outright for most workers.[13]

Discouraged Male Workers
in the Restructured Economy

The wave of deindustrialization was deeply demoralizing to male workers, as they saw the secure jobs held by their fathers and grandfathers disappearing. Susan Faludi captures this feeling of abandonment and disgrace in her book *Stiffed* (2000), where she documents the widespread pain and anger among male blue-collar workers. As deindustrialization shrank the numbers and the power of the older masculine job categories such as steelworker and machinist, feminist ideology attacked traditional masculinity as patriarchal. Groups such as the Promise Keepers expressed the resentment and even rage of male workers over this process of dethroning masculine privilege and called for the restoration of the male head of household to his former glory.

For many male workers affected by the decline in manufacturing jobs, a shift to less lucrative, service employment was a choice they refused to make. The dramatic change in employment patterns between men and women as the balance of the economy shifted toward service jobs can be seen from the rising percentage of men no longer seeking employment. The *New York Times* reports that as of 2006 "millions of men ... —in the prime of their lives, between 30 to 55—have dropped out of regular work. They are turning down jobs they think beneath them or are unable to find work for which they are qualified, even as an expanding economy offers opportunities to work. About 13 percent of American men in this age group are not working, up from 5 percent in the late 1960s. The difference represents 4 million men who would be working today if the employment rate had remained where it was in the 1950s and 1960s" (Uchitelle and Leonhardt 2006). This group of discouraged male workers represented a higher percentage of working-age men not in the paid workforce than at almost any time in the previous half-century. They included men with less than college educations, those living in "hard-hit industrial areas" or in rural states, and men emerging from prison.

But another way to accommodate the dramatic changes in male employment was for male workers to buy into a feminist analysis. Films such as *Bootmen* (2000), an Australian feature about men getting laid off from a steel mill who become tap dancers and organize a tap-dancing benefit for their laid-off fellow workers, or the English film *The Full Monty* (1997), where men become strippers when their traditional masculine steelworker occupation disappears, demonstrated the softening power of feminist ideology. Men no longer needed to be trapped in the masculinity of traditional, blue-collar, physical, typically male forms of labor. They could gracefully adapt to new, previously all-female roles in the service sector, such as dancing, stripping, or nursing. Thus, culturally, feminism could be used to ease the pain of economic restructuring. The widespread acceptance of mainstream feminist doctrines such as the abolition of gender and the obsolescence of sex roles was thus ideologically and practically useful to capital.[14]

ENDING WELFARE "AS WE KNOW IT"

The widespread acceptance of waged work for women did not go unnoticed by policymakers. The idea that women should be in the paid labor force was so hegemonic in the 1990s that the welfare "reform" legislation of 1996, the Personal Responsibility and Work Opportunity Reconciliation Act (PRWORA), made this its centerpiece. Carrying out a key element in the neoliberal agenda of undoing the social policies of the New Deal, welfare reform devolved responsibility to the states, removed the idea of welfare as an entitlement to any poor single mother needing assistance with taking care of her children, and, most importantly, instituted workfare as a requirement. Single mothers would no longer have the safety net of a government subsidy, no matter how inadequate, in exchange for raising their children.

The original precursor of the AFDC program was the system of pensions for single mothers, passed into law by most states and local governments from 1910 to 1920. As we saw in Chapter 2, this first modern public welfare program in the United States was the work of a generation of activist women—labeled *social feminists* by historians—who belonged to the "women's social reform network active in the Progressive Era" (Gordon 1994, 37, 323n71).[15] The relief provided was meager, intended only for "deserving" women such as white widows. In most cases, single mothers could not live on these pensions, so they were also expected to work. But work was supposed to be subordinated to their domestic duties, so that administrators forbade full-time work in factories in favor of piecework or the taking in of laundry at home. The women reformers of the Progressive Era and the 1920s expected the pensions to allow these women above all to perform their domestic duties.

In this they were motivated by an ideology of maternalism. This meant that they "regarded domestic and family responsibilities and identities as essential to the vast majority of women and to the social order, and strongly associated women's with children's interests." In addition, they saw themselves as in a motherly relationship to the poor, offering moral, spiritual, and economic help. And they defined their own social roles as deriving from their "work, experience, and/ or socialization as mothers," making them uniquely qualified as social reformers (Gordon 1994, 55).

The power of the "white women's reform community of approximately 1890–1935" extended into the New Deal era. Their power base in the Children's Bureau, established in 1912 within the Department of Labor as a concession to the "achievements and demands" of the Progressive Era women's network, gave them access to government policy circles. When the social movements challenging Roosevelt's New Deal government forced the creation of a social welfare state, however weak, for the United States, these women reformers were able to insert a provision in the Social Security Act of 1935 that enshrined the mothers' pensions (see Gordon 1994, 284).

When Aid to Families with Children (AFC, as this federal welfare program was first termed) was introduced, as part of the Social Security Act of 1935, it was still unthinkable to expect single mothers to enter the workforce while also caring for their children (Gordon 1994). But when, following the activism of the welfare rights movement, a major expansion of the welfare rolls in the 1960s took place, welfare began to be identified in the media and therefore in public consciousness primarily with black women. The black welfare mother became a major target of right-wing ideological critique. The issue of welfare became an entering wedge in the ideological delegitimization of government intervention in the market (see Nadasen 2004).

Ironically, the original AFC excluded black women, in a concession by President Franklin Roosevelt and his advisers to the Southern states, which did not want to lose their captive labor force of agricultural and domestic workers. But in the 1960s, influenced by the civil rights movement, a strong welfare rights movement emerged, expanding the welfare rolls with direct action. This movement also won some important Supreme Court cases that limited the powers of hostile welfare administrators, for example, to enter the homes of women at midnight checking for a male income supporter. The face of welfare began to change as more African American women became eligible for support, although at its peak AFDC always served more white women than black. In this expansive era, the addition of Medicare, Medicaid, food stamps, and antidiscrimination laws extended the reach of the welfare state. In a climate when government income support was under discussion even by right-wing politicians such as Richard Nixon, the welfare rights movement expressed the view that poor black women were just as entitled as white women to raise their children at home.

But an ideological attack on the black community and its so-called pathology was beginning to take shape. As we saw in Chapter 3, the influential Moynihan report of 1965 blamed many of the ills of the inner cities following deindustrialization, from crime to drugs, on the structure of the black "matriarchal" family. Moynihan's caricature of the strong and independent black matriarch, which delegitimized and stigmatized the survival skills of the black family, was an available ideological tool when the backlash was being formulated by conservative intellectuals and institutions.

As the economic climate turned chilly in the mid-1970s, business leaders began to question the costs of welfare programs, arguing that government spending "raised the cost of borrowing, increased the price of labor, deepened the deficit, and otherwise interfered with profits" (Abramovitz 1996b, 19). The AFDC program now became a target, a "stalking horse" for a broader attack on government spending. A barrage of publications from right-wing think tanks laid out a case against welfare and single mothers, turning the spotlight away from the ongoing restructuring of the U.S. economy and onto its most vulnerable victims. The American Enterprise Institute blamed U.S. social problems on a "culture of poverty," and argued that the poor were suffering from something called "behavior dependency." The Heritage Foundation echoed this analysis, pointing to a lack of education, single parenthood, illegitimacy, criminality, and drugs, all caused by the "social pathologies" among the poor. Reagan's White House Working Group on the Family argued in 1987 that welfare was becoming a force that destroyed family life by creating dependency and "an unhealthy sense of entitlement." And Charles Murray, of the American Enterprise Institute, and author of *Losing Ground: American Social Policy, 1950–1980* (1984), targeted programs for single mothers as particularly corrosive (see Abramovitz 1996b, 22–23).

The ensuing attacks on welfare were massive. The 1981 Omnibus Budget Reconciliation Act lowered benefits and tightened eligibility rules. The 1988 Family Support Act began requiring a portion of AFDC recipients to work for their benefits, and granted states "waivers" to begin a series of uncontrolled experiments with family caps, workfare, and time limits (Abramovitz 1996b, 23–29).

Some feminist activists fought very hard to stave off the welfare "reform" signed by President Bill Clinton, whose 1992 campaign pledge to "end welfare as we know it" stole an electorally popular issue from the Republicans.[16] But others regarded this fight as a lost cause. After a 1996 presentation at Queens College, in the informal gathering following her lecture, the president of the Feminist Majority, Eleanor Smeal, was asked why her organization had not tackled President Clinton on welfare "reform." Her answer was that "we" (the Feminist Majority leadership) thought this was an "unwinnable" fight.

And, indeed, a split between welfare organizers and mainstream feminist organizations had been visible much earlier. As the welfare rights movement grew in strength, mainstream feminist organizations, particularly the National Organization for Women, did not generally lend their strength to this movement. Even though the NOW leadership was attuned to issues of poverty and race, this was not the case for the majority of the membership:

> Due to its membership demographics—predominantly white, middle-class, well-educated women—welfare did not bear directly on the lives of these women. In fact, NOW's poverty activists had difficulty inciting interest among general members and planners of the 1970's national conference forgot to schedule a poverty workshop. Recognizing the need for a more public national campaign, NOW's leadership deemed 1973 "NOW's Action Year Against Poverty," hoping to inspire its members to hold rallies, protests, sit-ins, and other public acts intended to increase attention to poverty issues. Disappointingly, this only produced twelve actions, a mere ten percent of that year's total. (Snyder 2005, 9)

In addition to an interest gap, there was an ideological gap. When the attempts by Congress to "reform" welfare were renewed in the 1990s, a resurrected welfare rights movement, now called the National Welfare Rights Union, mobilized to defeat the proposed legislation. Its strategy involved an appeal to the right of poor women to raise their children at home: "[They] promoted their identities as mothers, placing a high priority on providing for the needs of their children. They demanded that social policy address the value of women's unpaid labor in the home and assist women in carrying out their domestic responsibilities. They emphasized the positive effects on children when mothers did not enter the paid labor force and worked outside the home" (Snyder 2005, 12). But this ideology—echoing the maternalist views of women's role as articulated in the early part of the century—ran directly counter to the beliefs of the NOW membership:

> Mainstream feminist organizations, such as NOW—organizations that wield the most power on Capitol Hill, who have allies in the White House [referring to the Clinton administration], and who helped elect the small number of female members of Congress—were hesitant to rally around these "traditional" views of women and motherhood, views they had been working to break down. In addition to their commitment to expanding access to the paid-labor market and protecting reproductive rights, NOW members were cautious to [*sic*] become engaged in a large-scale effort around the issue of welfare. (Snyder 2005, 12)

Despite the reluctance of the rank and file to engage in a fight to save "welfare as we know it," Patricia Ireland, president of NOW, waged a full-scale campaign against the new legislation. Ireland had reached out to the National Welfare Rights Union, joining its "Up and Out of Poverty Now!" campaign, and inviting Marian Kramer, their president, to address NOW's national conference in 1992. But her experience with this attempted coalition was bittersweet. As she recalls: "There was a great deal of anger from the poor women that the feminists in general had come to this issue late. One of the women ... asked, 'Where were you when our children were cold and hungry?'" (cited in Snyder 2005, 15).

Working both with (by meeting with officials) and against the government (by protesting) in a classic insider-outsider strategy, Ireland worked with Clinton administration officials to modify the legislation, trying without success to take out the most punitive provisions such as family caps (no benefits for extra children born) and time limits for the receipt of welfare over a lifetime. Ireland and her team were able to insert a family violence option, which meant that states were to screen for domestic violence and not force women off welfare back into abusive relationships. As the 1996 election approached, Ireland and other NOW leaders made it known that they would not support candidates who were going to vote for the legislation. Meanwhile, NOW led a full-scale public campaign, even participating in hunger strikes, organizing a national march, and publicly criticizing Clinton and other politicians for their support of "welfare reform."

But despite all these efforts, Clinton signed into law the Personal Responsibility and Work Opportunity Reconciliation Act of 1996 on August 22. "Even today," Bethany Snyder writes, "some critics within the feminist movement still wonder if NOW failed to be more successful because of their late entrance into the debate and the lack of grassroots support from their members" (Snyder 2005, 15). Gwendolyn Mink is more scathing in her assessment. As she notes:

> We had an elite-base chasm, where many women at the base—members of NOW or contributors to NOW-LDEF [the legal defense fund], for example— supported the idea of pushing welfare mothers into the labor market and agreed with Clinton and the Republicans that something should be done to stop "illegitimacy." These views were not inconsistent with their white, middle class version of feminism—a version that calibrated independence in terms of labor market attachment and that equated equality with fertility control, not with the right to have and care for children. To some degree, the national women's organizations that did oppose the punitive welfare bill were out of step with their constituencies. (Mink 2001, 7)

When the welfare legislation of 1996 was being voted on,

> one hundred fifty-nine House Democrats voted for this baleful assault on the rights of poor mothers including Democrats who call themselves feminists: the Democratic cochair of the Congressional Women's Caucus (Nita Lowey, D-NY), the former Democratic cochair of the Caucus (Patricia Schroeder, D-CO), the only woman in the Democratic leadership (Barbara Kennelly, D-CT), twenty-three of twenty-eight other Democratic women, and two past presidents of the liberal Americans for Democratic Action (Barney Frank, D-MA, and John Lewis, D-GA). As one congressional feminist admitted of her colleagues, when it comes to welfare "nobody cares about women." (Mink 1998, 3)

More broadly, it is arguable that the idea that women should be working made workfare acceptable to the broad American public: "If racism has permitted policymakers to negate poor single mothers as citizens and mothers, white middle-class feminism has provided those policymakers with an excuse. White middle-class feminists' emphasis on women's right to work outside the home— accompanied by women's increased presence in the labor force—gave cover to conservatives eager to require wage work of single mothers even as they championed the traditional family" (Mink 1998, 23–34). Mink, who cochaired the Women's Committee of 100, a group of feminist academics and activists opposing punitive welfare reform, argues that the leadership of the women's organizations needed to "sustain dialogue" with their memberships, to "try to disrupt the racism and solipsism that lured some feminists into the war against poor women" (Mink 2001, 7).

The abandonment of the New Deal entitlement to a safety net for poor women and the devolution of welfare—now renamed Temporary Assistance for

Needy Families—to the states, where a five-year limit was applied, were also a boon to employers. While the ideological assault on welfare by right-wing writers such as Charles Murray and think tanks such as the Heritage Foundation received widespread publicity, a less visible force in the welfare revolution of 1996 was the business community. Business lobbyists, especially the U.S. Chamber of Commerce, actively organized business leaders to help shape the 1996 legislation (Pimpare 2004, 4).

Why would these business owners work for the curtailment of welfare? The answer is that this legislation helped their bottom line in several ways. First, the payment of welfare benefits tends to set a floor for wages, so the lower the benefit, the lower the level of the floor. Second, cutting welfare payments drives new workers into the labor market, which lowers the overall wage level. And third, cutting welfare payments reduces the need for taxes, something employers always favor.

The interests of business in transforming the welfare system had been made explicit in the 1980s, when the continual growth in low-paid service sector jobs led to predictions of labor shortages. In 1986, the National Alliance of Business looked to welfare recipients as "an important source of needed workers," and opined that the economy could not afford "a growing underclass that cannot get or keep jobs, nor can the nation afford to suffer losses in productivity and world competitiveness because workers are unprepared for changes in the workplace" (cited in Abramovitz 1996b, 26).

The response to this pressure was the 1988 Family Support Act (FSA), which changed the welfare program from one that helped women stay at home with their children into a program that "mandated work as a condition of receiving aid." This legislation created the Job Opportunity and Basic Security (JOBS) Program, which meant that a person receiving aid had to be either working, searching for a job, or preparing for employment with education or training. The JOBS program gave AFDC mothers child care and Medicaid coverage for only one year, and to retain their matching funds from the federal government, states had to get 15 percent of their caseload enrolled in JOBS by 1995 (Abramovitz 1996b, 27).

Following the passage of the FSA in 1988, many states introduced workfare under the waivers issued to them by the federal government, and the impact of this was visible even before 1996, although it was accelerated by the passage of the PRWORA: "The economist Timothy Bartik estimated that welfare reform added 400,000 low-wage workers to the labor force from 1993–1997, one million by 2002, and predicted that waivers and the [Personal Responsibility Act] could be responsible for two million additional workers by 2008" (Pimpare 2004, 5). Economists differed as to the overall effect of this influx on the average wage. But they predicted that "a three percent increase in the number of less-educated women in the labor market . . . would lower the wages of a female high school dropout by between five and fifteen percent (Jared Bernstein estimated 13.2

percent, and even more for black women)" (Pimpare 2004, 5). In addition, those remaining on workfare could be used to replace unionized workers: "New York Mayor Rudolph Giuliani cut 22,000 municipal jobs between 1995 and 2000, and most were replaced by workfare workers. Part-time welfare workers constituted 75 percent of the labor force of the Parks Department and one-third of Sanitation. The average city clerical salary was $12.32 per hour, while it was $1.80 per hour for Work Experience Program workers, who received no benefits. The city's Department of Homeless Services itself replaced unionized city workers with welfare recipients fulfilling workfare obligations" (Pimpare 2004, 5). An official in Salt Lake City reported that "without the welfare people, ... we would have had to raise the wage, ... maybe 5 percent" (cited in Pimpare 2004, 5). Thus, both businesses and governments benefited from the availability of this new labor pool. The overall effect of the PRA was to "reduce the number of people able to refuse low-wage work" (Pimpare 2004, 5).[17]

In addition, women forced off welfare were pitted against illegal immigrants, whose claims to better working conditions were silenced by their uncertain status as noncitizens. This ensured even greater competition, and therefore lower wages, for these jobs (Chang 2000).

Why was the organized women's movement unable to stop the dismantling of "welfare as we know it"? One can argue that even the full strength of organized feminism could not have stopped the business and political juggernaut in 1996. But as we have seen, even though leaders of NOW and the Committee of 100 made a valiant effort, their rank and file were not prepared to follow them into battle. In the end, the attack on AFDC was persuasive to the majority of American women who work for wages outside the home. The U.S. welfare system has never provided American women with the kind of universal state supports (child allowances, government-funded child care, paid leaves) that European women (at least in the richest countries) enjoy. Hence, staying at home to care for children in the U.S. context had come to mean a privilege that a woman earned through the labor market efforts of her family (Orloff 2002, 109–110).

In addition, the ideology of mainstream feminism defined "employment and educational opportunity" (along with reproductive self-determination) as the keys to women's emancipation: "The dominant understanding is that if all must work to support households, and in addition this furthers women's prospects, women on welfare, too, should be employed. I would argue that this is why women's organizations and organizations of African Americans, including the Congressional Black Caucus, did not, in the end, make preventing welfare reform a high priority.... And once women, including mothers, are understood as workers, the logic of supporting their "choice" between employment and unpaid full-time care giving collapses" (Orloff 2002, 110). In this context, the demands of AFDC single mothers for taxpayer funds to raise their children at home fell on deaf ears.

EMERGENCE OF A CLASS DIVIDE AMONG WOMEN

Perhaps the most dramatic unintended impact of feminist activism has been the emergence of a serious class divide among women. Stephanie Luce and Mark Brenner ask the question, "Women and class: what has happened in the last 40 years?" Their major conclusion is that, although there were differences among women in the 1950s and 1960s, these were less significant than the similarities. But "after forty years of the women's movement, the gains of some segments have led to a greater class divide among women workers" (Luce and Brenner 2007, 120).

One class of women clearly has benefited significantly from the gains of the women's movement—female workers with higher education. "By 2005, women accounted for half of all managerial, professional, and related occupations, and this was the occupational category that saw the greatest growth for women in both absolute and relative terms." For women with college degrees, "whereas the average woman in this category earned $16.40 an hour in 1973 (in 2005 dollars), she earned $21.30 an hour in 2005, a 30 percent increase. By comparison, men with a college degree only experienced a 17 percent increase in wages over the same period. Women with advanced degrees have seen a 25 percent increase in their average hourly wage during this period" (Luce and Brenner 2007, 121). These changes translated into economic independence, the chance to enter occupations formerly open only to men, and the acquisition of status and authority.

What about women of color? "As of 2005, the median hourly wage for all women workers was $12.50. For a single mother with two children working full-time this represents about 153 percent of the federal poverty line for a family of three. Close to 60 percent of all black women and 67 percent of all Latina women earn hourly wages below this amount" (Luce and Brenner 2007, 122).

One significant variable here is access to a college education. Women are currently the majority of college students, but those who attend college still represent a minority of all women. Moreover, "in 2005, only 27 percent of all women aged 25 or older had a college degree. For black women in this age group, only 19 percent had a college degree or more. And for Hispanic women the figure is only 12 percent" (Luce and Brenner 2007, 122). These discrepancies are reflected in the figures by racial/ethnic origin for women reaching managerial and professional positions: "While 39 percent of all white women and 45 percent of all Asian women worked in management, professional, and related occupations in 2005, only 30 percent of black women and 22 percent of Hispanic women did so" (Luce and Brenner 2007, 122). But we should note that even women earning higher than average wages lost significant income during their years of childrearing: "A study by the Institute for Women's Policy Research shows that women between ages 26 and 59 earned only $273,592 over fifteen years, whereas the average man of that age earned $722,693 (in 1999 dollars) in the same time period" (Luce and Brenner 2007, 122).

There is no doubt that for a significant element of the female population, access to high-paying, glamorous, interesting, and exciting work has opened wide. These are the women whom the mainstream press celebrates. Consider the cover story of *Newsweek* for September 25, 2006: "Women and Leadership: The Next Generation. 20 Powerful Women on How to Take Charge." The featured women are Danica Patrick, race car driver; Queen Latifah, entertainer; Karenna Gore Schiff, lawyer and author (and daughter of Al Gore); Mary Cheney, political campaigner (and daughter of Dick Cheney); Marissa Mayer, vice president of search products, Google; Sarah Chang, violinist; Maria Celeste Arraras, broadcast journalist; Renee Reijo Pera, infertility researcher, University of California at San Francisco; Gwen Sykes, chief financial officer, NASA; Joyce Chang, managing director, J. P. Morgan; and Tracy Reese, fashion designer (see Kantrowitz, Peterson, and Breslau 2006).

The accompanying articles talk about how companies are addressing the problem of helping women who took time off for childrearing to get back on track; science and the gender gap; lessons from successful women leaders, including Ruth Simmons, president of Brown University, and Martina Navratilova, the tennis star; and "10 power tips" for women. The focus of this set of articles is on women as leaders. As one headline says, "These women are poised to be the next generation of leaders in their fields—whether it's sports, business, finance, politics or the arts" (Kantrowitz et al. 2006, 44). The language of the women reflects their acceptance of this role. And Anna Quindlen, in the column the "Last Word," summarizes the sense of achievement represented by the fact of this special issue. "In 1970, 46 women at this magazine charged it with workplace discrimination; today *Newsweek* publishes an annual issue on women's leadership" (Quindlen 2006, 84).

In Quindlen's interpretation, the successes of feminism have also been good for business: "Even the bottom line has benefited. Catalyst, the research organization that tracks women at work, reported in 2004 that the Fortune 500 corporations with the most women in top positions yielded, on average, a 35 percent higher return on equity than those with the fewest female corporate officers" (Quindlen 2006, 84).

But at the other end of the income scale, women are "more likely than men to be living in poverty," especially if they are heads of families: "Though the overall poverty rate of female-headed families has fallen over the past few decades, the rate began to increase in 2000, and it has been rising steadily since then. Today 36 percent of female-headed families with children under 18 years are living in poverty" (Luce and Brenner 2007, 123).

CONCLUSION

I have been arguing in this chapter that employer power was boosted enormously by the conjuncture of several different developments: (1) the counterrevolution against union power, starting with the Taft-Hartley Act in 1947 but accelerating in the 1970s and 1980s; (2) the breakdown of leftover remnants of the family wage system as women sought the market, rather than marriage, as their primary source of economic security; and (3) the restructuring of the economy that created a low-wage sector of about one-quarter of all workers. Even though government intervention helped to level the playing field somewhat in the affirmative action era (resumed briefly by Jimmy Carter, 1976–1980), this force diminished after the Reagan era began in 1981.

Is it hyperbole to speak of a marriage made in heaven between corporations and the mainstream women's movement? Married women formed a welcome reserve army of labor in the 1940s and 1950s, as the service sector grew rapidly along with manufacturing. When the service sector pulled away from manufacturing in terms of employment, the pool of women's labor, married and single, became an increasingly crucial part of the economy. The changes in attitudes and the explosion of feminist activism that followed had this market pull at their base. The result was a new concept of women's role—as independent financial actors rather than as dependent wives—just when the capacity of unions to protect wage levels and working conditions was weakening steadily.

Am I saying that I want a return to the limitations on women caused by the family wage system? Clearly not. This was a period when a labor aristocracy enjoyed a privileged existence. Most workers did not have this kind of protection. But the fact is that the remarkable increase in wage levels over the period from World War II to the 1960s has been reversed. The feminist movement was not able to prevent this. The energy that went into breaking down the barriers of sex discrimination did not act as a countervailing force on employer power. Instead, it helped to create a new pool of labor that employers were able to use to cut their costs.

We can try a mental experiment. What if the mainstream women's movement had concentrated on winning a minimum level of income for all women workers? What if the leadership of the women's movement had focused, not on gaining access to top levels of professional work—law, medicine, politics—but on addressing the economic needs of the poorest women? I am overstating the case here, and ignoring, for example, the campaigns for comparable worth, which were targeted at low-paid women's jobs, and for affirmative action to open areas such as construction and mining to women. But as Heather Booth notes, one of the mistakes of the feminist movement as a whole was that "we aimed at the top," rather than at the bottom, where the poorest women were, and are (Booth 2006).

5

In the Global South
"Women" Replace Development

❇

Thus far, I have been arguing that the central idea of mainstream U.S. feminism—paid work represents liberation for women—was deeply useful both to corporations and the governments backing them. We have seen two examples of this within the United States: the elimination of the family wage and the gutting of the welfare safety net. In this chapter, I will look at the ways in which mainstream feminist ideology has helped global capitalism to increase its inroads into the Global South. There are two interlinked elements in this process: first, the penetration of foreign capital into Global South economies; and second, the reduction of state-led development efforts. How have mainstream feminist ideas been useful in this process?

I will start by explaining the difference between state-led development and neoliberal "open door" development. The first, ideally, not only uses "massive capital-intensive, state-directed investments to build industries" but also mounts an "assault on the structures of inequality such as concentrated land ownership that systematically deprive the poor of resources to escape poverty" (Bello 2006, 1). The second drives the economy into depression and then selectively "develops" only those areas of the economy that are useful to generate export earnings, such as the production of electronic components. To facilitate this form of development, export processing zones (EPZs) are set up, with highly favorable conditions for multinational corporations that allow them, among other things, to utilize a largely female proletariat. The contrast between the two policies can be seen, for example, in the case of Mexico, where the shift from state-led industrialization to export-led maquiladora production is essentially a gender shift, from male to female labor, by the Mexican government (Cravey 1998).

Then, I will summarize the effects of structural adjustment programs (SAPs). These SAPs impoverish most people, but particularly women and children, because the reduction or elimination of free education, health care, and free water becomes a particular burden on women. This is especially the case in peasant economies where women are the water bearers, as in many parts of Africa. In addition, women who were drawn into paid employment in government service in the 1950s and 1960s are thrown back into the informal economy as government jobs and services are severely cut.

Compounding this are the effects of "free trade," which foster the import of cheap European and American agricultural products and which impoverish small farmers who are unable to compete on the basis of price. The supports that they used to get through government subsidies are now withdrawn by SAPs.

I then turn to the impact of this series of changes on women. Jean I. Pyle and Kathryn B. Ward identify four main work paths for women of the Global South (Pyle and Ward 2003).[1] They can enter the EPZs as exploited workers. They can emigrate, become domestic workers, and send remittances home. They can go into the informal sector and apply for microcredit. Or they can become sex workers.[2]

I argue that for each of these work paths, commentators have developed a celebratory rationale that glosses over women's suffering and exploitation. First, in the case of the EPZs, the idea that women ought to be working for wages gives support to governments establishing EPZs to attract foreign investment. Much feminist scholarship interprets this creation of a new female proletariat in the Third World as a form of emancipation, liberating women from patriarchal family structures in their rural places of origin.

Second, the introduction of microcredit, championed by agencies of the U.S. government and by the banking industry internationally, looks to women as microentrepreneurs. Microcredit, with its emphasis on women's "empowerment," is widely hailed as a key to development, most notably with the award of the Nobel Prize in October 2006 to Muhammed Yunus, the founder of the microcredit-based Grameen Bank in Bangladesh (Dugger 2006).

Third, the massive emigration by women from poor countries such as the Philippines to rich countries in the Middle East, Europe, and the United States is described by some observers as an opportunity for their emancipation and a contribution to the national development of their home countries. Their labor provides the "sending" countries with welcome infusions of hard currency, via remittances. Although the jobs they obtain can be exploitative and often dangerous, the work of these women permits other professional women to pursue their careers unimpeded by the demands of childrearing. In the Philippines, migrating women are celebrated as heroines of the nation, sacrificing the opportunity to raise their own children at home to contribute to national advancement.

Fourth, the rise of the tourist industry with its concomitant expansion of sex work is justified in some quarters of the women's movement as part of the feminist revolution. This ideological shift is symbolized by use among some writers of the term *sex worker* rather than *prostitute,* and by a view of this form of labor as a matter of free choice among women. The intensification of sexual trafficking as impoverished countries export unemployed women, often through criminal enterprises, is viewed by some feminist scholars as a sign of women's expanded economic choices.

I then turn to the rise of nongovernmental organizations (NGOs). Decades of structural adjustment have placed national governments under severe pressure to reduce their funding for social services such as education and health care. As a result, NGOs have stepped into the breach. Funded by international and national lending agencies in the North, NGOs, some of them devoted to women's issues, now carry out a wide range of functions that were formerly the responsibility of governments.

At the same time, the use of gender as a category has become ubiquitous in the development literature. The rhetoric of the international community has embraced feminist ideas, creating specialist positions in gender mainstreaming and pointing to women's education as the key to economic development.

Both at the level of rhetoric and at the level of global and local policy, then, I will argue that the "development" of women has become a substitute for state-led economic development in Third World countries. To eliminate poverty, it seems, it is no longer necessary to create an economy that meets people's needs. Now a focus on women's leadership is sufficient.

STATE-LED VERSUS NEOLIBERAL DEVELOPMENT

Before I explain the operation of structural adjustment policies and their impact on women, I want to define state-led development.[3] It means that the economic development of a country, that is, its transformation from a peasant-based agricultural economy (or, indeed, from a hunter-gatherer economy) into a modern industrial economy, is directed primarily by the government, rather than by the decisions of private investors. (In this discussion, I am leaving aside the issue of whether industrial development itself is a worthy goal for countries at this stage of history. I will address this issue in the Conclusion.) A state-led development process is by definition the prerogative of a sovereign country. Such development does not mean that the country is self-sufficient or autarchic, since it can accept foreign investment when useful, or that the government carries out all investment itself (it can rely on local investors). But state-led development does mean that the government has the decisionmaking power to channel that private investment along the lines of its own priorities.

The case of South Korea is illustrative here. As Alice Amsden shows, the remarkable industrialization process of South Korea under a military dictatorship beginning in the 1960s was the product of strong state policies that rewarded corporate groups (*chaebols*) that were successful in meeting state goals, while punishing those that failed. The government used state-owned banks to direct investment to those sectors of the economy that needed to be modernized; it restricted direct foreign investment, while welcoming joint ventures (in electronics, for example); and it protected domestic producers against foreign competition by restricting imports.

In short, the government acted as designer, instigator, director, and impresario of the whole range of sectors that brought South Korea to the level of a modernized economy that was so technologically advanced by the 1980s that it could offer assistance to older industrialized countries. (For example, South Korea was able to lend its model of technology to the U.S. shipbuilding industry.) "Ignoring the 1950s, when economic policy in Korea was for all practical purposes under foreign control, ... every major shift in industrial diversification in the decades of the 1960s and 1970s was instigated by the state" (Amsden 1989, 80). From cement, fertilizers, oil refining, synthetic fibers, iron and steel, to shipbuilding, heavy machinery, and chemicals, "major milestones in Korea's industrialization have been decided by the state" (Amsden 1989, 81).

Obviously, the categories of state-led development and development directed by private interests are ideal types: most governments represent a mix of these two models. During the cold war, the Soviet Union represented the extreme pole of state-led development, since by definition economic planning was directed by the government and there was no private industry to compete with. In the contemporary world, China might also be considered an example of state-led development. Although since its opening to "the capitalist road" in the 1980s the Chinese leadership has increasingly encouraged the growth of private enterprise, both indigenous and foreign, the governing regime still attempts to keep tight control over investment decisions and does not allow its currency to float freely on world markets. At this writing, the Chinese government struggles for control over independent decisions by local authorities to allow development, and tries to ride herd over the growing strength of the private sector. Hence, we might speculate as to whether in the near future China will still be considered a developmental state.

Although contemporary mainstream commentators treat the concept of state-led development as heretical, the truth is that the great industrial powers of the eighteenth and nineteenth centuries, Great Britain, Germany, and the United States, owed much of their industrial strength to state-led development policies. Great Britain was "an aggressive user, and in certain areas a pioneer, of activist policies intended to promote its industries." As early as the fifteenth century, in the case of woolen manufacture, the "leading industry of the time," when

England was exporting raw wool to the Netherlands, King Henry VII "sought to change this by taxing raw wool exports and poaching skilled workers from the Low Countries" (Chang 2003a, 10). More generally, between the reign of Prime Minister Robert Walpole in 1721 and the adoption of free trade around 1860, "Britain used very state-directed trade and industrial policies, involving measures very similar to those used later by countries like Japan and Korea to develop their industries" (Chang 2003a, 11).

Similarly, from the Civil War to World War II, "the United States had the most heavily protected economy in the world." Abraham Lincoln was a disciple of Henry Clay, an advocate of the so-called American System, "based on infrastructural development and protectionism." The American leaders "knew exactly what they were doing. They understood that Britain had reached the top through protection and subsidies, and they needed to do the same if they were going to get anywhere" (Chang 2003a, 12).

Criticizing the British for preaching free trade to his country, Ulysses S. Grant, Civil War general and U.S. president from 1869 to 1877, retorted that "within 200 years, when America has gotten out of protection all that it can offer, it too, will adopt free trade." Friedrich List, a major nineteenth-century German economist, noted that "Britain preaching free trade to less advanced countries like Germany and the United States was like someone trying to 'kick away the ladder' with which he had climbed to the top" (quoted in Chang 2003a, 11; see also Chang 2003b).

Flying in the face of this historical experience, the neoliberal, "free-market" regime imposed by the international financial institutions (IFIs) on the Global South countries since the 1980s has made state-led development impossible. Those countries that have been subjected to SAPs, in the guise of encouraging their economic development, instead have found themselves unable to direct their own economies. The net result of this process is a kind of distorted development that does not replicate the successful industrial development accomplished first by the original industrial powers of Europe, and second by the newly industrialized countries of the post–World War II period (Japan, South Korea, Taiwan, Hong Kong, and Singapore). In the absence of genuine industrial and agricultural development, it is illusory to think that poor developing countries can eliminate poverty and ill-health.

In this context, the "success" of feminist interventions has provided the industrialized countries and international agencies such as the United Nations with a way to disguise this reality by pointing to women as the key to economic development. Consider, for example, the words of outgoing UN chief Kofi Annan, in a speech marking the sixtieth anniversary of the United Nations Commission on the Status of Women: "The world is beginning to recognize that empowering women and girls is key to development thanks to a United Nations women's commission that is 'ahead of its time,' UN Secretary General Kofi Annan said.... 'The world is also starting to grasp that there is no tool for development more effective than the empowerment of women and girls,' Mr. Annan said.... 'Study after study has taught us that no other policy is as likely to raise economic productivity, or to reduce infant and maternal mortality'" ("Annan Praises UN Women's Panel" 2006).

It is gratifying to feminist activists for the former secretary-general of the United Nations to recognize the importance of support for women and girls around the world. But his statement is deeply misleading. There *is* a tool for development that is more effective than women's empowerment: namely, state-led development that directs investment toward the needs of everyone in the society.

The Origin of Structural Adjustment

The process of undermining state-led development has been carried out through the imposition of SAPs, which have been used to restructure the economies of 145 developing/emerging market countries across the globe (Nakatani and Herrera 2007, 1). As noted, the ideology of neoliberalism that undergirds the SAPs conveniently overlooks the key role played by state-led development policies in the history of Great Britain and the United States. Neoliberalism instead insists that underdeveloped countries abandon their policies of state-led development and the accompanying mechanisms, such as high tariffs and subsidies to industry.

The "debt crisis" that emerged in many Global South countries in the 1980s was met by the World Bank and the International Monetary Fund (IMF) with a "rescue package" of structural adjustment programs. Like any banker to whom money is owed, the IFIs had the power to set "conditionalities" for the use of their loaned money. The policies embraced by the IFIs in the 1980s and 1990s and imposed on the countries subjected to SAPs are, in effect, the negation of state-led development. The macroeconomic policies espoused by the IFIs deprive governments of the tools to direct investment internally. Instead, they are asked to selectively "develop" only those areas of the economy that are useful for bringing in export earnings.

Over the period since then, SAPs in various forms have been required of indebted countries in Latin America, Africa, Asia, the former Soviet Union, and the eastern European countries. The most visible of these was the so-called bailout of Mexico in 1982, when the country announced that it could no longer meet its debt repayment requirements. "Austerity" programs were also adopted by a series of developing countries, as financial crises loomed in Asia (1997), Russia (1998), and Argentina (2002).[4] As Bill Tabb concludes: "The debt crises in the 1980s and 1990s allowed the IMF and World Bank to impose the Washington consensus on the formerly nationalistic economic regimes of the Third World. Conditions imposed in exchange for preventing default on foreign debt included privatizing state enterprises, reduction or abolition of subsidies, opening markets to foreign competition, and more broadly, a shrunken role for governments" (Tabb 2001, 88–89).

In addition, a key feature of the SAPs has been their insistence on the free flow of capital in and out of countries. According to SAP theory, to attract foreign capital to invest, governments must keep interest rates high. Even though this does attract foreign capital, the high cost of capital internally also slows down local economic growth: "As Martin Khor, director of the Third World Network in Malaysia has described it, structural adjustment is 'a policy to continue colonial trade and economic patterns developed during the colonial period, but which the Northern powers want to continue into the postcolonial period. Economically speaking, we are more dependent on the ex-colonial countries than we ever were. The World Bank and IMF are playing the role that our ex-colonial masters used to play'" (Tabb 2001, 88).

THE FUNCTIONING OF SAPs

How do SAPs work in practice? Overall, First World financial institutions have applied their powerful economic machinery to Global South governments to reorient their economies and to transform their priorities. "How were sovereign countries brought under the tutelage of the international financial institutions? Because countries were indebted, the Bretton Woods institutions were able to oblige them through the so-called conditionalities attached to the loan agreements to 'appropriately' redirect their macroeconomic policy in accordance with the interests of the official and commercial creditors" (Chossudovsky 2003, 45). In laypersons' terms, the World Bank and the International Monetary Fund took advantage of the massive debt incurred by the developing countries to reorient their economies.

But why did these countries cooperate? Why did they not simply declare a default on their debts? The answer is at least twofold. First, the power of the IFIs is such that they can cause the reduction of most trade and financial flows from other creditors, something most countries could not afford to endure. But second, local bourgeoisies work hand in hand with foreign capital. Often the reforms are in the interest of the governing elites, which can emerge as the economic winners in the process. As one Bangladeshi activist and academic, Nilufa Ahmad explains: "It actually takes two parties to do it. Our government is complicit. The World Bank could not force all these policies on us if our government didn't agree to them. The government consents because government officials do not have enough political will and because they want to line their own pockets" (Ahmad 1994, 133).

In addition, Naomi Klein points out that often the imposition of austerity programs is preceded by a drastic economic or social shock that enables governments to introduce the policies against the will of the mass of the people. This was the case with the original neoliberal transformation carried out in the wake of the coup against Salvador Allende by Augusto Pinochet and his coconspirators in Chile in 1973. Similar situations of shock assisted neoliberal policymakers in Bolivia, the former Soviet Union, South Korea, and elsewhere (see Klein 2007, 75–280).

By the mid-1980s, developing countries were essentially exporting capital to the rich countries, because the outflow of funds to service the debt was exceeding the total inflow of capital from loans, foreign investment, and foreign aid combined. For the 1980–2006 period, the developing/emerging market economies taken together paid a cumulative $7.7 trillion in external debt service. Yet their total foreign debt actually increased by $2.6 trillion (from $0.6 trillion to $3.2 trillion). In other words, even though these countries already paid back far more than the original amount they borrowed, they now still carry a much larger burden of debt than they owed in 1980 (Nakatani and Herera 2007, 31). No wonder Michel Chossudovsky terms this situation "a Marshall Plan for the rich countries" (Chossudovsky 2003, 44).[5]

In order to even be allowed to keep financing their debts, Third World countries are required to undertake reforms, set out as a series of priorities in a "policy framework paper" (PFP). Although written as government documents, the PFPs are actually composed according to a preset format provided by the IMF and the World Bank. Thereafter, the IMF monitors the economic performance of the country to check whether it is conforming to the reforms it pledged to implement.

In this process, in some cases, representatives of the World Bank physically enter the government, working within the ministries of health, education, industry, agriculture, transportation, and the environment to supervise their activities (while themselves staying at luxury hotels). They oversee the privatization of state enterprises, and they monitor the national budget through a "public expenditure review." The changes that the IFIs are seeking are thus implemented through direct supervision of government activities (Chossudovsky 2003, 54–55).

The IMF also oversees the restructuring of a country's central bank, insisting that it be independent of both the executive and the legislative branches of the country's government. The agreement signed with the IMF provides that the government can no longer control domestic monetary policy. The IMF thus "is in a position virtually to paralyse the financing of real economic development," so that the country is increasingly dependent on external sources of funding. Furthermore, the central bankers' allegiance is often to the IFIs. "In many developing countries, senior officials of the Central Bank are former staff members of the IFIs and of the regional development banks. Moreover, Central Bank officials often receive 'salary supplements' in hard currency financed from multilateral and bilateral sources" (Chossudovsky 2003, 50–51).

Once in control of a country's budgetary process, what do the SAPs require? The process begins with what the IFIs deem to be "macroeconomic stabilization." The elements of this are as follows:

- Elimination of currency controls and devaluation of the currency, which raise import costs and hence cut the real value of wages and government expenditures
- Elimination of price controls and subsidies to get rid of "price distortions"
- Liberalization of the labor market, including such measures as phasing out minimum wage legislation and eliminating cost-of-living adjustment clauses in union agreements
- Reduction in the size of the public sector, which requires the dismissal of public employees and drastic cuts in social programs
- Withdrawal of the state from many basic educational and health services in favor of fee-for-service (that is, usually private) systems (Chossudovsky 2003, 56–57)

All of these economic stabilization measures, conceptually a first phase of reform, are to be followed by a second phase, fundamental structural reform (although more often both phases are carried out concurrently). The elements of the structural reform process are enumerated here. ·

Trade liberalization. The tariff structure has to be changed to eliminate import quotas and to reduce tariffs. This normally reduces customs revenues, which lowers revenue to the state. More importantly, it prevents the authorities from allocating the use of scarce foreign exchange. For example, a country might want to import food and limit the import of luxury goods. Instead, it has to increase imports of luxury goods such as automobiles and consumer durables, which particularly drain the country of its foreign exchange. At the same time, liberalized trade normally weakens domestic companies, which cannot compete with multinationals.

Free movement of foreign exchange in and out of the country. This includes the use of electronic transfers.[6]

Tax reform. This usually means introducing a value-added or sales tax, thereby raising the tax burden on the poor and on middle-income groups; registering small agricultural producers and members of the informal sector for tax purposes; and exempting joint ventures and foreign capital from taxes with "tax holidays," which are intended to encourage foreign investment.

Privatization of state enterprises. The most profitable are taken over by foreign capital or by joint ventures, while the money received by the state can be used to reduce government debt.

Land reform. This reform includes delegitimizing customary collective land rights, issuing land title to individual farmers (including corporations), and encouraging the concentration of farmland in fewer hands. This is where the "new enclosures" take place.[7]

Creation of social emergency funds (SEFs) to alleviate poverty. The theory here is that it is more efficient for governments to create "targeted" programs to help the poor, while delivering social programs to the rest of the population via privatization. (That is, the majority of citizens must now pay for health care, and education as well [Chossudovsky 2003, 54–58].)

Under these reform programs, "the state withdraws and many programmes under the jurisdiction of line ministries will henceforth be managed by the organization of civil society under the umbrella of the SEF.... The SEF officially sanctions the withdrawal of the state from the social sectors and the 'management of poverty' (at the microsocial level) by separate and parallel organizational structures [i.e., NGOs]" (Chossudovsky 2003, 67).

This is the entry point for NGOs. As public sector institutions are systematically dismantled, so that public education, health care, and other core government functions are crippled, outside funding has given rise to a proliferation of NGOs: "Various nongovernmental organizations (NGOs) funded by international 'aid programmes' have gradually taken over many of the functions of local level governments. Small-scale production and handicraft projects, subcontracting for export processing programs, community-based training and employment programmes, etc., are set up under the umbrella of the 'social safety net.' A meager survival to local level communities is ensured while at the same time the risk of social upheaval is contained" (Chossudovsky 2003, 67).

THE ECONOMIC AND SOCIAL IMPACT OF SAPs

The theory behind the package of economic stabilization measures is that countries will begin to export more than they import, and thus acquire enough foreign currency to pay back their debts and begin a process of economic growth. But exactly the opposite has occurred. Overall total foreign debt has increased, because trade liberalization has replaced domestic production with imports, including an increasing proportion of services, which further contributes to the imbalance of payments (see Chossudovsky 2003, 68). But above all, as I argued earlier, the SAP process fundamentally undermines the capacity of a country to control its own economic development.

In the official literature that touts the success of SAPs, much is made of the need to reduce the role of government in the economy. The World Bank's publications hail the end of the era of the developmental state, and welcome in the new era of the free market (see, for example, World Bank 1996). With the withdrawal of the state from economic planning, these writers argue, market forces can proceed to create wealth and increase productivity.

But the shift mandated by the IFIs in the 1980s and 1990s was not away from the state and toward the market, but rather toward a new use of the state. If the developmental state sought to increase wealth for the whole population by planning investment and directly running state enterprises, the structurally adjusted state increased wealth for the select few by shifting state resources in certain directions, usually away from services and subsidies for the poor and toward services and subsidies for the rich.

Take, for example, the case of Costa Rica. The goal of its SAP is to "systematically favor export over domestic production" (Korten 1994, 57). This means shifting farmers from growing staples such as beans, rice, and corn for domestic consumption to cultivating nontraditional agricultural exports such as ornamental plants, flowers, melons, strawberries, and red peppers. Industries that export their produce can receive tariff and tax exemptions whose value totals close to 5 percent of the country's annual budget. At the same time, the government is prohibited from buying grains from local producers at high prices, or selling to consumers at subsidized prices, and it can no longer shield grain farmers with the quotas that used to protect them from low international prices (Korten 1994, 57).

From Somalia in the early 1980s; Bolivia in 1985; Rwanda, Peru, Yugoslavia, and Brazil in 1990; India in 1991; the former Soviet Union in 1992; to Vietnam in 1993, the economic shock treatment meted out by the IFIs has created widespread poverty and devastation and, in some cases (notably, Somalia, Yugoslavia, and Rwanda), contributed to an explosion of ethnic tensions in civil war. Since the imposition of SAPs, communicable diseases that were thought to be under control have been resurging. In sub-Saharan Africa, cholera, yellow fever, and malaria; in Latin America, malaria and dengue; and in India, bubonic and pneumonic plague are all direct results of the degeneration of urban sanitation and public health infrastructure (Chossudovsky 2003, 72). To this list we could add the widespread pandemic of HIV/AIDS, the spread of which is intensified by the decline in public health infrastructure (Susser 2009).

A novel by Gil Courtemarche, set in Rwanda, paints a vivid picture of the impact of structural adjustment on health care:

> "Monsieur Lamarre, Structural Adjustment 101. Structural adjustment, which you've certainly heard has helped a number of poor countries stabilize their public expenditures, has in a way invented this hospital, which must look rather surreal to a Canadian like you. A gentleman from Washington tells the Rwandan government that it spends too much on public services, that its debt is too high, but it will be helped to repay that debt if—
>
> "Monsieur Valcourt, I did an internship with the International Monetary Fund. Spare me your leftist demagogy. The public finances of several African countries have been successfully stabilized this way."
>
> "Of course. When you're discussing these things in an office in Washington or drawing econometric curves on a computer, it all seems logical. In a hospital,

it doesn't hold up at all. You begin by charging admission fees. Half the patients stop coming to the hospital and go back to the leaf-doctors—that's what they call the witch doctors or charlatans. The cost of medications goes up because they're imported and structural adjustment devalues the local currency. This is how the pharmacy here has turned into an embroidery room. Staff reductions come next. Then you charge for meals, medications, dressings and so on. That's why all these people are swarming and finagling inside and around the hospital walls. Little restaurants selling food for patients, vendors of expired medicines, snake oil, filched antibiotics and various toiletries, and everywhere around you, these families too poor to pay for it all who've come to stay and prepare food for their patient and wash him, watch over him and comfort him. A structural adjustment hospital is a place where one pays for one's death ... because by the time patients come their condition is such that it would take a miracle or an accident for a cure to happen. (Courtemarche 2003,126–127)

THE EFFECTS OF SAPs ON POOR AND MIDDLE-CLASS WOMEN AND CHILDREN

The rise of SAPs around the world has been closely followed by feminist scholars, who have focused on the particular effects of SAPs on women and children (Afshar and Dennis 1992; Sparr 1994; Visvanathan et al. 1997, 263–264). As this body of work shows, for each element of the SAP adopted by an individual government, there are gender-specific repercussions. This literature does not, however, always differentiate among classes of women. In countries profoundly transformed by SAPs, the outcome for poor and middle-class women has usually been adverse; but for entrepreneurial women, as for entrepreneurial men, the outcome has been positive, mainly through the opening up of new opportunities. In this way, the category of gender is sometimes used misleadingly to mask increasing class differences among women.

In fact, the effects of structural adjustment on an economy are deeply uneven. For the bankers, investors, and CEOs of successful export-based industries; for the owners of export-based agricultural holdings; and for the ruling government elites, the changes have brought wealth and power. However, for small business owners, workers, small farmers, and peasants, the effects have been devastating. For poor women and children, the outcomes have been particularly disastrous. SAPs generally require the replacement of free medical, educational, and water services with services requiring fees. This places particular burdens on women, whose role in social reproduction is the care of children and families.

Vivid examples can be found in West Africa. In locations where the government does not provide running water—in slums, for example—women provide it. In Senegal in rural areas, it is a woman's job to go to the common pipe up to ten times a day. Women will walk up to ten kilometers to fetch water for the family. Given the power relationships in the household, they can be assaulted if they refuse this duty. Cooking, cleaning, bathing, or taking care of someone with AIDS requires a lot of water. The women make the water drinkable by pouring it out to take out the sediment. In Ghana, guinea worm disease is most prevalent among women, because they drink last from the water after first giving it to the husband and children: they drink from the more infected remaining sediment. Managing water is women's work.

SAP agreements force governments to cut financial aid to public water companies, and companies, in turn, dismiss skilled workers with long years of experience in water management. Water provision thus becomes inefficient, causing people to want privatization. But once water is privatized, the company raises its price to secure profits. Poor communities get ripped off by the owners of water tankers. The companies will not install pipes where the communities are poor. Public fountains are gone, and women go to unsafe wells (Fall 2003).

What are some other effects of SAPs that are specific to women?

Devaluation of the currency. The goal of devaluing a country's currency is to raise the price of imported goods (food, fuel, medicines, and spare parts) and thereby to reduce the consumption of these goods. This will in theory cut the country's balance-of-payments deficit, since it diminishes the flow of currency going abroad. But for women, whose job it is to buy essential items for the household, "devaluation can instantly wipe out their ability to ensure family survival. In Zambia, devaluation combined with other SAP measures to increase the cost of bread from 12 kwacha a loaf in 1990 to 350 kwacha in 1993. In describing what such a rapid and massive [decrease] in purchasing power seemed like to her, a woman from an eastern province in Uganda said, 'The government has stolen our money'" (McGowan 1995, 2).

Trade and market liberalization. SAPs have also hit hard at indigenous manufacturing, much of which in the Global South employs women. Opening the market to foreign goods leads to an influx of cheaper foreign agricultural and industrial products. In Sri Lanka, a strong handloom-weaving industry was established in the 1960s and 1970s by the government, which fixed prices, provided subsidies for raw materials, and restricted imports. Rural weaving centers were set up, and from a base of four thousand rural women employed in the early 1960s, the industry grew to more than sixty thousand women in the 1970s. But with the introduction of free-market policies in 1977, the state sold its four large textile mills to foreign private sector interests. "It was estimated that 40,000 handloom workers, mostly women, lost their livelihood" (Jayaweera 1994, 105). The closure of the village weaving centers took away the women's main source of income. Only younger women who were mobile and unmarried and had a secondary education were eligible to work in the new private export-processing industries. Similarly, in Tanzania, once imports were permitted in 1984, more than 90 percent of the textile mills, employing a majority of women, shut down (McGowan 1995, 5).

Labor market deregulation. Deregulation of the labor market is a euphemism for keeping labor costs low. In practice, to receive adjustment loans, countries must agree to keep both private and public sector wage increases below the level of inflation. Cutting wages, freezing wages while prices continue to rise, and reducing work-related benefits are all used to this end. As a result, according to the International Labour Organisation, in most African nations real wages have fallen between 50 and 60 percent since the early 1980s (McGowan 1995, 7). "A social worker in Uganda with a full-time job reports that in order to pay school fees for her four children she must also work evenings making bakery cakes and designing and sewing wedding dresses" (McGowan 1995, 7). Deregulation also implies a more "flexible" workforce, which includes women working in their homes as contractors (see Balakrishnan 2002).

Privatization and retrenchment of government workers. Government agencies must be privatized, that is, sold off to private owners, which invariably results in a reduction in the workforce. The goal of this policy ostensibly is to gain income for the government to enhance its capacity to pay off debt and to create a modernized economy. Neoliberal doctrines assume that private enterprise is more efficient than public, and that public sector spending through state enterprises represents a drag on the economy, rather than a stimulus, as Keynesians would argue.

For women in countries where the developmental-state economy had enhanced their status, this kind of policy has been disastrous. In the case of Egypt, early feminist organizing in the 1950s had persuaded the new government of Gamal Abdel Nasser (who overthrew the monarchy in 1952) to make room for women. "State feminism" was an important part of its reforming agenda. The 1956 constitution gave women the right to vote, to receive education, and to work outside the home. Women workers were to be provided with day care facilities, time off to breast-feed, and maternity leave. Jobs in the state sector were guaranteed to anyone who graduated from intermediate school (Hatem 1994, 40–42).

These changes made state sector employment very appealing to women. In the 1960s, many women left agriculture and shifted into state manufacturing and the social service sector. By 1970, women employed by government and public sector manufacturing constituted just over half of all women in the formal labor force.

Thus, when the IMF and the World Bank persuaded the new regime of Anwar Sadat, who came to power in 1970, to shrink the state sector, this "precipitated unprecedented levels of unemployment among women." From 1976 to 1986, the total unemployment rate doubled from 7.7 percent to 14.7 percent, but for women it reached 40.7 percent (Hatem 1994, 48).

Cutbacks in social services and the introduction of user fees. The introduction of user fees has had a particularly negative impact on women. Introducing these fees into hospitals inevitably reduces access to basic health care for both men and women. But not only is there a drop in hospital use by all, but also women become the backup as they have to care at home for those who are ill. As hospital-assisted childbirth becomes unaffordable, women increasingly give birth at home, where there is no recourse in the event of a difficult delivery. Hence, both maternal mortality and infant mortality have been rising. Similarly, although user fees in education have caused a decline in attendance levels for all, dropout rates are higher for girls:

> UNICEF's 1993 figures place maternal mortality rates in Ghana as high as 1,000 deaths to 100,000 births, one of the highest in sub-Saharan Africa. In Zimbabwe, the maternal mortality rate rose from 90 per 100,000 live births to 168 per 100,000 in 1993 following the introduction of user fees. More girls are also dropping out of school for lack of school fees, thus further increasing the educational gap between boys and girls.... Total public spending on education in sub-Saharan Africa fell in real terms between 1980 and 1988 from US$11 billion to US$7 billion. The withdrawal of state support resulted in a drop in gross enrolment rates at the primary school level, which fell from 77.1 per cent in 1980 to an estimated 66.7 per cent in 1990. In Africa in the 1980s, female school enrolment rates dropped and drop-out rates increased. On average, only 37 per cent of school-age girls were enrolled in first or second levels of education in 1990. (Amadiume 2000, 28)

Agricultural reform. Agriculture is another key area where SAPs have a particular impact on women. In Africa, women produce more than 70 percent of the food, and provide 90 percent of the labor hours spent processing and preparing it. Because most of their food production is consumed within the family or traded in local markets, women usually do not have the resources to switch to the export crops favored by SAPs. But even in the cases where they do, the change does not often benefit them. In Uganda, women taking on government incentives to produce beans for export report that they have no other food crops left to feed their families. In Kenya, women "speak of planting tobacco—an export crop—right up to their door, and yet not having enough money to buy food" (McGowan 1995, 4).

Similarly, in southern Ghana female farmers were encouraged to increase the production of cocoa. But since the World Bank "had led many cocoa-producing countries down the same road," there was soon a glut of cocoa on the world market. "As was the case in Tanzania and other countries in Africa, women still had to buy clothes and food, seeds and fertilizer, school fees and medical expenses, the price of all of which had increased. Thus even the gains women made through initially high cocoa prices were quickly wiped out by devaluation and increased prices for goods and services, leaving them worse off than before" (McGowan 1995, 4).

Reliance on women's unpaid labor. Finally, there is an unstated conditionality of SAPs: an increased reliance on women's unpaid labor. As feminist economists have pointed out, the neoclassical model adopted by the IFIs relies on the gender-biased statistical methods of traditional economists, whose national economic accounts notoriously do not factor in women's nonmarket labor.[8] Yet it is this work that supports the economic transformations that have taken away the underpinnings supplied by the older developmental state. As Dzodzi Tsikata notes, "SAPs assume the unlimited availability of women's unpaid labour and time and the efficiency approach of SAPs have tended to see women as a resource to be tapped to promote the efficiency of free market policies and to deal with the shortfall in access to social services" (Tsikata n.d., 5). MADRE, the international network of community-based women's organizations founded by Kathy Engel, points out: "When services become unaffordable, people's basic needs do not disappear; instead, the job of providing necessities shifts to women, who must intensify their work in social reproduction—hauling water, collecting wood, processing food, building community support networks, and providing their families with health care, day care, and the basic nutrition once guaranteed by public funding" (MADRE n.d., 3–4). The net result is that "the needs of girls and women are sacrificed first. In fact, women in poor countries have shown drastic drops in school enrollment, food intake, hospital admittance, and life expectancy since SAPs have taken hold" (MADRE n.d., 3–4).

HOW WORKING-CLASS AND POOR WOMEN RESPOND TO SAPS

In the face of the increasing pressures from SAP regimes, women have adopted various survival strategies. These include working in EPZs, using microcredit, engaging in sex work, and migrating to seek work elsewhere.

Export-Processing Zones

One option, at least for young women, has been the opportunity to work in EPZs, whose antilabor structures assure foreign investors a docile and not coincidentally largely female workforce. The use of cheap female labor for export industries was pioneered by South Korea during its so-called economic miracle, as women were drawn from farm to factory work. Indeed, Alice Amsden argues that the male-female gender wage gap was one of the keys to the success of South Korea's industrialization: "Korea's outstanding real wage increases and unrivaled gender wage disparities are related to one another insofar as an unlimited supply of women workers has allowed Korea's bifurcated wage structure to achieve dual ends. One end is the maintenance of international competitiveness in labor-intensive industries, which employ primarily females. The other is the entry into more skill-intensive pursuits on the basis of a relatively well-paid, highly motivated, male labor aristocracy" (Amsden 1989, 204).

In the electronics industry, shortly after the invention of the silicon chip in 1958–1959, Fairchild opened the first offshore semiconductor plant in Hong Kong; the company moved into South Korea in 1966. General Instruments moved its microelectronics production to Taiwan in 1964. In 1965, many high-tech firms moved their production to the U.S.-Mexico border, opening the first maquiladoras. In the next decade, Singapore, Malaysia, and the Philippines followed suit, and in the late 1970s they were joined by countries in the Caribbean and South America (Fernandez-Kelly 1989). In addition to high-tech production for computer parts, multinationals producing a wide range of goods shifted factories overseas, lured by government advertisements for the "nimble fingers" of their women workers (Froebel, Heinrichs, and Kreye 1980, 322ff.).

As information about the inhumane conditions experienced by women in these factories became widely known, there was widespread publicity about the return of sweatshop conditions around the world. Indeed, Naomi Klein argues that the global justice movement owed its origins in part to indignation over the conditions imposed by well-known brand name multinational corporations, such as Nike, on their workers (Klein 2000, 326ff.; see also Pollin 2003, 153–163).

There has been widespread debate over the advantages and disadvantages of EPZs (see Pyle and Ward 2003, 471). Some feminist scholars, such as Patricia Fernandez-Kelly (1983), have condemned the extreme exploitation of female workers. But others, such as Linda Lim and Naila Kabeer, have defended EPZs as a path for women to escape familial patriarchy, or as a way for women to earn incomes that exceed what they could get in domestic industries (Lim 1990; Kabeer 2000).[9] Thus, in her work on Japanese electronic companies in Malaysia, Aihwa Ong points out that the village girls they hired might be exploited workers, fired as soon as their keen young eyesight began to require the use of eyeglasses. But they were also being modernized, abandoning the peasant sarongs of their villages for blue jeans, and winning the right to choose their own husbands (Ong 1987; see also Beneria 2003, 77–78).

Diane Wolf notes the paradox for women workers: "Globalization is a double-edged process as far as women are concerned. On the one hand, employment opportunities derived from transformations in the global economy produce new kinds of patriarchal and capitalist controls over women" (Fernandez-Kelly and Wolf 2001, 1246). But on the other hand, the low-wage jobs, which are "often below subsistence standards," nonetheless give women "tools with which they [resist] patriarchy.... Women I interviewed [in Java, Indonesia] preferred work in 'global sweatshops' to the village rice fields" (Fernandez-Kelly and Wolf 2001, 1246).

Perhaps the extreme end on this spectrum of opinion is the view of Shelley Feldman, who has studied export-processing factories in Bangladesh. Feldman is critical of other feminist scholars for failing to acknowledge the power of women to make their own choices. According to Feldman, some analysts have explained that women left their homes for factories because of widespread rural poverty. In addition, these same analysts cite the fact that the Bangladeshi government had already decided to open EPZs to attract foreign investment into the textile industry.

But, says Feldman, such an explanation is simpleminded "economic determinism." Her research shows that the women were influenced, not by external factors such as structural adjustment programs, privatization, and the liberalization of the economy, but by their own choices, as "constituted through, and enabled by, the complex and contradictory histories of women's lives" (Feldman 2001, 1122). This argument seems to rely on a simplified either/or. Either the Bangladeshi women were motivated by the particularities of their own lives and needs, or they were pulled into paid employment by the policies of their government and of the textile factories. Obviously, there is an interaction here. But from this it is a leap to imply that rural peasant women on their own have conjured up the introduction of EPZs, not to mention structural adjustment policies!

Looking through the lens of a twenty-first-century feminism that sees work as the path to liberation, some feminist scholars perhaps equate the newly proletarianized women workers of the Global South with the "Lowell girls" of nineteenth-century Massachusetts, drawn from their farms into the first American textile factories. Under fairly mild working conditions (compared to those of their counterparts in Manchester, England), these young women developed both a worker and a feminist consciousness. (See Chapter 2.) There is no doubt that work in EPZs, which provides young women with an independent cash income, can have a liberating effect. These women are following the path prescribed by Karl Marx and Friedrich Engels: instead of doing unpaid and exhausting work on a farm, subject to feudal and patriarchal controls, a young woman can gain economic independence, and a consciousness of her own capacities.[10] But what may be true in theory can be less so in practice, given the harsh conditions under which most women in EPZs have to work.

Conditions in EPZs vary from country to country. But nearly all are exempt from national labor laws, and employers are ruthless in opposing any labor organizing. A report by the International Confederation of Free Trade Unions, which included case studies of Bangladesh, China, the Dominican Republic, Haiti, Honduras, Madagascar, Mauritius, Mexico, and Sri Lanka, documented the extensive efforts of EPZs to keep unions out and to go after labor organizers. (The exceptions were Honduras and Sri Lanka, where, after considerable pressure from international labor organizations, there have been some successful attempts to establish unions in EPZs [Perman et al. 2004].)

In addition, EPZ workers are subjected to constant harassment, whether or not they are attempting to organize. In Haiti, in CODEVI (Industrial Development Company), the free-trade zone in Ouanaminthe on the border with the Dominican Republic, where workers produce jeans for Levi's under the management of the clothing group Grupo M, "there have been cases of abductions, beatings, arbitrary dismissals, verbal abuse, unpaid overtime, intimidation with firearms, and interrogations" (Perman et al. 2004, 30). In Mexico, workers are usually on short-term contracts, with no job security. Women applying for jobs can be subjected to health tests, including pregnancy testing, which can include being examined naked and being "asked intrusive personal questions such as, 'Do you have a boyfriend?' 'How often do you have sex?' and 'Do you have children?'" (Perman et al. 2004, 47).

In a review of Naila Kabeer's study *The Power to Choose: Bangladeshi Women and Labor Market Decisions in London and Dhaka* (2000), Jeremy Seabrook notes that "Naila Kabeer sees the women workers of Dhaka as pioneers in an emancipatory process that goes with globalisation and industrialisation. The gains, both socially and economically, are tangible." Seabrook, who has observed the factories in Bangladesh, agrees with Kabeer that the women workers go through epic struggles to get into factory work, having to overcome the obstacles placed in their path by patriarchal families and communities. But they have no power to decide which industries settle in Bangladesh to take advantage of them. They are working fourteen-hour days, with wages often delayed, suffering brutality by overseers and management and extreme danger: he saw a fire in Dhaka on August 27, 2000, that killed a dozen people. More than two hundred have died in fires in recent years. As Seabrook remarks, "This is scarcely a model of self-determination" (Seabrook 2002, 80).

There is a further point to be made: Ellen Rosen argues that the nineteenth-century American pattern of industrialization is not being followed in the countries establishing EPZs: "Today's export-processing economy does not . . . transplant older forms of industrialization to the developing world. . . . Unlike in Western nations, where capital-intensive manufacture was central to economic growth, in many developing countries these low-wage industries have become central to the economic growth that is expected to occur. And unlike in the West, where the higher-paid men's industrial jobs were central to the economic welfare of families, in export-processing economies the low-paid women workers make up about 80 percent—the vast majority—of the workforce" (Rosen 2002, 245). Women receive a "woman's wage," but men do not receive a "man's wage." Thus, women working in EPZs have fewer chances of lifting themselves out of poverty.

Microcredit

A second option for women in countries dominated by SAPs is the use of microcredit or microfinance. As noted earlier, this strategy for alleviating poverty has received major publicity worldwide, with the awarding of the Nobel Peace Prize for 2006 to the founding pioneer of microcredit, Bangladeshi economist Muhammed Yunus. Women have been especially targeted for this form of loan, which has been widely promoted by international donor agencies as a way out of poverty for rural women. Proponents of microcredit wax eloquent about the possibility of drawing women into the mainstream economy by lending them small amounts, bundling the women into small groups who watch over each other, and charging them substantial interest rates. (The worldwide average interest rate for microloans is over 30 percent a year.)[11] This levying of a high interest charge follows microcredit's "cardinal rule" that, even though borrowers may lack collateral, they nonetheless should be considered serious businesspeople, "not charitable cases": "'Sixty dollars may not sound like much to us, but in a place like the Philippines it can be enough to get a family going, allowing them to buy a cow or goods to sell in the marketplace,' said Nancy Barry, president of Women's World Banking, a New York–based network and resource center for microfinancing organizations around the world. 'The hope over time is that the $60 becomes $100, then $500, and before you know it, these clients are integrated into the mainstream economy'" (Martinez 2003).

The origins of this idea of targeting women for microcredit lie, in part, with policies established in Washington. As early as 1973, the U.S. Agency for International Development (USAID), responding to critiques by feminist activists who saw development policies as directed only to men and not to women, introduced the Office of Women and Development after the Foreign Assistance Act was amended "to include the incorporation of women into national economies as part of the foreign aid policy" (Poster and Salime 2002, 194). Before long, microcredit lending became a major strategy of USAID, and women were specifically targeted for this form of credit.

Outside the United States, the idea of microcredit is widely attributed to an experiment in a local village in Bangladesh by Grameen Bank founder Muhammed Yunus, an economist and professor of economics at the University of Chittagong.[12] Concerned by the extreme poverty and suffering of the local peasantry, especially following a severe famine in 1974, Yunus began to observe the local economy closely. After watching how women villagers borrowed from middlemen to make bamboo stools and mats and then sold the products back to the middlemen at the end of each day, Yunus initially distributed microloans totaling $300 to forty-two people in the village of Jobra. (He borrowed the initial sum from a Bangladeshi bank.)

From this initial experience he developed the Grameen model (after the word *gram,* or "village"), in which groups of six nonrelated people from similar socioeconomic backgrounds are granted individual loans. These six are expected to meet good performance standards, which are defined as attending weekly meetings of their group and making weekly payments on time. If at the end of the loan cycle, everyone has repaid the loans consistently, the group can then seek a larger amount of money. The Grameen Bank Yunus founded in 1983, now headquartered in Dhaka, became the largest microlending institution in

Bangladesh, lending primarily to women. By 2005, Grameen had "4.3 million poor borrowers, 95 percent of whom were women, and a loan recovery rate of about 98 percent" (Isserles 2002, 210; see also Roy 2007, 31).

The Grameen model was picked up by banks and donor agencies worldwide. In 1997, the first international Microcredit Summit was held in New York City, setting a goal of reaching 100 million of the world's poorest families by 2005. As of 2002, more than twenty-five hundred institutions offering microcredit reached 43 million poor families worldwide, with the focus on "empowering women" (Semple 2003).[13] The United Nations declared 2005 to be the UN Year of Microcredit. "Today, the Grameen Bank model is being touted as a solution for everything from inner-city poverty in the United States to the reconstruction of Afghanistan" (Roy 2007, 31).

But what was the original relationship between the widespread availability of microcredit loans and the impact of structural adjustment policies? Anthropologist Julia Elyachar argues that microcredit schemes under the sponsorship of the World Bank began to be established precisely at the moment when SAPS failed to yield the results claimed for them by neoliberal theorists:

> Large-scale unemployment among public sector workers and state employees—
> as well as increasing levels of poverty among the poor due to the end of state
> subsidies—were supposed to have been a matter of "temporary suffering" until
> the private sector kicked in to take up the slack. But when the temporary suf-
> fering started to look permanent, new development programs were devised to
> relieve the suffering of groups negatively affected by structural adjustment. In
> a number of countries where SAPS were being enforced, the World Bank estab-
> lished Social Funds as the "social safety net" of choice. (Elyachar 2002, 501)[14]

Located in the Caribbean, Latin America, and Africa, the social funds contributed to microenterprise by granting funds to individual microentrepreneurs through local NGOs, which distributed these microloans while also supervising the collection of interest payments for banks. Even though the establishment of microcredit networks was an important innovation in helping to give individual women more economic options, in and of itself microcredit could not lift large numbers of women out of poverty. Introduced in areas where male unemployment was widespread, and where jobs were not being provided by an expanding economy, microcredit placed enormous burdens on the shoulders of women who were now in effect heads of households (Elyachar 2002, 498).

In its latest incarnation, microcredit has developed into an increasingly profitable enterprise, operating "through alliances among donor institutions, MFIs [microfinance intermediaries], national commercial banks, and international corporations such as Citigroup, Visa, and Hewlett Packard. In short, microcredit is like a microprocessor that runs the interlocked circuitries of development capital and finance capital" (Roy 2007, 33).

In recent years, the expansion of microcredit and microfinance has now been incorporated into a worldwide system where borrowers are instantly assessed for their level of risk: "The Microfinance Information eXchange (MIX)—a project funded by CGAP [the Consultative Group to Assist the Poorest, World Bank], Citigroup, Deutsche Bank, and the Open Society Institute—is a virtual online marketplace that connects various financial funds to NGOs around the world" (Roy 2007, 34). This flow of financial funds is accompanied by technological changes:

> A very poor woman in a remote rural region of Guatemala or Ghana goes to a point-of-sales kiosk—this could be a phone booth or a local store selling global commodities such as Coca-Cola. She swipes a smart card issued by VISA on a handheld device produced by Hewlett Packard. The smart card encapsulates her credit history, authorizing or deauthorizing a loan, and doing away with the need for loan officers or NGO workers. Her identity is verified by biometric identification: a fingerprint or an optical scan. The swipe of the VISA smart card links her instantaneously to the credit bureau of the country. The transaction is also registered at the MIX market across the street from the World Bank in Washington D.C., updating the information on the MFI with whom she is doing business.... This is also a geography that connects the hyperglobalized rural realm with the technofinancial power of development institutions in Washington D.C., lined up on Pennsylvania Avenue. (Roy 2007, 35)

Is microcredit a serious strategy for the elimination of women's poverty? Yunus himself, at least when he started out, did not see microcredit as a panacea for world poverty. It is certainly a strategy that has helped millions of women around the world, but it cannot in and of itself end poverty (Bello 2006, 1). In an interesting case study comparing microcredit on the islands of Cyprus and Trinidad and Tobago, Marina Karides shows that the use of microcredit can help to alleviate poverty among women when accompanied by strong government policies that protect local production from foreign competition, and that create economic safety networks for women. This was the case in Cyprus before it was forced to retract these policies in 1998 as the price of entry to the European Economic Community. In Trinidad, absent such policies, and in an economy subjected to neoliberal structural adjustment, microcredit programs, even with government support, did not alleviate women's poverty (Karides 2007).

Obviously, among the women who have benefited from microcredit programs there have been success stories, and I am not arguing against them per se. But the claim that microcredit offers a solution to the poverty in the Global South seems an exaggeration: "Do the activities of the Grameen Bank and other microlenders romanticize individual struggles to escape poverty? Yes. Do these programs help some women 'pull themselves up by the bootstraps'? Yes. Will microenterprises in the informal sector contribute to ending world poverty? Not a chance" (Feiner and Barker 2006, 11).

But more profoundly, microcredit is getting a lot of publicity and praise precisely because it does not challenge the neoliberal paradigm:

> For neoliberals the solution to poverty is getting the poor to work harder, get educated, have fewer children, and act more responsibly. Markets reward those who help themselves, and women, who comprise the vast majority of microcredit borrowers, are no exception. Neoliberals champion the Grameen Bank and similar efforts precisely because microcredit programs do not change the structural conditions of globalization—such as loss of land rights, privatization of essential public services, or cutbacks in health and education spending—that reproduce poverty among women in developing nations. (Feiner and Barker 2006, 10)

Microcredit will certainly benefit a woman farmer who can use the loan to buy a water buffalo for her rice fields. As a reader of this book in manuscript remarked to me, "What's wrong with getting a poor woman a buffalo?" But getting the wherewithal to pay off the loans presupposes a level of entrepreneurship that the majority of needy women probably will not attain.[15] In addition, the high rates of interest, and the absence of bankruptcy protections, can place the microborrower in severe financial jeopardy. An alternative mode of microcredit, not for profits but for community development, has been introduced in Venezuela as part of a general, state-led process. (I will discuss this in the Conclusion.) Thus, it is not microcredit in itself that I am critiquing here, but the failure by either governments or IFIs to link microcredit lending to a broader, state-led development effort that can move entire communities out of poverty.

Sex Work

A third, and time-honored, option for impoverished women is prostitution, or sex work. The rise in sex work is linked to the development of tourism as part of a strategy to bring in foreign currency and to encourage foreign investment. The Philippines is a good example of this strategy.

During the 1970s, the Ferdinand Marcos government in the Philippines adopted international tourism as part of its development planning. Among its calculations was that goodwill and political support could be created among foreign businesspeople and international bankers by providing them with luxury hotels. One year after the declaration of martial law in 1972, Marcos established a ministry of tourism, which oversaw the construction of fourteen first-class hotels plus a conference center in Manila, at a cost of over $450 million, financed with World Bank loans.

At the same time, the Philippine government touted the "beauty and generosity" of Filipina women to promote the tourist industry, and indeed, tourism in Manila and other tourist areas grew simultaneously with the sex industry. By the late 1970s, tourism brought in $300 million, and by the mid-1980s, the majority of tourists were men from Japan, Australia, and the United States drawn by sex-tourism packages that allowed the men to select women from a brochure, visit "girlie bars," and stay at the most luxurious hotels, usually owned or financed by government officials (Lacsamana 2004, 393).

The prostitution that traditionally flourished around the two major American military bases in the Philippines, Clark Air Force Base and Subic Naval Base, now had its parallel in the tourism industry. Although the lease for these original military bases was withdrawn by the Philippine Senate, under pressure from local activists, in 1991, a new agreement in 1998, the Visiting Forces Agreement, gave the United State twenty-two new ports of entry to conduct training exercises (called *Balikatan*) with the Philippine army. As the Philippine women's group GABRIELA notes, the renewed presence of U.S. troops has given further impetus to the sex industry, with these Balikatan camps serving American soldiers as a "take home sex delivery service." These twenty-two sites are transforming the Philippines once again into a country "where the selling of women and children" is sanctioned by the government (quoted in Lacsamana 2004, 390). In reaction to these developments, "grassroots groups in the country, notably GABRIELA and the Coalition against the Trafficking in Women—Asia Pacific (CATWAP), who use the term 'prostituted women' to highlight what they see as the exploitative nature of this industry, have been active in opposing sex tourism, and have succeeded in reducing the number of sex tours" (Lacsamana 2004, 394–395).

But the antitrafficking stance of these groups has come under attack from some feminist writers and activists. The debate over prostitution, or sex work, has a long history within the feminist movement, dating back at least to the nineteenth century. Do women who sell sex require rescuing, or are they women workers whose autonomy and agency should be respected? This ancient debate resurfaced within 1970s feminism. The self-proclaimed "pro-sex" feminists, such as the late Ellen Willis, argued for women's sexual autonomy, including the right to choose a wide range of sexual practices, including sadomasochism. The opposition saw women as sex objects unfairly and dangerously exploited by the pornography and sex industries. Among other venues, this debate exploded at the historic Barnard College Scholar and Feminist conference of 1982 in New York City, where speakers for a pro-sex stance, such as Amber Hollibaugh, were picketed by protesters wearing antisadomaschism T-shirts. (On this debate, see Vance 1984.)

Within the world of prostitution, women in the sex work industry influenced by feminism developed a number of organizations, such as COYOTE (Call Off Your Old Tired Ethics), founded by Margo St. James in 1973, to promote the view that laws against prostitution should be repealed; and that women choosing to sell sex should have the rights of other workers, including the right to unionize and to have their working conditions protected. This campaign has had some success, with the state of Victoria in Australia, New Zealand, the Netherlands, and Thailand having decriminalized prostitution. (On the rise of a globalized sex workers' rights campaign, see Kempadoo 1998.)

One wing of feminist writing and activism has called for the abolition of the terms *prostitution* and *prostitute* in favor of *sex worker*, because these writers view this area of work not as "an identity—a social or psychological characteristic of women, often indicated by 'whore'—but as an income-generating activity or form of labor for women and men" (Kempadoo 1998, 3, quoted in Lacsamana 2004, 396). This line of argument holds that sex work is a form of emotional labor, comparable to a range of service sector jobs that require the worker to provide commodified and commercialized care and feeling, from airline hostesses and child care workers to actors and psychotherapists. Sex workers distinguish real intimacy and love in their private lives from the act of selling sex, just as do actors and therapists (Kempadoo 1998a, citing Wendy Chapkis; Lacsamana 2004, 396–397).

A new and complex literature has emerged on the issue of international "trafficking," and the attempts to regulate it through national laws and international protocols (see Kempadoo with Sanghera and Pattanaik 2005). Within the debates over establishing international norms against trafficking, the same feminist arguments have emerged. "Abolitionists," on the one hand, see women as helpless victims of wicked male traffickers; defenders, on the other hand, view women sex workers as part of a broader spectrum of women seeking economic survival. One Hong Kong NGO working on behalf of sex workers expresses the issue in these terms: "From our local experience, we find no difference between people working as factory workers, domestic workers, sex workers, or people wanting to marry abroad. Sex work is a job or simply a way for women to increase their and their families' living standard. They are women who take initiatives to improve their living conditions. This is quite the opposite of the 'passive victim' stereotype that is widely circulated about them" (Kim Yuet-Lin and Anita Koo for ZiTeng, December 2003, quoted in Kempadoo et al. 2005, 151).

But what is missing from this analysis is a serious look at the relation between the rise of globalization and the deliberate encouragement of sex work as part of national policy on the part of governments in Thailand, the Philippines, and elsewhere. As Anne E. Lacsamana notes, those defending the rights of sex workers have not come up with "a tangible strategy for collectively organizing against the structural mechanisms that have led to the increase in the global sex trade. Instead, we are encouraged to negotiate prostitution/sex work within the existing social order by lobbying for unionization of prostitutes, recognition of prostitution as any other form of women's work, better 'working' conditions, and the overall *end* to laws that *prohibit* the traffic in women. In other words, there is no alternative (TINA). Has Margaret Thatcher been right all along?" (Lacsamana 2004, 400; emphasis in original).[16]

At a meeting of the "Facing Global Capital" seminar on December 5, 2002, one of the visiting Rockefeller Foundation scholars, Jacqueline Berman, presented a paper on the outflow of women from eastern European countries after the fall of the Soviet Union. (For details on this seminar, see the Preface; see also Berman 2003.) Berman sharply criticized the international literature that deplored this new market for sex work as somehow immoral and requiring regulation. In the discussion that followed, Berman reacted angrily to the suggestion that the women being trafficked might indeed require some form of state protection.

In her understanding of feminism, women's right to self-determination (including selling their own bodies) trumped any need for protection, which she saw as a dirty word. As Berman said vehemently, conflating herself with the trafficked women she was writing about, "I don't want to be protected!" But surely there is a complex class issue here. A young, rising scholar entering academe in the United States might not need protection. But the children being sold into sexual slavery in brothels in Southeast Asia or American cities might.

Feminist analysts such as Melissa Ditmore have done an effective job in exposing the hypocrisy of U.S. government initiatives against sex trafficking (Ditmore 2005). How likely is it that the U.S. State Department sincerely cares about the fate of women and children being trafficked across national borders? Yet to oppose this policy on the basis that it patronizes women and diminishes their right to economic self-determination leaves feminist organizers open to the charge that they are in effect protecting a free market in women's bodies. When the issue is posed as government "protection" versus women's "freedom," freedom looks like the obvious feminist choice. But the debate over sex work cannot stay within the framework of an assumed capitalist system, as Lacsamana argues (Lacsamana 2004). Otherwise, a feminist argument for women's "free" sexual choices winds up reinforcing the free-market doctrines of neoliberalism.

Migration and Remittances

Finally, women have the fourth option to leave their home countries and seek paid work elsewhere. In contrast to previous decades, when migration was primarily a male phenomenon, women have reportedly constituted almost half of all migrants since the 1960s (see Zlotnik 2003).[17] And there is reason to believe that the official figures, which are drawn from country records of legal migration, are an underestimate of the wave of female migration now under way.

In contrast to earlier periods, when women primarily left home as part of a family unit, increasingly women now migrate on their own or with their children in tow. And in some parts of the world, notably Asia, there is "significant evidence of the feminization of labor migration . . . where hundreds of thousands of women emigrate each year" (Yinger 2007, 2). In the case of the Philippines, successive governments have made it national policy to celebrate the heroism of women—nurses and other trained professionals—who leave to seek their fortune in First World countries. Thus, in June 2002 President Gloria Macapagal-Arroyo launched a program called "Filipinos for the World." She called these migrants "overseas Philippine investors" and "internationally shared resources" (Chang 2004, 242–243). At present, there are an estimated 8 million Filipino migrant workers in over 186 countries, of whom about 65 percent are women.

At least one organ of the United Nations offers a cheerful view of the migration of women from their home countries to the rich nations of the West and the Middle East. The official report of the United Nations Population Agency (UNFPA) for 2006 on international migration speaks of a growing "revolution," concerning the 95 million, or 49.6 percent of all, international migrants who are women. The UNFPA 2006 report notes that migration has "proven to be a positive experience for millions of women and their families worldwide." It "exposes women to new ideas and social norms that can promote their rights and enable them to participate more fully in society. It can also have a positive influence on gender norms in the country of origin" (United Nations Population Fund 2006, 21). In other words, migration is great because it teaches women to have a feminist consciousness.

An important subgroup of migrant women comprises those who leave home for First World countries, such as Italy or the United States, to become domestic workers. The UNFPA report is equally sanguine as to the benefits to women of entering domestic service in far away places:

> For millions of women and their families, the "global care chain" offers considerable benefits, albeit with some serious drawbacks, i.e., separation from children and other loved ones.... Aside from salaries that are several times higher than what they receive at home, international domestic workers also gain personal and social benefits, including improved educational and health opportunities for their children, gifts, extra cash to send back home and travel with employer families. In the case of Muslim domestic workers in the United Arab Emirates, the opportunity to make a pilgrimage to Mecca can lead to the fulfillment of a lifetime dream. (United Nations Population Fund 2006, 25)[18]

It is hard to read this with a straight face, given the testimonies of migrant domestic workers themselves. The "global nanny chain" is no bed of roses (to mix metaphors). This phenomenon is widespread enough to have given birth to a feminist literature on this category of women's work, where a woman leaves her children at home with their father or other family members while she becomes in effect a substitute mother to the children of her employer (see Ehrenreich and Hochschild 2004; Parrenas 2001). Migrant women organizations in First World countries have documented the stress, danger, and unprotected nature of migrant domestic labor, often accompanied by physical and psychological abuse (see Anderson 2004 on the work of Kalayaan, a London-based support group for migrant women workers organized in 1987).

The women driven out of their home economies because they can no longer survive as farmers, as industrial workers, or even as part of the informal economy are a major source of remittances to their families back home: "Despite a paucity of data, one thing is clear: The money that female migrants send back home can raise families and even entire communities out of poverty. Of the more than US $1 billion in remittances sent back to Sri Lanka in 1999, women contributed over 62 per cent of the total. Of the roughly US $6 billion remitted annually to the Philippines in the late 1990s, migrant women transferred one third" (United Nations Population Fund 2006, 29). Women send less money home than men do in absolute figures because they earn less. But they consistently send a higher proportion of their earnings.

"Remittances," notes the UNFPA report, "that is, migrant earnings sent back to countries of origin—are the main reason experts point to international migration as important for poverty reduction. . . . The World Bank estimates that, in 2005, formally transferred remittances rang in at about US $232 billion—of which developing countries received $167 billion" (United Nations Population Fund 2006, 12). (The actual number is higher, since some funds are transferred through nonformal channels.) The estimate of $167 billion represents "twice as much money as official development assistance" (Yinger 2007). In the Philippines, remittances (from both men and women) amount to about $7 billion annually and are the "largest source of foreign exchange—surpassing income from either sugar or minerals" (Chang 2002, 130). Worldwide, this flow of remittances is "fast becoming the cherished 'El Dorado' for micro financing promoters" (Martinez 2003).

Women forced out of their country by the absence of decent jobs, working long years away from their children and husbands, send home money to make up for their absence. The influx of funds from these remittances into the local banking system allows the microcreditors to draw poor local village women into entrepreneurship, overseeing their transformation into microentrepreneurs and responsible, interest-paying borrowers. This circuit of capital assists the government and the elite in continuing the policies that have created the poverty in the first place. And much of the cost is borne by women.

THE ROLE OF NGOS AND THE RISE OF "CIVIL SOCIETY"

Internationally, as the impact of SAPs began to register, they were "an important catalyst" for organizing by women activists, both locally and internationally: "It became clear to women activists that the burden of SAPs was being borne disproportionately by women, as they substituted their own reproductive labor for diminished social services; lost service sector jobs; became the breadwinners in the informal economy; or moved into the new export processing jobs as cheap labor" (Barton 2004, 170). As feminist economists built up an analysis of the impact of SAPs, feminist organizers formed or joined the rising number of NGOs being funded by international donors to intervene directly in improving women's lives at the grassroots level.

Thus, the era of SAPs has also been the era of the NGO.[19] There is now an international debate on the status and role of these organizations, which range from well-known groups, such as Oxfam, Greenpeace, and Amnesty International, to lesser-known specific issue–based organizations. Jim Paul credits NGOs, working in international coalitions, with important and successful campaigns, such as the treaty to eliminate land mines (1997), the creation of the International Criminal Court (1998), the defeat of the secret negotiations for a Multilateral Agreement on Investments (1998), and the Jubilee 2000 campaign to cancel Third World debt, which influenced both "thinking and policy" (Paul 2000, 3).

NGOs have been extremely active on gender issues, especially after the United Nations Development Fund for Women (UNIFEM) decided in the late 1970s to use NGOs to carry out funded projects, at a time when most UN agencies were still working through either national governments or their own UN institutions. NGOs have expanded rapidly since the 1980s in the postcommunist countries of Vietnam and China, as well as in newly "democratized" countries such as Mongolia and Indonesia (Bulbeck 2007).

The effectiveness of feminist organizing was soon reflected in the language of international organizations. When the Beijing UN women's conference of 1995 concluded that gender analysis "must be integrated into policy and programming in all areas," the result was a process of "gender mainstreaming" that "in practice has created a gender industry" (Barton 2004, 173). After meeting with World Bank president James Wolfensohn in Beijing in 1995, women activists were able to have the bank establish "internal gender monitoring mechanisms within the World Bank as well as an external monitoring group. The result has been a flurry of studies, new offices and bureaucracies, and new resources to women at the local level (particularly through microloans), but negligible change in the macroeconomic policies of the World Bank on borrowing countries" (Barton 2004, 174). Even if these concessions by the World Bank and other lending institutions are mostly window dressing, many women have nevertheless built careers in the arena of gender and development, reproductive rights, women and violence, and other feminist concerns. "Women professionals move back and forth between government posts, NGO agencies and multilateral institutions" (Barton 2004, 173).

With governments and institutions seeking "gender experts" to work within their official frameworks, and without any direct accountability to the women they are ostensibly serving, there is no small danger of co-optation. With the withdrawal of the state from responsibility for the social and economic well-being of the poor, NGOs funded by foreign donors have become, in effect, a partial substitute for the welfare functions of the state.

One clue to this development is the widespread use of the term *civil society* in documents produced by international institutions. For example, a set of Millennium Development Goals was announced by the United Nations in 2000 (I will discuss these goals later in this chapter). The corresponding policy document of the Commonwealth Education Fund, which officially seeks to reach the Millennium Development Goals in education (every child in the Commonwealth countries is to receive a primary school education by the year 2015), refers repeatedly to the role of civil society participation in reaching these goals (Wickramasinghe 2005, 460–461).

What is the meaning of the new celebration of civil society among donor organizations? In the political science tradition, civil society refers to the range of institutions located in society at large that are not part of government. The "proliferation" of NGOs is not a "flowering of civil society" in the Western sense, where the term refers to the widespread development of civic organizations, from the Red Cross to the Rotary Club, in the manner first described and admired by Alexis de Tocqueville (2002). There is reason to be suspicious of the concept of civil society, since it has been "embraced by the forces of capital." The World Bank, the Asian Development Bank, and even the World Trade Organization have all announced their support for civil society institutions (Wickramasinghe 2005, 466). Why are IFIs and donor groups so enamored of this concept? Many activists have suggested that "civil society is actively bannered not necessarily as an antidote to poverty, corruption or as a vehicle for democratization, but to steer grassroots organizations away from the radical influence of political organizations calling for radical comprehensive revolutionary reforms" (Aziz Choudry quoted in Wickramasinghe 2005, 465).

Nira Wickramasinghe suggests that the importation of the idea of civil society from the West into complex societies in the Global South with very different histories and class structures is a Trojan horse. Civil society in Africa is "an ideology that stems from the invocation by western donor countries—following the lead of the World Bank and the IMF—for a diminished role of the state, in the context of Structural Adjustment Programs" (Wickramasinghe 2005, 467).

Lenny Markovitz points out that the use of civil society, in the sense of an agency that counterbalances the state, is a misrepresentation of the history of capitalism. In fact, the growth of civil society in Europe was a process in which, as the modern capitalist state emerged from its feudal predecessor, "many coercive functions that once belonged to the state were relocated in the 'private' sphere, in private property, class exploitation, and market imperatives" (Markovitz 1998, 32–33, quoting Ellen Meiksins Wood). The economy that resulted was never separated from the state, but indeed was deeply intertwined with it in an intermingling of families and social networks that together constituted a bourgeois ruling group. Similarly, in the emerging capitalist economies of Africa, "through a process of struggle and conflict, emerging capitalist interests become embedded within the institutions of the state" (Markovitz 1998, 33). Therefore, the idea that civil society represents some kind of alternative to state power is ahistorical, and is being used in the service of the free-market ideology that promotes the idea of markets as existing somehow independently of the state.

This critique of the civil society concept as a Trojan Horse for permanently reducing the role of the state might come as a shock to the thousands of feminists working in NGOs worldwide, who see themselves as contributing to bettering the lives of poor women in the Third World. They would be indignant at the suggestion that they are being manipulated by international capitalist forces. And indeed it would be deeply unfair to question either the motives or the achievements of these feminist NGOs in raising consciousness, teaching reproductive self-determination, providing skills, offering microcredit, and helping women develop crafts and other businesses to make up for the virtual disappearance of formal sector employment. (For an excellent discussion of the role of women's NGOs, see Bulbeck 2007.) But the introduction of NGOs is a tacit acknowledgment by governments and donors alike that the activities of the 1960s and 1970s developmental state are not resuming anytime soon.

Some critics go further and argue that the NGOs have a second function. In addition to taking over the role of providing social services for the poor, they are a way of sopping up the energy of activists. Many observers have characterized the rise of NGOs throughout the developing world as an instrument of social control. As Patricia Fernandez-Kelly notes with irony, "Inspired by noble intentions, NGOs gave civil society a fresh face," promoting health care, education, credit associations, housing, and political participation. "If there ever was a potential for true sisterhood it dwelled within NGOs." But as William Robinson, James Petras, and others note as well, NGOs also bring with them ideologies and structures that impede worker organizing, and often become bureaucratized welfare providers rather than the locus of political protest (Fernandez-Kelly 2007, 514).

As Sonia Alvarez remarks in her analysis of the "NGO boom" in Latin America, neoliberal governments increasingly make use of feminist NGOs to carry out policies inspired by neoliberalism. These programs are "centered on incorporating the poorest of poor women into the market and promoting 'self-help,' civil society–led strategies to address the most egregious effects of structural adjustment.... Local governments and intergovernmental organizations (IGOs) increasingly have turned to feminist NGOs in particular to evaluate gender-focused policies and administer the targeted self-help, social service and training (*capacitacion*) programs for poor and working-class women currently in vogue throughout the region" (Alvarez 1999, 182). Feminist organizations that do not buy into the neoliberal paradigm are increasingly shut out of the action:

> Many feminists I interviewed maintained . . . that irrespective of their technical competence, NGOs that refuse to play by the rules of the game or whose discourses and practices run counter to the official orthodoxies of the day may be losing out in the gender projects market and are often silenced or marginalized from the public debate. . . . When feminist NGOs are critical of the government, they are, predictably, less likely to get contracts or grants, which some claim results in a tendency toward 'self-censorship beyond even that which the State requires of you.'" (Alvarez 1999, 198, citing an anonymous activist respondent)

Sylvia Marcos, a Mexican scholar and activist, discusses her experience working in the international feminist movement in equally critical terms. Attending the international forums on human rights at Vienna in 1993 and on population and health in Cairo in 1994, and the most recent UN conference on women in Beijing in 1995, she began as an enthusiastic participant, but ended with a great deal of disillusionment. While paying tribute to the activism of thousands of feminists in arenas such as reproductive rights, Marcos saw the issues of Third World women losing out to the agendas of funders from the North. Many feminist activists, both from the North and from Third World countries, were being co-opted. "From being very radical activists like myself, many of them have transformed into very able instruments of feminist imperialism" (Marcos quoted in Shih et al. 2005, 146).

Particularly in the area of reproductive rights, Marcos is critical of a single-minded focus on reducing the birthrate. Obviously, information about birth control is of value to Third World women and other women in poverty: "The focus on reproductive rights has increased the capacities of many women to make decisions. Many grassroots women suddenly find their voice and feel they have the right to decide about their bodies. . . . So there is a lot of positive outcome." But the "political implications" of this "became unbearable": "It is as if there is no other issue of women's health that exists. It is ridiculous. Poor women are dying of malnutrition, of diseases easily healed by adequate medical resources, and so many other things" (quoted in Shih et al. 2005, 147). But instead the result is a return to "a form of the eugenics discourse that underlay the older discourses of imperialism. . . . Poverty becomes the alibi to exercise a eugenic imperialism on 'Third World' countries'" (quoted in Shih et al. 2005, 148).

Carol Barton's report of her conversation with "a woman from the Global South working for a European government donor agency" is revealing in this regard (Barton 2004, 175). This woman was seeking to put development money into funding economic literacy for women, and to make sure World Bank economic reforms incorporated the input of local NGOs by mainstreaming gender concerns. She wanted to increase women's bargaining power in relation to local authorities; and she wanted women to gain knowledge of macroeconomic issues. To her, development assistance should be a transfer of knowledge and skills, rather than just a handing out of currency. And she thought that a process of "gender-budgeting" was a great way to get women engaged at a local level.

What, Barton inquired, was the source of her interest in so much economic and political participation by local women? "She candidly answered that the donors' goal is to 'reduce tensions by providing basic services and enabling women to become players at the local level so that they won't destabilize political systems.' She expressed concern that if people did not feel engaged they could become bomb-throwing fundamentalists." This particular donor representative "acknowledged that little would actually change in terms of these grassroots women's economic realities" (Barton 2005, 176).

MILD-MANNERED CRITIQUES BY FEMINIST ECONOMISTS

During the decades in which the developmental state was being virtually dismantled along neoliberal lines, what has been the role of feminist economists and development experts? One of the feminist interventions of the 1970s that has had a major international impact, winning recognition from UN organizations and donor agencies, is the rise of a feminist perspective within the field of economics. In particular, feminist economists have turned a gender lens onto the field of economic development, starting with the pathbreaking work of Ester Boserup (1970). Successive waves of feminist economists have critiqued mainstream development models for their failure to take account of the fundamental contribution of women to the creation of wealth, both through their productive labor in industry and agriculture, and in the unpaid reproductive labor that makes social continuity possible.[20]

This effort has born fruit. Organizations such as the World Bank now routinely promote the centrality of women in their analyses. The turn toward seeing women as the key to economic development occurred during the 1990s. A leading role in this change was played by Lawrence Summers, chief economist at the World Bank from 1991 to 1993, the U.S. secretary of the Treasury under President Bill Clinton, president of Harvard from 2001 to 2006, and named in 2008 to head President Obama's National Council of Economic Advisers. Summers argued in a 1992 paper, "Investing in *All* the People," that the variable most highly correlated with improvements in social indicators was female education. Education for women, Summers held, had a multiplier effect, since it empowered women to bring about other important social and economic changes (Summers 1992; Daniel 2008, 1).[21] "The irony that it took a powerful white man to make this case is not lost on Geeta Rao Gupta, president of the International Center for Research on Women. Nonetheless it made a difference. 'His statement on the returns on girls' education caught the attention of a higher level of policymakers,' she says. 'The evidence was known before he articulated it but it mattered who the messenger was'" (Daniel 2008, 1).

Since then, World Bank research has continued to claim that education for women has significant positive effects on health, welfare, and economic growth. For example, the bank recently published its gender action plan for 2007–2010 entitled, "Gender Equality as Smart Economics."[22] In the current era, reports such as that of the United Nations Development Programme on the problems with development in the Arab nations, or the United Nations Children's Fund on "The State of the World's Children 2007," regularly point to the need for girls' education and training and women's economic advancement as the key to economic development. Indeed the subtitle of the UNICEF report is "Women and Children: The Double Dividend of Gender Equality"(United Nations Development Programme 2006; United Nations Children's Fund 2006).

But at the same time, these UN bodies do not dissent from the overarching macroeconomic prescriptions of the Washington Consensus, which, as we saw, virtually guarantee the erosion of women and children's health and well-being. As Christa Wichterich notes, how is it possible to improve the opportunities for women "without changing the structures that again and again push subsistence farmers, street vendors, care workers, local industries, informal workers, household economies as well as migrants [into] marginal and precarious positions and poverty [?]" (Wichterich 2006, 2). This focus on gender is a sleight of hand in which the issue of women's empowerment is being substituted (surreptitiously) for the support of state-led development.

Feminist academics have been in the forefront of exposing the injuries caused by SAPs to women and children, pointing out the unequal burden placed on them by such austerity programs. But the remedies sought by these same academics are distressingly mild. Silvia Federici argues that most feminist analysts looking at the critical changes in the world economy have not understood that "the restructuring of the world economy is responsible not only for the global spread of poverty, but also for the emergence of a new colonial order, that deepens the divisions among women, and that this new colonialism must be a main target for feminist struggles if women's liberation is to be possible" (Federici 1999, 48). Most feminist economists, she argues, stop short of acknowledging the depth of the changes that will be required: "Even those who are critical of the global economy and of the policies pursued by international agencies like the World Bank and the International Monetary Fund (IMF), often settle for reformist positions that condemn gender discrimination, but leave the structural problems connected with the global hegemony of capitalist relations intact" (Federici 1999, 48).

As an example, here is a list by Joanna Kerr, a cofounder of the Association of Women's Rights in Development, of suggested points at which women can intervene to improve the development process in the Third World:

1. Feminist economists can contribute to the critique of neoliberalism with the aim of moving the field of mainstream economics to take more account of gender. For example, they can urge countries to revise their calculations of the gross domestic product (GDP) to more accurately reflect the enormous value created by unpaid women's work.

2. Feminist economists can participate in women's ministries or special offices created by governments to prepare women's budgets, as used by several African states.[23] By preparing a women's budget, which indicates the gender impact of government initiatives, feminists can intervene at the level of government policy to improve women's lives.

3. Feminist economists can participate in the international dialogue being carried out between agencies of the United Nations like UNIFEM and other international bodies and NGOs, as occurred in the run-up to the preparation of the final documents from the 1995 Beijing women's conference.

4. Feminist economists can gain influence by joining those groups that are directly lobbying the World Bank and the IMF to improve or change their policies toward women. (Kerr 1999, 191–202)

In this very mild-mannered list of interventions, all of them no doubt worthy of attention, no mention is made of using women's activism to build an alternative to the current economic system. None of these strategies challenges the main premises of the Washington Consensus or, more broadly, the workings of international capitalism in its globalized form. Nor do they challenge the role of governments in either setting the rules of the game (in the North) or following the rules (in the South). This is a respectful, well-behaved form of feminism, seeking approval from the powers that be.

In Kerr's very forgiving interpretation, the IFIs have left women out of their models due to oversight, or unconscious sexism, or an analysis based on a prefeminist version of neoclassical economics. These feminist interventions are reminiscent of the faculty development programs originated by the women's studies movement in the 1970s and 1980s. Just as women's studies practitioners earnestly sought to teach patriarchal male colleagues, through "faculty development programs," how to revise the curriculum so as to have a body of knowledge that was more sensitive to the new issues of gender, race, class, and sexuality, so these earnest feminists are seeking to reach the ear of their male colleagues and superiors in the IFIs. This is faculty development for technocrats. Gender-sensitive language, gender indicators, gender specialists—all these are ways to nudge the masters of the universe to include women and women's needs on the agenda. But none of this good faith educational effort expresses the need for a fundamental questioning of the neoliberal agenda.

CONCLUSION

In recent years, the growing international protest against the policies of neoliberalism has brought forth a series of responses from international institutions. Under pressure from groups such as Jubilee 2000 and Fifty Years Is Enough, international financial institutions and the G-8 governments have reached agreements to reduce the outstanding debt of the least-developed countries. Structural adjustment policies have been renamed and revamped to include measures ostensibly designed to reduce poverty.[24] The Human Development Reports produced by the United Nations Development Programme from 1993 onward, and most recently the UN Millennium Development Goals announced in September 2000, and reiterated at the 2005 Millennium + 5 Summit, are all responses to pressures brought by the international antiglobalization movement.

The Millennium goals, agreed to by the 191 member countries of the United Nations, represent targets for member states to be reached by the year 2015. Goal number three reads: "Promote gender equality and empower women. Eliminate gender disparity in primary and secondary education preferably by 2005, and at all levels by 2015" (Amin 2006, 14–15). It is presumably a measure of the influence of international feminist organizing that women's concerns—along with goals seeking to reduce child mortality, improve maternal health, and combat diseases such as HIV/AIDS—are front and center in the list. However, the scope of this goal was narrowed because "neoconservative Christian fundamentalists of the United States, Poland and elsewhere, the Muslims of Saudi Arabia, Pakistan and other countries, and the fundamentalist Hindus agree on eliminating any reference to the rights of women and the family" (Amin 2006, 3).

Of course, it is a victory for feminism that issues of concern to women and girls are included, however grudgingly, in the documents that are supposed to govern the behavior of governments and donors. (For a wide-ranging critique of the UN Millennium Development Goals from a feminist perspective, see Barton and Prendergast 2004.) But I am arguing that feminist ideas, however watered down by fundamentalist forces, have become useful to the powerful industrialized countries, and their instruments in the World Bank and the other IFIs, as a way of distracting attention from the devastation brought about by the policies of structural adjustment. To the extent that feminist economists and other activists do not unmask the hypocrisy of the neoliberal agenda and call for a fundamental alternative, they are acceding to the ideological sleight of hand that replaces real economic development with the "empowerment" of women.

6

Islamophobia and the Global War on Terror

✺

In previous chapters, I outlined the uses of mainstream feminism for global capitalism, both in pursuing class war in the United States and in carrying out the counterrevolution against the Third World. In this chapter, I will add a further use: the enlisting of feminist ideas and energies as part of the contemporary war on terrorism.

After the events of September 11, 2001, President George W. Bush, heavily under the influence of the neoconservative grouping of Douglas Feith, Richard Perle, and Paul Wolfowitz, among others, expressed an initial version of the goals of the global war on terrorism that displayed a broad imperial vision. He imagined a domino-like series of regime changes in the Middle East, tied to an expanded U.S. military and political presence in the region: first the Taliban, then Saddam Hussein, then regimes in Iran, Syria, and beyond would fall before the onslaught of an imperial democracy (Dreyfuss 2005, 335). The ideological machinery of the neocons echoed these aspirations. Lawrence Kaplan and Irving Kristol wrote that "the mission begins in Baghdad, but it does not end there.... We stand at the cusp of a new historical era." Similarly, stating that the war would not be limited to Iraq, Michael Ledeen declared that "it may turn out to be a war to remake the world" (quoted in Dreyfuss 2005, 336).

It is beyond the scope of this book to tackle the growing controversies over the events of 9/11.[1] But I agree with those who consider that the war on terrorism has become a useful replacement for the cold war, a justification for the continued pursuit of U.S. hegemony in the world. From this perspective, foreign policy under the administration of George W. Bush cynically made use of Islamic fundamentalism—in current parlance "Islamo-fascism"—to provide the government with convenient arguments for the prosecution of wars in Afghanistan and Iraq, for the support of the Israeli assault on Lebanon in 2006, and for possible future military adventures in the service of U.S. geopolitical and economic objectives.

What do I mean when I say the war on terrorism has "replaced" the cold war? With the fall of the Soviet regime in 1989–1991, the convenient enemy that justified so many military and economic interventions, such as the relatively recent war against the contras in Nicaragua under President Ronald Reagan, was no longer a plausible casus belli. I will turn in a moment to the specifics of the war on terrorism as they have been rolled out since the terrible events of September 11, 2001. But first, I want to note how readily the American public, by and large, initially accepted the rise of the new threat of Islamic terrorism.

Ira Chernus argues that Americans have been remarkably receptive to the war on terrorism, since it represents a return to the comfortable stance of "us versus them," with the United States in the role of the international good guys:

> Within two years after the Wall fell, the Soviet Union had simply disappeared. In the U.S., nobody really knew how to fight evil now, or even who the evildoers were. The world's sole remaining superpower was "running out of demons," as Colin Powell complained. Amid the great anguish of September 11, 2001, it was not hard to sense the paradoxical but very real feeling of relief that flooded across the country. After a decade adrift with no foes to oppose, Americans could sink back into a comfortingly black-and-white world, neatly divided into the good guys and the bad guys, the innocent and the guilty. In the hands of the Bush administration, "terrorists," modest as their numbers might have been, turned out to be remarkably able stand-ins for a whole empire-plus of "commies." They became our all-purpose symbol for the evil that fills our waking nightmares. (Chernus 2006)

The idea that the war on terror has replaced the cold war makes particular sense in the context of the United States seeking to maintain its economic and political dominance in the world. The war on communism was really a war on entities that were perceived as representing a threat to the reach of the capitalist system. To be sure, the Communist countries of the USSR and China had long ago taken themselves out of the capitalist orbit, and so the various military interventions carried on by the United States in the postwar era were presented as an attempt to stop further defections and a feared "falling dominoes" effect. This was the rationale of the war in Vietnam, for example. But Vietnam has now become an eager suitor of foreign investment, as has China itself. With the conversion of the Russian and eastern European governments to market capitalism, the list of plausible enemies for the United States was reduced to the "axis of evil": Iran, North Korea, and Iraq (State of the Union address, January 29, 2002).

One goal of the global war on terrorism (or the G-WOT, as it is referred to in the Pentagon)[2] is to preserve and expand the orbit of capitalism. This is the reason for the enmity evoked by Hugo Chávez of Venezuela, who is not a Communist but who continually calls for a twenty-first-century socialism and who has taken steps toward a national economic policy that is not dominated by neoliberal principles. (See the Conclusion for a discussion of Venezuela's Bolivarian revolution.)

Until recently, the concept of empire in the modern world was, in the U.S. view at least, reserved for the Soviet Union—witness Ronald Reagan's reference to the "Evil Empire." Now, however, particularly since the onset of the war in Iraq, the idea of the United States as an empire has regained wide currency, both on the left and on the right.[3] The Left considers that the imperial behavior of the United States endangers the planet, whereas the Right thinks that the United States has correctly assumed the mantle of empire to do good in the world.[4]

As we saw in Chapter 1, since 1945 the U.S. empire has become the hegemonic power, effectively governing the world economy by using financial and political methods where possible and covert or overt military means when these were deemed necessary. (On this point, see Perkins 2004.) The U.S. "imperium" is in effect an elaborate set of mechanisms seeking to control the world economy, in partnership with the other industrialized countries, which "share with American corporations the raw material, commodity, labor, and capital markets of the third world" (Gross 1980, 35–36).

The myriad "channels of influence" wielded by the United States include local subsidiaries of multinational corporations; foreign military bases; the Central Intelligence Agency (CIA) and a myriad of other intelligence agencies; the United States Agency for International Development (USAID), which provides economic and military aid and technical assistance; embassies and consulates; local armed forces trained and equipped by the United States; subordinate governments that do its bidding; transnational regional agencies such as the North Atlantic Treaty Organization (NATO); and the agencies of the United Nations, including the World Bank, the International Monetary Fund (IMF), and the World Trade Organization. Most recently, the National Endowment for Democracy, USAID, and other U.S. government agencies have engaged in "democracy building," openly intervening in national government elections in central and eastern Europe and elsewhere, to assure that these indigenous electoral events turn out in a way that favors U.S. interests.[5]

The American empire, then, is primarily based on economic and military hegemony.[6] What I will focus on in this chapter in particular is how, in the pursuit of U.S. foreign and domestic policy goals, American leaders lean heavily on a concept of democracy linked to the free market and opposed to various axes of evil that collectively either (1) reject free-market capitalism, as in Cuba and North Korea, or (2) represent centers of Islamic political aspirations, such as Iran, Syria, Hezbollah in Lebanon, or Hamas in Palestine. According to this reasoning, both of these categories of nations and subnational actors need to be swept into the orbit of "market democracy."

CONSTITUENTS OF THE GLOBAL WAR ON TERROR

What are the constituents of this so-called war on terrorism?[7] First are the actual military operations, including the invasion of Afghanistan in October 2001 and the invasion and occupation of Iraq in March 2003 (with the further threat of military actions in Iran and Syria). We could add to this, most recently, the U.S. air strikes in Somalia (January 2007) and Pakistan (ongoing), and tacit support by the United States for the Israeli invasions of Lebanon (July 2006) and of Gaza (January 2009).

Accompanying these military operations has been an expansion of the already vast network of U.S. bases. U.S. installations now extend to the borders of China. The United States has linked its Middle East and Persian Gulf locations, complete with an "archipelago of military bases" in the Gulf, the Indian Ocean, and points west, with "a new necklace of bases encircling Iraq, Afghanistan, and Central Asia" (Dreyfuss 2005, 246).[8] In addition, in 2007 the Bush administration announced the creation of a new Pentagon command for the entire continent of Africa, named AFRICOM (see Muwakkil 2007).

A second component of the war on terror is a concerted attack on civil liberties. From the passage of the PATRIOT Act, signed into law on October 26, 2001, and reauthorized on March 9, 2006, to the Military Commissions Act (passed in 2006), which eliminated the right of habeas corpus for "enemy combatants," the U.S. government has used the war on terror as a means to roll back constitutional rights. This has entailed not just overt restrictions, but also claims to an enormous expansion of federal power, including the right to wiretap and carry out surveillance of U.S. citizens and to detain and deport immigrants.[9] The war on terror has become an excuse for an enormous expansion of executive powers, which uses the rationale of the pursuit of "terrorists," enemy aliens, and U.S. citizens accused of aiding and abetting this new enemy.

Third, there has been an ideological conflation of terrorists with "illegal" immigrants, particularly in response to the rise of immigrants' rights activism bursting into public visibility during 2006 and 2007. In a revival of xenophobia, an explosion of deportations was aimed, initially after 9/11, at South Asian Muslim residents, thousands of whom suffered arbitrary and often secret deportations. More recently, an ideological campaign against "illegal" immigrant workers, including the agenda of sealing off the Mexican border, has been folded into the war on terror.

Raids on companies using immigrant labor and the deportations of immigrant workers have become high-profile examples of the work of the Immigration and Customs Enforcement (ICE) branch of the Department of Homeland Security.[10] For example, the raids against the Swift meatpacking plants, carried out simultaneously in Greeley, Colorado, and five other factories in Texas, Iowa, Nebraska, Utah, and Minnesota on December 12, 2006, were aimed allegedly at workers with stolen identities. Representatives of ICE arrived at the plants in riot gear, rounding up parents and driving them off in buses to faraway detention centers, leaving children at school with nowhere to go and no one to take them home. The parent company of Swift itself was apparently not at all penalized in this operation. This sweep was defended by the head of Homeland Security, Michael Chertoff, as a way of finding terrorists, and, more specifically, as a way of finding people with stolen identity documents. But as union leaders pointed out, this was obviously a means of keeping undocumented immigrant workers in a state of fear (see Cooper 2007). Similar raids have been carried out regularly in subsequent years.

A fourth element of the war on terrorism has been a conflation of activism with terrorism. The worldwide antiglobalization movement had reached a peak in the months prior to September 11, 2001, most notably with the convening of a UN conference against racism in Durban, South Africa, in August–September, 2001; there activists "placed the fight against racism, xenophobia and other related intolerances at the center of [the] antiglobalization critique" (Beal 2001). With the launching of the global war on terror, antiglobalization as well as antiwar, animal rights, death-penalty-opposing, and other categories of activists risked being identified as dangerous terrorists.[11]

The final element, and my major focus here, is the use of *Islamophobia*, a term that has sufficient currency to have its own entry in Wikipedia: "Islamophobia refers to the fear and/or hatred of Islam, Muslims, or Islamic culture. Islamophobia can be characterized by the belief that all or most Muslims are religious fanatics, have violent tendencies toward non-Muslims, and reject ... equality, tolerance, and democracy" (cited in Ralph 2006, 282–283). Despite efforts by President Bush and many of his spokespeople to disavow a general animus toward Islam and/or toward people of Muslim faith, the rhetoric of the Bush administration's war on terror was filled with "Islamophobic assertions" (Ralph 2006, 283).

The spread of Islamophobia is bolstered by a "clash-of-civilizations" ideology, first developed by Bernard Lewis in the 1950s and elaborated upon by Samuel Huntington in the 1990s.[12] A debate on citizenship, which has been developed in the media and through statements by government spokesmen both in the United States and in Europe, has been framed by Huntington's thesis, which specifies that there is a fundamental conflict of civilizations between the West and Islam. His claim is that countries in the West that "fail to control immigration and/or preserve civilisational coherence and homogeneity" are deeply threatened (Fekete 2006, 8).

As Liz Fekete points out, "Within days of the New York and Washington attacks of September 11, key players on the Right were popularising Huntington's themes by establishing a binary between western, European, Enlightenment values (based on the Judaeo-Christian tradition) and those of the 'other' (i.e., Islam)" (Fekete 2006, 8). European leaders such as Silvio Berlusconi, prime minister of Italy, and Pia Kjaersgaard, a Danish parliamentarian, spoke publicly on the need to preserve the integrity and superiority of Western civilization. Pope Benedict XVI himself created a media firestorm around the world in September 2006 with his claim that Islamic culture is intrinsically violence-prone. "If radical Islam posed a threat abroad, Muslim communities within western countries also needed to be strictly monitored. 'Islam is the biggest threat to world peace since the fall of Communism,' commented the DFP's Kristian Thulesen Dahl, comparing it to the cuckoo in the nest. 'It is eating us [from within] and destabilizing [our societies]'" (Fekete 2006, 9; brackets in original; the DFP is the Danish People's Party, located on the far right).[13]

FEMINISM AS A CONSTITUENT ELEMENT OF THE GLOBAL WAR ON TERROR

I propose to add feminism to the constituent elements of the war on terror. Indeed, if we define the word to mean the image of women's rights and women's freedoms that is being projected as part of the virtues of U.S. and European "civilization," mainstream feminism is essential to this war. It is particularly useful for the purposes of Islamophobia that Islamic societies, in general, be perceived and portrayed as uniquely oppressive to women.

What could be more convenient than the hostility toward women's rights of extreme Islamist tendencies, such as the versions of Wahhabi Islam cultivated by the Saudi regime and practiced by the Taliban in Afghanistan?[14] Never mind that the modern international movement of political Islam is largely the product of Western funding and encouragement, intended as a weapon against secular and Left nationalist regimes and movements. (For this history, see Amin 2001; Dreyfuss 2005.) Now that Muslim extremism had become the international target of the war on terrorism, the rights of women, linked inextricably to modern industrial capitalism, were a made-to-order part of the propaganda machine of the Bush administration.

It goes without saying that the Bush administration's embrace of women's rights as part of the justification for the war in Afghanistan and the occupation of Iraq was beyond cynical. As detailed earlier, the Bush administration was demonstrably hostile to the wide range of major women's issues and used a series of anti–women's rights positions—from rolling back abortion rights to opposing gay marriage; from restoring the global gag order on abortion counseling to supporting abstinence in lieu of condoms to prevent the spread of HIV/AIDS—as a means of keeping its base in the fundamentalist Christian Right. Laura Bush herself was presented as an emblem of traditional womanhood, implicitly countering the feminist First Lady stance of her predecessor, Hillary Clinton. But this does not mean that the Bush administration was not prepared to use women's rights as part of its international propaganda.[15] It is in this context that the ideology and the activism of the women's movement became useful to the U.S. imperial project.

Ironically, the very success of the women's movement in the United States was now being used by the very people who fought against it to sell capitalism around the world. If terrorism was the overriding threat, and if Islamic fundamentalism was the core of the terrorist network, and if the suppression of women was crucial to Islamic fundamentalism, then logically the emancipation of women became a keystone of the U.S. ideological framework for the war on terror.

The liberation of women was self-evidently part of the project of modernization and democratization claimed by the Bush administration as it brutally reshaped the landscape of Afghanistan and Iraq. The conventional wisdom linked democracy, the free market, and the emancipation of women. Indeed, the equation was that "modern" equaled women's rights, the Judeo-Christian heritage, and democracy, whereas "traditional" equaled patriarchal suppression of women's rights, the Islamic heritage, and terrorism. From the point of view of the official war on terror, the terrorists were those who are at war with the "free world" of modernity, industrialism, democracy, that is, with capitalism. This paradigm incorporates women as part of modernity and freedom. In contrast, the Islamic world is denominated by its very nature as a part of nonmodernity and therefore as part of the terrorist threat. This rhetoric deftly folds feminism into modernity and assimilates terrorism to patriarchy. For the women of the world, then, there is a clear path: be modern, be democratic, and escape the clutches of patriarchal terrorists.

The rights of women were given center stage in the Bush administration's war on terrorism. The war in Afghanistan was justified in part as an effort to save Afghani women from the Taliban, and both Laura Bush and Cherie Blair (British prime minister Tony Blair's wife) made this explicit in public statements: "Following the invasion of Afghanistan, Laura Bush was paraded before the UN Commission on the Status of Women on International Women's Day 2002, to celebrate the U.S. attack as a new chapter of 'rebuilding' Afghani women's lives'" (Chew 2005a, 2). The president himself claimed credit for liberating millions of women as the result of the U.S.-initiated wars in Afghanistan and Iraq. Thus, speaking in 2004 with Laura Bush and other highly ranked administration women by his side, he boasted about his achievement in "advancing human rights for women": "'Just think about it,' Bush said at the White House in a speech marking the close of International Women's Week. 'More than 50 million men, women, and children have been liberated from two of the most brutal tyrannies on earth—50 million people are free. And for 25 million women and girls, liberation has a special significance. Some of these girls are attending school for the first time. Some of the women are preparing to vote in free elections for the very first time'" (quoted in Finley 2006, 89).

The media accepted this set of ideas and illustrated it in their news coverage, treating these assumptions about modernity and tradition as legitimate news items. Thus, in Afghanistan in December 2003 a dispute over the representation of women in the leadership of the constitutional convention was interpreted by the *New York Times* reporter as a self-evident struggle between the ancient and the modern. According to this account, the chairman, Sebaghatullah Mojadeddi, told the women not to put themselves on a level with men. "Even God has not given you equal rights ... because under his decision two women are counted as equal to one man" (quoted in Waldman 2003). In saying this, the reporter commented, the chairman "managed to expose the tensions that underlay not just this assembly but also this nation, over the role of women and the role of Islam, the fealty to tradition and the push for modernity" (Waldman 2003).

The same direction is evident in the attempt to reconstruct the Middle East by the neoconservative cabal around President Bush, starting with the invasion and occupation of Iraq in 2003. Indeed, Vice President Dick Cheney's daughter, Liz, was tasked in the State Department with a project called the Middle East Partnership Initiative, with a brief to "modernize" the Middle East by, among other things, encouraging the full participation of women in public life (Bumiller 2003).

The U.S. State Department showed its concern for Iraqi women by organizing an "Iraqi women's democracy initiative," allocating $10 million to train women for participating in the election of January 2005. Some of this money was awarded to the Independent Women's Forum, a notoriously right-wing antifeminist organization founded in 1991 by Cheney's wife, Lynne, Labor secretary Elaine Chao, and the right-wing editor of *National Review*, Kate O'Beirne. This group opposes paid maternity leave, government-provided child care, equal pay for equal work, "quotas" for women in government service (that is, affirmative action), and the Violence Against Women Act! (see Chew 2005a, 7).

As Haifa Zangana writes:

There has been no shortage of initiatives to "enlighten" Iraqi women and encourage them to play an active role in the country's reconstruction. In one, the Department for International Development and the Foreign Office declared "the need, urgently, for a women's tent meeting in Baghdad with a declaration in compliance with [U.N. Resolution] 1325." Condoleezza Rice opened a center for women's human rights in Diwanya. In her opening speech—delivered via satellite—she assured Iraq women that "we are with you in spirit." ... Meanwhile in Diwanya itself, local farmers (many of them women) were unable to start the winter season because of unexploded cluster bombs on their land. (quoted in Chew 2005a, 7)[16]

In reality, the occupation of Iraq and the policies followed by U.S. authorities since the invasion have given rise to a situation of extreme danger and vulnerability for women. The U.S. decision to support Iraq's Shiite Islamists has led to a rollback of women's legal rights in the constitutional provisions that return authority over family law to clerics, with the United States trading "women's rights for cooperation from Islamist political parties" (Susskind 2007, 5). At the same time, the U.S. use of the "Salvador" option, giving material support for armed militias, which have mobilized against the Sunni-led resistance and which have official standing with the Interior Ministry, has helped to create a situation where the militias are "using gender-based violence to impose a theocracy" (Susskind 2007, 12).

The consequent rise in attacks on women, including rapes, forced prostitution, and murders, places Iraqi women "squarely within the paradigm of feminicide," that is, "the sum total of various forms of gender-based violence against women, characterized by impunity for perpetrators and a lack of justice processes for victims.... Feminicide occurs in conditions of social upheaval, armed conflict, violence between powerful rival criminal gangs and militias, rapid economic transformation, and the demise of traditional forms of state power. All of these conditions apply to Iraq" (Susskind 2007, 13).

Increasingly, too, feminists as well as feminist ideas are being used as a weapon against Islam and Islamic communities. In Europe, attacks against immigrant communities are being ideologically supported by claims that these communities are a threat to the values of European civilization. A new coalition of right-wing forces is using the war on terror to revive anti-immigration policies, exploiting fears of "backward" Islamic practices to bar immigration under the rubric of "family reunion." These forces are explicitly enlisting feminist ideology, portraying Europe as the home of sexual freedom and women's self-determination.

In a development that she terms *cultural fundamentalism*, Liz Fekete (2006) shows that European right-wing parties that are making use of the war on terror to push an anti-immigrant agenda are pulling in feminist arguments and feminist spokespersons to advance their ideas. A focus on the perceived crimes of Islamic communities—from "honor killings" to forced marriages to the wearing of the hijab—allows these parties to argue that, due to irreconcilable cultural differences, the assimilation of Islamic immigrant neighbors by Europeans is nearly impossible.[17]

The cultural fundamentalists are those who hold that the integrity of European civilization rests on its Enlightenment values: individual autonomy, equality, and freedom. In some countries, this is taking the form of an attack on ideas of multiculturalism. For example, the German feminist Alice Schwarzer, a TV personality who founded the feminist journal *Emma*, has stated that multiculturalism is a threat to these Enlightenment values. She argues for the banning of the hijab for Islamic schoolgirls, and she scolds other Germans for a failure to value their own heritage. As Fekete writes, "An assimilationist, monocultural society needs its feminist cheerleaders" (Fekete 2006, 15).

Similarly, in France the 2003 legislation that banned the wearing of the hijab in state schools (along with other conspicuous religious symbols, including the Sikh turban and the Christian crucifix) was justified by an appeal to women's emancipation: "An open letter addressed to president Chirac, signed by dozens of prominent women, appeared in the glossy magazine *Elle*, expressing support for the ban on the grounds that the 'Islamic veil sends us all—Muslims and non-Muslims alike—back to a discrimination against women that is intolerable'" (Fekete 2006, 17). In 2008, France took this one step further by denying citizenship to a Moroccan woman, Faiza Silmi, a legal immigrant, on the basis of her refusal to stop following her religious practices as a Muslim, including wearing a *niqab*, an Islamic robe that includes a facial veil. Silmi pointed out that she wore the *niqab*, not because her husband told her to, but because it was her choice. "Yes, I am a practicing Muslim, I am orthodox. But is that not my right?" But the French Council of State noted, in upholding a ruling against the woman, that she had "adopted a radical practice of her religion, incompatible with essential values of the French community, particularly the principle of equality of the sexes" (quoted in Bennhold 2008).

Some American academic feminists have been even more outspoken, supporting all aspects of the war on terror. Thus, Jean Bethke Elshtain, a noted feminist political scientist, defends American policies since 9/11 unflinchingly. Drawing on the tradition of the "just war," elaborated first by St. Augustine, in *The City of God*, then by medieval thinkers, down through the ages to Hugo Grotius and then Carl von Clausewitz, she includes both the illegal invasion of Afghanistan and the equally illegal invasion and occupation of Iraq in this category (Elshtain 2004).[18] I will come back to the role of U.S. feminist academics later in this chapter.

FEMINISM IN THE SERVICE OF EMPIRE: PRECEDENTS IN EARLIER CENTURIES

These stances by mainstream feminists represent a revival of "imperial feminism" (see Sudbury, 2000; Chew 2005a, 2005b). Feminism in the service of empire is not a new phenomenon. Part of the arsenal of the European colonial regimes in the nineteenth and early twentieth centuries was the use of "colonial feminism"

(Ahmed 1992). This was a doctrine devised to bolster the narrative of the legitimacy of domination by colonial regimes, the "White Man's burden" of Rudyard Kipling's poetry. Such a narrative was tailored to fit the individual cultures being ruled, showing how the gender arrangements of the targeted population demonstrated its cultural inferiority to the colonizing powers.

The concern with the gender arrangements of colonized cultures goes back to the earliest years of European expansion. European colonial powers sought, and in many cases succeeded, in transforming the gender arrangements of precolonial societies. Contrary to the traditional findings of male anthropologists, who "found" male dominance to be nearly universal throughout the premodern world, feminist anthropologists have uncovered the existence of many alternative gender arrangements. These studies "illustrate the reality of female-male complementarity" in many premodern cultures, and "document the clash between this egalitarian principle and the hierarchical organization that European colonization brought about in many parts of the world" (Etienne and Leacock 1980a, 10).

The agents of colonization—Jesuit and other Christian missionaries, soldiers, and colonial administrators—understood that the gender arrangements they encountered had to be restructured. In the case of missionaries, this was both a prerequisite to, and a mechanism for, the conversion of "native" peoples to Christianity. "The seventeenth-century Jesuits recognized that if they were to achieve their goal of converting the native Canadians, they had to deal directly with women's independence, and they explained the resulting problems in their reports to their superiors" (Etienne and Leacock 1980a, 10).

The process of establishing colonial control varied with the social structures of the peoples to be colonized. These ranged from egalitarian cultures where the roles of men and women were complementary, to stratified cultures where the beginnings of state formation had already established patriarchal and hierarchical social structures (as, for example, with the Aztecs; see Nash 1980). But whatever the preexisting culture, along with the economic transformation wrought by colonial powers came a profound change in the status of women, generally in the direction of their losing economic, cultural, and political power (see Etienne and Leacock 1980b).

Leila Ahmed's classic study on women and Islam points out that, in the case of Islam, nineteenth-century British and French colonizers could draw on "a rich vein of bigotry and misinformation." In fact, "the peculiar practices of Islam with respect to women had always formed part of the Western narrative of the quintessential otherness and inferiority of Islam, going back as far as the Crusades" (Ahmed 1992, 149, 151). Ahmed shows the uses of colonial feminism, particularly in the case of Lord Cromer (Evelyn Baring), the British banking scion and consul-general in Egypt in the late nineteenth century.[19] Even as he remained a leading figure in the antisuffrage movement at home, supporting Victorian ideas of women's proper place, Cromer launched an ideological attack on the treatment of women in Egyptian (that is, Ottoman) customs as a way of discrediting local culture:

> [That] the Victorian colonial paternalistic establishment appropriated the language of feminism in the service of its assault on the religions and cultures of Other men, and in particular on Islam, in order to give an aura of moral justification to that assault at the very same time as it combated feminism within its own society ... can easily be substantiated by reference to the conduct and rhetoric of the colonizers. The activities of Lord Cromer are particularly illuminating on the subject, perfectly exemplifying how, when it came to the cultures of other men, white supremacist views, androcentric and paternalistic convictions, and feminism came together in harmonious and entirely logical accord in the service of the imperial idea. (Ahmed 1992, 152)

Cromer believed in a doctrine of inferiority of the "Oriental," which inferiority could be traced primarily to the treatment of women: "It was essential to change the position of women in Islam, for it was Islam's degradation of women, expressed in the practices of veiling and seclusion, that was 'the fatal obstacle' to the Egyptian's 'attainment of that elevation of thought and character which should accompany the introduction of Western civilization'" (Cromer quoted in Ahmed 1992, 153). Colonial feminism drew on contemporary anthropology to demonstrate the inferiority of the native peoples. Both missionaries and feminists at this time acted as handmaidens of colonialism, using women's subordinated role within Islam as a point of attack to condemn the entire culture (Ahmed 1992, 151–155).

In light of the contemporary attacks in Europe on the use of the hijab, it is worth tracking Ahmed's account of how this battle of the veil originally played out in the early twentieth century. In that earlier era of globalization, for modernizing leaders in Egypt, Iran, and Turkey, the attack by Western powers on the position of women under Islam, and most symbolically, the wearing of the hijab, or "veil," convinced them that this practice must be abolished. For these countries to enter the modern capitalist world, they needed to emulate the West and abolish what seemed backward practices. But this acceptance of dress reform by modernizing national leaders produced a strong domestic backlash. In Ahmed's language, the result was a "counternarrative." If the "civilizing" West pointed to the veil as the symbol of women's oppression and of Muslim cultural inferiority, then, in response, some of the defenders of Islam became apologists for the veil.

This split over whether to embrace European culture or to fight it was deeply related to class issues. An economic transformation was expanding Egyptian cotton production, using modernized agricultural techniques, while forcing the acceptance of European products to the detriment of local production. Those who benefited from these changes, the elite and the new middle class, embraced both the new political economy of colonialism and the European culture that came with it. In sharp contrast, the peasants who were being driven off their land resented and opposed both.

The new "feminist" writings by modernizing leaders in the Middle East represented the interests of those who, like Kamal Ataturk of Turkey, Reza Shah of Iran, and the writer Qassim Amin, Egypt's so-called first feminist, saw their fate as tied to the colonizing West. These leaders wanted to refute the idea that they were uncivilized. They reacted to the critique of the veil by calling for unveiling as a way of repudiating the perceived weaknesses of Muslim culture. Others defended Islam, but then in a mirror image defended the veil uncritically (Ahmed 1992, 165–168). Thus, one either echoed the Western narrative or one resisted it. But in this debate, both sides essentially accepted the premise that women's customs were a stand-in for the entire culture.

Why did leaders such as Ataturk, Reza Shah, and Egyptian writer Qassim Amin accept this equation? According to Ahmed, this was the logical corollary of the perception by nationalist modernizers that there was an intrinsic connection between women's relative emancipation in the West and the power of Western science, technology, and industrialism. Like their counterparts in Japan and China, Egyptian and Turkish leaders in the early twentieth century perceived the need to acquire Western technology. But in the Islamic case, along with Western technological capacities, they also embraced a version of feminism to go along with modernization.

Opponents of the Europeanization process rejected this view. If women's veiling and subordination were isolated as the key to national inferiority, then in defense these writers took up the opposite position. The veil and the seclusion of women were embraced as indeed intrinsic to Islam, which they posed as a counterweight to modernization. This stance contains the roots of modern Islamic fundamentalism, and of course ignores many other strains of Islamic thought and practice that honor women's rights, as modern Islamic feminists have been pointing out. (On this point, see section "The Space for Muslim Women, Feminist and Otherwise" later in this chapter.)

If we now fast-forward to the twenty-first century, we see this battle of the veil being reenacted, beginning with the events of the Iranian Revolution of 1979 (see Sedghi 2007), and the imposition of the burqa under the Taliban regime in Afghanistan. After the overthrow of the shah of Iran, a key U.S. ally, the forces of Ayatollah Khomeini instituted an openly Islamist government. The Iranian Revolution initially had the support of the Left, as the shah's brutal regime had created a broad-based opposition. But as the Islamic forces within the regime strengthened themselves, a repressive period began in which the rights of women were severely curtailed. "The Iranian Revolution introduced a new political development on the world scene: here was an Islamist regime that was not only Islamist and anticommunist but at the same time fervently nationalist, determined to act independently of all foreign influences, particularly the United States" (Mamdani 2004, 122). When the United States allowed the deposed shah into New York for medical treatment, Khomeini characterized the United States as "the Great Satan," and three thousand students stormed the U.S. Embassy in Tehran, taking ninety hostages. The hostage struggle, which lasted for 444 days, was the cover under which Khomeini's forces strengthened their hold on Iranian society. During this crisis, they imprisoned and executed thousands of opponents of the regime and strictly limited the opportunities for women to work outside the home or, indeed, to appear in public without a full black covering known as a chador (see Mamdani 2004, 121–122). With Islamic Iran now an official enemy of the United States (which proceeded to arm Iraq and encourage its eight-year war against Iran), the chador became a central element in the identification of the Iranian Islamic regime as antiwoman.

Similarly, in Afghanistan the rise of the Taliban, which was a law-and-order movement arising in reaction to the chaos and depredations of the warlords, who had successfully ended the Soviet occupation of their country and then began fighting among themselves, represented another Islamist regime with draconian provisions for women. The forced wearing of the burqa became a cause célèbre among U.S. feminists, with the Feminist Majority under the leadership of Eleanor Smeal establishing the Campaign to Stop Gender Apartheid, which raised thousands of dollars seeking to dissuade President Bill Clinton from his support for the regime. (See "Mavis Leno to Chair" 1998. On the antiburqa campaign, and its ethnocentrism, see Tripp 2006, 304–305, who points out that "starvation, war, militarization, and lack of security loomed as much larger problems in the eyes of women in Afghanistan at the time.")

The Iranian Revolution and the takeover by the Taliban revived the equation in the minds of Westerners between Islamist fundamentalism and the repression of women's rights, symbolized by the "veil." The burqa and the chador came to represent the suppression of women's rights, and this laid the groundwork for the equation of women's rights with capitalist democracy, once the global war on terror was launched.

IMPERIAL FEMINISM: THE CASE OF YUGOSLAVIA

In the context of the global war on terror, I am arguing that, as in the nineteenth and early twentieth centuries, contemporary feminism is once again being enlisted in the service of imperialism. Dolores E. Janiewski observes that U.S. white feminist scholars have by and large avoided confronting the United States as an empire, and the role of U.S. feminism within it (see Janiewski 2001).[20] Why is this the case? Whereas British black feminists raised the issue of "imperial feminism" as early as the 1980s,[21] U.S. feminists have generally stayed more innocent, with the exception of African American writers such as Hazel Carby and Third World feminist scholars such as Chandra Mohanty and Jacqui Alexander.

It might be more accurate to say that one can divide women's studies scholars based in the United States into two groups. One group writes from the premise that the United States is a democracy and that mainstream feminist activism simply seeks to extend this democracy to women around the world. In this category are writers such as Martha Nussbaum and Jean Bethke Elshtain. Thus, Nussbaum argues for foreign intervention by the United States to defend women's rights, saying, for example, that "the complete exclusion of women from political processes would provide a moral case for economic sanctions or some other form of coercion" (Nussbaum 2006, 260). The second group, in contrast, consists of those who, like Alexander, Carby, Mohanty, and Zillah R. Eisenstein, seek to understand U.S. mainstream feminism as part and parcel of U.S. global hegemony (Alexander and Mohanty 1997a; Carby 1987; Eisenstein 2007).

The war on terror is not the first instance where mainstream feminism became useful to U.S. foreign policy. This is a complicated issue. There is no doubt that the intense research and activism by feminist legal scholars and their allies to promote the cause of women's rights as human rights have transformed the international legal landscape. The official acknowledgment of such crimes against humanity as rape during war are no doubt major advances for the world community. But invariably some of this work runs parallel to stated goals of U.S. foreign policy. For example, the State Department regularly rates countries on their human rights records, although human rights in this context strictly refer to political, rather than economic or social, rights. It is beyond the scope of this book to trace the history of this entry of women's rights into the international discussion of human rights since World War II. (On the legal and political campaigns to establish women's rights as human rights, see Agosin 2001; Bunch and Reilly 1994; Cook 1994.) But in the context of U.S. foreign policy, it is crucial to recognize that women's rights have been incorporated into the arsenal of "humanitarian imperialism" (Bricmont 2006).

To illustrate this point, let me focus on the series of wars that resulted in the dismantling of the state of Yugoslavia into its component parts.[22] The dominant view in the United States is that we intervened in Yugoslavia to prevent a humanitarian catastrophe and to curb the dangerous violence of the Serbian leader Slobodan Milosevic. After a failed peace meeting at Rambouillet, France, in February 1999, the United States was forced to conduct a brutal air war under the auspices of NATO from March 24 to June 10, 1999. I will argue here for an alternative interpretation: namely, that the war in Yugoslavia was part of an American and European effort to dismantle the mixed economy there, which after the fall of the Soviet Union and its eastern European allies represented the only remaining bastion of quasi-socialist state-directed national development in Europe; the war was also for the purpose of gaining access to the natural resources of the Balkans (see Chossudovsky 1996, 243ff.; Gervasi 1996; Johnstone 2002; Parenti 2000).

The story of the breakup of Yugoslavia as a multiethnic federation into a group of states seeking to be defined by ethnicity is extremely complex, involving both the machinations of nationalist leaders within the states of the former federation, and those of foreign powers, including Germany, England, and the United States, among others, with their own interests in the conflict. After the death of longtime leader Josip Broz Tito in May 1980, and after being subjected to the process of structural adjustment by the International Monetary Fund, Yugoslavia over a period of ten years went from a united, prosperous multiethnic federation with free medical care and high life expectancy to a state with massive unemployment and high inflation (see Lucas 2005). This was followed by chaos, multiple civil wars, and extreme cases of ethnic cleansing, as the multiethnic composition of the states, especially Bosnia-Herzegovina, was transformed through warfare into enclaves separating the formerly integrated populations of Muslims, Catholics, and other religious and ethnic groups. (For a detailed account, see Woodward 1995.)

The Balkan civil wars began with the secession of Croatia and Slovenia from the Yugoslav federation in 1991; this triggered the outbreak of war, as national troops from the Yugoslav army resisted these breakaways with force. The wars concluded with the dismantling of Yugoslavia after a period of bloody internal conflicts. During this period, the United States intervened using CIA personnel and retired U.S. military officers under contract to the Pentagon to support the breakaway governments of Aleja Izetbegovic in Bosnia-Herzegovina and Franjo Tudjman in Croatia. The United States also actively supported the Kosovo Liberation Army, an Albanian group deeply involved in drug smuggling, in its attempt to carve a separatist nation out of a former province of Serbia. The covert role of the United States, along with Germany, in supplying air power, ground forces, training, and even military uniforms was hidden from public view (see Gervasi, 1996, 5; Parenti 2000, 31).

Instead, another version of events was disseminated through an elaborate propaganda campaign propagated by journalists and underwritten by public relations firms. This effort painted the situation in Yugoslavia, not as a civil war led by a series of opportunistic neonationalist leaders with the encouragement of Western powers, but as a unique response to a vicious expansionist campaign by Serbian nationalists led by Slobodan Milosevic. To establish this view of the events in Yugoslavia, a process of delegitimizing the cause of Serbia, which was fighting to preserve Yugoslav national unity, was undertaken: "The Albanian secessionists in Kosovo or 'Kosovars,' the Croatian secessionists and the Bosnian Muslims hired an American public relations firm, Ruder Finn, to advance their causes by demonizing the Serbs. Ruder Finn deliberately targeted certain publics, notably the American Jewish community, with a campaign likening Serbs to

Nazis. Feminists were also clearly targeted by the Croatian nationalist campaign directed out of Zagreb to brand Serbs as rapists" (Johnstone 1998, 5).

This public relations campaign intended to bring the Jewish community on board by painting an analogy between the persecution of the Jews under the Nazis and the alleged persecution of Muslims in Bosnia by the Bosnian Serbs. Similarly, American feminists were targeted for indignation over the "mass rapes" (as they were characterized in the mainstream media) of Bosnian Muslim women by Serbian troops. In this way, both groups would be drawn into endorsing the U.S. and German position of supporting the breakaway states of Slovenia and Croatia, whose decision to pull out of the Yugoslav federation had precipitated the civil war.

The success of Ruder Finn Global Public Affairs in influencing U.S. public opinion was an open secret. James Harff, the Ruder Finn executive in charge of these Balkan contracts, publicly boasted to French television journalist Jacques Merlino that his greatest achievement in this operation was in transforming the reputation of Croats and Bosnian Muslims, whose heavy involvement in the persecution of the Jews in World War II might have tarnished their image, into worthy victims:

> In the first days of August 1992, the Long Island newspaper *Newsday* published reports from its Bonn correspondent Roy Gutman, based on interviews in Zagreb, telling of horrendous conditions in Serb-run internment camps in Bosnia. Seeing the potential impact of comparison with Nazi "death camps," Ruder Finn immediately contacted three major Jewish organizations, the B'nai B'rith Anti-Defamation League, the American Jewish Committee, and the American Jewish Congress, suggesting they publicly protest. They did. This launched the demonization of Serbs as the new Nazis. (Johnstone 2002, 66–70)

The accounts of mass rapes by Bosnian Serb soldiers became a major part of U.S. propaganda against Serbian president Slobodan Milosevic, formerly a strong U.S. ally and recipient of IMF funding when Yugoslavia was still an intact state.[23] Like most of the rest of the media, and many writers on the political Left, many feminist organizations accepted the view that it was Serb troops, and especially Bosnian Serbs, who were the major demonic figures in the several civil wars that raged in the Balkans from 1992 to the Dayton Peace Accords signed in 1995. The claims of systematic mass rape in rape camps became part of the reason to attribute blame for the Yugoslav civil war to aggression by Serbs, rather than to a struggle between breakaway states and a federal government seeking to maintain national unity.

There is no doubt that in the course of the conflicts, which mingled regular armies, militias, and street criminals being drawn into the violence, there was enormous carnage. In particular, in the patriarchal countryside where much of the fighting took place, with an aim of identifying people as outsiders in order to exclude them from their rights to land, "women became particularly vulnerable, regardless of age, because the culture of patriarchy viewed their sexual purity and shame as essential to the honor and unity of the family—to violate women is to destroy the family's ability to resist" (Woodward 1995, 239). As Diana Johnstone notes:

> No one denies that many rapes occurred during the civil wars in Croatia and Bosnia-Herzegovina, or that rape is a serious violation of human rights. So is war, for that matter. From the start, however, inquiry into rape in Bosnia-Herzegovina focused exclusively on accusation[s] that Serbs were raping Muslim women as part of a deliberate strategy. The most inflated figures, freely extrapolated by multiplying the number of known cases by large factors, were readily accepted by the media and international organizations. No interest was shown in detailed and documented reports of rapes of Serbian women by Muslims or Croats. (Johnson 1998, 13n12)

Investigations into the claims of mass rape were carried out by the journalist Nora Beloff:

> The late Nora Beloff, former chief political correspondent of the *London Observer*, described her own search for verification of the rape charges in a letter to the *Daily Telegraph* (January 19, 1993). The British Foreign Office conceded that the rape figures being bandied about were totally uncorroborated, and referred her to the Danish government, then chairing the European Union. Copenhagen agreed that the reports were unsubstantiated, but kept repeating them. Both said that the EU had taken up the "rape atrocity" issue at its December Edinburgh summit exclusively on the basis of a German initiative. In turn, Fran Wild, in charge of the Bosnian Desk in the German Foreign Ministry, told Ms. Beloff that the material on Serb rapes came partly from the Izetbegovic government and partly from the Catholic charity Caritas in Croatia. No effort had been made to seek corroboration from more impartial sources. Despite the absence of solid and comprehensive information, a cottage industry has since developed around the theme. (Johnstone 1998, 13–14n12)

To make the conflict in Yugoslavia understandable, the media emphasized the role of ancient ethnic tensions and cultural incompatibilities, rather than the role of the Western powers in the dismantling of the former Balkan state. Some feminist scholars elaborated on this theme (see, for example, Boose 2002). In this literature women's rights were encapsulated within a U.S. foreign policy framework, with no critical inquiry into the good faith of the U.S. government as a champion of feminism. Some U.S. academic feminists (along with substantial portions of the U.S. Left, to be sure) had no hesitation in accepting at face value the need for humanitarian intervention in Yugoslavia and elsewhere. And others readily accepted the U.S. version of why and how these events occurred.[24]

Even writers who acknowledged the need to locate feminist inquiry within the context of U.S. militarism and imperialism fell into this trap. Thus, Cynthia Enloe discussed the Bosnian rapes (for which estimates vary widely, from three thousand to thirty thousand; see Enloe 2004, 117) as evidence for the view that the Balkans crisis represented an upsurge of ancient, tribal enmities, rather than a calculated set of interventions by interested Western powers. She presented the case of one convicted Bosnian Serb rapist in an analysis advancing the notion that "the warrior is a central element in the modern cultural construction of the Serbian ideal of masculinity" (Enloe 2004, 107).

Feminist activists within the former parts of Yugoslavia who were seeking to heal the wounds of war, and to offer support for rape victims and refugee women regardless of nationality, tried to counter attempts by some external feminist individuals and groups from the United States, Germany, and elsewhere to express their outrage over particular forms of ethnic violence toward women.

> Even though they were well aware that Bosnians had been most victimized by rape . . . local feminists regarded the mixing of ethnic and gender representation through symbols and images as inflaming hostilities and generating even greater violence. They had seen how claims of rape had been exaggerated and manipulated by all sides to provoke conflict in this region. The symbolic metanarratives about ethnicity and the victimization of women as symbolic of a disgraced people were being used to incite people to fight and to inspire even greater violence. . . . Many Yugoslav women activists from all ethnic groups were especially concerned because all the governments involved in these wars manipulated and politicized rape and inflated the numbers of victims. (Tripp 2006, 301)

But more broadly, an interpretation of the Yugoslav civil wars as primarily caused by presumed ancient tribal and ethnic rivalries obscures the role of the United States, and other Western powers, in helping to foment these bitter conflicts, during which horrific atrocities, including rapes, were committed on all sides.

THE FOCUS OF RELIGIOUS FUNDAMENTALISM ON WOMEN'S PLACE

In analyzing the rise of a new form of imperial feminism, I am not defending religious fundamentalisms. But I think we need to ask why religious fundamentalist ideologies place women at the center of their worldview. One answer is suggested by the late activist and writer Bina Srinivasan, using the case of the Hindu fundamentalist party and movement the Bharatiya Janata Party, which was in power in India under Prime Minister Atal Bihari Vajpayee from 1998 to 2004. [25] Srinivasan traced the rise of Hindu fundamentalism in India to the long-term impact of colonization and the more recent impact of modernization.

The outcome of these processes, she argued, was the disruption and breakup of the "economic, social, and cultural fabric of communities and the individuals within them." For example, she pointed to the impact of development projects such as major dams in India, which created massive dislocations and disruptions that extended down to the level of individual and community identity. These "multiple mutations ... affected the cohesion of communities, their very basic organization" (Srinivasan 2004, 136).

Religious fundamentalism is "one of the forces that steps in to restore a cohesion that has been thrown into disarray." Seeking to create a "new hegemonic order," fundamentalism "invokes mythical memories of a perfect age where religious principles were followed to the book and all was well with the world. It relies on the constant creation of a set of enemies who were/are responsible for all that went wrong with this perfect world. Therefore the only way to rectify this situation is to eliminate the enemies one by one and at the same time to adhere to the religious principles it describes as the only correct ones" (Srinivasan 2004, 136–137). In the propaganda of the Hindu Right, its publications, speeches, and videos show "a concerted effort to invoke a Golden Age where Hinduism reigned supreme and Hindu principles were firmly in place, governing all of society. Women, in this mythical age, enjoyed a high status and were free from fear of rape. The situation deteriorated for a number of reasons, but chiefly because of the corruption of morality brought about by the increasing presence and takeover of political power by the 'enemies'" (Srinivasan 2004, 137).

The history used to evoke this Golden Age and how it has deteriorated is somewhat creative. It includes "the constant invocation of events like the plunder of Hindu temples by Moghul warlords and kings, and the heroic exploits of feudal lords like Shivaji, the Maratha king. The plunder of Hindu temples is likened to the plunder of Hindu women; especially remembered are the 'sacrifices' of Rajput women, who threw themselves into the funeral pyres rather than face death and rape at the hands of marauding Moghuls. From this point, it is yet another easy move that brings the Partition of the subcontinent [creating Pakistan as a separate Islamic state in 1947] into focus" (Srinivasan 2004, 137). All of these historical and in some cases mythical details are used to portray the Islamic communities within India and next door in Pakistan as the mortal enemies of Hindu life and, not so incidentally, of Hindu political legitimacy.

In order to shape the us versus them ideology that has been so effective in stimulating communal aggression of the kind carried out in the Indian state of Gujarat since February 2002, creating a "fear psychosis" that gave rise to the notorious massacres in that state, the incendiary propaganda produced by the Hindu Right focuses on women and sexuality: "Women are perceived to be the property of the community, of men, and therefore have to subscribe to the appropriate rules. Women are not seen as autonomous beings, which is why the issue of community 'honor' being tied up with women's bodies is so crucial"

(Srinivasan 2004, 139). In the case of the Hindu Right, patriarchy has been art-fully reshaped to legitimize the participation of women in the nationalist project: "While there is a 'looking back' to a golden age, there is a clever refashioning of the new roles expected of women.... Therefore women can legitimately attend training camps for 'self-defense,' participate in all public 'religious' processions ... and can represent communities to various state bodies if necessary" (Srinivasan 2004, 139). At the same time, women can also act as emissaries to neighborhoods and temples to carry the message to other women.

The case of Hindu fundamentalism, with its central focus on the restora-tion of women's proper place, is replicated in many other religious fundamentalist movements. What explains the centrality of women and gender arrangements in these social movements? As Valentine Moghadam notes, "In periods of rapid social change, gender assumes a paramount position in discourses and political programs." This is because, in response to "new values and ideas that are perceived to be threatening," fundamentalists turn to a concept of a "better or more moral past," with more traditional social roles: "As women are seen as the main trans-mitters of societal values, the changing role of women is associated with changes in values and behavior that are felt to be at odds with religious or moral beliefs. As a result, efforts are made to try to reimpose traditional behaviors for women as a remedy for crisis and destabilization" (Moghadam 2003, 152).

In the case of religious fundamentalisms, women's place is contested precisely because that place has been so deeply challenged and altered by the processes of modernization. We could argue that in this respect Hindu right-wing nationalist fundamentalism is not far from Christian Evangelical right-wing fundamentalism in the United States. For Hindu, Islamic, and Christian fundamentalists, there is a common effort to "restore" the place of women to a mythic Golden Age. If for Hin-dus this dates back to the centuries before Islamic influence in India, for Christians the nostalgia can date all the way back to the Garden of Eden. Among the victories of the Christian Right, as we saw in Chapter 2, was the defeat of the Equal Rights Amendment, equated in the rhetoric of the Radical Right with the defeat of femi-nism itself: "Phyllis Schlafly, a Roman Catholic leader whose 'Eagle Forum' often held joint events with the Moral Majority, chastised feminism as a 'disease,' the cause of the world's illness. Ever since Eve disobeyed God and sought her own liberation, she said, feminism had brought sin into the world and with it 'fear, sickness, pain, anger, hatred, danger, violence, and all varieties of ugliness'" (Mamdani 2004, 43).

THE SPACE FOR MUSLIM WOMEN, FEMINIST AND OTHERWISE

The targeting of Islamic fundamentalism has created a cottage industry of Mus-lim women seeking to show that they are in fact moderates. A spate of books has appeared arguing that Islam must be "reformed" to accommodate modern ideas about women's rights.[26] The media scour the landscape for indicators of enlightened Muslim women. Thus, for example, the story of the election of Canadian professor Ingrid Mattson as the first woman president of the Islamic Society of North America, "the largest umbrella organization for Muslim groups in the United States and Canada, [made] her a prominent voice for a faith ever more under assault by critics who paint it as the main font of terrorism.... To her supporters, Professor Mattson's selection comes as a significant breakthrough, a chance for North American Muslims to show that they are a diverse, enlightened community with real roots here—and not alien, sexist extremists bent on the destruction of Western civilization" (MacFarquhar 2006). Similarly, the enlistment of an Islamic woman in the U.S. Army is an occasion to show how U.S. institutions can remold even the most conservative Muslim woman into a leader of men: "Stomping her boots and swinging her bony arms, Radwa Hamdan led a column of troops through this bleak Texas base. Only six months earlier, she wore the head scarf of a pious Muslim woman and dropped her eyes in the presence of men. Now she was marching them to dinner" (Elliott 2006, 1).

Where does all of this leave Muslim women who wish to retain their faith but not be victimized as dangerous religious fanatics who foster terrorism? In this landscape, there is little or no space to offer alternative interpretations of Islam. There is no way to present the wearing of the hijab as an expression of faith, as a way of remaining modest, or as a matter of personal religious choice. As Lila Abu-Lughod points out, the veil marks the symbolic separation of men's and women's spheres as part of the association of women with family and home.

> Twenty years ago the anthropologist Hanna Papanek, ... who worked in Pakistan, described the burqa as "portable seclusion." She noted that many saw it as a liberating invention because it enabled women to move out of segregated living spaces while still observing the basic moral requirements of separating and protecting women from unrelated men. Ever since I came across her phrase "portable seclusion," I have thought of these enveloping robes as "mobile homes." Everywhere, such veiling signifies belonging to a particular community and participating in a moral way of life in which families are paramount in the organization of communities and the home is associated with the sanctity of women. (Abu-Lughod 2002, 785)

Abu-Lughod argues that the push by U.S. women to liberate Afghani women from their burqas fits into a long line of imperialist and colonialist use of women as a way to control and dominate. From the French in Algeria to the English in India, this is imperialist feminism. In contrast to the assumption of Western feminists that all women want the same things, Lughod asks: "Might other desires [besides western liberation] be more meaningful for different groups of people? Living in close families? Living in a godly way? Living without war?

I have done fieldwork in Egypt over more than 20 years and I cannot think of a single woman I know, from the poorest rural to the most educated cosmopolitan, who has ever expressed envy of U.S. women, women they tend to perceive as bereft of community, vulnerable to sexual violence and social anomie, driven by individual success rather than morality, or strangely disrespectful of God" (Abu-Lughod 2002, 788).

Similarly in Algeria, where a rise in Islamist fundamentalism has coexisted with a remarkable increase in women's workforce participation, women adopt the hijab as a form of protection against those who would object to the presence of women in the public sphere. "Sociologists and many working women say that by adopting religion and wearing the Islamic head covering called the hijab, women here have in effect freed themselves from moral judgments and restrictions imposed by men. Uncovered women are rarely seen on the street at night, but covered women can be seen strolling the city after attending the evening prayer at a mosque. 'They never criticize me, especially when they see I am wearing the hibjab,' said Denni Fatiha, 44, the first woman to drive a large city bus through the narrow, winding roads of Algiers" (Slackman 2007, 2).

In fact, the Muslim world has produced a wide variety of Islamic feminisms in recent decades. Just as feminists within Judaism, Roman Catholicism, and the many branches of Protestantism have created a range of possible positions for believing women who choose to remain within their faith, so, too, have Islamic women sought to carve out a position that improves the situation of women, while seeking to retain the religion that constitutes their emotional and ideological home base.

The debate over Islamic feminism, or feminism within the Islamic framework of belief, is now a global discussion. One way to think about this is to see Islamic feminists as seeking reform within the compass of their religious beliefs. This is an endeavor with serious real-world consequences in those regimes that espouse a Muslim ideology as part of their governing codes. In countries where the government is avowedly Islamic, rather than secular, family codes and other legal provisions can have a strong influence on the status of women. The impact of Islamic feminists within Iran, for example, has been considerable, creating improvements in the situation of working mothers and divorced women and increasing the number of women elected to parliament and to local councils (see Moghadam 2003, 193ff.; Sedghi 2007).

Of course, to have this political impact, these women have had to stay within the framework of their own political system, with its establishment of Islam as the official state religion, which gives enormous political authority to the religious leadership (as is also the case, we may note, in Israel). But in this respect, "Iran's Islamic feminists are not substantially different from liberal feminists, particularly those in the United States, who work within the existing political system and seek to improve women's positions through the discursive framework of liberal capitalism. . . . Both groups of feminists work within and maintain the legitimacy of their respective political systems" (Moghadam 2002, 1159). If the more traditional Islamic feminists in Iran do not challenge the fundamental principles of their government, neither do liberal feminists in the United States, who "have not called for economic and political transformation." Indeed, "one may suggest provocatively that those Islamic feminists who question the exclusive right of clerics and the *faqih* to interpret the Islamic texts and to define and implement Islamic jurisprudence are more subversive to the existing political system than are their U.S. liberal-feminist counterparts" (Mogaham 2002, 1159).[27]

Because the G-WOT has declared Islamic fundamentalism to be the mortal enemy of the West, people all over the world have been drawn into an argument over whether Islam as a religion does or does not oppress women, and/or whether Islam as a religion does or does not advocate violence. A whole literature has grown up starting from the premise that, unlike Christianity, Islam never underwent a reformation and therefore is somehow locked into a medieval style of orthodoxy that does not admit of questioning or of modernization. Mahmood Mamdani captures this search for acceptable Muslims in the title of his book, *Good Muslim, Bad Muslim*: "Democracy lags in the *Muslim* world, concludes a Freedom House study of political systems in the non-Western world. As if taking a cue from Bernard Lewis, Stephen Schwartz, director of the Islam and Democracy project for the Foundation for the Defense of Democracies, claims that the roots of terrorism really lie in a sectarian branch of Islam, the Wahhabi. Even the pages of the *New York Times* now include regular accounts distinguishing good from bad Muslims: good Muslims are modern, secular, and Westernized, but bad Muslims are doctrinal, antimodern, and virulent" (Mamdani 2004, 24).

Nicholas D. Kristof, a liberal columnist for the *New York Times*, similarly is "looking for Islam's Luthers" and finding Islamic feminists: "Islamic feminists often argue that the Koran generally raised the status of women compared to earlier Arabian society—banning female infanticide, for example, and limiting polygamy—and that what is needed today is that larger spirit of progress and enlightenment rather than precise seventh-century formulations that would freeze human society." Kristof notes that "female Muslim scholars like Fatima Mernissi of Morocco have also turned up evidence that Prophet Muhammad's youngest wife (and the person he said he loved most in the world), Aisha, vigorously contested the chauvinism of early clerics. Indeed, she sometimes comes across as the first Islamic feminist" (Kristof 2006).

Why is a major "liberal" columnist for the *New York Times* discovering Islamic feminism? In my view, it is because he wants to support the ideological stance that the trouble with the world today is Islamist fundamentalist terror, and that one way to combat this is through a "reformation" within Islamic traditions. But I want to argue that this focus on the inherent qualities of Islam as a world religion is a red herring. If we leave aside the many varieties of Islamic belief and practice that exist in so many different countries, among the more than 1 billion Muslims worldwide, the character of Islam as a religion is not the main issue.

The conflation of Islam as a world religion with traditionalism and pre-modern culture is really a political and intellectual sleight of hand. Certainly, it is legitimate to interpret Islamic fundamentalist activism, whether at the level of government, as in Iran, or at the level of individual or group actions, as in part at least a cultural reaction to the neocolonial modernity represented by the West. This is explicit in the ideology of the most openly anti-Western leaders of the Iranian government, such as President Mahmood Ahmadinejad. But what is really at stake here is the intention by the ideologists of capitalist globalization, such as Thomas Friedman and Samuel Huntington, to depict as primary features of the modern world a sharp dichotomy between Islam and the West.

These ideologists characterize Islam as fundamentally antimodern and dangerous, and the West as fundamentally modern and benevolent. This formulation hides another reality, which is the goal of capitalist interests to pry open *all* forms of premodern traditional political economies. In attempting to make the world safe for foreign investment, and to reproduce the individualistic culture that will guarantee the rise of consumerism, Western globalizing interests (corporations and governments) are opposed to major economic elements of premodern culture, such as land held in common and subsistence agriculture. And they are equally opposed to religious elements of premodern culture, such as indigenous belief systems, that hold that it is impossible to own land. The framework of a capitalist economy requires the establishment of private property, and of a legal system that protects it. Hence, for example, land held in common within African villages represents an obstacle to this process. (On this point, see Federici 2000, 156; Gordon 1996.)

Thus, it is not Islam that is the target, but all premodern economic formations that are perceived as unreceptive to the rise of a capitalist economy. The global war on terror has taken Islam as a stand-in for traditional cultural practices of all kinds. This ideological framework conceals the enormous variety of cultural practices and legal regimes that come under the heading of Islamic societies. As Val Moghadam illustrates for the countries of the Middle East, the degree of modernization and, concomitantly, the degree of women's emancipation vary with the political regime and specifically with elements of how the state is organized, rather than with the presence of Islam.

It is a mistake to attribute the position of women in the Middle East to the "presumed intrinsic properties of Islam." Generally, Islam is patriarchal; but so are the other major world religions, including Hinduism, Judaism, and Christianity (Moghadam 2003, 5). In addition, there are many other areas of the world in which women's status is low. These are the areas where the impact of industrialization and other aspects of modernization have had the least effect. Hence, this lower status of women needs to be understood as a feature, not of the effects of a particular patriarchal religion, but of the remaining influence of "kin-ordered, patriarchal and agrarian structures" (Moghadam 2003, 6).

The "belt of classic patriarchy," as described by Deniz Kandiyoti and other writers, in North Africa, the Muslim Middle East, and South and East Asia remains based on the tribe or communal group, which maintains property within families through the "control of women in tightly interrelated lineages." These are the areas where control of women through the association of family honor with female virtue constrains the life options of women severely. "Patriarchy, therefore, should not be conflated with Islam but rather should be understood in social-structural and developmental terms" (Moghadam 2003, 122–123).

In addition, the status of women within the Muslim world varies considerably, since "adherence to Islamic precepts and the applications of Islamic legal codes differ throughout the Muslim world" (Moghadam 2003, 6). Thus, Tunisia is a secular state, which for some time in the 1980s had the most progressive family law in the Middle Eastern region (Moghadam 2003, 209). This is in strong contrast to the more regressive aspects of family law in Iran, for example. Similarly, in Algeria, where the scars of the civil war between government forces and Islamist militants that killed more than 100,000 people are still deeply felt, a sea change is now reported in the status of women. In 2007, women made up 70 percent of the lawyers, 60 percent of the judges, and 60 percent of university students, and they were also dominant in medicine (see Slackman 2007, 1). Since Islamic belief is a common feature of the countries in the Middle Eastern region, variations in women's condition within these countries are due, not to the precepts of Islam, but to "developmental issues—the extent of urbanization, industrialization, and proletarianization," as well as to policy decisions by state managers (Mogahadam 2003, 6).[28]

FEMINIST IDEAS AS A SOLVENT OF TRADITIONAL CULTURES

It is easy to dismiss the feminist sentiments of the Bush administration in the service of the war on terrorism as a cynical exercise. But there is an important kernel of truth in this propaganda. If a central goal of globalization is to break up the bonds that hold a traditional society together, then feminist ideas constitute a powerful solvent. The modern process of globalized capitalism, as it expands into new territories or deepens its grip on older ones, encounters cultures that are organized in ancient ways. The bottom line is that contemporary feminism as shaped by capitalism is a way to dismantle ancient cultures.

One could, perhaps, make an analogy to the functions of Christianity in the centuries of European exploration. Christian missionaries accompanied Western traders, and their evangelism helped to transform the traditional cultures they encountered, whether in Africa, Asia, or the Americas. Consciously or unconsciously, the effect of missionary preaching was to weaken and to delegitimize the assumptions underlying the ancient ways of doing and being that had held these cultures together (Wolf 1997, 145ff.).

In the late twentieth and early twenty-first centuries, for better or worse, mainstream feminism functions in a similar way. As Martha Gimenez notes: "The rise of the abstract individual, the bearer of economic, political, civil and human rights, is both a precondition for the development of capitalism, and a continuing capitalist structural effect that contributes to its ongoing reproduction. Feminism is one of the important expressions of Western individualism" (Gimenez 2004, 92). Ideologically, feminism encourages women to be individuals, rather than members of families or communities. At the same time, the proletarianization of peasant women modernizes their consciousness and their sense of identity. As William Greider observes, the managers for Motorola in Kuala-Lumpur have to "change the culture" of the Islamic women it hires to make silicon chips. The company teaches them to speak up for themselves, and to use ATMs, instead of handing their wages over to their families (Greider 1997, 82–84).

The glittery modern form of capitalism, with its television, video games, and high-rise buildings, is expanding into territory where patriarchal, tribal, kinship-based life found in small, undeveloped communities is still powerful. In some of the areas to which the United States has turned its attention, such as Afghanistan and the Islamic countries carved out of the former Soviet Union (such as Kazakhstan), Western economic interests are encountering societies where the preindustrial feudal or tribal cultural structures are barely touched by modern life, or coexist unevenly with it. (The same is true of many countries in sub-Saharan Africa; on this point, see Gordon 1996.)

A professional investment adviser who is working on a project to bring socially responsible investment to Afghanistan told me that most of her colleagues have no idea of how intensely patriarchal Afghan culture still is. My informant noted that, even though the men she was dealing with presented themselves as European and Westernized, this was a thin patina that barely concealed a deeply held set of ancient feudal and tribal attitudes. She recounted one incident in which the current president, Hamid Karzai, was seeking to persuade a certain warlord, located as it happened in the town of Karzai's family, to take a particular course of action. The warlord was resisting, and to make his point, he threatened to exhume Karzai's father's body and hang it in public in the town if Karzai did not desist. Karzai abandoned his argument and returned empty-handed to the capital (personal communication, August 2006).

If the goal of globalization is to create investment and marketing opportunities, and therefore acceptance of Western products along with Western norms, then in this context an image of a liberated Western woman becomes part of the sale. Western experience is made equivalent to individualizing women, freeing them from their cultural (patriarchal) constraints, and giving them enormous opportunities for self-advancement.

The attraction of this freeing up of women's potential is illustrated in the film *Bend It like Beckham* (2002), where a young Sikh Indian immigrant girl is transformed into a champion soccer player, much to the dismay of her traditional family. Whereas her sister is married off conventionally and is pregnant at the end of the movie, the heroine is selected to go to the United States to play soccer, with a romantic attachment to her Irish-English coach lingering unresolved at the end of the movie. This movie encapsulates the promise of Western feminism: escape from the constraints of tradition into the unlimited possibilities of a gender-free, competitive lifestyle.

Thus, feminism, defined as women's liberation from patriarchal constraints, is made the equivalent of participating in the market as a liberated individual. Feminist-inspired gender ideology is used to enforce the idea of Western cultural superiority, and thus to facilitate the penetration of multinational corporations into the preindustrial areas of the world. The new imperial feminism, supporting the war on terrorism in the name of European Enlightenment, works for the same goals. I will turn in the Conclusion to the project of developing a feminism that is not intrinsically linked to the twin goals of capitalist globalization and imperial domination.

Conclusion

❀

Some who have been following my argument thus far might be tempted to resign from the practice of feminism. I have been painting a picture of a world capitalist system whose leaders thoroughly absorb progressive ideas and transform them into propaganda and strategies in pursuit of their own interests. It might appear, therefore, that all activism, feminist or otherwise, is hopeless, since it will just feed into the giant maw of corporate expansionism.

It is certainly not news that capitalist interests are expert in co-opting social movements, using their language and their ideas to enhance profitability, while at the same time suppressing the really radical features of these movements, either through ideology or through the use of force. (Thanks to Mike Locker for this point; personal communication 2008.) But I have been dwelling on one particular phenomenon, which is that certain aspects of mainstream feminism are thoroughly congruent with neoliberal capitalism and have been used to facilitate its expansion.

The argument I have been making in this book is that in the 1970s, a counterrevolution against the gains of the 1960s in both the developed world and the Third World was successfully undertaken, and that this counterrevolution is still going on. If we accept the idea of a global class war, then the winners to date have been the elites, the managers of the global economy across the globe, and the losers have been both the middle class and the poor. The poorest of the poor, in every country, are the women and children.

In Chapter 1 I detailed the elements of this counterrevolution, which has involved a complex series of political and economic changes, or restructurings, as major corporations and their national governments jockey for position in an increasingly competitive world market. The developed powers simultaneously compete with one another while uniting to preserve their competitive advantage against Third World countries; these powers use the ideology of neoliberalism and the mechanisms of the international financial institutions (IFIs) to preserve their privileges in trade and their access to cheap labor.

This competition by the United States, Europe, and Japan against the rising economic powers of East and Southeast Asia, especially China and India, is currently being carried on in the context of a war on terrorism. This war is directed by the United States with the enthusiastic assistance of Great Britain, and with greater or lesser degrees of participation by other world powers. If, as Carl von Clausewitz famously said, war is the continuation of politics by other means, then the war on terror is the continuation of the counterrevolution against the middle class and the poor in the First World and against most of the population in the Third World.

My aim in this book has been to take the achievements and the aspirations of feminism as a world movement and to place them in the context of this larger struggle. I have tried to show those arenas in which mainstream feminist ideologies have been taken up and used by governments, corporations, and nongovernmental organizations (NGOs); I have also demonstrated the ways in which the use of women's labor has been a crucial part of the counterrevolution.

In Chapter 2 I explored the development of the women's movement in the United States as it exploded onto the scene in the late 1960s. I looked at the themes of the legitimation of paid work for women and what I call the abolition of gender, as feminist interventions took down a series of barriers, from protective legislation to unequal legal access to credit and education, creating a level playing field for women, in theory if not in practice.

In Chapter 3 we saw how the fault lines of race and class weakened the women's movement. In the struggle over abortion, in the campaigns against violence against women, and in the First World–Third World debate over female genital cutting, the divergent interests and perspectives of different categories of women made the goal of a unified feminist movement difficult to reach.

In Chapter 4, I traced the changes in the United States as the economy was radically restructured, with a steady rise in the low-wage, unorganized service sector. With 72 percent of its employees women, Wal-Mart replaced General Motors as the prototypical U.S. corporation. Manufacturing jobs steadily moved overseas, and investment shifted into the FIRE industries—finance, insurance, and real estate.

The increasing appetite for women's labor soon used up the pool of available single, divorced, and widowed women. The taboo against hiring married women was effectively broken, first among the working class during the 1950s, and then in the middle class during the 1960s. The elimination of the family wage as an aspiration, let alone a requirement, meant that women, married or single, mothers or not, now entered the labor market on their own.

Concomitant with the increasing use of women in low-waged service jobs came an unrelenting battle against the power of unions, which drove down union membership to its lowest point in history. Corporations could now substitute female labor for male labor without the constraints of protective legislation or the family wage ideology, and so they did. As we saw, the good news for women, as the result of the long and hard struggles by unions and by antidiscrimination lawsuits, was the opening up of access to virtually all areas of work. The bad news was that with overall economic restructuring, wage levels stagnated for decades. We saw, too, that government officials were quick to use feminist ideology, interpreted as women's right to paid employment, as a way to gut the welfare legislation of 1935, thereby removing a crucial safety net that had helped to provide a floor for wages.

Finally, we saw that one outcome of the economic restructuring of the neoliberal period was the consolidation of a serious class divide among women. On one end of the spectrum were those who benefited significantly from the gains of the women's movement by entering managerial and professional occupations and increasing their earnings more rapidly than their male counterparts. At the other end, women remained more likely than men to be in poverty, especially if they were single heads of families.

In Chapter 5 we saw that the application of structural adjustment programs (SAPs) by Third World governments had devastating impacts on poor women and children. SAPs have been used to restructure the economies of countries in Africa, Latin America, South and Southeast Asia, as well as in eastern Europe, using the requirements of debt repayment as a lever to redirect investment and other resources toward an export-based economy. All of the elements of this process, from currency devaluation to privatization to market liberalization, ended up placing greater and greater burdens on women. We saw, too, that relying on the unpaid labor of women was an unstated "conditionality" that undergirded all the rest of the changes. For with the defunding of public services, from education to hospitals to provision of water and other utilities, the slack was taken up by women's labor.

Women's options included working in export-processing zones (EPZs), as international corporations transferred some of their production to Third World countries; accepting microcredit loans; migrating overseas; or choosing sex work. Meanwhile, international agencies, as they responded to the growing world anger over the decline in living standards, the increase in preventable diseases, and the increases in maternal and infant mortality that were the result of neoliberal economic policies, increasingly focused on gender, and specifically, on women's empowerment as the new key to economic development.

Finally, in Chapter 6, we saw that in the war on terror, the governments of the United States and Europe were openly enlisting the ideas and the writings of feminists to defend the policies that, among other things, prolonged brutal wars in Yugoslavia, Iraq, and Afghanistan, and threatened the opening of other fronts, in Iran, Syria, and elsewhere.

To make these arguments, I have, of course, been selective in my focus, and I have ignored the progressive achievements and potential of feminist activism around the world. In this chapter I want to lift my gaze from the gloom and doom of the preceding chapters, and counterbalance this with some accounts of feminist activism that can give us hope for the future. But the whole point of this book has been to say to my sisters and colleagues in the women's movement (and to our brothers in the struggle): "Red alert! Red alert! The globalizers are using our ideas to further their goals and to frustrate ours." To me, feminism was and is about global justice, about taking care of those in need, giving a voice to the voiceless, letting people determine their own destiny. All of these goals are in danger of being defeated by a system of global imperialism that tells the Iraqis and the Afghanis and so many other peoples around the world how they must live.

Am I saying that there is no place for feminists to argue for women's rights in societies where women have been subjected to patriarchal domination? Not at all. But the rights of women cannot be imposed by military force. They have to be developed by women within their own societies. The propaganda of globalization has mesmerized us, making us feel that the only real engine of women's liberation is the expansion of corporate capitalism to every corner of the globe. I want to challenge the equation of capitalist modernity with the emancipation of women. As I will discuss in the following pages, the socialist tradition, for all of its historical errors, also sought to emancipate women and succeeded in many ways.

The structure of my argument in this book has been deliberately provocative. I seem to be implying that it was the shape that mainstream feminism took in the United States, with its fateful disregard of issues of class and race, that opened the door to the global juggernaut that has so dramatically reshaped the world economy. Am I not imputing enormous powers to a social movement that holds not a single lever of real power, whether political, economic, social, or religious? Is the women's movement responsible for the Bretton Woods institutions, corporate leadership, and the military-industrial complexes of the world powers? Surely not!

Yet let us recall the words of writer Virginia Woolf on the eve of World War II. She said that women were innocent because they were out of power. But woe betide them when the doors of power started opening to them. Speaking on behalf of the "daughters of educated men," at the moment when the doors to professional life had begun to open to women, Woolf wrote: "We ... are between the devil and the deep blue sea. Behind us lies the patriarchal system; the private house, with its nullity, its immorality, its hypocrisy, its servility. Before us lies the public world, the professional system, with its possessiveness, its jealousy, its pugnacity, its greed. The one shuts us up like slaves in a harem; the other forces us to circle, like caterpillars head to tail, round and round the mulberry tree, the sacred tree of property. It is a choice of evils" (Woolf 1938, 113). Is there a third choice, between exclusion from public life and absorption into it in its current corrupt form?

Along with so many other writers and activists, I would like to see the construction of "another world," one where the failed or incomplete attempts at women's liberation could be remedied, and one where the dreams that women have for their own self-determination would be an integral part of the overall social project. It would be both arrogant and foolish of me to attempt any kind of blueprint for feminist organizing toward such a project. But I want to briefly address some issues that grow out of the analysis I have been making, as a contribution to the worldwide debate stimulated by the antiglobalization, or global justice, movement. I list them here in the form of seven questions.

First, how can feminists put the critique of capitalism and the discussion of socialism back on the agenda?

Second, can the break between feminism and the Left be mended?

Third, how can feminism be both antiracist and anti-imperialist?

Fourth, how can the women's movement address class issues effectively?

Fifth, is there a way to decouple modernity from capitalism?

Sixth, can we rethink the role of the state, looking at state development and the case of Venezuela?

Seventh, is there a way to keep the gains from the abolition of gender while avoiding the losses from a reversion to essentialism?

PUTTING SOCIALISM BACK ON THE FEMINIST AGENDA

In the Introduction to this book, I called for feminists to put the critique of capitalism and the possibility of socialism back on the agenda. But what does this mean in practical terms? Alternatives to capitalism do not seem within reach in the current U.S. situation, although they are under active discussion in some parts of the globe (see my discussion of the Bolivarian revolution in Venezuela later in this chapter). But if large-scale social change does not seem to be forthcoming in the near term, this is no reason not to talk about it. The World Social Forum (WSF) slogan "Another world is possible" is an invitation to think about this other world.

How would one go about ultimately replacing the present system with an economic framework that would really meet all people's needs for food, shelter, environmental sustainability, intimacy, sexual self-determination, children, education, employment, leisure, and political participation (I'm sure readers will add to this list with their own priorities)? I want to argue that this process needs to begin with a full and detailed understanding of how capitalism, and particularly how globalized capitalism, actually works now, particularly in relation to women and women's labor. How can people educate themselves further on the political economy of gender?

Here I want to point to the work of the Women of Color Resource Center (www.coloredgirls.org) in creating a workbook that can be used by small groups of women (or men) to educate themselves as to how the global economy works, both in the United States and around the world. Miriam Ching Louie and Linda Burnham's *WEdGE: Women's Education in the Global Economy* (2000) is an example of how to bring the extensive scholarship on globalization to people who might not have the level of education or the time to inform themselves on the economic forces that impinge on their lives. Using simple workshop tools such as butcher paper and marking pens, the individual modules teach participants about the revival of sweatshops globally, the impact of the Temporary Assistance to Needy Families program on the family budget, and how women's "unpaid, underpaid, contingent, and informal-sector work" affects their daily lives (Louie and Burnham 2000, 101).

This is only one example of the flood of information being produced by women's organizations on how the global financial infrastructure affects the lives of women and girls. Despite my earlier criticism of the political role of some women's NGOs (see Chapter 5), there is no doubt that the research by groups such as the Women's Environment and Development Organization (WEDO, New York, www.wedo.org), the Association for Women in Development (AWID, Toronto, www.awid.org), MADRE (New York, www.madre.org), and the Center for Women's Global Leadership (Rutgers University, New Brunswick, New Jersey, www.cwgl.rutgers.edu) (to mention just some North American–based examples) provides extensive political and economic information about the role of women and gender in the process of globalization. These websites and their publications provide important teaching tools that can help students and activist groups understand what are admittedly complex issues.

I wish to argue, then, that a first step in resisting globalization lies in advancing the spread of what we might call *economic literacy*. The increasing number of courses in university curricula introducing a Marxist perspective on globalization is a good indicator of progress. Infusing these courses with an intelligent, radical, gender perspective, in my view, would be an even better indicator. But this raises the issue of whether Marxism and feminism are actually compatible frameworks, which brings me to my next question.

Mending the Break of Feminism with the Left

I entitled this book "Feminism Seduced," because I felt that in the process of selling globalization, corporate leaders and other elites have been systematically trying to seduce women into embracing the expansion of capitalism. We have seen how the IFIs have embraced the idea of gender as central to economic development and how corporate media publicize the achievements of women in high places. All of this has seemed to me to be an overall effort to smoothly fold feminism and feminist ideas into the corporate embrace. In sharp contrast, the male Left has seemed historically to be hostile or indifferent to women's issues, as encapsulated in the "unhappy marriage" concept coined by Heidi Hartmann (1981). Metaphorically speaking, has capitalism been a better husband for women than socialism?

In the 1970s, a painful break between feminism and the Marxist Left developed that has yet to be healed. The unhappy marriage between Marxism and feminism referred then primarily to the failure of the Marxist tradition to take adequate account of women's issues. (On this debate, see Gimenez and Vogel 2005; Sargent 1981.) If we revisit the unhappy marriage of Marxism and feminism in the early twenty-first century, we can perhaps see this problem with new eyes. On the one hand, there is a need for a gendered, feminist perspective to correct the failures of Marxism/communism as a political experiment. On the other hand, there is a need to avoid the tendency within much of contemporary feminism to dismiss revolutions, socialism, and Marxism as no longer relevant, as passé, and, indeed, as useless traditions, due to their slighting of women's concerns.

Even though the Marxist tradition did tackle the issue of women, labeled the *woman question*, both in theory and practice Marxism saw the solution to women's oppression as including women in industrial production. Drawing on the doctrines of Karl Marx and Friedrich Engels, male revolutionaries assumed that "both the evolution of women's consciousness and the material bases for its transformation would be the direct result of the massive entry of women into the world of waged work and workers' struggles" (Kruks, Rapp, and Young 1989, 9). All of the issues surrounding sexuality, reproduction, patriarchal relations, and the myriad of other questions raised by first- and second-wave feminism were either ignored or inadequately incorporated into the successive Marxist revolutions of the twentieth century, although the more recent the revolution, the more women's issues have been addressed by national policy (Kruks et al. 1989).

There is no doubt that revolutionary governments in the twentieth century contributed substantially to women's emancipation, although this was not an end in itself, but part of a broad project of modernization as Communist states competed with their capitalist rivals. "Formulated as responses to the perceived need to realize the potential of modernity and to pursue and win an international rivalry against the antagonistic capitalist world beyond, such states [as China, Albania, Yemen, and Afghanistan] sought to mobilize women and transform their social position as part of the planned reorganization of society" (Molyneux 2001b, 125).

But a rigid adherence to Marxist doctrine often undermined these attempts. Jennifer Disney's analysis of the revolutionary governments in Mozambique and Nicaragua shows in detail how male revolutionary leaders designed programs that were incapable of succeeding, precisely because the leadership was ignorant of the actual lived reality of women's dual roles in economic production and family-based reproduction: "the emphasis both FRELIMO and the FSLN placed on large-scale state farms, the subsequent devaluation of subsistence and family farming, the gendered access to paid agricultural labor on state farms and to full cooperative membership, and the perpetuation of the sexual division of labor in the sphere of reproduction all reveal the limitations of a productivist, economistic model of emancipation that does not consider the reality of the intersections of production and reproduction in women's lives" (Disney 2004, 11).[1]

As Delia Aguilar writes about her comrades within the Philippines revolutionary struggles during the 1970s and 1980s, Third World movements for national liberation were "sidelining" women's issues: "It wasn't that women were ignored or were not considered important for the revolution, because they could be found in organizations of various kinds and proved to be dependable and committed workers. It also was not that the platform for national liberation failed to articulate a position on women, because it did. But ... women's oppression was conceptualized almost exclusively along productivist lines so that male chauvinism—or the everyday conduct of men, both as individuals and as a group—could easily escape scrutiny or criticism and, therefore, correction or redress" (Aguilar 2006, 1).

Filipino writings at this period certainly pointed to the subjugation of women as factory workers, prostitutes, and domestic workers forced overseas as the result of the neocolonial status of the Philippines. But the analysis highlighted class at the expense of gender issues: "Precious little was observed or remarked about the home or family and the gender inequality spawned by the division of labor occurring within this site. Nor was there any questioning of male authority and male privilege, or attention to quotidian gender interactions.... Without the necessary interrogation, gender asymmetry would remain naturalized, accepted as the normal state of affairs, and continue to place women in a materially and psychologically disadvantaged position" (Aguilar 2006, 1).

Even among revolutionaries who explicitly take women's issues into account, the record is spotty, as in Chiapas, Mexico: "Among the Zapatistas, women's 'issues' tend to come behind national issues, and demands for greater equality in the community behind demands placed on the state; patriarchy, in other words, will once again be dealt with only after capitalism and racism. And the 'solutions' therefore do not go far enough: child care centers, hospitals, facilities to make food—all essential demands—do not add up to what indigenous women have eloquently called 'the right to rest,' and beyond that, to think and to do, to feel and to love" (Foran 2003, 4).

If the Marxist political and theoretical traditions have been found wanting, so, too, is the left literature on globalization. Major male writers simply exclude or gloss over issues of gender, even though feminist scholarship shows the centrality of gender and, particularly, of women's labor and feminist ideology to the political economy of the neoliberal era. My sampling of the indexes of some of these volumes for entries on gender, women, sexuality, women and work, and related topics reveals a glaring paucity.

The lack of understanding of feminist analysis has cost previous revolutions enormously in strength and in staying power (see Randall 1992). In the contemporary period, some of the same failures are being repeated in the venues of the World Social Forum. For example, despite steady and occasionally successful efforts by a coalition of feminist groups, including Development Alternatives with Women for a New Era, the World March of Women, the Women's International Coalition for Economic Justice, and the Articulacion Feminista Marcosur, to have women's voices heard in the main forums of the World Social Forum for 2003, gender issues overall were marginalized. Only where feminist groups took responsibility for organizing thematic areas could one find feminist analysis. "In short, the integration of feminist concerns into antiglobalization discourses remained dependent on the concrete presence of self-declared feminists" (Eschle 2005, 1759).

Similarly, Ana Elena Obando, reporting on the 2005 World Social Forum meeting in Porto Alegre, Brazil, shows once again that the leadership of the Left is not yet prepared to take on board the issues that are central to the organizing goals of feminist activism. Of the 570 events on the first day of the forum, 25 were devoted to women's rights, that is, only 4 percent of the total. But more profoundly, the other major panels throughout the conference did not include gender in their discussion of central issues such as war, neoliberal globalization, militarism, and, especially, the rise of fundamentalisms. Issues crucial to women were discussed in venues for feminists, but marginalized or omitted in the "mainstream" venues.

More distressingly, in the International Youth Camp, which drew about 35,000 participants and was intended as a "socially progressive microcosm of political relationships and life in society" and designed as "a space where the values of the WSF were practiced," there were "90 reported cases of violence against young women," from harassment to rape. As Obando notes: "The women I spoke with in the camp reacted with sadness, frustration and rage. They said that a space that permits or tolerates violence against women cannot struggle for another world. They were angered that the perpetrators were not arrested. Others asked if 'another camp was possible'; in this one they felt invaded, disrespected and abused" (Obando 2005, 4).

In contrast, Catherine Eschle reports that at the fourth World Social Forum held in Mumbai in 2004, the strength of the Indian women's movement was reflected in a much greater "visibility and power.... Many panels were feminist organized and women dominated and provided complex feminist analyses of war, communalism, and coalition building. It is notable that 'patriarchy' was included among the five key thematic areas for official panels. We were further surprised by our encounter with a small but highly articulate core of feminist activists in the Mumbai Resistance, a Marxist-Leninist alternative to the forum, who drew our attention to the exclusions generated by an emphasis on nonviolent direct action in the Indian context" (Eschle 2005, 1761). Obviously, it is possible to bring women's issues to the fore at a World Social Forum if women's groups are sufficiently organized, powerful, and effective. How can the successes of the Indian women's movement be replicated elsewhere?

On another front, the publication of the brave memoir by Bettina Aptheker (2006), daughter of the renowned Communist historian Herbert Aptheker, and the vitriolic response to her work by some writers on the Left suggest the difficulties for feminists and leftists in healing the breach. Aptheker, a longtime activist and professor of feminist studies at the University of California, Santa Cruz, revealed that her father had sexually molested her during her early adolescence. This provoked a firestorm from Left writers, who were outraged that Aptheker was sullying the reputation of her famous father. Some even imagined that she had invented these events. The doubters were courageously tackled by Left male historian Jesse Lemisch, who pointed out that those attacking the younger Aptheker had clearly failed to absorb the most elementary lessons of feminism about personal politics and abuses of patriarchal power at the level of the family. In addition, he argued that the failure to encompass emotional and personal issues, as explicated particularly by feminists, was a source of weakness, both for the old Communist Party and for the contemporary political Left (Lemisch 2006a, 2006b).

That this episode erupted in 2006 might indicate that the objective of teaching Left men about the significant issues raised by thirty-plus years of feminist theorizing and activism is in fact unattainable. Yet in this sequence of events, I find myself dwelling on the intervention of Lemisch (married to the psychologist and feminist pioneer Naomi Weisstein), as an exemplar of progressive Left male consciousness, rather than on the Neanderthal reactions of his colleagues. And, indeed, I collect examples of Left male writers who have incorporated and understood feminist writings and who actively collaborate with feminist organizers and theorists in their own work.

Doug Henwood, one of the few Left economists writing in the U.S. context today who has understood the crucial importance of feminist insights, regularly includes feminist publications and concerns on his weekly radio show, "Behind the News," on WBAI-Pacifica New York (99.5 FM, Thursdays at 5 p.m.). Former Special Forces officer Stan Goff uses his extensive military experience to critique the elements of masculinity, white supremacy, and sexism that go to make up what he calls the rise of American fascism (Goff 2004). Social theorist Manuel Castells recognizes feminism as the most important revolution of the modern era.[2] And sociologist John Foran enjoins the Left to incorporate the ideas and critiques by feminist and antiracist activists: "The feminist revolution, along with the antiracist revolution, may thus well prove the longest revolutions, but a new Marxism attuned to feminism and antiracism at its core, linking with women's and other movements with an irreducible global and class edge may help us get there in the end" (Foran 2003, 4).

But healing the breach is a two-way street. The feminist divorce from the Left leaves feminists in the camp of the reformers rather than the revolutionaries.[3] Ideologically, this position feeds into the campaign by ruling international elites to dismiss or invalidate any proposed alternatives to globalized capitalism. So there is much work to be done on both sides of the fence.

In the body of this book, I have emphasized the elements of feminist ideology and practice that have been found useful by the forces of corporate globalization. I have pointed to the individualism and self-determination that have been so much a part of hegemonic feminism over the past few decades. But, of course, there is another strand coming out of 1970s feminism, which is the notion of collectivism and solidarity.

As noted in Chapter 3, I have been critical in my previous writing of the glib assumptions behind the "all women" theme that ran through 1970s white feminism, from Susan Brownmiller to Robin Morgan. The divisions of race and class made it impossible for feminists of color to sign on to the priorities set by white feminist leadership. The aspiration to unite all women regardless of divisions of race and ethnicity was naive, and the process of consciousness-raising that it led to created a limited agenda for feminism, as I argued, because it was constrained by the social networks of a racist society. But if we return to the idea of consciousness-raising, we can see some elements that are promising for the future.

The process of consciousness-raising was exhilarating because it illuminated commonalities among women, where before as individuals they had experienced the pain and sense of shame on their own, without support or acknowledgment. The capacity of women's groups to develop an analysis of rape, incest, and other kinds of sexual abuse relied on this sharing of information, based on a sense of trust and openness that overcame the competitiveness traditionally felt by women toward one another.

So one element in the treasure chest of items that the women's movement can offer to a world movement is this experience of solidarity through the sharing of experience. I am not speaking here of the sensationalism provided by the commercialization of feminist ideas through venues such as the Oprah Winfrey show. This facile sharing of pain, to be somehow alleviated by confessing to Oprah or her counterparts in front of a live television audience, is a distortion of the original feminist goals in the service of consumerism.[4] But the core skill and the capacity of sharing experience, and thus creating bonds for future action, are something that the women's movement can teach the Left.

There is one major difficulty with this proposal, of course, which is that a lot of the pain and damage being reported is pain inflicted on women by their fathers, husbands, brothers, and lovers. Much female solidarity in women's movement activism has up to now been in the service of creating female solidarity against men. Indeed, the charge of male-bashing has been very common in critiques of hegemonic feminism. For this form of feminist solidarity to extend to male comrades, they must be willing to engage in their own forms of consciousness-raising and to incorporate respect for women into their own revolutionary program.

In the context of a discussion of activism against the contemporary war and occupation in Iraq, Huibin Amee Chew writes a most eloquent and reasoned appeal to male-led antiwar organizations to incorporate women's issues into their campaigns. She reproaches leftist groups, "from the Nader campaign to the Campus Antiwar Network," with "failing to take seriously the predicament of Iraqi women." In her view, antiwar activists "have failed to imagine and articulate an alternative that incorporates Iraqi women as equal political actors." Even though it would be inappropriate for American organizations to instruct Iraqis either in how to resist U.S. occupation or in how to organize as Iraqi women, says Chew, "the inability to dream, to think of the possibility for better alternatives, weakens our antioccupation message—as well as our ability to find Iraqi actors to work in solidarity with towards a truly progressive vision" (Chew 2005b, 3).

This phrase—"the inability to dream"—encapsulates so brilliantly and with such heartfelt passion what progressive feminists would like to find in their male Left companions. It articulates the deep desire of feminist progressives to have their ideas, their aspirations, their analysis, and their worldview acknowledged and understood by their compañeros. Indeed, it is a serious call for change. Male leftists must heed this message and overcome their "inability to dream."

But dream of what? If I might take liberties with Chew's suggestive phrase, I think she means learning to dream of a world in which the dignity of women is taken for granted alongside the dignity of men. The work of consciousness-raising that women activists have carried out so painstakingly is a task that male analysts and activists must also undertake, however difficult or unpleasant this work might turn out to be. That this represents a sacrifice of much that has constituted hegemonic masculinity (in Raewyn Connell's phrase) goes without saying. For feminists, equally, it requires the willingness to go beyond anger toward constructive education and sharing of ideas.

Many veterans of women's struggle may resent this requirement, just as women of color are tired of explaining themselves to their white sisters. To quote Ana Elena Obando again: "As feminists we again have [the] added duty of ensuring a gendered perspective in the building of an alternative world, that is, the resistance within the resistance. Therefore, we must continue to fight against many forms of capitalistic patriarchy while strengthening the movement from the inside and raising the consciousness of those who believe the revolution is possible. 'Revolutionary patience,' as Brazilian women say, 'or a form of forced maternity? You decide'" (Obando 2005, 3).

CREATING AN ANTIRACIST
AND ANTI-IMPERIALIST FEMINISM

The triumphalist accounts of feminism that I am challenging with this book point to the rise of women's influence and access as in and of itself a matter for celebration. In contrast, there is an increasing awareness, at least among women of color, that the international feminist movement must pay attention to the fundamental divide in the world between the rich North and the impoverished Global South. As globalization has incorporated the giant economies of China and India, the coexistence of glittering, rich capitalist enclaves with Third World favelas increasingly characterizes the situation within countries as well as in the great North-South divide.

What does this mean in practical terms for feminist activists? I am arguing that it means a rethink of the allocation of one's energies. What is the vision of feminism for the future? Surely, this is not an era when the be-all and end-all of feminist organizing is to simply get a bigger piece of the pie for women. Or to put this another way, the concept of organizing only on behalf of gender oppression is bankrupt, since, other things being equal, the system proceeds unimpeded. The great successes of this mode of feminist organizing turn out to be the appointment of Condoleezza Rice at the State Department, avidly pursuing the global war on terror, and Jean Bethke Elshtain, from her perch in the academy, endorsing as national policy certain forms of "light" torture (see Lazreg 2008, 245ff.).

In this context it is instructive to reconsider the rise of women's liberation from its origins in the civil rights movement and the anti–Vietnam War movement. Although women's liberationists of the time were rebelling against the hopeless sexism of their brothers in the movement, they nonetheless retained the ideological framework of their erstwhile allies. They were clear that the United States was an imperialist power, and that their radicalism as women was connected to antiracist struggles at home and to anti-imperialist struggles around the world. They then proceeded to the necessary work of analyzing patriarchy and the role of women, which led to the incredibly rich body of literature that has transformed our thinking about women, gender, sex roles, and social reproduction.

Now, with the tragic wars raging in Afghanistan and Iraq, perhaps we have come full circle, and it is time to go back to conceptualizing what real women's liberation would mean in the current conjuncture. I am not so naive as to think that feminism is one big thing, rather than the myriad of currents, eddies, and whirlpools that make up the fast-flowing river of women's movement activism around the world. But a touchstone, for me, of a newly radical form of feminism would be the consciousness of our location within the capitalist world system, and a linkage with the various forms of current opposition to it.

The brilliant work of CODEPINK comes to mind in this context. With its title a parody of the level of threat color codes introduced by the masterminds of the war on terrorism,

> CODEPINK was launched as a women's preemptive strike for peace when Medea Benjamin, Starhawk, Jodie Evans, Diane Wilson and approximately 100 other women marched through the streets of Washington, D.C. on November 17, 2002 and set up a four-month vigil in front of the White House.... On March 8th, 2003, International Women's Day, the growing PINK movement celebrated women as global peacemakers with a week of activities, a rally and a march to encircle the White House in pink. Over 10,000 people participated, among them Alice Walker, Maxine Hong Kingston, Jody Williams, Susan Griffin, Amy Goodman and Rachel Bagby. ("About Us," www. codepink4peace.org)

Since its inauguration, CODEPINK has become a global network, with over 250 local groups, and has sent peace delegations to Iraq, Jordan, Syria, Iran, and Afghanistan. With an imaginative use of posters, T-shirts, and courageous demonstrations, the CODEPINK group embodies a feminist-inspired activism against the war in Iraq and against U.S. imperialism more generally.

Similarly, I am endorsing the calls by women of color and their sympathetic allies for a feminism that acknowledges its location in the belly of the beast and looks at the issues that arise from this imperialism at home and abroad. One example of this kind of feminism comes from the organizing around reproductive justice led by women of color in the United States. We saw in Chapter 3 that the issue of abortion became a wedge between white women and women of color, because mainstream feminist organizations by and large did not contest the Hyde Amendment. As a result of these differences, women of color began to organize their own groups for reproductive justice.

This struggle took on an international flavor when a small delegation of women of color attended the International Conference on Population and Development in Cairo in 1994, and learned how women in other countries were able to use a human rights framework to advocate for reproductive health and sexual rights. At a meeting of the Illinois Pro-Choice Alliance in Chicago, this group formed the informal Black Women's Caucus, seeking to "bring Cairo home" by adapting these human rights agreements to a U.S. context. Forming groups in 1997, called Women of African Descent for Reproductive Justice, and then SisterSong Women of Color Reproductive Health Collective, they challenged the priorities of the mainstream movement.

In 2004, the leadership of a major march on Washington, principally the National Abortion Rights Action League (NARAL), invited SisterSong to be part of the endorsing organizations. In the ensuing negotiations, SisterSong was able to compel NARAL and the other mainstream leadership organizations to welcome organizations of women of color onto the steering committee, and to change the title of the march from "March for Freedom of Choice" to "March for Women's Lives."

But more broadly, with the newly enlarged leadership of the march, organizers reached out to "women of color, civil rights organizations, labor, youth, antiwar groups, antiglobalization activists, environmentalists, immigrant rights' organizations, and many, many others" (Ross 2006, 65). These women-of-color advocates were able to address a range of issues of concern to their constituencies, from the right to bear wanted children to the impact of HIV/AIDS on reproductive choices.

This set of events is instructive. The mainstream organizations of the women's movement were challenged on their political agenda, and the women-of-color organizations won the day. The result was a broadening out of the agenda to place the issues confronted by women of color front and center for the entire march. I want to suggest that for a whole range of issues, the experience of women of color and of working-class women needs to become the basis for agenda-setting in future activism.

In a discussion of black feminism, historian Barbara Ransby points to the linkages among economic, sexual, and racial issues:

> Radicals within the feminist, lesbi-gay-trans, and people of color communities generally see fighting against economic exploitation as intimately related to, and inseparable from, the fight against racism, sexism, and heterosexism as a critical component of their political agenda. Thus, these forces are potentially the connective tissue between various social change movements and constituencies, rather than the wedge that divides them.... It is no coincidence, then, that black feminist organizers around the country have deeply immersed themselves in struggles that incorporate but are not isolated to gender issues. (Ransby 2000, 1219)

Ransby cites "Beth Richie's ... work on domestic violence[, which] has connections with larger antiviolence, antipoverty, and prisoners' rights movements, as does Angela Davis's work on the prison-industrial complex. Atlanta-based black feminist Loretta Ross and Washington, D.C.–based organizer and law professor Lisa Crooms have worked on international and domestic human rights projects that incorporate many issues in addition to gender" (Ransby 2000, 1219n5). In this perspective, issues of gender are not isolated, but are linked to other crucial issues related to how class and race impinge on the experience of women of color (see Davis 2005; Richie 1996; Silliman et al. 2004).

A further point: in the years of the growth of the international women's movement, leadership has come from women in the Global South, who reinterpreted Northern women's movement goals in the light of their own experiences in the

Third World. This has broadened the agenda of what feminism is about, and points the way toward a link between feminism and anti-imperialism. In saying this, I am by no means seeking to diminish the ideological and political contributions of the second wave on key issues such as domestic violence, incest, rape, women's right to paid work, access to political power, and sexual harassment. But the cross-pollination of these feminist ideas from the Global North with the experiences and knowledge of feminists from the Global South gave rise to an understanding that a women's movement agenda was necessarily linked to the larger political and economic structures governing the world economy. This led directly back to a challenge to the neocolonialism of the rich countries and their powerful grip on the economies of the Global South.

This experience points to the responsibility of those of us in the center of the global U.S. empire to learn about and to oppose the policies of our own government. An anti-imperial feminism means in the first instance a clear knowledge of how U.S.-led global capitalism works, and then an effort to educate others about this powerful and dangerous system. As Pakistani feminist Nighat Said Khan points out: "The onus of a global movement, including a global women's movement, lies with the North since even the combined struggle of the South will not, and cannot, be successful in bringing about global change in what is called the new world order, since this ordering is determined by a handful of countries and significantly by the United States. We in the South can do our best but until the women's movement and feminist academics in the North are also against their respective states and the international world order, we will never see a global women's movement" (Khan 2004, 86).

For academic feminists, this means turning away from postmodern analyses that focus on individual and private acts of resistance, and back toward a structural analysis of global capitalism. There has been, in Delia Aguilar's words, "a domestication or taming of feminism" that has "rendered it unable to come to grips" with the realities of global capitalism. Thus, for example, the body of recent academic work on the experiences of domestic workers in relation to their overseas employers focuses, for the most part, on the alleged "agency" of workers who are able to manipulate the authority of their bosses, rather than on the "complex dynamics of class, race, and nation in mistress/housemaid relationships" (Aguilar 2006, 3, analyzing Constable 1997 and Hondagneu-Sotelo 2001). "The current state of feminist theorizing ... not only severely limits our understanding of how the global market works but also circumscribes the field of feminist action. That it is unequal to the task of explaining how globalization is built on the backs of Third World women, as it allows a few to move up the class ladder, is an understatement. This task ought to be paramount if feminism is to restore its emancipatory project" (Aguilar 2006, 4).

If feminist researchers were to turn away from their "current preoccupation with nuance and complexity" and move toward "illuminat[ing] the ways in which gender, race, and nationality are ultimately grounded in production relations, the resulting findings would likely depart radically from those of current studies, for these would unavoidably recognize the necessity of mass political mobilization, not merely the celebration of individual oppositional acts. It would be a theoretical enterprise that could open up the possibility of collective action, with social justice as the primary item on the feminist agenda once again" (Aguilar 2006, 5).[5]

RECOGNIZING THE SIGNIFICANCE OF CLASS

How can the women's movement address class issues effectively? Let us look at one aspect of the co-optation of feminism within the United States: corporations encouraging some women to enter management, thereby in effect creating a form of "managerial feminism." Indeed, Karen Nussbaum argues that the acceptance of some women into management was a maneuver by employers to derail the increasing demands of working women:

> To contain the growing demands of working women, employers created op-portunities for some women, opening up professional and managerial jobs for college graduates while resisting the demands for institutional changes that would improve jobs for all women. Women at both ends of the workforce continued to share common concerns of equal pay and work-family policies, but the intensity of the issues differed as the conditions of the two groups changed. Employers had created a safety valve. College-educated women who had been bank tellers were becoming branch managers; clericals in publishing companies were becoming editors. The percentage of women who were manag-ers or professionals doubled between 1970 and 2004, from 19 to 38 percent. (Nussbaum 2007, 165)[6]

To counter this division of women by class, I want to argue for a new class consciousness, something that is essential to the success of the women's movement. A cross-class alliance was part of the secret of the political power of the women's movement in the Progressive Era (see Chapter 2). Such a cross-class alliance is equally necessary now. In the current era, middle-class women's issues are closer to working-class issues, namely, longer hours, the conflict between work and parenting, and the lack of social support for caregiving work. But as Dorothy Sue Cobble argues, the U.S. women's movement "has a 'class' problem." This is "a failure to incorporate 'class' as a continuing and central category of analysis. What is needed is a more class-conscious approach, one that acknowledges class as a still salient, lived experience that shapes the needs and perspectives of *all* women. For left unaddressed, class reproduces itself in social relations and in social policy. And without such a class-conscious approach, the problems of one group of women end up being solved at the expense of another" (Cobble 2004,

227; emphasis in original). As Stephanie Luce and Mark Brenner point out, even though many individual women have gained access to higher education, economic independence, and meaningful work,

> it isn't enough for a few women, or even a lot of women, to succeed. Because under capitalism, their success in leaving the [working] class only means others are left behind. Under capitalism, you can't have a manager without the managed, and you can't have a winner without a loser. And who is losing? It remains primarily women and people of color who lose the most under capitalism, overrepresented among the working class and the poor. In addition, many of those women who are "winners" by virtue of their new degrees and higher-paying jobs aren't really winning, either. They may have more money and more power, but because of our privatized system of social reproduction, capitalism still constrains their options for caring for others and being cared for. In this way, the women who "win" under capitalism, as well as those who lose, have an incentive to build a cross-class women's movement to fight for a different model of production and social reproduction that allows us to construct our lives around human needs. (Luce and Brenner 2007, 130)

It is arguable that the divisions between women of color and poor women, on the one hand, and mainstream feminists, on the other, that I chronicled in Chapter 3, come down to an issue of class. In a well-known formulation, Maxine Molyneux distinguishes between strategic gender interests and practical gender interests. Strategic interests are those that seek "to overcome women's subordination, such as the abolition of the sexual division of labor, the alleviation of the burden of domestic labour and childcare, the removal of institutionalized forms of discrimination, the attainment of political equality, the establishment of freedom of choice over childbearing and the adoption of adequate measures against male violence and control over women" (Molyneux 2001a, 43). Practical gender interests are formulated by women "by virtue of their place within the sexual division of labour as those primarily responsible for their household's daily welfare.... When governments fail to provide these basic needs, women withdraw their support; when the livelihood of their families—especially their children—is threatened, it is women who form the phalanxes of bread rioters, demonstrators and petitioners" (Molyneux 2001a, 44). Molyneux goes on to note that "gender and class are closely intertwined; it is, for obvious reasons, usually poor women who are so readily mobilized by economic necessity. Practical interests, therefore, cannot be assumed to be innocent of class effects. Moreover, these practical interests do not in themselves challenge the prevailing forms of gender subordination, even though they arise directly out of them" (Molyneux 2001a, 44).

This distinction between practical and strategic interests has entered the literature (see, for example, Peterson and Runyan 1999, 177ff.). But it is not always identified as a class issue, and scholars have spilled much ink trying to decide which campaigns by women around the world are genuinely feminist, as opposed to those that are "merely" representing the interests of poor women in defending their families. Thus, for example, are the Mothers of the Plaza de Mayo in Buenos Aires, seeking information about their disappeared loved ones in Argentina, acting as feminists or "just" as mothers? (On this point, see Stephen 1997, 10ff.).[7] This line of inquiry presupposes the intrinsic superiority of a Western feminist viewpoint and is therefore suspect from the outset!

But I suggest that this debate go back to basics and look again at the issue of class. Rather than using the term *feminist* as a term of approbation, and implicitly blaming poor women for being more interested in the welfare of their families than in their own self-advancement as women, we need to acknowledge that the goals laid out by liberal feminism in the context of the developed industrial countries represent, in part, the "strategic interests" of those women who have the resources, education, and wherewithal to conceive of themselves as independent economic actors. The tensions and political disagreements that have characterized feminist debates in the United States and around the world are in part due to a reluctance on the part of some writers and activists to let go of the romantic view that the experience of being female automatically unites all women. The level of economic development of a society and the class position of women within it dictate the degree to which they can seek to be independent actors without relying on the protections of kinship and marriage.

Women in Third World situations, whether located in advanced industrial countries or in countries of the Global South, are forced to focus on what the late Bina Srinivasan called survival struggles (Srinivasan 2004). It requires a certain level of education and political consciousness, not to mention economic security, to begin to consider issues of the kind laid out by mainstream feminism. But it may be that, in the contemporary scene, these streams of practical versus strategic interests have begun to flow together, since so many activists around the world have incorporated feminist ideas into their local struggles. (On this point, see Rowbotham and Linkogle 1994a.) The ongoing battles taking place in Oaxaca, Mexico, for example, in defense of public education, led by schoolteachers of indigenous peasant background, have seen extraordinary leadership by women, who incorporate many forms of what we might think of as feminist consciousness into what is essentially a class struggle.

As Lynn Stephen notes, the presence of women working to

> remove a governor from power, running barricades and neighborhood committees, taking over radio and TV stations and then defending them on security duty—these are not traditional "female" tasks. What was striking—both to participants and to observers—was the number of women who were involved and who acted in coordination, creating a very strong female, public political presence that severely challenged the Oaxacan political elite. This presence of

the "short, the fat and the brown" was evident not only in the public spaces in the center of the city but also on television and radio. (Stephen 2007, 110)

In this popular struggle, long-standing activist teachers were allied with working-class and middle-class housewives having their first experience of political activism. In this configuration, the streams of strategic gender interests (seeking equality of women with men) and practical gender interests (survival struggles) flowed together into one larger river: "The ways in which women activists ... presented themselves and their demands suggests that their organizing is consistent with other hybrid contemporary social movements that combine the strategic demands of achieving women's equality with the practical demands of access to food, healthcare, housing, democratic representation, respect, and simply the right to speak in public" (Stephen 2007, 110).

One way for the women's movement to address class issues effectively is through the infusion of energy that women activists have brought into union organizing. Traditionally, unions have been an important counterweight to corporate power.[8] We saw how, in the period since the 1970s, corporate leaders have carried on an unremitting campaign to weaken unions. Manufacturing unions, in particular, have felt the effects of deindustrialization and this concerted corporate campaign, both of which have seriously reduced union membership and union political power. (See Chapter 4.)

But an unexpected result of the shift to a service economy is the expansion of a female workforce that is increasingly union-friendly. Public sector unionism grew rapidly in the 1960s and 1970s and peaked in the early 1980s, with two-fifths of government workers organized. This growth continues for large public sector unions such as the American Federation of State, County, and Municipal Employees and the American Federation of Teachers. "With close to 7 million women covered by union contracts, organized labor arguably is the largest working women's movement in the country" (Cobble 2007, 6). As Ruth Milkman notes: "Even as the nation's overall unionization rate has declined, the female share of union membership has expanded rapidly. In 2004, 43 percent of all the nation's union members were women—a record high, up from 34 percent only twenty years earlier, and just slightly below the 48 percent female share of the nations' wage and salary workforce" (Milkman 2007, 68).[9]

Service sector women represent a different kind of workforce from the old blue-collar model of unionism. In response, new kinds of organizing have been emerging, both inside and outside of organized labor. One example is the work of the Harvard Union of Clerical and Technical Workers (HUCTW), which gained its first contract in 1988. This union reflects its "female-dominated service-worker constituency," both in its bargaining agenda and in its institutional structures. In fact, lead organizer Kris Rondeau refers to a "feminine style of organizing," whose goals are "self-representation, power, and participation" (Rondeau quoted in Cobble 2004, 226). This mode of negotiation is modeled on Polish Solidarity negotiations, with workers sitting around in small teams at tables and focusing on specific issues. Collective bargaining also includes people telling their life stories. "Management needed to know the realities of our lives and to know that our lives were as important as theirs."[10] As a result of member involvement, commitment and creativity emerged. In the early 1990s, HUCTW won a 30 percent wage increase, improved benefits including more paid leave for family and community time, and raises and increased job security, plus benefit parity for part-time employees. The union also introduced skills training classes for clerical workers in dealing with students, faculty, and university personnel (Cobble 2004, 226–227).

Other service-based unions are also breaking with traditional models of organizing and representing workers. In 1999 in Los Angeles County, 74,000 home care workers, predominantly Latina, black, and immigrant women, joined the Service Employees International Union (SEIU) Local 434B in the largest single increase of union membership since the 1930s (Boris and Klein 2007, 177). The rapid growth of unionism among home care workers in recent years depended on unions such as 1199 and the SEIU recognizing that the predominantly female workforce carrying out home care could not be approached in the manner of traditionally male industrial workers. Instead, these women first needed to develop a sense of identity as workers. At the same time, the public and governmental agencies paying their wages had to be made aware that home care work was not identical with the unpaid caring work of women everywhere, but rather that this work deserved recognition for employees, with entitlements to health care, social security, workers compensation, and other benefits.

The Los Angeles victory, and others like it, depended on a mode of organizing that drew in a coalition of interests, including the elderly and disabled who were "consumers" of home health care. It also developed techniques that drew on the role of women workers as community members. Thus, SEIU 880 in Chicago "cultivated rank and file leaders from among female home attendant members, who were drawn in through tens of thousands of house visits. The women created a social world around the union, with regular meetings, parties, barbeques, recognition ceremonies, letter-writing campaigns, marches, and neighborhood alliances. They held 'speak outs' and 'honk-ins,' stopping traffic.... The ACORN model enabled the union to address women's whole lives as workers, kin, caregivers, and community members" (Boris and Klein 2007, 189).[11] Drawing on the experience of welfare reform organizing, this "new social movement unionism" allowed the low-wage immigrant and black workers a leadership role by acknowledging their complex identities as women doing care work in individual homes.

Other avenues of organizing—including attempts to organize welfare-to-work recipients—have served to expand the horizons of traditional union activities:

The ideals embodied in workfare and welfare organizing—the right to a decent job at livable wages, support for children and families, and gender and racial equality—are crucial to the labor movement's revival and growth. They create possibilities for a compelling vision of social justice at a time when the labor movement most desperately needs to reframe its beliefs and goals, and they capture the high ground in the national debate about economic and social justice. For trade unions, organizing that takes into account workers' issues outside of purely employment-based concerns offers a way to join with other movements for social justice. For community-based groups working for welfare rights, women's rights, and racial/ethnic justice, putting their energies into labor organizing builds bridges with those unions whose work has centered on traditional employment-based organizing. (Tait 2007, 208)

The influence of feminist leadership is visible in the style of organizing, and the creative use of gender consciousness, in the highly successful campaigns being waged by the California Nurses Association (CNA). The leader of the CNA, Rose Ann DeMoro, "an earthy, fifty-seven-year-old, Teamster-trained, water-skiing grandmother," is a women's studies graduate who abandoned her graduate studies in sociology when her professors told her that her heart was in organizing (Breslau 2006, 2). After thirteen years under her leadership, the union tripled in size, to 70,000 members, most of them female, and has become a major political force within California. Now the CNA is seeking to organize registered nurses in forty states and is pushing for campaign finance reform along with universal health care.

The union's innovative tactics were most visible in its campaign against Governor Arnold Schwarzenegger of California:

Schwarzenegger's aura of invincibility began evaporating in December 2004, after an episode that has become legendary in California political circles. A band of nurses, upset that the newly elected governor had sided with the hospital industry in the long-running legal battle over staffing ratios, infiltrated a women's conference hosted by Schwarzenegger's wife, Maria Shriver. As the governor spoke, the nurses stood up, unfurling large squares of red-lettered cloth they had tucked under their blouses. They swiftly assembled a giant banner reading "Hands Off Our Ratios," a none-too-subtle reference to the charges of sexual harassment that had dogged Schwarzenegger during the final days of California's madcap 2003 recall election. "Those are the special interests," Schwarzenegger cracked as security forces ejected the chanting nurses. "They're just angry because I'm always kicking their butts." Even Shriver looked stunned at the remark. (Breslau 2006, 3)

This confrontation was a turning point: "From that moment, nurse power was born. 'I love Arnold, in a way,' DeMoro says with a hearty cackle, still savoring the moment. 'He articulates publicly what they say behind closed doors.' With his wisecrack, says DeMoro, 'he woke up a sleeping giant. I mean, think about it: This guy standing up in front of a conference of working women and saying that?'" (Breslau 2006, 3). Using public relations techniques that drew on the public's deep respect for the role of nurses, the CNA was able to rout Schwarzenegger, not only on the issue of respecting reasonable staff ratios of nurses to patients, but on his antilabor electoral propositions:

> Over the next year, protesting squads of women in surgical scrubs, waving signs that read "Patients are our special interest," dogged Schwarzenegger at nearly every public appearance. They buzzed his Super Bowl party in a rented plane they dubbed "Air Arnold," trailing a banner that read, "It's no party for nurses." They showed up at his fundraisers, including a Rolling Stones concert in Boston, where a plane dragged an "Arnold's Beast of Burden: Corporate Cash" banner over Fenway Park, and a tony event in New York, where California nurses snuck in as guests and chastised him in front of the paying customers. They put Arnold up for auction on eBay: Bidding reached $3.6 million before the site took the auction down. (Breslau 2006, 3)

In 2007, the CNA joined forces with filmmaker Michael Moore. At a rally held in Sacramento, California, more than one thousand nurses "swarmed the west steps of the Capitol to urge passage of Senate Bill 840, sponsored by Sen. Sheila Kuehl, D-Santa Barbara," intended to supply affordable health care for every Californian. They were addressed by Michael Moore, whose movie *Sicko* (2007), which indicts the profit-based health care system, was being previewed for the nurses and for the California State Assembly, and by Rose Ann DeMoro, who focused in her remarks on the destructive role played in the health care system by insurance companies (see Calvan 2007).

I don't want to romanticize the role of women in unions or the political impact of unions more broadly. Indeed, in 2008 a bitter dispute between the CNA and the SEIU roiled the service sector union movement and brought to light so many of the ugly power struggles and compromises that have made many turn away from unions altogether (see Gluckman 2008; Kaplan 2008).[12] The union movement has a long way to go in incorporating and accepting leadership, not only from women, but also from the many new actors in the immigrant community that have been creating workers' centers and other alternative institutions as part of the struggle for labor rights as well as for citizenship (see Moody 2008). Welcoming innovative strategies by groups traditionally excluded from union organizing must be part of the agenda: for example, the June 2008 National Domestic Workers Congress, held in New York City, which threw its support behind a proposed New York State domestic workers' bill of rights, which if passed would be the first in the country (Buckley and Correal 2008). Nonetheless, I would argue that the revival of unions, both domestically and internationally, is one of the most significant sites of resistance to corporate power, and the infusion of women's energy and feminist consciousness into labor unions is a hopeful aspect of an otherwise bleak picture.

DECOUPLING FEMINISM
FROM CAPITALIST MODERNITY

I want here to begin articulating a strategy for disentangling the project of women's emancipation from its tight embrace with capitalist modernization. The germ of this idea came to me in the wake of one of the passionate discussions in the "Facing Global Capital" seminar at CUNY. (For details of this seminar, see the Preface.) This was a group of some thirty to forty people, primarily academics (faculty and graduate students), but with a sprinkling of activists. The discussion was lively to the point of active verbal hostilities. The disputes stemmed from the ideological differences among the participants, whom I mentally divided into three categories.[13]

First were the liberal feminists, who happily envisaged the spread of hegemonic U.S. feminism to the rest of the world and who uncritically believed that the ideas of U.S. feminism would genuinely benefit the lives of other women, if only they had access to them. Second were the postmodernists, whose governing ideological mode was active despair about the ravages of contemporary globalization, along with a skepticism about feminism as being simply another hollow "grand narrative," and a conviction that there was no "outside" of capitalism to repair to. Third were the Marxist feminists, who continued to insist that another world was possible. This group (including myself) agreed with the despair of the postmodernists about the contemporary ravages of globalization: the increasing immiseration of the majority of the world, along with the decline in health, life expectancy, and access to education and a viable future for so many millions of the world's population. But we did not agree with the premise that there was no "outside" of capitalism, that is, no alternative way of organizing society. Indeed, I felt that the postmodernists in a curious way were ideologically wedded to their worst enemies in that they saw continued globalization as inevitable.

This set of disagreements came to a head (not for the only time) at a meeting of the seminar on November 21, 2002, devoted to the theme "cultures of violence." As it happened, we had read one piece on the abject situation of people with AIDS in Brazil, who are subjected to the bureaucratic rigidities of the state health system (Biehl 2001). And we had read another piece on female genital cutting among one of the indigenous peoples of the Sudan (Abusharaf 2001). What I observed in the discussion that followed was that speakers pointed either to the misery and abjection of the people being spit out by the bureaucracies of modernity or to the cruelty of the traditional tribal requirements toward young girls.

We seemed to be facing a stark set of choices. On the one hand, there was the choice of leaving unaltered the harshness of a traditional culture toward its female children on the theory that indigenous cultures had their own integrity. On the other hand, the choice was to intervene in this system through modernization, via the structures of globalization, and thus bring to bear the new ultra-cruel violence of bureaucratized capitalism. In other words, one was forced to choose between a respect for traditional patriarchy, with so many of its costs born by young women and girls, and an uncritical acceptance of corporate globalization, with its modern ideas of female empowerment and all of the accompanying baggage of consumerism, individualism, and radical inequalities of life chances, not to mention environmental degradation.

What was missing from the discussion was a third choice, namely, a renewed dream of an alternative world in which health care would not be rationed and in which indigenous wisdoms would be preserved in tandem with modern knowledge. The example that came to my mind during this discussion was an instance of combining indigenous knowledge and practices with the knowledge provided by modern science: the practice of midwifery in Nunavik, the Inuit region of the Quebec Arctic. The practice of the Quebec government had been to fly pregnant mothers out of their community all the way to Montreal, where they received medical care in total isolation from their family and community. "Inspired by community organizing by Inuit women and growing activism for Inuit cultural revival and self-government," a health care center, the Inuulitsivik Health Centre, established a midwifery service in 1986 to train Inuit midwives. "The community expressed a strong desire to reclaim midwifery skills and traditional knowledge about birth and to combine both traditional and modern approaches" (Epoo and Wagner 2005, 1–2).

These Inuit midwives in northern Quebec receive modern medical training. They use this up-to-date scientific training, along with their knowledge of traditional practices, to deliver babies using their traditional language. If all goes well, the babies are born uneventfully, immersed in the language of their traditional culture. If they are endangered, they get modern medical care on the spot, rather than having to be flown four to eight hours to Montreal, although this is still the case for severe emergency procedures:

> Birth in the community is seen as part of restoring skills and pride and building capacity in the community. Participating in birth builds family and community relationships and intergenerational support and learning. It can be part of both "re-Inuitization," through promoting respect for traditional knowledge, and of teaching transcultural skills both within the local community and with nonlocal health care providers. The Inuit midwives play a vital role in promoting healthy behavior and in health education and can be effective in this role in ways that

health care workers who do not speak the language or know the culture could not hope to be. (Epoo and Wagner 2005, 4)

This project, which combined modern feminist ideas about health care and the proper role of women as midwives with the language and wisdom of an ancient indigenous culture, encapsulated for me a way to escape from the either/or trap of tradition versus modernity. We have seen that the global war on terror relies on a stark dichotomy between modernity and tradition, where the first encapsulates the values of Western civilization, equated with market democracies, while the second encapsulates "our" terrorist enemies, who are mired in patriarchal traditions that lead them inexorably to become Western-hating terrorists. Beyond this grotesque caricature of the world, there is the reality that, as I have argued, Western feminism carries with it the liberal ideas of individual autonomy and self-determination that grow from the Enlightenment traditions of the seventeenth and eighteenth centuries in Europe. But as many have pointed out, these traditions of human rights, enshrined in UN documents and national constitutions around the world, are no longer the exclusive patrimony [*sic!*] of the West.

Is it not possible, now, to decouple the cluster of ideas that constitute contemporary feminisms from the battering ram of U.S. imperialism? One goal, then, for a newly radical feminism would be the achievement of self-determination for peoples, with women's rights encapsulated in that process. Even though I have been relentlessly critical of globalization throughout this book, I do want to note a positive side—that the globalization of information has produced an interpenetration of ideas and concepts that renders the old dichotomy of tradition versus modernity, if not utterly obsolete, at least an inadequate descriptor of the present reality.

Certainly, the ideas of feminism have become so widespread and so universally familiar that we can imagine the creation of as many feminisms as there are languages and cultures. As noted earlier, it is clear from their writings and proclamations that the Zapatista struggle for indigenous rights now incorporates a sophisticated set of claims for women's rights that has become part and parcel of the revolutionary goals of this movement. (On the cosmology and the activism of indigenous women's movement among the Zapatistas in Chiapas, Mexico, see Marcos 2005.)

So instead of assuming that one has to choose between capitalist modernity and patriarchal traditionalism, we can think of a third option, which would represent community autonomy and self-determination, where people are free to choose what elements of tradition and what elements of modernity will make up their own vision of the future. In this project those cultures that were ravaged by colonialism can look back into their own past to resurrect the elements of women's autonomy that were suppressed or destroyed by colonial regimes.

RETHINKING THE ROLE OF THE STATE: THE CASE OF VENEZUELA

Here I want to rethink attitudes toward the state and state-led economic development. In the current crisis, the Left in the United States and around the world is divided as to strategy and goals and uncertain about a path to the future. While acknowledging the brave achievements of the Cuban revolution, most Left writers see the blueprint of Soviet-model economic development as discredited and agree that the only possible socialism for the future is one that is deeply democratic.

But how do we build this new socialism? James Petras and Henry Weltmeyer make a case for a return to state-led development, with nations redirecting resources toward food sufficiency and a vibrant local economy (Petras and Weltmeyer 2001). But much feminist scholarship proceeds on the assumption that women's interests and state or government interests are opposed because governments are inevitably patriarchal. Thus, Rosalind Petchesky places her faith in a new international civil society mediating between nation-states and international institutions (Petchesky 2003). Arturo Escobar sees the possibility of creating some kind of a hybrid culture and economy that would restore the autonomy and health of indigenous peoples (Escobar 1995). And Maria Mies and Veronica Bennholdt-Thomsen go further, calling for a rollback of industrialization and a return to a subsistence economy (Bennholdt-Thomsen and Mies 1999).

But Doug Henwood is scathing about calls for a return to a presumed pre-capitalist Golden Age, which disregard the complexity of modern production and distribution and overlook the achievements of industrialization: "the lengthening of lives, the reduction in infant and maternal mortality, the far-from-complete liberation of women (accomplished in part by the availability of factory jobs, which offer them a way out of rural patriarchy), the spread of literacy—in the First and Third Worlds over the long sweep of things" (Henwood 2003, 165–166).

Some writers have been arguing that it is possible to create a new world within the structures of the old. John Holloway, a student and advocate of the Zapatista movement, argues against the idea that seizing state power can ever create social justice, advocating instead a myriad of individual and collective acts that reject capitalism. Similarly, J. K. Gibson-Graham argues for a "postcapitalist politics," encouraging feminist economic alternatives to capitalism, such as cooperatives, that spring up within the system. In other words, these writers are skeptical of the traditional idea that one has to seize and hold state power to create workable alternatives to capitalism (Gibson-Graham, 2006a, 2006c; Holloway, 2005).[14] Thus, there is no consensus as to either means or ends among those who are seeking an alternative to the current system.

But if we take seriously the analyses of writers such as Vincent Navarro, Jeff Faux, and Ed Herman, which suggest that the current period has been characterized by a counterrevolution against the working class and the poor by the elites of a globalized world, then the process of reversing this inevitably means the development of solidarity against the elites. In other words, we are looking at a return to class struggle or, rather, to the reversal of the class struggle that is now being waged against the poor. Navarro puts it this way: "The left-wing alternative must be centered in alliances among the dominated classes and other dominated groups, with a political movement that must be built upon the process of class struggle that takes place in each country. As Hugo Chávez of Venezuela said, 'It cannot be a mere movement of protest and celebration like Woodstock.' It is an enormous struggle, an endeavor in which organization and coordination are key, calling for a Fifth International. This is the challenge to the international left today" (Navarro 2007, 34).[15]

Whether or not one is convinced by Navarro's proposal for a Fifth International, are there places in the world today where the class struggle against the poor is in the process of being reversed? I want to argue that in the current political and economic scene, the Bolivarian revolution of Hugo Chávez merits our attention.

If we cut through the fog of disinformation and bias produced by the U.S. media, we can see that the work that the Chávez government has been carrying out in creating state-led development as an alternative to neoliberalism has enormous significance for feminism. The influence of the Chávez experiment is magnified through the Venezuelan President's links with a cluster of left-leaning leaders, including Cristina Fernández de Kirchner in Argentina, Evo Morales in Bolivia, Luiz Inácio Lula da Silva in Brazil, Rafael Correa in Ecuador, Fernando Lugo of Paraguay, and even Michelle Bachelet in Chile (not to mention his close ties to Fidel and Raul Castro in Cuba).[16]

The historical juncture that brought Hugo Chávez to power through a series of intensely democratic processes, including at this writing nine separate elections where he received about 60 percent of the vote, has created a new opening for state-led development, defined in the broadest possible way (Ellner 2006, 103). In the "missions" Chávez's government has established in the poorest neighborhoods, establishing jobs, health care, housing, subsidized foodstuffs, and education, he is using the state to create a newly expansive kind of development where individual human needs are being given priority.

Although this is not evident from most media coverage, the role of poor women in the Bolivarian revolution has been crucial. When an attempted coup against Chávez was launched in April 2002 by a coalition of right-wing forces with the tacit consent and encouragement of the U.S. government, it was reversed through massive street organizing: "Women were the first to mobilize: not just at Fort Tiuna and Miraflores but right across the country. In Venezuela there is a Plaza Bolivar in each town and village, and this is where people gathered, with women at the forefront" (Nora Castañeda quoted in Lopez 2006, 37). As millions mobilized by taking to the streets, "women had a great presence across the country, making calls, organizing, forming a chain of information which replaced the disinformation of the private media" (Castañeda quoted in Lopez 2006, 37). Why? "Because they were the ones with the most to lose, I think. Men were deeply affected by the coup, but it was the women who were most affected. Grassroots women have managed to survive conditions of terrible poverty and with the revolution they have gained so much that to lose it would be truly unbearable. It was like the loss of a precious loved one; we were in mourning, but ready to fight at the same time" (Castañeda quoted in Lopez 2006, 37).

It was the organized women's movement that persuaded the Chávez government to incorporate into the revised constitution of 1999 a provision, Article 88, that requires housewives to receive a government pension as a reward for their household labor. The article reads: "The State will guarantee equality between men and women in exercising the right to work. The State will recognize housework as an economic activity that creates added value and produces wealth and social welfare. Housewives are entitled to social security in accordance with the law" (cited in Lopez 2006, 53). The decades-long campaign of activists in the worldwide Wages for Housework movement has thus borne perhaps its first real fruit in the Bolivarian revolution.

In addition, the Chávez government has created the Women's Development Bank, the Banmujer, a public microfinancial system financed by the state. The first president of the bank, appointed in March 2001, Nora Castañeda, is an economist and longtime feminist activist who was a lecturer at Venezuela's Central University for more than thirty years. Bank representatives conduct grassroots economic training workshops, and then set up organized women's groups within individual communities, assist them with preparing their projects (including a budget that calculates the value of women's unpaid labor), and then grant credit for an enterprise to be carried out by women in the community.

The women are organized into cooperatives (Unidades Económicas Asociativas, or Associative Economic Units), and they monitor their progress in cooperation with the bank through a network of Banmujer users (Red de Usuarias de Banmujer). Instead of the bank setting up regional offices, bank representatives travel to remote rural regions to assist women, including indigenous women, offering small loans but also workshops on basic business principles and on broader issues such as health, community organizing, leadership, and the prevention of domestic violence (Walker 2008, 2).

The goal of establishing these cooperatives is to begin the process of bringing women out of poverty. As Nora Castañeda remarks: "The purpose of credit is not to grant it to people who may or may not spend it, so they end up indebted to the Bank and therefore not only in poverty, but in debt.... The purpose is to improve the quality of life of women and their families" (cited in Lopez 2005, 59). The microcredit scheme is publicly funded and is intended as an antipoverty measure, not a profit-making enterprise, as is the case with most microcredit programs:

Typical loan projects range from a cooperative farm to a craft workshop to a bakery to a hair salon. The credits average between 500,000 and 1,000,000 [old] bolivares (US $260 to $520) and are subsidized by the government, allowing the bank to charge interest as low as 1 percent.... Rather than measure success by profits alone, the bank prefers to focus on the progress it has made in empowering women and helping to break the cycle of poverty. In the pursuit of these goals it has indeed been successful; according to one estimate, the credits issued by the bank have created more than 260,000 jobs and assisted more than 1.3 million people. (Walker 2008, 2)

The Banmujer model encapsulates the goals of Chávez's Bolivarian project, which is, in Castañeda's words, "creating a caring economy, an economy at the service of human beings, not human beings at the service of the economy" (quoted in Walker 2008, 3).

It could be that this difference in philosophy is what engenders so much hostility. As Kristen Walker notes:

Perhaps what the United States so intensely dislikes about Venezuela is not so much its political system (which is, after all, democratic—Chávez won 56 percent of the popular vote in 1998, compared to Bush's 48 percent in 2000), but rather its rejection of free-market capitalism as the ruling economic paradigm. Instead, Chávez is using programs like the Women's Development Bank to encourage the formulation of what Castañeda terms a "popular economy." This economy is intended to serve average people instead of large corporations by mirroring on a larger scale the cooperative work that Banmujer encourages for the groups of women with whom it collaborates. Just as the individual women work together to run their business or workshop, the "popular economy" promotes larger economic actors to work together, complementing each other instead of competing for resources. An article in *The Guardian* commented that "the mini-entrepreneurs [given loans by Banmujer] are encouraged to cooperate with other small businesses rather than competing with them. If one group is given money to rear chickens, another nearby will be given a loan to slaughter the chickens." Thus, Banmujer uses financial and nonfinancial services to empower women, enabling them to overcome poverty sustainably, while also promoting Venezuela's vision of a "popular" or "caring" economy. (Walker 2008, 3; brackets in original)

The Chávez model of state-led development insists on national sovereignty in economic decisionmaking. But it goes well beyond this, toward an expanded concept of human development. Under this model, Venezuela uses state power to create the conditions of welfare and education necessary to help build a new socialism, a goal Chávez has publicly embraced on many occasions. To be sure, the Venezuelan experience is built on oil wealth and is not easily replicable in countries lacking such a plentiful and profitable natural resource. But the contrast with other oil-rich countries is noteworthy: unlike countries such as Angola and Nigeria, where the presence of oil has been diagnosed as the "resource curse," keeping these countries more impoverished on average than comparable countries that lack oil, the government of Venezuela under Chávez has consciously and deliberately turned substantial proportions of its oil wealth into the basis of social programs in education, health, subsidized consumption, and housing (see Hammond 2008).

As one U.S. expert on Venezuelan events notes, "Chávez's six and a half years in power demonstrate that third-world governments can forcefully uphold national sovereignty and at the same time promote a nationalist, progressive agenda in opposition to powerful economic interests" (Ellner 2006, 101). Little wonder that *The Economist*, the *Wall Street Journal*, *BusinessWeek*, and other business outlets fulminate about the ways in which Chávez's antineoliberal policies challenge the dominant paradigm of decisionmaking by, for, and to the profit of international corporate interests. In the debate, then, about building another world, the case of Venezuela is extremely important, worthy of attention, close study, and international solidarity.[17]

ABOLISHING GENDER VERSUS REHABILITATING MATERNALISM

Finally, I want to raise again what I have called the abolition of gender. I have argued that hegemonic feminism in the United States sought to abolish gender. (See Chapter 2.) That is, in the struggle to establish the right of women to enter all areas of work, especially those areas that had been delineated as male since the Industrial Revolution, feminist activists had to emphasize the capacities of women as equivalent to those of men. Indeed, in recent years some feminist scholars have presented the need to abolish gender as the most fundamental element in feminist-inspired social change and the key to revolutionizing all of society. Thus, Judith Lorber argues that what is required is a process of degendering all aspects of social life, from parenting to politics (Lorber 2005).

I have further argued that this abolition of gender became part of the vocabulary and the assumptions of the media and of academe. From the casting of Demi Moore as a Navy SEAL to the gender-neutral coverage of the assassination of the Russian journalist Anna Politkovskaya,[18] it was accepted that being a woman was not relevant to performing a professional job. The concerted attack by feminist writers on chivalry as a form of condescension, masking a belief in female inferiority, was well and truly absorbed by the mainstream.

This apparent acceptance of women in all areas of the workforce and more broadly in all kinds of public roles, from politics to the military, is the good news.

But to me the bad news is that all "womanly virtues" have now been banished from our vocabulary. Feminist scholars detecting a trace of maternalism are quick to label this *essentialism*, a return to the bad old days when women (at least, women of a certain race and class) were relegated to the kitchen and the bedroom. Similarly, female corporate leaders and heads of state are congratulated on their successful renunciation of such "female" virtues as compassion.

The most extreme evidence of the "success" of integrating women into male-dominated professions is the horrific story of the role of women soldiers in the atrocities of Abu Ghraib. But with the banishing of maternalism has also gone the possibility of an appeal to nurturance and to mutual dependence. Very few feminist scholars—with the honorable exception of Martha Fineman (1995, 67ff.)—have dared to raise the issue of what has become of the female virtues of mothering and tenderness, all of the qualities formerly attributed to women, from the Virgin Mary on down, by Western culture.

An exception here is the growing literature on care by writers such as Joan Tronto and Nancy Folbre (Tronto 1993; Folbre 2001). They ask the question, "What becomes of caregiving in a society where most women are in the workforce full-time?" A glib short answer might be that we now expect men to have these virtues as well, and we could point to the growth of "house husbands" as exemplars. But a more radical reply might be to note that the qualities of nurturance and care have indeed been the domain of women in the past, but that they now need to be the domain of society as a whole.

Rather than the abolition of gender, then, could we not consider a return to maternalism, but writ large? We could raise something that we—correctly, in my view—associate with mothers to the level of a social principle. Of course, the meaning would have to be transmuted. The critique by feminist scholars of the maternalism of the Progressive Era means that this form of social policy is severely discredited. (See Chapter 4.) One would not want to see again elite white women presiding over the lives of immigrant and African American women, teaching them to be "real" Americans. But I am envisaging a transformed kind of maternalism, meaning a sense of compassion and a responsibility to nurture on the part of all social and political organizations.

One model for this revived maternalism is to be found in the Nordic countries, which, although under pressure from neoliberal forces, have largely managed to maintain their welfare states. The history of these states is linked to the efforts of first-wave feminists to capture state power in the interests of women and children. Indeed, Hilkka Pietila argues that activist women played a key role in helping to build the welfare state in Finland, and that this model of using the state to advance women's interests is linked to the extraordinary economic development of Finland, a country that still provides its population with remarkable levels of income and social protections. As she notes:

Finland approaches the state as a caring and sharing institution from the point of view of gender equality and the status of women. The feminist notion of "domestication of the state" is very close to the terms often used about the welfare society in Nordic countries in general. *Folkshemmet*, "a/people's home," was politically popular in Sweden for decades, and idea [*sic*] of "the public family" as parallel to the private family was introduced by Swedish researcher Ulla Olin in the 1970s.... Anneli Anttonen ... speaks about a "maternalist citizenship" in Finland. Since the welfare state here shares with families both the burden and the expenses of raising children, it is sometimes called "the third parent in every family" (Pietila 2006, 175–176).

This is what I mean by reviving a transformed maternalism, not as an essentialist definition of women's roles, but as a set of claims on the state, as pursued, for example, by the femocrats in Australia. As noted earlier, mainstream economic publications in the United States, England, and elsewhere continue to speak with contempt of the "nanny state." This should give us a clue to what they do not want us to think about. What is wrong with looking to government, as people did in the 1930s, for protection from a raging and violent corporate system?

Obviously, this suggestion is fraught with difficulties. How could impoverished states in the Third World ever aspire to the kind of wealth that undergirds the Finnish welfare state? Such a concept presupposes that the struggles currently being waged by countries in the Global South for equitable trade arrangements and the cancellation of debt would have been successfully concluded, and that food sovereignty had been restored to Global South nations. It also presupposes that the battles by feminists for an equal voice in government around the world could be won, so that women's voices were intrinsically a part of social decision-making. And finally, it presupposes that it would be possible to balance meeting the needs of all citizens, female and male, of all ethnic and racial backgrounds, with ensuring sufficient autonomy and independence for each individual to feel at once both economically secure and individually self-determining.[19] A tall order! But let us assume that such a transformation is possible.

What would this kind of transformed maternalism look like at the local, state, national, and international levels? I am not wedded to the word, although I use it because it evokes a long historical memory. We could call this transformed government *a parental state*, if this would be less offensive to some feminist thinkers. Folbre suggests the term *a family state* (Folbre 2001). But whatever expression we use, would this concept not involve caring for children and ensuring health care for everyone, along with sufficient nutrition and adequate housing? Would it not mean meeting the needs of women, as mothers, along with those of fathers, and those in alternative relationships of all kinds? Would it not, then, eventually, if carried out in every country, mean a world where disease, poverty, and war were abolished? This is at least something to think about as we consider how to develop a set of feminist principles for the long, hard struggle ahead of us.

Notes

❋

The Introduction was previously published as "Scouting Parties and Bold Detachments: Toward a Postcapitalist Feminism," in *The Global and the Intimate*, edited by Geraldine Pratt and Victoria Rosner, a special issue of *WSQ: Women's Studies Quarterly* 34, nos. 1–2 (Spring–Summer 2006): 40–62. Chapters 1, 2, 4, 5, and 6 include short sections that originally appeared in "A Dangerous Liaison? Feminism and Corporate Globalization," *Science and Society* 69, no. 3 (July 2005): 487–518. All previously published material is reprinted here with permission.

Notes for the Preface

1. See Agrell 2008. Zapatero's first cabinet in 2004 was half women. See Socolovsky 2004.

2. From announcement for Womenomics Part I: Women and the Global Economy, Thursday, January 31, 2008, Demos Forum, New York City. Series sponsored by the Women's Leadership Initiative. See "Guide to Womenomics" 2006; "Importance of Sex" 2006; "Womenomics Revisited" 2007; World Bank 2006; and World Economic Forum 2007.

3. "In the wake of the cold war, there is a mood of triumphalist Americanism in the United States. 'Democratization,' code name for the transformation of (efficient through inefficient to wild) state capitalisms and their colonies to tributary economies of rationalized, global financialization—carries with it the aura of the civilizing mission of earlier colonialisms. Again, the talk is of 'transformation.' And it is now more specifically in terms of gender than anything else. This is the globalized subject. The rationalization of sexuality, the invasive restructuring of gender relations, poor women's credit-baiting without infrastructural involvement in the name of women's micro-enterprise, the revision of women-in-development (modernization) to gender-and-development (New World Economic Order)—all this is seen as global sisterhood" (Spivak 1999, 223n42).

4. The NICs usually include Hong Kong, Malaysia, Singapore, South Korea, and Taiwan (the list varies with different authorities and criteria for inclusion). Brazil, Russia, India, and China are currently referred to as the *BRIC countries,* seen as leaders among the world economies; the phrase is attributed to Jim O'Neill, chief economist of Goldman Sachs. See Smale 2008.

5. The second half of this famous slogan was added in Caracas, Venezuela, when the forum met there in 2006. On the history of the World Social Forum, see Smith et al. 2008.

6. I am borrowing Stuart Ewen's expression from *Captains of Consciousness* (2001) to avoid speaking of capitalism itself as an agent.

7. Max Weber, the famous German intellectual and founding father of sociology, introduced the notion of an "ideal type" as a way to model social reality. I draw on Raewyn Connell's concept of "hegemonic masculinity" here. See Connell 1995. Chela Sandoval uses a related term, "hegemonic feminist theory," following Gayatri Spivak (2000, 41 ff.) Women's studies orthodoxy now insists on the locution *feminisms* to stress the wide range of sometimes conflicting ideologies that all claim the same title.

8. I use this somewhat more neutral term instead of female genital mutilation or female circumcision. For a full discussion, see Chapter 3 of this volume.

Notes for the Introduction

1. My original academic training was at Yale University, where I received a (gender-free) Ph.D. in French history. My feminist academic training was self-taught from around 1970 onward.

2. Although the struggle for ecological sustainability is highly relevant to the issues here, I have not tackled these questions in this book.

3. The events of Seattle brought into consciousness in the North a range of movements against globalization that had been developing in the Global South over the decades since the 1970s. See Smith et al. 2008, 14ff.

4. For a more precise account of the ideological positions of World Social Forum participants, which range from anarchist to Marxist to reformist, see Smith et al. 2008, 79ff.

5. See Stacey 2006 for her very courteous response to my criticism.

6. See "Learning to Speak Australian," in Eisenstein 1991b, 6–15.

7. Patricia Ticineto Clough and I were among the faculty advisers; the students included Jennifer Leigh Disney, Mitu Hirshman, Yvonne Lasalle, Kriemeld Saunders, and Kimberly Flynn, at the CUNY Graduate Center ("Which Way for Women and Development? Debating Concepts, Strategies, and Directions for the 21st Century," October 15-17, 1998, the Borough of Manhattan Community College and the Graduate Center, the City University of New York).

8. On the debates within the women and development literature, see Chapter 5.

9. The student body of over nineteen thousand includes students from more than 140 countries. Among freshmen in 2006, 44 percent were born outside the U.S. mainland. Forty-four percent of undergraduates are first-generation college students, and a majority of students work either full- or part-time. See Queens College 2006.

Notes for Chapter 1

1. Cf. Fernandez-Kelly 2007, 509: as of 1978, "women were becoming the new face of the international proletariat." For an introduction to the literature on globalization, see Sklair 2002. For an overview of women, work, and globalization, see Beneria 2003; Rai 2002; and Visvanathan et al. 1997.

2. In this book I am accepting the use of the term *globalization* since it has become so widely used, although many writers on the Left consider *neoimperialism* a better expression.

3. "Macroeconomic" refers to the performance of an economy as a whole (as opposed to the "microeconomics" of individual firms, industries, or markets). Macroeconomic policies, including levels of taxation, interest rates, and money supply, can be used to influence employment, inflation, and economic growth. In this book I use the term *Third World* or *Global South* to designate those

countries still struggling with the aftereffects of colonialism. The mainstream press uses the term *emerging markets* to refer to countries that are seen as promising targets of international investment.

4. For details of the struggle over attempts to privatize Medicaid, see www.ncpssm.org.

5. See Levitt 1993. "The underlying concept may be traced back to McLuhan's (1960) notion of the 'global village' but was explicitly introduced into the management literature in Levitt's (1983) paper on the globalization of markets" (Dicken 1998, 15n1). Cf. Feder 2006: "His concept that business was becoming globalized, which Mr. Levitt defined as the changes in technologies and social behaviors that allow multinational companies like Coca-Cola and McDonald's to sell the same products worldwide, first appeared in a 1983 *Harvard Business Review* article 'The Globalization of Markets.'"

6. See, for example, Byron 2007 on how Procter & Gamble is targeting 1 billion very poor women in developing countries by packaging shampoo and other products into tiny single-use packets that they can afford.

7. The mortgages were bundled into tradable securities owned by banks, hedge funds, and other investment institutions. The disputed value of some of these "toxic" mortgages led to mutual distrust and an unwillingness to grant credit.

8. GDP is the sum of all goods and services produced annually within a country. It is used to compare the total value of one country's economy against another. Feminist economists have pointed to the inadequacy of these figures, which exclude all of the unpaid work performed by women in households and the work of women in the "informal" sector, such as street vending. GDP figures are also tilted against environmental policies: a forest that is cut down counts, but not a forest left standing. On this point, see Folbre 2001, 68–71.

9. A third international financial institution was established in 1948: the General Agreement on Trade and Tariffs (GATT), which was designed to reduce tariff rates on trade in manufactured goods. GATT was succeeded by the World Trade Organization in 1995 (McMichael 2004, 168–172).

10. The First Estate was the clergy; and the Second Estate, the nobility. The Third Estate comprised the remainder of the entire population, led by the bourgeoisie, whose claims for political representation were a starting point of the revolutionary process.

11. Keynesianism is named for the influential British economist John Maynard Keynes, who argued in the 1930s that government spending was necessary to counter the underconsumption that was helping to prolong the Great Depression. The term *neoliberalism* is confusing to most Americans as it sounds like liberalism, that is, the left of the political spectrum as opposed to conservatism on the right. But it refers to a return to a free-market ideology, labeled *liberalism* in the context of English politics.

12. Of course, the "consensus" in the United States was hard fought, and labor historians are now emphasizing the intensity of labor conflict during the years from 1945 to the mid-1970s (see, for example, Lichtenstein 2002).

13. "In fact, it was economist Milton Friedman, who said ... 'In one sense, we are all Keynesians now; in another, nobody is any longer a Keynesian.' (*Time* magazine, February 4, 1966). What Nixon said in 1971 was 'I am now a Keynesian in economics' (*New York Times,* January 4, 1971)" (Bartlett 2008).

14. "Dhaka muslin was in demand in the court of the Mughal emperor and among the aristocracy of Europe as the finest textile in the world and description of its delicacy and beauty abound in the historical literature" (Kabeer 2000, 55). As the British textile industry mechanized, the British first limited the sale of Bengal cloth at home with prohibitive tariffs, and eventually the competition from British textiles ended the production of both local cotton and muslin. Dhaka was reduced to a ghost town, and the governor-general of the East India Company told London in 1835 that "the misery hardly finds a parallel in the history of commerce. The bones of the cotton

weavers are bleaching the plains of India" (cited in Kabeer 2000, 56). This is also the quote made famous by Karl Marx in *Capital I* (1909, Chapter 15, Section 5, 471).

15. See Perman et al. 2004, 4.

16. U.S. Census Bureau 2002, 416, Table 653: "Employment by Industry, 1970–1994," and 385, Table 591: "Employment by Industry, 1980–2001."

17. White House 2002. Calculated from Table B-12: "Gross Domestic Product by Industry, 1959–2000."

18. Petrodollars are the dollars received by the members of OPEC from Western countries in exchange for their oil, which are then deposited in Western banks.

19. This shock was named for Paul Volcker, chair of the Federal Reserve Board under Presidents Jimmy Carter and Ronald Reagan, from 1979 to 1987.

20. These were called the Bretton Woods institutions after the name of the town in New Hampshire where representatives of the British and U.S. treasuries designed the founding bodies of the postwar economic order: the World Bank and the International Monetary Fund.

21. The WTO succeeded the GATT agreement signed in 1944 in Havana, Cuba, and implemented in 1947; this was an international treaty that sought to assure free trade among member nations. Regular international negotiations on the terms of free trade have continued and have become the site of renewed contestations between the developing and the rich countries (McMichael 2004, 194–195). In 2008, the "Doha" round of WTO negotiations launched in 2001 ended in failure as the newly intensified demands by developing countries for protections against imports were rejected by the United States (see Loyn 2008).

22. Just to take the case of agribusiness: "Three agribusiness firms headquartered in the United States operate meat-packing operations across the world, raising cattle, pigs, and poultry on feedstuffs supplied by their own grain marketing subsidiaries elsewhere in the world. Cargill, headquartered in Minnesota, is the largest grain trader in the world, operating in 70 countries with more than 800 offices or plants and more than 70,000 employees. It has established a joint venture with Nippon Meat Packers of Japan called Sun Valley Thailand, from which it exports U.S. corn-fed poultry products to the Japanese market. ConAgra, headquartered in Nebraska, owns 56 companies and operates in 26 countries with 58,000 employees. It processes feed and animal protein products in the United States, Canada, Australia, Europe, the Far East, and Latin America. Tyson Foods, headquartered in Arkansas, runs a joint venture with the Japanese agribusiness firm C. Itoh, which produces poultry in Mexico for both local consumption and export to Japan" (McMichael 2004, 104–105).

23. The *Washington Consensus* is "a term coined in 1990 by John Williamson of the Institute for International Economics, a think tank in that city" ("Wanted: A New Regional Agenda" 2003, 2). Of course, the term refers not to Washington, DC, the city, as disingenuously suggested by *The Economist,* but to Washington, the seat of U.S. economic and military power.

24. The OECD comprises thirty member countries in Europe plus the United States, Japan, and South Korea, all considered developed economies. Reagan's expansion of public spending was paid for by an increase in the deficit and an increase in taxes for the majority (while he dramatically reduced taxes for the 20 percent of the population with the highest incomes) (Navarro 2007, 21).

25. The informal economy refers to forms of income that are not usually part of the official economy: they are not taxed or regulated, but are off the books, including everything from street vendors and sex workers to drug traffickers.

26. For China, the figures are 4.5 percent versus 9.8 percent and 2.5 percent versus 8.4 percent, reflecting the impact of continued state-led development.

27. "George Caffentzis, the philosopher of money, and his colleagues in the Midnight Oil Collective were the first, in the early 1980s, to develop the idea that the neoliberal project is, in its essence, a form of 'new enclosures,' taking the tactics of the English enclosures to a planetary level and creating this time a fully globalized proletariat" (Boal 2007, 3).

28. "Five of South Africa's nine provinces have now reported cases of cholera. The country's department of health announced on Friday that there have been 64 deaths and nearly 18,000 infections since the outbreak began last August.... Critics have accused the government of exacerbating the problem by introducing charges for access to clean water—a move that has prompted some people to save money by getting their water from contaminated sources" ("Cholera in South Africa Spreads" 2001).

29. The G-8 was originally the Group of 7—the United States, the United Kingdom, France, West Germany, Japan, Italy, and Canada. Founded in 1975, it holds annual meetings in which finance ministers set economic policy for the world economy. Russia was admitted in 1996, hence the G-8.

NOTES FOR CHAPTER 2

1. By "hegemonic" feminism, as noted in the Preface, I mean a commonsense, everyday understanding of feminism that permeates the media and is widely accepted as what feminism connotes in the mind of the public. I am modeling this expression on "hegemonic masculinity," the locution coined by Raewyn Connell (1995).

2. As noted in the Preface, my argument in this chapter parallels the analysis set forth by Judith Stacey in her work on postindustrial society. As she writes: "In the late 1980s, I suggested that second-wave feminism had served as an unwitting midwife to postindustrial society.... Legitimate feminist critiques of women's economic dependency and mandatory domesticity in the 1950s modern family, I argued, had provided unintended ideological support for the massive entry of women into the labor force and its complex interaction with rising divorce rates and family instability that were already under way. In that sense feminism unwittingly had abetted the shift from industrial to postindustrial labor practices that ultimately eroded real wages, weakened labor unions, undermined public support for welfare entitlements, and increased class inequality. Paradoxically, therefore, women's efforts to achieve gender equality with men contributed to forces that yielded the feminization of poverty and increased inequality among women (and men)" (Stacey 2006, 63; see also Stacey 1987, 1990).

3. See "ABC Impeaches *Commander in Chief*" 2006.

4. Palin was preceded in this role by Geraldine Ferrraro, nominated by Walter Mondale at the Democratic convention of 1984 as the first woman vice presidential candidate; both were defeated in a landslide for the incumbent president Ronald Reagan and vice presidential candidate George H.W. Bush.

5. See Amott and Matthei 1991 for a detailed history of the very different experiences of Native American, African American, Asian, and Hispanic women.

6. This account relies heavily on Kessler-Harris 1982.

7. The establishment of dormitories and the concern for parental attitudes reappear in this century. For Malaysia, on the treatment of peasant girls in Japanese electronic factories, see Ong 1987. For Mexico, see Cravey 1998.

8. Barbara Welter (1966) documents the separate spheres ideology of the pre–Civil War period; for a more class conscious account, see Lerner 1969.

9. *Social feminists* is a term coined by historians to refer to the several generations of middle-class women reformers whose concern was to better the conditions of women and children under industrial capitalism. For the maternalism of these women, see Gordon 1994. By and large, the social feminists saw wives and mothers as in need of protection, either from husbands or from government, rather than envisioning them as independent wage-earners. On the strengths and weaknesses of maternalism as a political strategy, see Koven and Michel 1993. On the cross-class alliance of women workers with the WTUL, see Buhle 1983, 190 ff.; Roark et al. 2006, 536–537; Tax 2001.

10. Some supporters of the *Muller v. Oregon* decision saw protecting women first as paving the way to gain protection for male workers later on. "Much of the energy behind attempts to limit the hours of women and children in the 1880s and 1890s came from those who believed that women could be an 'opening wedge' in obtaining laws for all the unorganized. Shorter hours for some, they argued, along with adequate factory sanitation and safety devices, would inevitably lead to better conditions for all workers." Kessler-Harris quotes the economist Elizabeth Brandeis as concluding, sarcastically, that "workers had decided to 'fight the battle behind the women's petticoats'" (Kessler-Harris 1982, 184).

11. See May 1982. The wage was actually allocated on a sliding scale, according to an elaborate evaluation of workers' domestic situation and their suitability for assembly-line work. Hence, only a portion of Ford workers would be receiving a genuine family wage.

12. The first wave of feminism generally refers to the period from the alliance with abolitionists in the 1830s to the winning of the vote primarily for white women in 1920. The second wave refers to the rebirth of feminism in the 1960s and 1970s, drawing on a phrase coined by Martha Weinman Lear in a widely read 1966 article in the *New York Times Magazine* (cited in Eisenstein 1983, 147). As Sue Cobble (2004) points out, the "trough" between the two waves from the 1920s to the 1960s referred to by many women's history scholars was in fact a period of intense labor feminism.

13. Carter et al. 2006, 2–103, Table Ba688-705, "Major Industrial Groups of Labor Force Participants—Females: 1910–1990."

14. Carter et al. 2006, 2–135, Table Ba1061-1074, "Major Occupational Groups—Females: 1860–1990." This calculation omits occupational categories not clearly identifiable by class: "farmers," "other service workers," and "unclassified."

15. U.S. Census Bureau 2003, 52, Table HS-30, "Marital Status of Women in the Civilian Labor Force: 1900–2002." In 1947, "married" women included widowed, divorced, and separated women. In 1965, "married" women excluded these categories, which were moved to "other," perhaps reflecting the influence of feminist attitudes toward marriage and work. The category of single women did not change. Hence the figure for "total" minus the figure for "other" was used in calculating the numbers of married women.

16. Cobble (2004) touches on the turmoil within the labor movement during the purges of communist and radical union leaders in the 1940s and 1950s, but does not focus particularly on the effects of this taming of labor radicalism on issues for women workers.

17. Mary Anderson, a former garment and shoe worker, labor organizer, and cofounder of the Women's Trade Union League, was director of the federal Women's Bureau from 1919 to 1944.

18. Carter et al. 2006, Table Ba1033-1046, Major Occupational Groups—All Persons: 1860–1990.

19. On this history, see Cobble 2004 and Harrison 1988. In fact, Esther Peterson and her allies postponed the consideration of the Equal Rights Amendment as long as they could and sought to have the state laws on protection of women workers considered individually, so as not to throw out the baby with the bathwater. But the emergence of the National Organization for Women in 1966, under the leadership of Betty Friedan, impatient with the foot-dragging of the EEOC on sex-based discrimination, pushed hard to eliminate state laws, and many were found unconstitutional under Title VII of the Civil Rights Act of 1964.

20. The mobilization against the ERA by the right wing was part of a strategy of using the gains of the women's movement as an entering wedge for undermining the Democratic majority, along with attacks on abortion rights, affirmative action, and civil rights. See Chapter 4. Even though, as noted, the Equal Rights Amendment had been part of the Republican agenda for decades, it now became a weapon against the advances of feminism and an entering wedge for the new Republican coalition. On the evolution of the ERA and the role of Phyllis Schlafly, see Spruill 2008.

21. This borrows from Richard Sennett's famous book *The Hidden Injuries of Class*. See Rosen 2002, 432ff.

22. In Daly's vocabulary, "biophiliac," or loving of life, describes women, whereas "necrophiliac," or death loving, describes men. See Daly 1978 and Eisenstein 1983, 107–115.

23. The antipornography legislation movement holds that pornography is injurious to women's civil rights because it causes them harm; the opposition holds that limiting pornography is a curtailment of free speech. The Minneapolis City Council passed the first civil rights antipornography ordinance, written by Catharine MacKinnon and Andrea Dworkin, in 1983 and in 1984; both ordinances were vetoed by the mayor. In Indianapolis, the city council passed and the mayor signed a similar ordinance, but the law was struck down by the U.S. Court of Appeals for the Seventh Circuit in 1985, a ruling upheld without comment by the Supreme Court. In 1988, a similar voter initiative with 62 percent of the vote was passed in Bellingham, Washington, again to be struck down by Federal District Court judge Carolyn Dimmick. But in February 1992, in a victory for the antipornography campaigners, the Canadian Supreme Court ruled unanimously that obscenity should be defined by the harm it causes to women. "Materials portraying women as a class of objects for sexual exploitation and abuse have a negative impact on the individual's sense of self-worth and acceptance" (Hill and Silver 1993, 283, citing the Supreme Court opinion).

24. See Osborn 2001: "Mass rape and sexual enslavement in time of war will for the first time be regarded as a crime against humanity, a charge second in gravity only to genocide, after a landmark ruling from the Yugoslav war crimes tribunal in The Hague yesterday which sentenced three Bosnian Serbs to a combined tariff of 60 years in jail."

25. "By far, the single greatest impact of the women's movement was in the American workforce. Beyond housing, beyond day care, beyond issues of housework between husbands and wives, it was issues of career and work opportunities that allowed women to remake the nation. Whether they worked in factories, in offices, or as professionals, the politics of work was an abiding concern for feminists" (Evans 2003, 81–82).

26. Calculated from U.S. Census Bureau 2001, 373, Table 577, "Employment Status of Women by Marital Status and Presence and Age of Children: 1970–2000."

27. Title IX of the Education Amendments of 1972, introduced by U.S. Reps. Patsy T. Mink and Edith Green, prohibited discrimination on the basis of sex in any education programs receiving federal financial assistance; its most visible impact has been on high school and college athletics.

28. *Ms.* was introduced in 1972 as a special supplement to *New York Magazine,* then edited by Clay Felker. On the history of the magazine, see Thom 1997.

29. "Among the more than 117 million women over the age of 15, according to the marital status category in the Census Bureau's latest American Community Survey, 63 million are married. Of those, 3.1 million are legally separated and 2.4 million said their husbands were not living at home for one reason or another. That brings the number of American women actually living with a spouse to 57.5 million, compared with the 59.9 million who are single or whose husbands were not living at home when the survey was taken in 2005" (Roberts 2007, 2).

30. Of course, these figures tell us nothing about the growth in lesbian relationships and their centrality in the lives of so many women.

31. "The Future of the Women's Movement: Class, Race, and Globalization," Socialist Scholars Conference, Cooper Union, New York City, April 12–14, 2002. The conference has been renamed the Left Forum, and is the largest annual socialist academic and activist conference in the United States. See www.leftforum.org.

32. See MacLean 2006, 185ff. MacLean traces the backlash, in part, to elements in the organized Jewish community led by neoconservatives such as Nathan Glazer. Their concerted attack on affirmative action as representing special preferences, rather than an assault on a centuries-old

wall of exclusion, served to break up the historic black-Jewish alliance over fears of black advances in professions such as teaching (as in the Ocean Hill–Brownsville dispute with the American Federation of Teachers), medicine, and law.

33. The Supreme Court decision of April 19, 2007, in the combined cases of *Gonzales v. Planned Parenthood* and *Gonzales v. Carhart,* upholding the constitutionality of a ban on the rare late-term procedure of intact dilation and evacuation, dubbed "partial-birth abortion" by the fundamentalist Right, represents a high-water mark in this campaign. This procedure is carried out only when the mother's life is at stake; the callous cynicism of the partial-birth campaign is breathtaking.

34. "Eighty-seven percent of all U.S. counties lacked an abortion provider in 2005; 35 percent of women live in those counties" (Guttmacher Institute 2008).

35. This did not stop the Reagan administration from slowing down the efficacy of the antidiscrimination agencies by underfunding their administrative budgets and staffing them with ideological opponents such as Clarence Thomas at the EEOC (MacLean 2006, 311ff.).

36. As I write this, I am aware that this claim is belied by so many aspects of contemporary U.S. life, from the persistence of domestic violence, an expression of men's feudal concept of their wives as personal property, to the prevalence of near-sharecropping conditions in the poorest farm areas of the U.S. South. Obviously, feudalism and even slavery describe many aspects of contemporary life. I am speaking here at the level of popular ideology.

NOTES FOR CHAPTER 3

1. This point was made philosophically by Elizabeth Spelman (1988). The concept of intersectionality was introduced by legal scholar Kimberle Crenshaw (1991).

2. The black-white divide has diminished in some respects since the civil rights movement. For example, college-educated black women working full-time earned more than their white female counterparts in 2005. But in 2006, about 25 percent of all blacks lived below the poverty line compared with 8 percent of all whites (Swarns 2008). In 1968, the black graduation rate from college was 41 percent of the white rate; in 2004 it was 61 percent (19 percent of all blacks graduated from college versus 31 percent of all whites). But per capita income for blacks was about $17, 000, as compared with $29,000 for whites in 2005, and median household wealth for blacks in 2004 was 10 percent that of whites ($11,800 versus $118,300). A startling indicator of lack of change is that black per capita income as a percent of white per capita income was 54 percent in 1967 and 57 percent in 2005: an increase of 3 cents on the dollar after nearly four decades (Muhammad 2008a, 7–11). The figures are similar for Latino families. "African American families ... have a median net worth of $20,600, only 14.6 percent of the $140,700 median white net worth. The median net worth for Latino families is $18,600, only 13.2 percent of median white net worth. Between 1983 and 2004, the most recent year for which official federal data are available, median black and Latino wealth inched up from 7 percent to 10 percent of median white wealth. At this rate, we will not achieve wealth equality for 634 years" (Muhammad 2008b, 26).

3. For the sequel volume to *This Bridge,* see Anzaldúa and Keating 2002. For a good introduction to the literature on feminism and race, see Bhavnani 2001.

4. For a definitional discussion of global feminism, see Ferree 2006.

5. This opening section relies heavily on Omi and Winant 1986.

6. On Ella Baker, see Ransby 2003.

7. The contemporary experience of the war in Iraq underscores this interpretation if we consider the vocabulary of U.S. soldiers, who are encouraged to call Iraqis "hajis" or "sand niggers" (Braga 2005; see also Herbert 2004).

8. Significantly, the doctrine of *terra nullius* as it was applied to Aboriginal Australia was repudiated by the Australian Supreme Court only in response to the *Mabo v. Queensland* case in 1992. See *Mabo v. Queensland* 1992.

9. Sara Evans documents the experiences of white women in the black freedom struggle, and how these led directly to the rise of women's liberation (Evans 1979).

10. In the discussion that follows I will be using primarily material from the work of black feminists, neglecting the elaboration of related ideas in the work of Native American, Hispanic, Asian, and other women of color. For a contemporary overview that highlights the issues of immigrant women, see Hernandez and Rehman 2002.

11. Ironically, while matriarchal families were seen as the source of poverty for African Americans, Mexican families were being blamed as the source of poverty because they were too patriarchal! See Bridenthal 1989.

12. See Fried 2006 for further details. In 1980 the Supreme Court decided, in a case originally brought by Rhonda Copelon with the Center for Constitutional Rights, that the Hyde Amendment was constitutional. See *Harris v. McCrae* 1980.

13. The state law outlawing abortion, with no exception for rape, incest, or a woman's health, signed into law by Governor Mike Rounds in March 2006 was repealed via a referendum on the November 2006 ballot after a remarkable grassroots campaign.

14. "Black women are 4.8 times as likely as non-Hispanic white women to have an abortion, and Hispanic women are 2.7 times as likely.... The abortion rate among women living below the federal poverty level ($9,570 for a single woman with no children) is more than four times that of women above 300 percent of the poverty level (44 versus 10 abortions per 1,000 women)" (Guttmacher Institute 2008).

15. The book was published in 2005 with a new foreword, prior to the elections of November 2006 in which the Democrats took back both the House and (more narrowly) the Senate. See Frank 2005.

16. Frank's analysis ignores black voters, who were much more likely than white voters to vote along the lines of their own economic interests. "Only white evangelicals elevate their provincial moral concerns above classical conceptions of self-interest. Black evangelicals ... voted against Bush by margins of anywhere from 6 or 7 to 1, despite often agreeing with his politics on certain issues like abortion, gay rights, or prayer in schools. But 78 percent of white evangelicals and 'born-again Christians' voted for Bush" (Wise 2005, 2).

17. See www.unifem.org/campaigns/vaw.

18. The Central Park defendants were not cleared of all charges until 2005, after the renowned civil rights attorney Lynn Stewart persuaded the actual perpetrator of the crime, who was serving time for another offense, to confess to authorities. On this case, see Bumiller 2008, 48ff.; and Omolade 1994, 179–192.

19. "One in nine black men ages 20 to 34 is behind bars. For black women ages 35 to 39, the figure is one in 100, compared with one in 355 for white women in the same age group" (Aizenman 2008).

20. A similar history of the use of state power to "protect" white women against violence from men of color can be seen in British colonial history. For example, the White Women's Protection Ordinance, passed in Papua, New Guinea, introduced the death penalty for the crime of rape or attempted rape against any European female. This was aimed against the so-called Black Peril, the fear of the "strong sex instincts" of native men. Meanwhile, white men were tacitly encouraged to satisfy their "natural desires" on the bodies of native women, since raping a native woman was seen as totally acceptable (Amos and Parmar 1984, 14, quoting Vron Ware).

21. A 2008 fund-raising letter for CARE on the campaign to eradicate this practice uses "female genital cutting." See "Proclamation to Stop the Practice of Female Genital Cutting Now," insert in fund-raising letter from Helene D. Gayle, MD, president and CEO, August 2008.

NOTES FOR CHAPTER 4

1. The liberal coalition was not unique to the Democrats, as moderate Republicans also broadly accepted the consensus on progressive taxation, although they were harsher on labor issues.

2. The Taft-Hartley Act of 1947 severely limited the reach and power of unions with a number of restrictions on union activities, including a prohibition of wildcat strikes and closed shops (where the employer must hire only union members), and with a provision that permitted states to pass "right-to-work" laws that prevented collective bargaining, among other measures. The act also required union leaders to sign affidavits that they did not belong to the Communist Party, a provision held unconstitutional by the Supreme Court in 1965.

3. See, for example, Maher 2008 on the techniques used by Starbucks to track union organizers. When management discovered that two prounion employees had graduated from a labor program at Cornell University, they downloaded the names of graduates from an online discussion group and the school's website and crosschecked them with employee lists nationwide, informing store managers of the employees who were Cornell alumni. The telltale e-mails were revealed in discovery during a 2008 National Labor Relations Board case in New York that found Starbucks guilty of nearly thirty labor violations. On how union-busting firms work, see Levine 2007.

4. For a detailed and sophisticated account of the rise of the Religious Right and its influence on the Republican Party, see Phillips 2006. The author of the Southern Strategy now regrets the extreme direction his party took under the Bush dynasty.

5. Under the influence of environmental and consumer interest reformers, by 1974 Congress had already established the Environmental Protection Agency (1970), the Occupational Health and Safety Administration (1970), the Consumer Product Safety Commission (1972), and the Mine Safety and Health Administration (1973). It had also increased funding for food stamps, raised social security payments by 20 percent, and passed the Employee Retirement Income Security Act.

6. Other groups in this coalition included the Hoover Institution on War, Revolution, and Peace at Stanford University; the Center for the Study of American Business at Washington University; and the American Council for Capital Formation in Washington, DC.

7. Proposition 13 was the brainchild of Californians Howard Jarvis and Paul Gann.

8. See Wagner 2002.

9. Remarkably, the set of issues put together in this family values package, as early as the first direct-mail campaigns of Richard Viguerie in response to the *Roe v. Wade* decision of 1973, continues to have legs although the 2008 election of President Obama and a Democratic majority in the House and Senate reflected a strong swing to the left.

10. Since that time, the inequality between black and white women's wages has increased again. Black women's median earnings were 85 percent of their white women counterparts in 2008, and Hispanic women earned 77 percent of white women's earnings (U.S. Department of Labor 2008).

11. Even before the deregulation was authorized by law, a major merger linked Citibank, under John Reed, with Travelers Group, Inc., the insurance giant that owned Salomon Smith Barney, a major brokerage, under Sanford Weill. "That merger was negotiated despite the fact that the merged company, Citigroup, was in violation of the Glass-Steagall Act, because billionaire Travelers boss Sanford Weill and Citibank CEO John Reed were confident of bipartisan support for repeal of the 60-year-old law" (McLaughlin 1999, 1).

12. "The city's disastrously low-performing school system was almost entirely washed away in the flood—many of the buildings were destroyed, the school board was taken over and all of the teachers were fired. What is being built in its place is an educational landscape unlike any other, a radical experiment in reform. More than half of the city's public school students are now being

educated in charter schools, publicly financed but privately run" (Tough 2008, 32). Charter schools receive public funds but are organized by a variety of entities, including for-profit corporations, and are permitted to evade many of the regulations and requirements of public schools, especially the requirement to hire only unionized teachers. The claim is that poor African American kids can be taught properly only in charter schools rather than in a revitalized public education system with sufficient funding. But many observers see the charter school movement as an attempt to delegitimize and ultimately to replace the public education system.

13. "For more than two decades now, real wages in America have been stagnating or falling, the distributions of earnings and income have become increasingly unequal, and the bulk of financial wealth has been accumulating among fewer and fewer families. Since 1973, real average weekly earnings for the more than 80 percent of the workforce who are counted as production or nonsupervisory workers have fallen by 19 percent; median family income is no higher than twenty years ago; and the share of total marketable net worth accruing to the top 1 percent of all households has increased from about 20 percent to nearly 39 percent" (Bluestone 1995, 1).

14. For a more optimistic account of the cultural meaning of *The Full Monty,* see Gibson-Graham 2006c, 9–21, who argue that the film "shows us a process of reeroticization, the forging of new desires, satisfactions, and masculinities freed from an anchor in a certain form of work" (Gibson-Graham 2006c, 13). Gibson-Graham is the pen name for the authorial collective of two feminist economic geographers: Katherine Gibson, Australian National University, and Julie Graham, University of Massachusetts. In Gibson-Graham's view, the "freeing" of these men from traditional, highly paid, secure men's work represents an opportunity for the creation of a new sense of community "energized by pleasure, fun, eroticism, and connection" (Gibson-Graham 2006c, 18). Presumably, the pleasure and energy thus released are an adequate substitute for major losses in pay and job security for individuals, their families, and the wider community.

15. Social feminists themselves rejected the term *feminist,* which they reserved for those who were seeking to equalize the roles of men and women.

16. See Boris 1998 on the coalition of activists and academics known as the Women's Committee of 100, which brought together feminist scholars and grassroots activists, and the rest of the special issue of *Feminist Studies* 24, no. 1 (1998) devoted to this topic.

17. Pimpare notes that simultaneously with the abolition of the AFDC, the Earned Income Tax Credit was expanded. This subsidized the wages of low-paid workers with children, shifting public expenditure away from those not working to those in the low-wage labor market and "acting as a reward and incentive to the prospective employee and as a wage subsidy to his or her employer" (Pimpare 2004, 4; see also Pimpare 2006).

NOTES FOR CHAPTER 5

1. "Over the past three decades, increasing numbers of women have become sex workers, maids, workers in export production, or microfinance recipients to earn incomes in the restructured global economy. Many must migrate domestically or internationally to obtain this work.... These 'industries' now span the globe, occurring in most areas of the developing world as well as throughout industrialized countries" (Pyle and Ward 2003, 470).

2. These can be overlapping categories, by the way, as the new literature on trafficking makes clear (see Kempadoo et al. 2005).

3. The literature refers variously to state-led development or the developmental state, which covers the period from the 1950s, when most states in Africa and Asia won their independence, to the crisis years of the 1970s (see Tabb 2001). In South Africa, an urgent debate over the role of the developmental state reemerged in response to the draconian neoliberal policies of the African National Congress under Thabo Mbeki; see www.amandla.org.za.

4. "Since the mid-1990s, austerity programs ceased to be referred to as structural adjustment policies, perhaps because SAPs had become very controversial and contested terrain, despite the fact that they continued to be adopted in different countries" (Beneria 2003, 49). As MADRE notes in its position paper: "The IMF ... has tried to deflect opposition to its discredited Structural Adjustment Programs (SAPs) by echoing the concerns and language of economic justice advocates. SAPs have undergone a series of cosmetic changes and been infused with more inclusive, humane language. They are now called 'Poverty Reduction Strategy Papers' (PRSPs) and are being used to assess and implement development strategies for many poor countries. But PRSPs merely reassert the goals of the original SAPs: to ensure that poor countries make debt payments to northern creditors, orient their economies toward a global market, and create favorable conditions for foreign investors. In this framework, the rights of poor working women remain impediments to 'economic growth' and 'development'" (MADRE n.d.).

5. The Marshall Plan was a massive investment program undertaken by the United States to restore the economy of Europe, which had been devastated by World War II.

6. This liberalization of capital movements allows "dirty money" (from illegal trade or criminal activity) and "black money" (money escaping taxation), deposited by Third World elites in offshore bank accounts, to be laundered and used to purchase state assets, with the proceeds earmarked for debt-servicing.

7. "The tendency is towards the forfeiture and/or mortgaging of land by small farmers, the growth of the agro-business sector, and the formation of a class of landless seasonal agricultural workers.... The[se] measures often contribute—under the disguise of modernity—to the restoration of the rights of the 'old-time' landlord class, ... often the champion of economic 'liberalization'" (Chossudovsky 2003, 64).

8. On this point, see Waring 1999. See Beneria 2003, 131ff., on the various attempts to quantify the value of women's unpaid labor over the past two decades.

9. Lim 1990, 101, dismisses the critique by feminist scholars of EPZs as ideologically biased and disproportionate given the small percentage of all women workers in EPZs compared to "the several hundred million working women in the Third World."

10. Thanks to Val Moghadam for this point; comments at Global Studies Association Annual Meeting, Pace University, New York, June 7, 2008.

11. But, for example, in Mexico the range is from 50 percent to 120 percent annually! See Epstein and Smith 2007, 40.

12. My account here draws heavily upon Isserles 2002.

13. For 2006, the latest year for which figures are available, the number of borrowers had grown to 133 million. This is equal to about 5 percent of the number of people in the world who live on less than $2 a day. These borrowers had received a total of $13.5 billion (Worldwatch Institute 2008).

14. Social funds were originally termed Social Emergency Funds (SEFs) as we saw earlier. But as it became clear that the damage caused by SAPs was not temporary the term was changed to Social Investment Funds or Social Funds more generally. See Huque and Zafarullah 2006, 448 ff.

15. See Bello 2006. To put microcredit efforts in some perspective, note the following: in 2006, the 133 million families with microloans had received a total amount of $13.5 billion (World Watch Institute 2008). This figure is less than 0.5 percent of the $3.2 trillion in total debt held by the Global South in that year.

16. Great Britain's neoliberal Prime Minister Margaret Thatcher and her supporters in Parliament were famous for repeating that "There is no alternative," or TINA for short, meaning, no viable alternative to free market capitalism such as socialism or communism.

17. As of 2007, there are an estimated 191 million people living in a country other than the one they were born in, a number equivalent to about 3 percent of the world's population (Yinger 2007, 1). This number does not include the enormous internal migrations going on within

countries: refugees displaced by war in the Congo, for example, or by economic transformation, as in China.

18. To be fair, the UNFPA report goes on to document the myriad difficulties and dangers encountered by migrant women both in their passage to the First World and during their employment there.

19. "The United Nations system uses this term to distinguish representatives of these agencies from those of governments. While many NGOs dislike the term, it has come into wide use because the UN system is the main focus of international rule-making and policy formulation in the fields where most NGOs operate" (Paul 2006, 1).

20. On feminist economics, see the journal by that name published by the International Association for Feminist Economics (IAFFE), www.iaffe.org. On the rise of feminist economics, see Beneria 2003, 31ff. The literature on women and development is vast. For an introduction, see Visvanathan et al. 1997.

21. Ironically, in the light of his championing of education for Third World women while at the World Bank, Summers was forced to resign from the presidency of Harvard University in 2006, due at least in part to remarks that cast aspersions on women's innate capacities in math and science (see Bombardieri 2005).

22. World Bank 2006. For a scathing response to the World Bank gender action plan for 2007–2010, see Wichterich 2006.

23. This is an initiative that was pioneered by Australian femocrats and has been imitated widely across the world (see Eisenstein 1996, 57ff.).

24. The World Bank even agreed to cosponsor a comprehensive research report on the impact of SAPs, but after an elaborate process of research and assessment, the bank officially withdrew from the project as the final report was being delivered (see Structural Adjustment Participatory Review International Network 2004).

Notes for Chapter 6

1. See Zarembka 2006.

2. See Dreyfuss 2005, 304. "In the Pentagon, the Global War on Terrorism is known by its acronym, G-WOT, pronounced 'gee what,' thus neatly rhyming with 'jihad.'"

3. A mainstream example of this is "The American Empire Project," the name of the contemporary series of books coming out from the Metropolitan Books division of Henry Holt (see www.americanempireproject.com).

4. Interestingly, a similar debate broke out in the context of the war in Vietnam, with Harry Magdoff (1969) arguing that the United States was indeed an empire, and right-wing commentators in effect agreeing, with approving titles such as Richard Van Alstyne's *The Rising American Empire* (1960), George Liska's *Imperial America* (1967), Amary de Riencourt's *The American Empire* (1968), and Raymond Aron's *The Imperial Republic* (1974) (see Gross 1980, 35). My approach joins that of other Left critics, from Noam Chomsky and Zillah Eisenstein to Greg Grandin and David Harvey, in seeing the U.S. imperial role in the twenty-first century as a major impediment to a peaceful and, indeed, to a viable world.

5. "Promoted as 'democracy building,' electoral interventions are critically important to U.S. policy objectives, contributing to long-term state and corporate planning by solidifying U.S. linkages to foreign governments and helping establish economic and military alliances" (Sussman 2006, 16).

6. Giovanni Arrighi identifies the United States as the latest and most powerful hegemonic world economic power. He places it in the context of previous such hegemonies from the early modern period onward, from the Italian city-states to Amsterdam to Great Britain (Arrighi 2005).

Each era in the development of modern capitalism has had a dominant economic power that presided over a system of international trade, acting as banker and imposing its will through military and, especially, naval power. These have not all been empires on the model of ancient Rome, where the central power extended its reach by direct military rule. Whereas Great Britain prided itself on actually administering its territories so that the sun never set on its holdings, the United States has limited its territorial reach to the land acquired through Manifest Destiny, whether by conquest (over the Native Americans and Mexico) or by acquisition (Alaska, the Louisiana Purchase, Hawaii, Puerto Rico). Even though many writers have addressed the question of what kind of empire the United States is, it is perhaps a historical cul-de-sac to endlessly debate the ways in which the United States is different from Rome or even from nineteenth-century Great Britain.

7. This is a partial list. No doubt many more elements could be added.

8. A U.S. State Department briefing gives the total number of U.S. military installations at 5,458. "Trying to put the whole picture into perspective, the senior defense official noted, 'There are only 230 major U.S. military bases in the world, 202 of which are in the United States and its territories. But there are 5,458 distinct and discrete military installations around the world, and … many of them are 100 acres or less.' He termed these small installations a legacy from the Cold War. 'We don't need those little pieces of property anymore,' he said" (U.S. Department of State 2004).

9. On June 12, 2008, the Center for Constitutional Rights successfully challenged the Military Commissions Act provision that eliminated habeas corpus for enemy combatants. "In *Boumediene v. Bush*, the [Supreme] Court held that the Center's clients detained at Guantánamo have a constitutional right to file petitions for habeas corpus in U.S. federal court challenging the lawfulness of their detention" (Center for Constitutional Rights 2008). Habeas corpus, literally, "you have your body," means the traditional right inherited from British common law to challenge in open court the authority of those who have imprisoned you.

10. The ICE was created in March 2003, combining the law enforcement arms of the former Immigration and Naturalization Service (INS) and the former U.S. Customs Service (see www .ice.gov/about/index.htm).

11. See, for example, the debate concerning the Animal Enterprise Protection Act introduced in 2006 to combat the effectiveness of animal rights advocates. "The War on Terrorism has come home. Corporations and politicians are labeling activists 'eco-terrorists' and national security threats" (Potter 2006, 11). Similarly, death penalty opponents in Takoma Park, Maryland, were infiltrated and spied on in an operation run by the Maryland State Police and the Department of Homeland Security from 2005 to 2006; these agencies devoted nearly "300 hours and thousands of taxpayer dollars … to harassing people whose only crime was dissenting on the question of the war in Iraq and Maryland's use of death row" (Zirin 2008).

12. See Dreyfuss 2005, 334. "In the period after September 11, 2001, Lewis was ubiquitous, propagating his view that Islam was unalterably opposed to the West." Bernard Lewis, a former British intelligence agent, professor emeritus at Princeton, and close associate of the neoconservative alliance brought to power under George W. Bush, introduced the term *clash of civilizations* in a 1956 article in the *Middle East Journal* (Dreyfuss 2005, 332, 81). See also Huntington 1996; Mamdani 2004, 20ff.

13. See Fisher, 2006, 1, on the pope's remarks, quoting a "fourteenth-century Byzantine emperor, Manuel II Paleologus, in a conversation with a 'learned Persian' on Christianity and Islam.… 'Show me just what Muhammed brought that was new, and there you will find things only evil and inhuman, such as his command to spread the sword by the faith he preached.'"

14. On the growth and cultivation of Wahhabism in the Middle East, under Saudi sponsorship and with U.S. support, see Dreyfuss, 2005, 3ff.

15. For a comprehensive account of the widespread policy assault on women's interests and rights under the Bush administration, see Finlay 2006.

16. UN Resolution 1325, adopted on October 31, 2000, in response to commitments in the Beijing Declaration and Platform for Action of 1995 and the Special Session of the United Nations General Assembly entitled "Women 2000: Gender Equality, Development and Peace for the Twenty-first Century," recognizes that women and children are the majority of those "adversely affected by armed conflict" and calls for an increased role for women in the "prevention and resolution of conflicts and in peace-building," among other provisions.

17. The hijab, or headscarf, is often used in Western media as equivalent to veiling. Actually, there is a very great variety of Islamic dress adopted by women, from a full-body covering and veil to a decorative headscarf. Although, as discussed herein, the issue of dress for women in Islam has been a political flashpoint, in the matter of dress women are also making individual choices that express their personal religious faith.

18. On Elshtain and her defense of "just war," see Chomsky 2003, 95, 199, 203.

19. From 1883 until he retired in 1907, Evelyn Baring, who became Lord Cromer, was the real ruler of Egypt. "A member of the great banking dynasty, Baring could be trusted to look after British financial interests" (Newsinger 2008, 72).

20. A notable exception to this rule is the writing of Cynthia Enloe; see, for example, Enloe 2004.

21. See Amos and Parmar 1984.

22. These components are Slovenia, Croatia, Bosnia-Herzegovina (now partitioned into the Muslim-Croat Federation of Bosnia, and the Republika Srpska, or Serb Republic), and the rump states of Macedonia and Serbia/Kosovo. With the support of Europe and the United States, the parliament of Kosovo declared its independence from Serbia on February 18, 2008, risking further conflict.

23. See Parenti 2000, 177: "It should be remembered that Yugoslav president Slobodan Milosevic was not always consigned to this rogue's gallery [along with Manuel Noriega of Panama, Muammar El-Qaddafi of Libya, and Saddam Hussein of Iraq]. As late as 1995, the Clinton administration accepted Milosevic as a negotiating partner and guarantor of the Dayton Accords in Bosnia, even praising him for the many concessions he made. Only later, when they saw him as an obstacle rather than a tool, did U.S. policymakers begin to depict him as having been all along the demon who 'started all four wars.'"

24. On the widespread acceptance of the NATO intervention by the U.S. Left, see Bricmont 2006. Ed Herman and his colleagues make a similar point about the role of Human Rights Watch in supporting a U.S.-centric view of the events in Yugoslavia and the trial of Milosevic at the International Criminal Tribunal for the Former Yugoslavia (Herman, Peterson, and Szamuely 2007).

25. Bina Srinivasan, who died in 2007, was an activist based in Colombo, Sri Lanka, with INFORM (inform@lanka.gn.apc.org); she worked against trafficking in women, sought to expose the state-sponsored violence in the Indian state of Gujarat, and took part in the anti–large dams movement in India, China, and elsewhere. She was a participant in the Human Security seminar at CUNY (see the Preface).

26. See, for example, the book by Irshad Manji (2003), an openly lesbian Canadian journalist and broadcaster.

27. The *faqih* is an Islamic jurist, the supreme authority in Iran. "The preamble to the Constitution vests supreme authority in the *faqih*. According to Article 5, the *faqih* is the just and pious jurist who is recognized by the majority of the people as best qualified to lead the nation." The first *faqih* was Ayatolleh Khomeini himself. See http://countrystudies.us/iran/82.htm.

28. Moghadam is drawing here on the framework developed in an anthology edited by Deniz Kandiyoti, *Women, Islam, and the State* (1991b). These essays show the variety of conditions for women in different Islamic nations, revealing that the major variables are not the presence of Islam, but the history of state formation and economic development for each country. "The unifying argument of this volume is that an adequate analysis of the position of women in Muslim societies

must be grounded in a detailed examination of the political projects of contemporary states and of their historical transformations. In this respect, the countries covered illustrate very different paths of evolution. Some have emerged from declining empires (Turkey, from the Ottoman empire), or dynastic rule (Iran, from the Qajar) and others from direct colonial domination (Egypt, Lebanon, Iraq, the People's Democratic Republic of Yemen, and the countries of the South Asian subcontinent). Some, like Turkey and Egypt, have a long history of modernization of state and society, while others are relatively new territorial entities. Their current political regimes likewise cover a wide spectrum. However, they have all had to grapple with the problems of establishing modern nation states and forging new notions of citizenship. This has led them to search for new legitimizing ideologies and power bases in their respective societies.... The postindependence trajectories of modern states and variations in the deployment of Islam in relation to different nationalisms, state ideologies, and oppositional social movements are of central relevance to an understanding of the condition of women. The ways in which women are represented in political discourse, the degree of formal emancipation they are able to achieve, the modalities of their participation in economic life, and the nature of the social movements through which they are able to articulate their gender interests are intimately linked to state-building processes and are responsive to their transformations" (Kandiyoti 1991a, 2–3).

Notes for the Conclusion

1. See also Disney 2008. FRELIMO is the acronym for the Liberation Front of Mozambique; FSLN stands for the Sandinista Liberation Front of Nicaragua.

2. "Only since the last quarter of the twentieth century have we witnessed what amounts to a mass insurrection of women against their oppression throughout the world.... Such a consciousness is rapidly extending throughout the planet. This is the most important revolution because it goes to the roots of society and to the heart of who we are" (Castells 2004, 194).

3. This has turned out to be a long-lasting separation, one which I was deploring as early as 1983 (see Eisenstein 1983, 125ff.).

4. On the media consumption and distortion of feminist ideology as confessionalism, see the work of feminist media critic Elayne Rapping 1997.

5. See also Aguilar 2004b on the need to reinstate the category of class into feminist theorizing.

6. See also Nussbaum 2007, 159: "A working women's movement emerged. Across the board, women came to think of themselves as providers and to rely on themselves. They pressed demands, often banding together in groups, associations, and unions. As a result, employers provided new opportunities for women, both as a legitimate response to women's demands and as a way to drive a wedge into the growing movement. A split in the workforce emerged between college-educated and non-college-educated women. Business created a safety valve to siphon off the growing demands of some women through new opportunities for careers as professionals and managers for college-educated women while holding the line on wages and reducing benefits for non-college-educated women and immigrants."

7. In this context, Stephen also cites the well-known article by Temma Kaplan, which set forth a theory of "female consciousness" in her discussion of women's collective action in early-twentieth-century Barcelona: "When women who have internalized their designated roles as domestic providers and caretakers are unable to carry out their duties, they will be moved to take action in order to fulfill their social roles as females. This may even include taking on the state when it impedes their day-to-day activities. Kaplan has extended this analysis to women's participation in grassroots movements within contemporary Latin America" (Stephen 1997, 10–11; see also Kaplan 1982, 1990).

8. The other counterweight is government, in periods such as the New Deal when leaders accepted the need to curb corporate power.

9. Of female union members, 70.9 percent are in three industry groups: education, health care, and public administration. See detailed figures in Milkman 2007.

10. A similar technique has been adopted by the Professional Staff Congress of the City University of New York, under the leadership of feminist scholar Barbara Bowen, with representatives of all sectors of the union, from senior professors to part-time faculty to higher education officers and other staff members, attending contract negotiation sessions and setting forth their own painful experiences in working for the university.

11. ACORN (the Association of Community Organizations for Reform NOW) is "the largest community organization of low- and moderate-income families, working together for social justice and stronger communities" (http://www.acorn.org).

12. Gluckman (2008) analyzes the conflict as being, in part, over "density versus democracy" (8). The SEIU has been negotiating deals directly with the employer, often in secret and without consultation with members, in order to increase labor density by bringing in more and more worksites, whereas De Moro and other critics of the SEIU believe in direct organizing of the rank and file.

13. I beg the indulgence of any former seminar members who happen to read these words if I have turned your ideas into too much of a caricature.

14. See also Gibson-Graham responding to Eisenstein 2006: "A postcapitalist politics involves working collaboratively to produce alternative economic organizations and spaces in place.... We can foster the growth of a feminist political economy by enrolling women in actively practicing 'noncapitalism' rather than primarily opposing capitalism" (Gibson-Graham 2006b, 77).

15. In proposing a Fifth International, Navarro is referring to the history of international organizations established to spread socialism and then communism throughout the world. The First or International Workingman's Association was founded in London in 1864. The Second International, an association of socialist and labor parties, was founded in Paris in 1889 and dissolved in 1916 over the issue of supporting or opposing World War I. The Third International refers to the international communist organization founded in Moscow in 1919 following the Russian Revolution. The Fourth International was established by Leon Trotsky in 1938 to oppose both capitalism and Stalinism.

16. Although these leaders vary in their approach to neoliberalism, they are united in refusing to oppose the reforms of Chávez and Morales. Furthermore, they are cooperating on various joint projects. For example, the proposed creation of a Latin American pipeline system for oil and gas may signal the beginning of a new economic and political union.

17. For informed and sympathetic updates on the Bolivarian revolution, see www.venezuelanalysis.com. See also the videos available from www.globalwomenstrike.net, especially *Venezuela: A 21st-Century Revolution* (2003) and *Journey with the Revolution* (2006), for vivid illustrations of the multiple roles of women.

18. See *G.I. Jane* (1997); "Anna Politkovskaya" 2006.

19. Thanks to Mike Menser for his comments on this section (personal communication, July 8, 2008).

References

Note: All websites were accessed prior to September 30, 2008.

"ABC Impeaches *Commander in Chief.*" 2006. *Zap2It.com,* May 2. http://www.zap2it .com/tv/news/zap-commanderinchiefpulled.0.7217400.story.

Abramovitz, Mimi. 1996a. *Regulating the Lives of Women: Social Welfare Policy from Colonial Times to the Present.* Boston: South End Press.

———. 1996b. *Under Attack, Fighting Back: Women and Welfare in the United States.* New York: Monthly Review Press.

Abu-Lughod, Lila. 2002. "Do Muslim Women Really Need Saving? Anthropological Reflections on Cultural Relativism and Its Others." *American Anthropologist* 104, no. 3: 783–790.

Abusharaf, Rogaia Mustafa. 2001. "Virtuous Cuts: Female Genital Circumcision in an African Ontology." *Differences* 12, no. 1: 112–140.

Afshar, Haleh, and Carolyne Dennis, eds. 1992. *Women and Adjustment Policies in the Third World.* New York: St. Martin's Press.

Agosin, Marjorie, ed. 2001. *Women, Gender, and Human Rights.* New Brunswick, NJ: Rutgers University Press.

Agrell, Siri. 2008. "Politics Gender Shift: Large and in Charge." April 16. http://www .theglobeandmail.com/servlet/story/RTGAM.20080416.wl.

Aguilar, Delia D. 2004a. "Introduction." Pp. 11–23 in *Women and Globalization,* edited by Delia D. Aguilar and Anne E. Lacsamana. Amherst, NY: Humanity Books.

———. 2004b. "Questionable Claims: Colonialism Redux, Feminist Style." Pp. 405–419 in *Women and Globalization,* edited by Delia D. Aguilar and Anne E. Lacsamana. Amherst, NY: Humanity Books.

———. 2006. "Current Challenges to Feminism: Theory and Practice." *MRZine, Monthly Review.* http://mrzine.monthlyreview.org/aguilar181006p.html.

Ahmad, Nilufar. 1994. "Battling the World Bank." Pp. 128–134 in *Fifty Years Is Enough: The Case Against the World Bank and the International Monetary Fund,* edited by Kevin Danaher. Boston: South End Press.

Ahmed, Lila. 1992. *Women and Gender in Islam: Historical Roots of a Modern Debate.* New Haven, CT: Yale University Press.

Aizenman, N. C. 2008. "New High in U.S. Prison Numbers: Growth Attributed to More Stringent Sentencing Laws." *Washington Post,* February 29.

Akale, Catherine Mudime. 1999. "Who Has the Right to Name Female Genital Mutilation a Crime?" Paper presented at Women's Worlds, Seventh International Interdisciplinary Congress on Women, Tromso, Norway, June 20–26. www.skk.uit.no/WW99/papers/Akale_Catherine_Mudime.pdf.

Alexander, M. Jacqui, and Chandra Talpade Mohanty, eds. 1997a. *Feminist Genealogies: Colonial Legacies, Democratic Futures.* New York: Routledge.

———. 1997b. "Introduction: Geneaologies, Legacies, Movements." Pp. xiii–xliii in *Feminist Genealogies: Colonial Legacies, Democratic Futures,* edited by M. Jacqui Alexander and Chandra Talpade Mohanty. New York: Routledge.

"All-Female Peacekeeper Squad to Deploy." 2007. Associated Press, January 19. http://www.usatoday.com/news/world/2007–01-liberia-women_x.htm.

Alperowitz, Gar, and Jeff Faux. 1984. *Rebuilding America.* New York: Pantheon.

Alvarez, Sonia E. 1999. "Advocating Feminism: The Latin American Feminist NGO 'Boom.'" *International Feminist Journal of Politics* 1, no. 2: 181–209.

Amadiume, Ifi. 2000. *Daughters of the Goddess, Daughters of Imperialism: African Women Struggle for Culture, Power, and Democracy.* London: Zed Books.

Amin, Samir. 2001. "Political Islam." *Covert Action Quarterly* (Winter): 3–6.

———. 2006. "The Millennium Development Goals: A Critique from the South." *Monthly Review* 57, no. 1: 1–15.

Amos, Valerie, and Pratibha Parmar. 1984. "Challenging Imperial Feminism." *Feminist Review* 17 (Autumn): 3–19.

Amott, Teresa L. 1993. *Caught in the Crisis: Women and the U.S. Economy Today.* New York: Monthly Review Press.

Amott, Teresa L., and Julie Matthei. 1991. *Race, Gender, and Work: A Multicultural History of Women in the United States.* Boston: South End Press.

Amsden, Alice H. 1989. *Asia's Next Giant: South Korea and Late Industrialization.* New York: Oxford University Press.

Anderson, Bridget. 2004. "Who Needs Yehudi Menuhin? Costs and Impact of Migration." Pp. 262–277 in *Women and Globalization,* edited by Delia D. Aguilar and Anne E. Lacsamana. Amherst, NY: Humanity Books.

"Anna Politkovskaya." 2006. *The Economist,* October 14, 91.

"Annan Praises UN Women's Panel on 60th Anniversary for Being 'Ahead of Its Time.'" 2006. UN News Service, November 10. http://www.un.org/apps/news/pringnews.asp?nid=20571.

Antrobus, Peggy. 2004. *The Global Women's Movement: Origins, Issues, and Strategies.* London: Zed Books.

Anzaldúa, Gloria E., and Analouise Keating, eds. 2002. *This Bridge We Call Home: Radical Visions for Transformation.* New York: Routledge.

Aptheker, Bettina F. 2006. *Intimate Politics: How I Grew Up Red, Fought for Free Speech, and Became a Feminist Rebel.* Emeryville, CA: Seal.

Arrighi, Giovanni. 2005. "Hegemony Unravelling—1." *New Left Review* 32 (March–April): 23–80.

Australian Bureau of Statistics. 2008. "6310.0—Employee Earnings, Benefits, and Trade Union Membership, August 2007." Media release, April 14. http://www.abs.gov.au/AUSTATS/abs@nsf/Latestproducts/6310.0.

Automobile Workers v. Johnson Controls, Inc., 499 U.S. 187 (1991). http://www.law.cornell.edu/supct/html/89-1215.ZO.html.

Bacchi, Carol Lee. 1990. *Same Difference: Feminism and Sexual Difference.* Boston: Allen and Unwin.

Balakhrishnan, Radhika. 2002. *The Hidden Assembly Line: Gender Dynamics of Subcontracted Work in a Global Economy.* Bloomfield, CT: Kumarian.

Barnett, Thomas P.M., and Henry H. Gaffney Jr. 2003. "The Global Transaction Strategy." Reprinted from *Military Officer* (May). http://www.thomaspmbarnett.com/published/gts.htm.

Barry, Kathleen. 1984. *Female Sexual Slavery.* New York: New York University Press.

Bartlett, Bruce. 2008. "Hoary Myth Laid to Rest." Letter to *The Nation,* December 1, 2.

Barton, Carol. 2004. "Global Women's Movements at a Crossroads: Seeking Definition, New Alliances, and Greater Impact." *Socialism and Democracy* 35, no. 1: 151–184.

Barton, Carol, and Carol Prendergast, eds. 2004. *Seeking Accountability on Women's Human Rights: Women Debate the UN Millennium Development Goals.* Women's International Coalition for Economic Justice. Nerul, India: Information Company. www.ticworks.com.

Basu, Amrita, ed., with the assistance of C. Elizabeth McGrory. 1995. *The Challenge of Local Feminisms: Women's Movements in Global Perspective.* Boulder, CO: Westview Press.

Baxandall, Rosalyn, and Linda Gordon, eds. 1995. *America's Working Women: A Documentary History, 1600 to the Present.* Rev. and updated ed. New York: Norton.

———. 2000. *Dear Sisters: Dispatches from the Women's Liberation Movement.* New York: Basic Books.

Beal, Frances M. 2001. "NGOs at Durban Target Globalization." *Alternet,* September 12. http://www.alternet.org/module/printversion/11478.

Bello, Walden. 2006. "Microcredit, Macro Issues." *The Nation,* October 14, 1–2. www.thenation.com/doc/20061030/bello.

Bend It like Beckham. 2002. Directed by Gurinda Chadha. Fox Searchlight Pictures.

Beneria, Lourdes. 1998. "In the Wilderness of One's Inner Self: Living Feminism." Pp. 249–267 in *The Feminist Memoir Project: Voices from Women's Liberation,* edited by Rachel Blau Du Plessis and Ann Snitow. New York: Three Rivers.

———. 2003. *Gender, Development, and Globalization: Economics As If All People Mattered.* New York: Routledge.

Bennhold, Katrin. 2008. "A Veil Closes France's Door to Citizenship." *New York Times,* July 19.

Bennholdt-Thomsen, Veronika, and Maria Mies. 1999 [1997]. *The Subsistence Perspective: Beyond the Globalised Economy.* London: Zed Books/Spinifex.

Berman, Jacqueline. 2003. "(Un)Popular Strangers and Crises (Un)Bounded: Discourses of Sex Trafficking, the European Political Community, and the Panicked State of the Modern State." *European Journal of International Relations* 9, no. 1: 37–86.

Bernstein, Aaron. 2003. "Waking Up from the American Dream: Dead-End Jobs and the High Cost of College Could Be Choking Off Upward Mobility." *BusinessWeek,* December 1, 54–58.

Bhavnani, Kum-Kum, ed. 2001. *Feminism and "Race."* Oxford, UK: Oxford University Press.

Biehl, João. 2001. "Vita: Life in a Zone of Social Abandonment—Dead Language." *Social Text* 19, no. 3: 131–149.

Bluestone, Barry. 1995. *The Polarization of American Society: Victims, Suspects, and Mysteries to Unravel.* New York: Twentieth Century Fund.

Bluestone, Barry, and Bennett Harrison. 1982. *The Deindustrialization of America: Plant Closings, Community Abandonment, and the Dismantling of Basic Industries.* New York: Basic Books.

Boal, Iain. 2007. "Specters of Malthus: Scarcity, Poverty, Apocalypse: Iain Boal in Conversation with David Martinez." *Counterpunch,* September 11. www.counterpunch.org/boal09112007.html.

Bombardieri, Marcella. 2005. "Summers' Remarks on Women Draw Fire." *Boston Globe,* January 17.

Boose, Lynda E. 2002. "Crossing the River Drina: Bosnian Rape Camps, Turkish Impalement, and Serb Cultural Memory." *Signs* 28, no. 1: 71–78.

Booth, Heather. 2006. Remarks, Meeting of the Veteran Feminists of America, Columbia University Faculty House, New York City, November 13.

Bootmen. 2000. Directed by Dein Perry. Bootmen Productions.

Boris, Eileen. 1998. "Introduction: Scholarship and Activism—the Case of Welfare Justice." *Feminist Studies* 24, no. 1: 27–31.

Boris, Eileen, and Jennifer Klein. 2007. "'We Were the Invisible Workforce': Unionizing Home Care." Pp. 177–193 in *The Sex of Class: Women Transforming American Labor,* edited by Dorothy Sue Cobble. Ithaca, NY: ILR Press.

Boserup, Esther. 1970. *Women's Role in Economic Development.* New York: St. Martin's Press.

Boston Women's Health Book Collective. 1971. *Our Bodies, Ourselves: A Book by and for Women.* Boston: New England Free Press.

———. 1992. *The New Our Bodies, Ourselves: A Book by and for Women, Updated and Expanded for the '90s.* New York: Simon and Schuster.

Boumediene v. Bush, 128 S.Ct. 229 (2008).

Braga, Fernando. 2005. Testimony at Queens College Professional Staff Congress Antiwar Committee speakout, Queens, New York, May 9.

Breines, Winifred. 2006. *The Trouble Between Us: An Uneasy History of White and Black Women in the Feminist Movement.* Oxford, UK: Oxford University Press.

Brenner, Johanna. 2000a. "The Best of Times, the Worst of Times: U.S. Feminism Today." Pp. 220–292 in *Women and the Politics of Class,* by Johanna Brenner. New York: Monthly Review Press.

———. 2000b. *Women and the Politics of Class.* New York: Monthly Review Press.

———. 2003. "Transnational Feminism and the Struggle for Social Justice." *New Politics* 9, no. 2 (new series), whole no. 34. http://www.wpunj.edu/newpol/issue34/brenne34.htm.

Breslau, Karen. 2006. "Rose Ann DeMoro: Labor Leader and Political Player." *More .Com: Celebrating Women 40+,* September 3. www.more.com/more/printableStory.jsp;jsessionid=ZEBDHTUINTT2JQFIBSB42.

Bricmont, Jean. 2006. *Humanitarian Imperialism: Using Human Rights to Sell War.* New York: Monthly Review Press.

Bridenthal, Renate. 1989. "The Family Tree: Contemporary Patterns in the United States." Pp. 47–100 in *Families in Flux,* edited by Amy Swerdlow, Renate Bridenthal, and Joan Kelly. New York: Feminist Press.

Brownmiller, Susan. 1975. *Against Our Will: Men, Women, and Rape.* New York: Simon and Schuster.

———. 1999. *In Our Time: Memoir of a Revolution.* New York: Dial.

Buckley, Cara, and Annie Correal. 2008. "Domestic Workers Organize to End an 'Atmosphere of Violence' on the Job." *New York Times,* June 9.

Buhle, Mari Jo. 1983. *Women and American Socialism, 1870–1920.* Urbana-Champaign: University of Illinois Press.

Bulbeck, Chilla. 2007. "Hailing the 'Authentic Other': Constructing the Third World Woman as Aid Recipient in Donor NGO Agendas." Pp. 59–74 in *Sustainable Feminisms,* edited by Sonita Sarker. Amsterdam: Elsevier/JAI.

Bumiller, Elizabeth. 2003. "White House Letter: A Diplomatic Success, and Cheney's Daughter." *New York Times,* June 16.

Bumiller, Kristin. 2008. *In an Abusive State: How Neoliberalism Appropriated the Feminist Movement Against Sexual Violence.* Durham, NC: Duke University Press.

Bunch, Charlotte, and Niamh Reilly. 1994. *Demanding Accountability: The Global Campaign and Vienna Tribunal for Women's Human Rights.* New York: UNIFEM.

Butler, Judith. 1999. *Gender Trouble: Feminism and the Subversion of Identity.* New York: Routledge.

Byron, Ellen. 2007. "Emerging Ambitions—P&G's Global Target: Shelves of Tiny Stores." *Wall Street Journal,* July 16.

Calvan, Bobby Caina. 2007. "Filmmaker Moore, Nurses Rally for Health-Care Bill." *Sacramento Bee,* June 12. http://www.sacbee.com/101/story/218615.html.

Carabillo, Toni, Judith Meuli, and June Bundy Csida. 1993. *Feminist Chronicles, 1953–1993.* Los Angeles: Women's Graphics.

Caraway, Nancie. 1991. *Segregated Sisterhood: Racism and the Politics of American Feminism.* Knoxville: University of Tennessee Press.

Carby, Hazel. 1987. *Reconstructing Womanhood: The Emergence of the Afro-American Woman Novelist.* New York: Oxford University Press.

Carter, Susan B., Scott Sigmund Carter, Michael R. Haines, Alan L. Olmstead, Richard Sutch, and Gavin Wright, eds. 2006. *Historical Statistics of the United States: Earliest Times to the Present.* Vol. 2, Part B: "Work and Welfare." New York: Cambridge University Press.

Castells, Manuel. 2004. *The Power of Identity.* 2nd ed. Vol. 2: *The Information Age: Economy, Society, and Culture.* Malden, MA: Blackwell.

Center for Constitutional Rights. 2008. "CCR Legal Analysis: *Boumediene v. Bush/ Al Odah v. United States.*" http://www.ccrjustice.org/learn-more/faqs/legalanalysis%3A-boumediene-v.-bush/al-odah-v.-unitedstates.

Center for Reproductive Rights. 2004. "Briefing Paper: Legislation on Female Genital Mutilation in the United States." http://www.reproductiverights.org/pdf/pub_bp_fgmlawusa.pdf.

Chang, Grace. 2000. *Disposable Domestics: Immigrant Women Workers in the Global Economy.* Boston: South End Press.

———. 2004. "Globalization in Living Color: Women of Color Living Under and Over the 'New World Order.'" Pp. 230–261 in *Women and Globalization,* edited by Delia D. Aguilar and Anne E. Lacsamana. Amherst, NY: Humanity Books.

Chang, Ha-Joon. 2003a. "Kicking Away the Ladder: Neoliberals Rewrite History." *Monthly Review,* 54, No. 8 (January): 10-15.

———. 2003b. *Kicking Away the Ladder: Development Strategy in Historical Perspective.* London: Anthem.

Chernus, Ira. 2006. "The Day That Changed Everything Wasn't 9/11." www.portside.org, reprinted from www.TomDispatch.com.

Chesler, Ellen. 1992. *Woman of Valor: Margaret Sanger and the Birth Control Movement in America.* New York: Simon and Schuster.

Chew, Huibin Amee. 2005a. "Occupation Is Not (Women's) Liberation—Part I."

Znet, March 24. http://www.zmag.org/content/print_article.cfm? itemID=7518& sectionID=1.

———. 2005b. "Occupation Is Not (Women's) Liberation—Part II." *Znet,* March 24. http://www.zmag.org/content/print_article.cfm?itemID=7519&section ID=1.

"Cholera in South Africa Spreads." 2001. BBC News Online. http://news.bbc.co.uk/2low/africa/113995.stm.

Chomsky, Noam. 2003. *Hegemony or Survival: America's Quest for Global Dominance.* New York: Henry Holt.

Chossudovsky, Michel. 1996. "Dismantling Former Yugoslavia, Recolonizing Bosnia-Herzegovina." *Covert Action Quarterly* 56 (Spring). http://www.globalresearch.ca/articles/CHO202Gp.html.

———. 2003. *The Globalisation of Poverty and the New World Order.* 2nd ed. Shanty Bay, ON: Global Outlook.

Clarren, Rebecca. 2006. "Showdown on the Plains." *Ms.* (Fall): 34–37.

Cobble, Dorothy Sue. 2004. *The Other Women's Movement: Workplace Justice and Social Rights in Modern America.* Princeton, NJ: Princeton University Press.

———. 2007. "Introduction." Pp. 1–12 in *The Sex of Class: Women Transforming American Labor,* edited by Dorothy Sue Cobble. Ithaca, NY: ILR Press.

Coffman, Jennifer E. 2007. "Producing FGM in U.S. Courts: Political Asylum in the Post-Kasinga Era." *Africa Today* 53, no. 4: 59–84.

Combahee River Collective. 1995. Pp. 231–240 in *Words of Fire: An Anthology of African-American Feminist Thought,* edited by Beverly Guy-Sheftall. New York: New Press.

Connell, Raewyn W. 1995. *Masculinities.* Berkeley and Los Angeles: University of California Press.

Constable, Nicole. 1997. *Maid to Order in Hong Kong: Stories of Filipina Workers.* Ithaca, NY: Cornell University Press.

Cook, Rebecca J., ed. 1994. *Human Rights of Women: National and International Perspectives.* Philadelphia: University of Pennsylvania Press.

Cooper, Anna Julia. 1988. *A Voice from the South.* New York: Oxford University Press.

Cooper, Marc. 2007. "Lockdown in Greeley: How Immigration Raids Terrorized a Colorado Town." *The Nation,* February 26, 11–16.

Cott, Nancy. 1987. *The Grounding of Modern Feminism.* New Haven, CT: Yale University Press.

Courtemarche, Gil. 2003. *A Sunday at the Pool in Kigali,* translated by Patricia Claxton. New York: Knopf.

Cravey, Altha J. 1998. *Women and Work in Mexico's Maquiladoras.* Lanham, MD: Rowman and Littlefield.

Crenshaw, Kimberle. 1991. "Mapping the Margins: Intersectionality, Identity Politics, and Violence Against Women of Color." *Stanford Law Review* 43, no. 6: 1241–1299.

"Crises: One After Another for the Life of the System." 2002. *Monthly Review* 54, no. 6: 47–59.

Daly, Mary. 1978. *Gyn/Ecology: The Metaethics of Radical Feminism.* Boston: Beacon Press.

Danaher, Kevin, ed. 1994. *Fifty Years Is Enough: The Case Against the World Bank and the International Monetary Fund.* Boston: South End Press.

Daniel, Caroline. 2008. "The New Class Struggle." *Financial Times,* September 27–28, "Life and Arts" section, 1–2.

Davies, Margery W. 1984. *Woman's Place Is at the Typewriter: Office Work and Office Workers, 1870–1930.* Philadelphia: Temple University Press.

Davis, Angela. 1983. *Women, Race, and Class.* New York: Random House.

———. 2005. *Abolition Democracy: Beyond Empire, Prisons, and Torture.* New York: Seven Stories.

Davis, Flora. 1999. *Moving the Mountain: The Women's Movement in America Since 1960.* 2nd ed. Urbana: University of Illinois Press.

Davis, Mike. 2006. *Planet of Slums.* London: Verso Books.

de Tocqueville, Alexis. 2002 [1831]. *Democracy in America,* translated by Harvey Mansfield and Debra Winthrop. Chicago: University of Chicago Press.

De Veaux, Alexis. 2005. *Warrior Poet: A Biography of Audre Lorde.* New York: Norton.

Defunis v. Odegaard. 1974. 416 U.S. 312.

Dembele, Demba Moussa. 2003. "PRSPs: Poverty Reduction or Poverty Reinforcement?" *Pambazuka News: An Information Service for Social Justice in Africa,* December 11. http://www.pambazuka.org.

Desai, Manisha. 2002. "Transnational Solidarity: Women's Agency, Structural Adjustment, and Globalization." Pp. 15–33 in *Women's Activism and Globalization,* edited by Nancy Naples and Manisha Desai. New York: Routledge.

Dicken, Peter. 1998. *Global Shift: Transforming the World Economy.* London: Guilford.

Disney, Jennifer Leigh. 2004. "Incomplete Revolutions: Gendered Participation in Productive and Reproductive Labor in Mozambique and Nicaragua." *Socialism and Democracy* 18, no 1: 7–37.

———. 2008. *Women's Activism and Feminist Agency in Mozambique and Nicaragua.* Philadephia: Temple University Press.

Ditmore, Melissa. 2005. "Trafficking in Lives: How Ideology Shapes Policy." Pp. 107 126 in *Trafficking and Prostitution Reconsidered: New Perspectives on Migration, Sex Work, and Human Rights,* edited by Kemala Kempadoo. Boulder, CO: Paradigm Publishers.

Downie, Andrew. 2005. "A Police Station of Their Own." *Christian Science Monitor,* July 20. http://www.csmonitor.com/2005/0720/p15s02-woam.html.

Dreyfuss, Robert. 2005. *Devil's Game: How the United States Helped Unleash Fundamentalist Islam.* New York: Henry Holt.

Duberman, Martin, and Alisa Solomon, eds. 2003. *Queer Ideas: The Kessler Lectures in Lesbian and Gay Studies.* New York: Feminist Press.

Dugger, Celia W. 2006. "Peace Prize to Pioneer of Loans to Poor No Bank Would Touch." *New York Times,* October 14.

Edsall, Thomas Byrne. 1984. *The New Politics of Inequality.* New York: Norton.

Ehrenreich, Barbara. 2002. *Nickel and Dimed: On (Not) Getting By in America.* New York: Henry Holt.

Ehrenreich, Barbara, and Arlie Russell Hochschild, eds. 2004. *Global Woman: Nannies, Maids, and Sex Workers in the New Economy.* New York: Metropolitan Books/Owl Books.

Eisenstein, Hester. 1983. *Contemporary Feminist Thought.* Boston: G. K. Hall.

———. 1991a. "Encountering Simone de Beauvoir." *Women and Politics* 11, no. 1: 61–74.

————. 1991b. *Gender Shock: Practicing Feminism on Two Continents.* Boston: Beacon Press.

————. 1996. *Inside Agitators: Australian Femocrats and the State.* Philadelphia: Temple University Press.

————. 2005. "A Dangerous Liaison? Feminism and Corporate Globalization." *Science and Society* 69, no. 3 (July): 487–518.

————. 2006. "'Scouting Parties and Bold Detachments': Toward a Postcapitalist Feminism." *WSQ: Women's Studies Quarterly* 34, nos. 1–2: 40–62.

Eisenstein, Hester, ed. 2004. "Gender and Globalization: Marxist-Feminist Perspectives." *Socialism and Democracy* 18, no. 1: 1–184.

Eisenstein, Zillah R., ed. 1979. *Capitalist Patriarchy and the Case for Socialist Feminism.* New York: Monthly Review Press.

————. 1981. *The Radical Future of Liberal Feminism.* New York: Longman.

————. 2007. *Sexual Decoys: Gender, Race, and War in Imperial Democracy.* Melbourne, Australia: Spinifex/Zed Books.

Elliott, Andrea. 2006. "From Head Scarf to Army Cap, Making a New Life." *New York Times,* December 15.

Ellner, Steve. 2006. "Venezuela: Defying Globalization's Logic." Pp. 93–103 in *Dispatches from Latin America: On the Frontlines Against Neoliberalism,* edited by Teo Ballve and Vijay Prashad. Boston: South End Press.

Elshtain, Jean Bethke. 2004 [2003]. *Just War Against Terror: The Burden of American Power in a Violent World.* New ed. New York: Basic Books.

Elyachar, Julia. 2002. "Empowerment Money: The World Bank, Non-governmental Organizations, and the Value of Culture in Egypt." *Public Culture* 14, no. 3: 493–513.

Enloe, Cynthia. 2004. *The Curious Feminist: Searching for Women in a New Age of Empire.* Berkeley and Los Angeles: University of California Press.

Epoo, Brenda, and Vicki Van Wagner. 2005. "Bringing Birth Back to the Community: Midwifery in the Inuit Villages of Nunavik." Paper presented at the Twenty-seventh Congress, International Confederation of Midwives, Brisbane, Australia, July. www .naho.ca/inuit/midwifery/documents/2005–07NunavikICMkeynotefinal.pdf.

Epstein, Keith, and Geri Smith. 2007. "The Ugly Side of Micro-Lending: How Big Mexican Banks Profit as Many Poor Borrowers Get Trapped in a Maze of Debt." *BusinessWeek,* December 24, 39–44.

Eschle, Catherine. 2005. "'Skeleton Women': Feminism and the Antiglobalization Movement." *Signs* 30, no. 3: 1741–1769.

Escobar, Arturo. 1995. *Encountering Development: The Making and Unmaking of the Third World.* Princeton, NJ: Princeton University Press.

Etienne, Mona, and Eleanor Burke Leacock. 1980a. "Introduction." Pp. 1–24 in *Women and Colonization: Anthropological Perspectives,* edited by Mona Etienne and Eleanor Burke Leacock. New York: Praeger.

Etienne, Mona, and Eleanor Burke Leacock, eds. 1980b. *Women and Colonization: Anthropological Perspectives.* New York: Praeger.

Evans, Sara M. 1979. *Personal Politics: The Roots of Women's Liberation in the Civil Rights Movement and the New Left.* New York: Vintage Books.

————. 2003. *Tidal Wave: How Women Changed America at Century's End.* New York: Free Press.

Ewen, Stuart. 2001. *Captains of Consciousness: Advertising and the Social Roots of the Consumer Culture.* 25th anniversary ed. New York: Basic Books.

Ezeilo, Joy Ngozi. 2007. "Amazons Go to War Without Weapons: Women and the Conflict in Scaravos, Niger Delta." Pp. 190–203 in *The Wages of Empire: Neoliberal Policies, Repression, and Women's Poverty,* edited by Amalia L. Cabezas, Ellen Reese, and Marguerite Waller. Boulder, CO: Paradigm Publishers.

Fall, Yassine. 2003. "The Privatization of Water from Johannesburg to Jersey City." Roundtable at the Brecht Forum, New York City, June 5.

Faludi, Susan. 1991. *Backlash: The Undeclared War Against American Women.* New York: Crown.

———. 2000. *Stiffed: The Betrayal of the American Man.* New York: HarperPerennial.

Fausto-Sterling, Anne. 1992. *Myths of Gender: Biological Theories About Women and Men.* New York: Basic Books.

Faux, Jeff. 2006. *The Global Class War: How America's Bipartisan Elite Lost Our Future— and What It Will Take to Win It Back.* New York: Wiley.

Featherstone, Liza. 2004. *Selling Women Short: The Landmark Battle for Workers' Rights at Wal-Mart.* New York: Basic Books.

Feder, Barnaby J. 2006. "Theodore Levitt, 81; Coined the Term 'Globalization.'" *New York Times,* July 6.

Federici, Sylvia. 1999. "Reproduction and Feminist Struggle in the New International Division of Labor." Pp. 47–81 in *Women, Development, and Labor of Reproduction: Struggles and Movements,* edited by Mariarosa Dalla Costa and Giovanna F. Dalla Costa. Trenton, NJ: Africa World Press.

———. 2000. "War, Globalization, and Reproduction." *Peace and Change* 25, no. 2: 153–161.

———. 2001. "The Debt Crisis, Africa, and the New Enclosures." *Commoner* (September). http:commoner.org.uk/02federici.pdf.

Feiner, Susan F., and Drucilla K. Barker. 2006. "Microcredit and Women's Poverty." *Dollars and Sense* 268: 10–11.

Fekete, Liz. 2006. "Enlightened Fundamentalism? Immigration, Feminism, and the Right." *Race and Class* 48: 1–22.

Feldman, Shelley. 2001. "Exploring Theories of Patriarchy: A Perspective from Contemporary Bangladesh." *Signs* 26, no. 4: 1097–1127.

Fernandez-Kelly, M. Patricia. 1983. *For We Are Sold, I and My People: Women and Industry in Mexico's Frontier.* Albany: State University of New York Press.

———. 1989. "International Development and Industrial Restructuring: The Case of Garment and Electronics Industries in Southern California." Pp. 147–165 in *Instability and Change in the World Economy,* edited by Arthur MacEwan and William K. Tabb. New York: Monthly Review Press.

———. 2007. "The Global Assembly Line in the New Millennium: A Review Essay." *Signs* 32, no. 2: 509–521.

Fernandez-Kelly, M. Patricia, and Diane Wolf. 2001. "A Dialogue on Globalization." *Signs* 26, no. 4: 1244–1249.

Ferree, Myra Marx. 2006. "Globalization and Feminism: Opportunities and Obstacles for Activism in the Global Arena." Pp. 3–23 in *Global Feminism: Transnational Women's Activism, Organizing, and Human Rights,* edited by Myra Marx Ferree and Aili Mari Tripp. New York: New York University Press.

Ferree, Myra Marx, and Beth B. Hess. 1994. *Controversy and Coalition: The New Feminist Movement Across Three Decades of Change.* Rev. ed. New York: Macmillan.

Ferree, Myra Marx, and Aili Mari Tripp, eds. 2006. *Global Feminism: Transnational Women's Activism, Organizing, and Human Rights.* New York: New York University Press.

Fineman, Martha. 1995. *The Neutered Mother, the Sexual Family, and Other Twentieth-Century Tragedies.* New York: Routledge.

Finlay, Barbara. 2006. *George W. Bush and the War on Women: Turning Back the Clock on Progress.* London: Zed Books.

Fisher, Ian. 2006. "Pope Calls West Divorced from Faith, Adding a Blunt Footnote on Jihad." *New York Times,* September 13.

Flanders, Laura. 2004. *Bushwomen: Tales of a Cynical Species.* London: Verso Books.

Folbre, Nancy. 2001. *The Invisible Heart: Economics and Family Values.* New York: New Press.

Foran, John. 2003. "Feminism and Global Marxism: Making a Commitment." *From the Left: The Newsletter of the Section on Marxist Sociology of the American Sociological Association* 24, no. 2: 3–4.

Fortunato Jr., Stephen. J. 2007. "The Imperative of an International Guaranteed Income." *Monthly Review* 58, no. 11. http://www.monthlyreview.org/0407/fortunato.htm.

Frank, Thomas. 2005. *What's the Matter with Kansas?* New York: Metropolitan Books.

Fraser, Nancy, and Linda Gordon. 2003. "A Geneaology of Dependency: Tracing a Keyword of the U.S. Welfare State." Pp. 14–39 in *The Subject of Care: Feminist Perspectives on Dependency,* edited by Eva Feder Kittay and Ellen K. Feder. Lanham, MD: Roman and Littlefield.

Freedman, Estelle B. 2002. *No Turning Back: The History of Feminism and the Future of Women.* New York: Ballantine Books.

Freeman, Carla. 2000. *High Tech and High Heels in the Global Economy: Women, Work, and Pink-Collar Identities in the Caribbean.* Durham, NC: Duke University Press.

Freeman, Jo. 1975. *The Politics of Women's Liberation: A Case Study of an Emerging Social Movement and Its Relation to the Policy Process.* New York: McKay.

Fried, Marlene. 2006. "The Hyde Amendment: The Opening Wedge to Abolish Abortion." *New Politics* 11, no. 2. www.wpunj.edu/newpol/issue42/Fried42.htm.

Friedan, Betty. 2001 [1963]. *The Feminine Mystique.* New York: Norton.

Frieden, Jeffrey A. 2006. *Global Capitalism: Its Fall and Rise in the Twentieth Century.* New York: Norton.

Friedman, Thomas L. 2000. *The Lexus and the Olive Tree.* New York: Random House.

Froebel, Folker, Jurgen Heinrichs, and Otto Kreye. 1980 [1977]. *The New International Division of Labor: Structural Unemployment in Industrialized Countries and Industrialization in Developing Countries,* translated by Pete Burgess. Cambridge, UK: Cambridge University Press.

Full Monty, The. 1997. Directed by Peter Cattaneo. Redwave Films.

Funk, Nanette, and Magda Mueller, eds. 1993. *Gender Politics and Postcommunism: Reflections from Eastern Europe and the Former Soviet Union.* New York: Routledge.

George, Susan. 2002. "A Short History of Neoliberalism." Pp. 1–6 in *Real World Globalization: A Reader in Economics and Politics from* Dollars and Sense, edited by Alejandro Reuss, Thad Williamson, Jeanne Winner, and the Dollars and Sense Collective. 7th ed. Cambridge, MA: Dollars and Sense Economic Affairs Bureau.

Gervasi, Sean. 1996. "Why Is NATO in Yugoslavia?" www.emperors-clothes.com/articles/gervasi/why.htm.

G.I. Jane. 1997. Directed by Ridley Scott. Hollywood Pictures.

Gibson-Graham, J. K. 2006a. *The End of Capitalism (As We Knew It): A Feminist Critique of Political Economy—with a New Introduction.* Minneapolis: University of Minnesota Press.

———. 2006b. "Imagining and Enacting a Postcapitalist Feminist Economic Politics." *WSQ: Women's Studies Quarterly* 34, nos. 1–2: 72–78.

———. 2006c. *A Postcapitalist Politics.* Minneapolis: University of Minnesota Press.

Giddings, Paula. 1996 [1984]. *Where and When I Enter: The Impact of Black Women on Race and Sex in America.* New York: Morrow.

———. 2008. *Ida: A Sword Among Lions—Ida B. Wells and the Campaign Against Lynching.* New York: Amistad.

Gimenez, Martha E. 2004. "Connecting Marx and Feminism in the Era of Globalization: A Preliminary Investigation." *Socialism and Democracy* 18, no. 1: 85–105.

Gimenez, Martha E., and Lise Vogel, eds. 2005. *Marxist-Feminist Thought Today.* Special issue of *Science and Society* 69, no. 1.

Gindin, Sam, and Leo Panitch. 2002. "Exchange: 1. Rethinking Crisis." *Monthly Review* 54, no. 6: 34–45.

Glater, Jonathan D. 2004. "Offshore Services Grow in Lean Times: Consultants Help Companies Shift Their Operations." *New York Times,* January 3.

Gluck, Sherna Berger, with Maylei Blackwell, Sharon Cotrell, and Karen S. Harper. 1998. "Whose Feminism, Whose History? Reflections on Excavating the History of (the) U.S. Women's Movement(s)." Pp. 31–56 in *Community Activism and Feminist Politics: Organizing Across Race, Class, and Gender,* edited by Nancy A. Naples. New York: Routledge.

Gluckman, Amy. 2008. "Dust-up at the Labor Notes Conference: SEIU and CNA at Loggerheads." *Dollars and Sense* 276 (May–June): 8–9.

Goff, Stan. 2004. *Full Spectrum Disorder: The Military in the New American Century.* Brooklyn, NY: Soft Skull Press.

Gonzales v. Carhart, Gonzales v. Planned Parenthood, 550 U.S. 124 (2007).

Gordon, April A. 1996. *Transforming Capitalism and Patriarchy: Gender and Development in Africa.* Boulder, CO: Lynne Rienner.

Gordon, Linda. 1994. *Pitied but Not Entitled: Single Mothers and the History of Welfare, 1890–1935.* Cambridge, MA: Harvard University Press.

Grandin, Greg. 2006. *Empire's Workshop: Latin America, the United States, and the Rise of the New Imperialism.* New York: Metropolitan Books/Henry Holt.

Greenberg, Ilan. 2006. "Almaty Journal: Up, Up, and Away: New Towers and Ambitions to Match." *New York Times,* June 22.

Greenhouse, Steven. 2008. "Union Membership Sees Biggest Rise Since '83." *New York Times,* January 26.

Greenwald, Maurine Weiner. 1989. "Working-Class Feminism and the Family Wage Ideal: The Seattle Debate on Married Women's Right to Work, 1914–1920." *Journal of American History* 76: 118–149.

Greider, William. 1997. *One World, Ready or Not: The Manic Logic of Global Capitalism.* New York: Simon and Schuster.

Grewal, Inderpal, and Caren Kaplan. 2000. "Postcolonial Studies and Transnational Feminist Practices." http://socialclass.ncsu.edu/jouvert/v5il/grewal.htm.

Griggs v. Duke Power Co., 401 U.S. 424 (1971).

Gross, Bertram. 1980. *Friendly Fascism: The New Face of Power in America.* Boston: South End Press.

Gross, Harriet Engel, Alice J. Dan, Nona Glazer, Judith Lorber, Martha McClintock, Niles Newton, and Alice Rossi. 1979. "Considering 'A Biosocial Perspective on Parenting.'" *Signs* 4, no. 4: 695–717.

"Guide to Womenomics, A." 2006. *The Economist,* April 12, 1–4. www.economist.com/finance/PrinterFriendly.cfm?story_id=6802551.

Guttmacher Institute. 2008. "Facts on Induced Abortion in the United States." January. http://www.guttmacher.org/pubs/fb_induced_abortion.pdf.

Guy-Sheftall, Beverly. 1995a. "Introduction: The Evolution of Feminist Consciousness Among African-American Women." Pp. 1–22 in *Words of Fire: An Anthology of African-American Feminist Thought,* edited by Beverly Guy-Sheftall. New York: New Press.

Guy-Sheftall, Beverly, ed. 1995b. *Words of Fire: An Anthology of African-American Feminist Thought.* New York: New Press.

Hammond, Jack. 2008. "The Resource Curse and Social Spending in Angola and Venezuela." Paper presented at the Global Studies Association Annual Conference, New York City, June 6–8.

Harris v. McCrae, 448 U.S. 297 (1980).

Harrison, Cynthia. 1988. *On Account of Sex.* Berkeley and Los Angeles: University of California Press.

Hartmann, Heidi I. 1981. "The Unhappy Marriage of Marxism and Feminism: Towards a More Progressive Union." Pp. 1–41 in *Women and Revolution: A Discussion of the Unhappy Marriage of Marxism and Feminism,* edited by Lydia Sargent. Boston: South End Press.

———. 1987. "Changes in Women's Economic and Family Roles in Post–World War II United States." Pp. 33–64 in *Women, Households, and the Economy,* edited by Lourdes Beneria and Catharine R. Stimpson. New Brunswick, NJ: Rutgers University Press.

Hartmann, Susan S. 1982. *The Home Front and Beyond: American Women in the 1940s.* Boston: Twayne.

Harvey, David. 1989. *The Condition of Postmodernity.* Oxford, UK: Blackwell.

———. 2003. *The New Imperialism.* New York: Monthly Review Press.

Hatem, Mervat R. 1994. "Privatization and the Demise of State Feminism in Egypt." Pp. 40–60 in *Mortgaging Women's Lives: Feminist Critiques of Structural Adjustment,* edited by Pamela Sparr. London: Zed Books.

Heilbrun, Carolyn G. 1973. *Toward a Recognition of Androgyny.* New York: Knopf.

Henwood, Doug. 2003. *After the New Economy.* New York: New Press.

Herbert, Bob. 2004. "'Gooks' to 'Hajis.'" *New York Times,* May 21.

Herman, Edward S. 2006. "Notes on the Progress of the Counterrevolution." *Z Magazine* (July–August). www.zmag.org/zmag/viewArticle/13827.

Herman, Edward S., David Peterson, and George Szamuely. 2007. "A Review of 'Weighing the Evidence: Lessons from the Slobodan Milosevic Trial' (*Human Rights Watch* [December 2006]." *Zmag.org,* February 25. www.globalresearch.ca/PrintArticle.php?articleId=5021.

Hernandez, Daisy, and Bushra Rehman, eds. 2002. *Colonize This! Young Women of Color on Today's Feminism.* Emeryville, CA: Seal.

Hill, Steven, and Nina Silver. 1993. "Civil Rights Anti-pornography Legislation: Addressing the Harm to Women." Pp. 283–300 in *Transforming a Rape Culture,* edited by Emilie Buchwald, Pamela R. Fletcher, and Martha Roth. Minneapolis: Milkweed Editions.

Holloway, John. 2005. *Change the World Without Taking Power: The Meaning of Revolution Today.* London: Pluto.

Holmstrom, Nancy, ed. 2002. *The Socialist-Feminist Project: A Contemporary Reader in Theory and Politics.* New York: Monthly Review Press.

Hondagneu-Sotelo, Pierrette. 2001. *Domestica: Immigrant Workers Cleaning and Caring in the Shadow of Affluence.* Berkeley and Los Angeles: University of California Press.

hooks, bell. 1981. *Ain't I a Woman? Black Women and Feminism.* Boston: South End Press.

Horowitz, Daniel. 1998. *Betty Friedan and the Making of* The Feminine Mystique: *The American Left, the Cold War, and Modern Feminism.* Amherst: University of Massachusetts Press.

Hosken, Fran. 1993. *The Hosken Report: Genital and Sexual Mutilation of Females.* 4th ed. Lexington, MA. Women's International Network News.

Huntington, Samuel P. 1996. *The Clash of Civilizations and the Remaking of World Order.* New York: Simon and Schuster.

Huque, Ahmed Shafiqul, and Habib Mohammed Zafarullah, eds. 2006. *International Development Governance.* Boca Raton, FL: CRC.

"Importance of Sex, The." 2006. *The Economist,* April 12, 1–2. www.economist.com/opinion/PrinterFriendly.cfm?story_id=68.

Isserles, Robin G. 2002. "Ideology, Rhetoric, and the Politics of Bureaucracy: Exploring Women and Development." Ph.D. diss., Program in Sociology, Graduate School, City University of New York.

Jacobe, Monica F. 2006. "Contingent Faculty Across the Disciplines." *Academe: Bulletin of the American Association of University Professors* 92, no. 6: 43–49.

James, Stanlie M., and Claire C. Robertson. 2005. "Introduction: Reimaging Transnational Sisterhood." Pp. 5–15 in *Genital Cutting and Transnational Sisterhood: Disputing U.S. Polemics,* edited by Stanlie M. James and Claire C. Robertson. Urbana: University of Illinois Press.

Janeway, Elizabeth. 1971. *Man's World, Woman's Place: A Study in Social Mythology.* New York: Dell.

Janiewski, Dolores E. 2001. "Engendering the Invisible Empire: Imperialism, Feminism, and U.S. Women's History." *Australian Feminist Studies* 16, no. 36: 279–291.

Jardine, Alice. 1985. *Gynesis: Configurations of Woman and Modernity.* Ithaca, NY: Cornell University Press.

Jayawardena, Kumar. 1986. *Feminism and Nationalism in the Third World.* London: Zed Books.

Jayaweera, Swarna. 1994. "Structural Adjustment Policies, Industrial Development, and Women in Sri Lanka." Pp. 95–115 in *Mortgaging Women's Lives: Feminist Critiques of Structural Adjustment,* edited by Pamela Sparr. London: Zed Books.

Johnstone, Diana. 1998. "Seeing Yugoslavia Through a Dark Glass: Politics, Media, and the Ideology of Globalization." *Covert Action Quarterly* 65 (Fall). http://ourworld.compuserve.com/homepages/grattan_healy/johnston.htm.

———. 2002. *Fool's Crusade.* London: Pluto Press.

Journey with the Revolution. 2006. Directed by Finn Arden and Nina Lopez. Produced by Global Women's Strike. www.globalwomenstrike.net.

Kabeer, Naila. 2000. *The Power to Choose: Bangladeshi Women and Labor Market Decisions in London and Dhaka.* London: Verso Books.

Kandiyoti, Deniz. 1991a. "Introduction." Pp. 1–21 in *Women, Islam, and the State,* edited by Deniz Kandiyoti. Philadelphia: Temple University Press.

Kandiyoti, Deniz, ed. 1991b. *Women, Islam, and the State.* Philadelphia: Temple University Press.

Kantrowitz, Barbara, Holly Peterson, and Karen Breslau. 2006. "Leadership for the 21st Century: Leading the Way." *Newsweek,* September 25, 44–60.

Kaplan, Caren, Norma Alarcon, and Minoo Moallem, eds. 1999. *Between Women and Nation: Nationalisms, Transnational Feminisms, and the State.* Durham, NC: Duke University Press.

Kaplan, Esther. 2008. "Labor's Growing Pains: SEIU Battles the California Nurses—and Dissidents Within Its Own Ranks." *The Nation,* June 16, 17–23.

Kaplan, Temma. 1982. "Female Consciousness and Collective Action: The Case of Barcelona, 1910–1918." *Signs* 7, no. 3: 545–560.

———.1990. "Community and Resistance in Women's Political Cultures." *Dialectical Anthropology* 15, nos. 2–3: 259–267.

Karides, Marina. 2007. "Macroeconomics and Microentrepreneurs: Comparing Two Island Nations' Responses to Neoliberalism and Its Impact on Women's Lives." Pp. 73–85 in *The Wages of Empire: Neoliberal Policies, Repression, and Women's Poverty,* edited by Amalia L. Cabezas, Ellen Reese, and Marguerite Waller. Boulder, CO: Paradigm Publishers.

Kempadoo, Kamala. 1998. "Introduction: Globalizing Sex Workers' Rights." Pp. 1–28 in *Global Sex Workers: Rights, Resistance, and Redefinition,* edited by Kamala Kempadoo and Jo Doezema. New York: Routledge.

Kempadoo, Kamala, with Jyoti Sanghera and Bandana Pattanaik. 2005. *Trafficking and Prostitution Reconsidered: New Perspectives on Migration, Sex Work, and Human Rights.* Boulder, CO: Paradigm Publishers.

Kerr, Joanna. 1999. "Responding to Globalization: Can Feminists Transform Development?" Pp. 190–205 in *Feminists Doing Development: A Practical Critique,* edited by Marilyn Porter and Ellen Judd. London: Zed Books.

Kessler-Harris, Alice. 1982. *Out to Work: The History of Wage-Earning Women in the United States.* Oxford, UK: Oxford University Press.

———. 2001. *In Pursuit of Equality: Women, Men, and the Quest for Economic Citizenship in 20th-Century America.* Oxford, UK: Oxford University Press.

Khan, Nighat Said. 2004. "Up Against the State: The Women's Movement in Pakistan and Its Implications for the Global Women's Movement." Pp. 86–99 in *Feminist Politics, Activism, and Vision: Local and Global Challenges,* edited by Luciana Ricciutelli, Angela Miles, and Margaret McFadden. A Project of the Feminist Journals Network. Toronto: Inanna/Zed Books.

King, Deborah K. 1988. "Multiple Jeopardy, Multiple Consciousness: The Context of a Black Feminist Ideology." *Signs* 14, no. 1: 42–72.

Klein, Naomi. 2000. *No Logo: Taking Aim at the Brand Bullies.* New York: Picador.

———. 2004. "Risky Business: Hanging with Halliburton at Rebuilding Iraq 2." *The Nation,* January 5, 11–16.

————. 2007. *The Shock Doctrine: The Rise of Disaster Capitalism.* New York: Metropolitan Books/Henry Holt.

Koedt, Anne. 1973. "The Myth of the Vaginal Orgasm." Pp. 198–207 in *Radical Feminism,* edited by Anne Koedt, Ellen Levine, and Anita Rapode. New York: Quadrangle Books.

Koppel, Nathan. 2007. "Remembrances 1923–2007: Judith P. Vladeck—Fiery Lawyer Advanced Rights in the Workplace." *Wall Street Journal,* January 13–14.

Korten, Alicia. 1994. "Structural Adjustment and Costa Rican Agriculture." Pp. 56–61 in *Fifty Years Is Enough: The Case Against the World Bank and the International Monetary Fund,* edited by Kevin Danaher. Boston: South End Press.

Koven, Seth, and Sonya Michel. 1993. *Mothers of a New World: Maternalist Politics and the Origins of Welfare States.* New York: Routledge.

Kristof, Nicholas D. 2006. "Looking for Islam's Luthers." *New York Times,* October 15.

Kruks, Sonia, Rayna Rapp, and Marilyn B. Young, eds. 1989. *Promissory Notes: Women in the Transition to Socialism.* New York: Monthly Review Press.

Kuhn, Sarah, and Barry Bluestone. 1987. "Economic Restructuring and the Female Labor Market: The Impact of Industrial Change on Women." Pp. 3–32 in *Women, Households, and the Economy,* edited by Lourdes Beneria and Catharine R. Stimpson. New Brunswick, NJ: Rutgers University Press.

Kwong, Peter. 2006. "China's Neoliberal Dynasty." *The Nation,* October 2, 20–22.

Lacsamana, Anne E. 2004. "Sex Worker or Prostituted Woman? An Examination of the Sex Work Debates in Western Feminist Theory." Pp. 387–403 in *Women and Globalization,* edited by Delia D. Aguilar and Anne E. Lacsamana. Amherst, NY: Humanity Books.

Lazreg, Marnia. 2008. *Torture and the Twilight of an Empire: From Algiers to Baghdad.* Princeton, NJ: Princeton University Press.

Leigh, Andrew. 2005. "The Decline of an Institution." *Australian Financial Review,* March 7. http://econrsss.anu.edu.au/~Leigh/pdf/Deunionization.pdf.

Lemisch, Jessie. 2006a. "About the Herbert Aptheker Sexual Revelations." *History News Network,* October 4. http://www.hnn.us/articles/30519.html.

————. 2006b. "Shhh! Don't Talk About Herbert Aptheker." *History News Network,* October 8. http://www.hnn.us/articles/30522.html.

Lerner, Gerda. 1969. "The Lady and the Mill Girl: Changes in the Status of Women in the Age of Jackson." *American Studies Journal* 10, no. 1: 5–15.

Levine, Arthur. 2007. "Unionbusting Confidential." *In These Times* 31, no. 10 (October): 20–23.

Levitt, Theodore. 1993. "The Globalization of Markets." Pp. 249–266 in *Readings in International Business: A Decision Approach,* edited by Robert Z. Aliber and Reid W. Click. Cambridge, MA: MIT Press.

Lichtenstein, Nelson. 2002. *State of the Union: A Century of American Labor.* Princeton, NJ: Princeton University Press.

————. 2006. "Wal-Mart: A Template for Twenty-First-Century Capitalism." Pp. 3–30 in *Wal-Mart: The Face of Twenty-First-Century Capitalism,* edited by Nelson Lichtenstein. New York: Free Press.

Lim, Linda Y. C. 1990. "Women's Work in Export Factories: The Politics of a Cause." Pp. 101–119 in *Persistent Inequalities: Women and World Development,* edited by Irene Tinker. New York: Oxford University Press.

Lorber, Judith. 2000. "Using Gender to Undo Gender: A Feminist Degendering Movement." *Feminist Theory* 1, no. 1: 79–95.

———. 2005. *Breaking the Bowls: Degendering and Feminist Change.* New York: Norton.

Lopez, Nina, ed. 2006. *Creating a Caring Economy: Nora Castañeda and the Women's Development Bank of Venezuela.* London: Crossroads.

Lorde, Audre. 1983. "An Open Letter to Mary Daly." Pp. 94–97 in *This Bridge Called My Back: Writings by Radical Women of Color*, edited by Cherrie Moraga and Gloria Anzaldúa. New York: Kitchen Table/Women of Color Press.

Louie, Miriam Ching, and Linda Burnham. 2000. *WEdGE: Women's Education in the Global Economy—a Workbook of Activities, Games, Skits, and Strategies for Activists, Organizers, Rebels, and Hell Raisers.* Berkeley, CA: Women of Color Resource Center.

Loyn, David. 2008. "Trade Talks' Failure Ends Doha Dreams." BBC News, July 29. http://news/bbc.co.uk/go/pr/fr-/-/business/7532168.stm.

Lucas, James A. 2005. "Media Disinformation on the War in Yugoslavia: The Dayton Peace Accords Revisited." *Global Research*, September 7. http://www.globalresearch.ca/index.php?context=viewArticle&code=LUC20050907&artic.

Luce, Stephanie, and Mark Brenner. 2007. "Women and Class: What Has Happened in Forty Years?" Pp. 119–130 in *More Unequal: Aspects of Class in the United States*, edited by Michael D. Yates. New York: Monthly Review Press.

Luker, Kristin. 1984. *Abortion and the Politics of Motherhood.* Berkeley and Los Angeles: University of California Press.

Maathai, Wangari Muta. 2006. *Unbowed (a Memoir).* New York: Knopf.

"*Mabo v. Queensland*: A Question of Morality." 1992. www.convictcreations.com/history/mabo.htm.

MacFarquhar, Neil. 2006. "Putting a Different Face on Islam in America." *New York Times*, September 20.

MacLean, Nancy. 2002. "Postwar Women's History: The 'Second Wave' or the End of the Family Wage?" Pp. 235–259 in *A Companion to Post-1945 America*, edited by Jean-Christophe Agnew and Roy Rosensweig. Malden, MA: Blackwell.

———. 2006. *Freedom Is Not Enough: The Opening of the American Workplace.* Cambridge, MA: Harvard University Press.

MADRE. n.d. "Economic Justice and Women's Human Rights: A MADRE Position Paper." www.madre.org/print-/articles/int/b10/econjustice.html.

Magdoff, Harry. 1969. *The Age of Imperialism: The Economics of U.S. Foreign Policy.* New York: Monthly Review Press.

Maher, Kris. 2008. "Starbucks Emails Describe Efforts to Stop Unionization." *Wall Street Journal*, January 9.

Mama, Amina. 2001. "African Women's Voices: Talking About Feminism in Africa." Interviewed by Elaine Salo. *Agenda, African Feminisms* 1, no. 50: 58–63. www.wworld.org/programs/regions/africa/amina_mama_p.htm.

Mamdani, Mahmood. 2004. *Good Muslim, Bad Muslim: America, the Cold War, and the Roots of Terror.* Johannesburg, South Africa: Jacana Media.

Manji, Irshad. 2003. *The Trouble with Islam Today: A Muslim's Call for Reform in Her Faith.* New York: St. Martin's Press.

Marable, Manning. 2004. "Global Apartheid and America's New Racial Domain." *Along the Color Line* (August). http://www.manningmarable.net/works/aug04d.html.

Marcos, Sylvia. 2005. "The Borders Within: The Indigenous Women's Movement and Feminism in Mexico." Pp. 81–112 in *Dialogue and Difference: Feminisms Challenge Globalization,* edited by Marguerite Waller and Sylvia Marcos. New York: Palgrave Macmillan.

Markovitz, Irving Leonard. 1998. "Uncivil Society: Capitalism and the State in Africa." Pp. 21–53 in *Civil Society and Democracy in Africa: Critical Perspectives,* edited by Nelson Kasfir. Portland, OR: Cass.

Martinez, Andres. 2003. "How a Seed-Money Loan of $60 Turned Melanie Pico into an Entrepreneur." *New York Times,* July 8.

Marx, Karl. 1909. *Capital: A Critique of Political Economy.* Volume I: *The Process of Capitalist Production,* translated from the 3rd German ed. by Samuel Moore and Edward Aveline and edited by Friedrich Engels. Chicago: Kerr.

Mather, Mark. 2007. "Closing the Male-Female Labor Force Gap." *Population Reference Bureau.* http://www.prb.org/Articles/2007/ClosingtheMaleFemaleLaborForceGap .aspx?p=1.

Matthews, Nancy A. 1994. *Confronting Rape: The Feminist Anti-rape Movement and the State.* New York: Routledge.

"Mavis Leno to Chair Feminist Majority Foundation's Campaign to Stop Gender Apartheid." 1998. *Ms.* October 21. http://www.msmagazine.com/news/printnews .asp?id–4542.

May, Elaine Tyler. 1990. *Homeward Bound: American Families in the Cold War Era.* New York: Basic Books.

May, Martha. 1982. "The Historical Problem of the Family Wage: The Ford Motor Company and the Five-Dollar Day." *Feminist Studies* 8, no. 2: 399–424.

———. 1985. "Bread Before Roses: American Workingmen, Labor Unions, and the Family Wage." Pp. 1–21 in *Women, Work, and Protest: A Century of U.S. Women's Labor History,* edited by Ruth Milkman. London: Routledge and Kegan Paul.

McGowan, Lisa. 1995. "The Ignored Cost of Adjustment: Women Under SAPs in Africa." A Development Gap Paper prepared for the Fourth United Nations Conference on Women. Washington, DC: The Development GAP (The Development Group for Alternative Policies).

McLaughlin, Martin. 1999. "Clinton, Republicans Agree to Deregulation of U.S. Financial System." November 1. http://www.wsws.org/articles/1999/nov1999/ bank-no1_prn.shtml.

McMichael, Philip. 2004. *Development and Social Change: A Global Perspective.* 3rd ed. Thousand Oaks, CA: Pine Forge/Sage.

Mies, Maria. 1998 [1986]. *Patriarchy and Accumulation on a World Scale: Women in the International Division of Labor.* 2nd ed. London: Zed Books.

Milkman, Ruth. 1985. "Women Workers, Feminism, and the Labor Movement Since the 1960s." Pp. 300–322 in *Women, Work, and Protest: A Century of U.S. Women's Labor History,* edited by Ruth Milkman. London: Routledge and Kegan Paul.

———. 1987. "Women Workers and the Labor Movement in Hard Times: Comparing the 1930s with the 1980s." Pp. 111–131 in *Women, Households, and the Economy,* edited by Lourdes Beneria and Catharine R. Stimpson. New Brunswick, NJ: Rutgers University Press.

———. 2007. "Two Worlds of Unionism: Women and the New Labor Movement." Pp. 63–80 in *The Sex of Class: Women Transforming American Labor,* edited by Dorothy Sue Cobble. Ithaca, NY: ILR Press.

Millett, Kate. 1970. *Sexual Politics.* New York: Avon.

Mink, Gwendolyn. 1998. *Welfare's End.* Ithaca, NY: Cornell University Press.

———. 2001. "Feminism Today: An Interview with Gwendolyn Mink." *New Politics* 8, no. 31: 1–9. www.wpunj.edu/~newpol/issue31/mink31.htm.

Moghadam, Valentine M. 2002. "Islamic Feminism and Its Discontents: Toward a Resolution of the Debate." *Signs* 27, no. 4: 1135–1171.

———. 2003. *Modernizing Women: Gender and Social Change in the Middle East.* 2nd ed. Boulder, CO: Lynne Rienner.

———. 2005. *Globalizing Women: Transnational Feminist Networks.* Baltimore, MD: Johns Hopkins University Press.

Mohanty, Chandra Talpade. 1991a. "Cartographies of Struggle: Third World Women and the Politics of Feminism." Pp. 1–50 in *Third World Women and the Politics of Feminism,* edited by Chandra Mohanty, Lourdes Torres, and Ann Russo. Bloomington: Indiana University Press.

———. 1991b. "Under Western Eyes: Feminist Scholarship and Colonial Discourses." Pp. 51–80 in *Third World Women and the Politics of Feminism,* edited by Chandra Mohanty, Lourdes Torres, and Ann Russo. Bloomington: Indiana University Press.

———. 2003a. *Feminism Without Borders: Decolonizing Theory, Practicing Solidarity.* Durham, NC: Duke University Press.

———. 2003b. "Under Western Eyes Revisited: Feminist Solidarity Through Anticapitalist Struggles." Pp. 221–252 in *Feminism Without Borders: Decolonizing Theory, Practicing Solidarity,* by Chandra Talpade Mohanty. Durham, NC: Duke University Press.

Mohanty, Chandra Talpade, Lourdes Torres, and Ann Russo, eds. 1991. *Third World Women and the Politics of Feminism.* Bloomington: Indiana University Press.

Molyneux, Maxine. 2001a [1985]. "Mobilization Without Emancipation? Women's Interests, the State, and Revolution in Nicaragua." Pp. 38–59 in *Women's Movements in International Perspective: Latin America and Beyond,* by Maxine Molyneux. New York: Palgrave Macmillan.

———. 2001b. *Women's Movements in International Perspective: Latin America and Beyond.* New York: Palgrave Macmillan.

Moody, Kim. 2008. "Harvest of Empire: Immigrant Workers' Struggles in the USA." Pp. 315–334 in *Socialist Register 2008: Global Flashpoints—Reactions to Imperialism and Neoliberalism,* edited by Leo Panitch and Colin Leys. London: Merlin/Monthly Review/Fernwood.

Moraga, Cherrie, and Gloria F. Anzaldúa, eds. 1983. *This Bridge Called My Back: Writings by Radical Women of Color.* 2nd ed. New York: Kitchen Table/Women of Color Press.

Morgan, Robin, ed. 1970. *Sisterhood Is Powerful: An Anthology of Writings from the Women's Liberation Movement.* New York: Vintage Books.

Morgen, Sandra. 2002. *Into Our Own Hands: The Women's Health Movement in the United States, 1969–1990.* New Brunswick, NJ: Rutgers University Press.

Muhammed, Dedrick. 2008a. "Forty Years Later: The Unrealized American Dream." Paper presented to the Program on Inequality and the Common Good, Institute for Policy Studies, Washington, D.C. April. www. ips-dc.org.

———. 2008b. "Race and Extreme Inequality." *The Nation,* June 30, 26–27.

Muller v. Oregon, 208 U.S. 412 (1908).

Mullings, Leith. 1997. *On Our Own Terms: Race, Class, and Gender in the Lives of African American Women.* New York: Routledge.

Murray, Charles. 1984. *Losing Ground: American Social Policy, 1950–1980.* New York: Basic Books.

Muwakkil, Salim. 2007. "Globalism with Combat Boots." *In These Times,* 31, no.5 (April 19). http://www.inthesetimes.com/article/3127/globalism_with_combat_boots.

Nadasen, Premilla. 2004. *Welfare Warriors: The Welfare Rights Movement in the United States.* New York: Routledge.

Nakatani, Paulo, and Remy Herrera. 2007. "The South Has Already Repaid Its External Debt to the North: But the North Denies Its Debt to the South." *Monthly Review* 59, no. 2: 31–36.

Naples, Nancy A., ed. 1998. *Community Activism and Feminist Politics: Organizing Across Race, Class, and Gender.* New York: Routledge.

Nash, June. 1980. "Aztec Women: The Transition from Status to Class in Empire and Colony." Pp. 134–148 in *Women and Colonization: Anthropological Perspectives,* edited by Mona Etienne and Eleanor Burke Leacock. New York: Praeger.

Nasser, Alan G. 2003. "The Tendency to Privatize." *Monthly Review* 54, no. 10: 23–37.

National Manpower Council. 1957. *Womanpower: A Statement by the National Manpower Council with Chapters by the Council Staff.* New York: Columbia University Press.

Navarro, Vincent. 2007. "The Worldwide Class Struggle." Pp. 19–34 in *More Unequal: Aspects of Class in the United States,* edited by Michael D. Yates. New York: Monthly Review Press.

Newsinger, John. 2008. "Liberal Imperialism and the Occupation of Egypt in 1882." *Race and Class* 49, no. 3: 54–75.

Nicholson, Linda, ed. 1990. *Feminism/Postmodernism.* New York: Routledge.

Nussbaum, Karen. 2007. "Working Women's Insurgent Consciousness." Pp. 159–176 in *The Sex of Class: Women Transforming American Labor,* edited by Dorothy Sue Cobble. Ithaca, NY: ILR Press.

Nussbaum, Martha. 2006. *Frontiers of Justice: Disability, Nationality, Species Membership.* Cambridge, MA: Belknap Press.

Obando, Ana Elena. 2005. "Sexism in the World Social Forum: Is Another World Possible?" Women's Human Rights.Net, Association for Women's Rights in Development. www.whrnet.org/docs/issue-sexism_wsf.html.

Omi, M., and H. Winant. 1986. *Racial Formation in the United States.* London: Routledge and Kegan Paul.

Omolade, Barbara. 1990. "Writing the History of Women's Liberation: Alice Echols' *Daring to Be Bad.*" Roundtable at Berkshire Conference on the History of Women, June 1–4, Douglass College, Rutgers University, New Brunswick, New Jersey.

———. 1994. *The Rising Song of African American Women.* New York: Routledge.

Ong, Aihwa. 1987. *Spirits of Resistance and Capitalist Discipline: Factory Women in Malaysia.* Albany: State University of New York Press.

Oppenheimer, Valerie K. 1970. *The Female Labor Force in the United States: Demographic and Economic Factors Governing Its Growth and Changing Composition.* Westport, CT: Greenwood.

O'Reilly, Jane. 2002 [1972]. "Click! The Housewife's Moment of Truth." *Ms.* (Spring). http://www.msmagazine.com/spring2002/fromtheissue.asp.

Orloff, Ann. 2002. "Explaining U.S. Welfare Reform: Power, Gender, Race, and the U.S. Policy Legacy." *Critical Social Policy* 22: 96–118.

Osborn, Andrew. 2001. "Landmark Ruling for Women's Human Rights: Mass Rape Ruled a War Crime." *Guardian*, February 23. http://www.commondreams.org/cgi-bin/print.cgi?file=/headlines01/0224–02.htm.

Oza, Rupal. 2006. *The Making of Neoliberal India: Nationalism, Gender, and the Paradoxes of Globalization*. New York: Routledge.

Parenti, Michael. 2000. *To Kill a Nation: The Attack on Yugoslavia*. London: Verso Books.

Parrenas, Rachel Salazar. 2001. *Servants of Globalization: Women, Migration, and Domestic Work*. Palo Alto, CA: Stanford University Press.

Pateman, Carole. 1988. *The Sexual Contract*. Palo Alto, CA: Stanford University Press.

Paul, James A. 2000. "NGOs and Global Policy-Making." *Global Policy Forum*. www.globalpolicy.org.ngos/analysis/anal00.htm.

Perkins, John. 2004. *Confessions of an Economic Hit Man*. San Francisco: Berrett-Koehler.

Perman, Sarah, with Laurent Duvillier, Natacha David, John Eden, and Samuel Grumiau. 2004. *Behind the Brand Names: Working Conditions and Labor Rights in Export Processing Zones*. International Confederation of Free Trade Unions. www.icftu.org. www/PDF/EPZreportE.pdf.

Petchesky, Rosalind P. 1990. *Abortion and Women's Choice: The State, Sexuality, and Reproductive Freedom*. Rev. ed. Boston: Northeastern University Press.

———. 2003. *Global Prescriptions: Gendering Health and Human Rights*. London: Zed Books/UN Research Institute for Social Development.

Peterson, V. Spike, and Anne Sisson Runyan. 1999. *Global Gender Issues*. 2nd ed. Boulder, CO: Westview Press.

Petras, James, and Henry Weltmeyer. 2001. *Globalization Unmasked: Imperialism in the 21st Century*. Halifax, NS: Fernwood/Zed Books.

Phillips, Kevin. 2006. *American Theocracy: The Peril and Politics of Radical Religion, Oil, and Borrowed Money in the 21st Century*. New York: Viking.

Pietila, Hilkka. 2006. "Women as Agents for Development: Learning from the Experiences of Women in Finland?" Pp. 166–184 in *Global Feminism: Transnational Women's Activism, Organizing, and Human Rights*, edited by Myra Marx Ferree and Aili Mari Tripp. New York: New York University Press.

Pimpare, Stephen. 2004. "What Business Wanted from Welfare Reform." *CounterPunch* 11: 4–5.

———. 2006. *New Victorians: Poverty, Politics, and Propaganda in Two Gilded Ages*. New York: New Press.

Plessy v. Ferguson, 163 U.S. 537 (1896).

Polanyi, Karl. 1944. *The Great Transformation*. Boston: Beacon Press.

Pollin, Robert. 2003. *Contours of Descent: U.S. Economic Fractures and the Landscape of Global Austerity*. London: Verso Books.

Poster, Winifred, and Zakia Salime. 2002. "The Limits of Microcredit: Transnational Feminism and USAID Activities in the United States and Morocco." Pp. 189–219 in *Women's Activism and Globalization: Linking Local Struggles and Transnational Politics,* edited by Nancy A. Naples and Manisha Desai. New York: Routledge.

Potter, Will. 2006. "Analysis of the Animal Enterprise Terrorism Act." *GreenIstheNewRed.com*. www.greenisthenewred.com/blog/aeta-analysis-109th.

Prasad, Vijay. 2007. *The Darker Nations: A People's History of the Third World.* New York: New Press.

Pyle, Jean L., and Kathryn B. Ward. 2003. "Recasting Our Understanding of Gender and Work During Global Restructuring." *International Sociology* 18, no. 3: 461–489.

Queens College. 2006. "Queens College Announces Fund-Raising Campaign Goal of $100 Million." Office of Communications, March 30. http://www.qc.cuny.edu/nis/Releases/viewNews.php?id=198.

Quindlen, Anna. 2006. "The Last Word: Everyday Equality." *Newsweek,* September 25, 84.

Rai, Shirin M. 2002. *Gender and the Political Economy of Development: From Nationalism to Globalization.* Cambridge, UK: Polity.

Rajendra, Dania, and Peter Hogness. 2008. "Bad for Adjuncts and Students: Exploitation of Part-Timers Hurts Both." *Clarion: Newspaper of the Professional Staff Congress, City University of New York,* January 4.

Ralph, Diana. 2006. "Islamophobia and the 'War on Terror': The Continuing Pretext for U.S. Imperial Conquest." Pp. 261–298 in *The Hidden History of 9-11-2001,* edited by Paul Zarembka. Research in Political Economy Series, vol. 23. Amsterdam: Elsevier/JAI.

Randall, Margaret. 1992. *Gathering Rage: The Failure of Twentieth-Century Revolutions to Develop a Feminist Agenda.* New York: Monthly Review Press.

Ransby, Barbara. 2000. "Black Feminism at Twenty-one: Reflections on the Evolution of a National Community." *Feminisms at a Millennium,* special issue of *Signs* 25, no. 4: 1215–1221.

———. 2003. *Ella Baker and the Black Freedom Movement: A Radical Democratic Vision.* Chapel Hill: University of North Carolina Press.

Rapping, Elayne. 1997. *The Culture of Recovery.* Boston: Beacon Press.

Regents of the University of California v. Bakke 438 U.S. 265 (1978).

Remick, Helen, and Ronnie J. Steinberg, eds. 1984. *Comparable Worth and Wage Discrimination.* Philadelphia: Temple University Press.

Reskin, Barbara, and Patricia A. Roos. 1990. *Job Queues, Gender Queues: Explaining Women's Inroads into Male Occupations.* Philadelphia: Temple University Press.

Rich, Adrienne. 1980. "Compulsory Heterosexuality and Lesbian Existence." *Signs* 5, no. 4: 631–660.

Richie, Beth E. 1996. *Compelled to Crime: The Gender Entrapment of Battered Black Women.* New York: Routledge.

Roberts, Dorothy E. 1997. *Killing the Black Body: Race, Reproduction, and the Meaning of Liberty.* New York: Pantheon.

Roberts, Sam. 2007. "51% of Women Are Now Living Without Spouse." *New York Times,* January 16.

Roark, James L., Michael P. Johnson, Patricia Cline Cohen, Sarah Stage, Alan Lawson, and Susan M. Hartmann. 2006. *The American Promise: A Compact History,* 3d ed. New York: Macmillan.

Rodney, Walter. 1972. *How Europe Underdeveloped Africa.* London: Bogle-L'Overture.

Roe v. Wade, 410 U.S. 113 (1973).

Rosen, Ellen Israel. 2002. *Making Sweatshops: The Globalization of the U.S. Apparel Industry.* Berkeley and Los Angeles: University of California Press.

Rosen, Fred. 2003. "Mercosur's Hope." *NACLA* 37, no. 1: 7.

Rosen, Ruth. 2000. *The World Split Open: How the Modern Women's Movement Changed America.* New York: Viking.

Ross, Loretta J. 2006. "The Color of Choice: White Supremacy and Reproductive Justice." Pp. 53–65 in *Color of Violence: The Incite Anthology,* edited by Incite! Women of Color Against Violence. Boston: South End Press.

Rossi, Alice. 1977. "A Biosocial Perspective on Parenting." *Daedalus* 106, no. 2: 1–31.

Roth, Benita. 2004. *Separate Roads to Feminism: Black, Chicana, and White Feminist Movements in America's Second Wave.* Cambridge, UK: Cambridge University Press.

Rowbotham, Sheila, and Stephanie Linkogle. 1994a. "Introduction." Pp. 1–12 in *Women Resist Globalization: Mobilizing for Livelihood and Rights,* edited by Sheila Rowbotham and Stephanie Linkogle. London: Zed Books.

———, eds. 1994b. *Women Resist Globalization: Mobilizing for Livelihood and Rights.* London: Zed Books.

Roy, Ananya. 2007. "In Her Name: The Gender Order of Global Poverty Management." Pp. 28–39 in *The Wages of Empire: Neoliberal Policies, Repression, and Women's Poverty,* edited by Amalia L. Cabezas, Ellen Reese, and Marguerite Waller. Boulder, CO: Paradigm Publishers.

Roy, Arundhati. 1999. *The Cost of Living.* New York: Modern Library.

———. 2003. "Instant-Mix Imperial Democracy (Buy One, Get One Free)." Speech at the Riverside Church, New York City, May 13. http://cesr.org/arundhatiroytranscript.

Rubin, Gayle. 1975. "The Traffic in Women: Notes on the Political Economy of Sex." Pp. 175–210 in *Toward an Anthropology of Women,* ed. Rayna Reiter (Rapp). New York: Monthly Review Press.

Ruddick, Sara. 1995 [1989]. *Maternal Thinking: Toward a Politics of Peace.* Boston: Beacon Press.

Rupp, Leila J., and Verta A. Taylor. 1990. *Survival in the Doldrums: The American Women's Rights Movement, 1945 to the 1960s.* Columbus: Ohio State University Press.

Sandoval, Chela. 2000. *Methodology of the Oppressed.* Minneapolis: University of Minnesota Press.

Sargent, Lydia, ed. 1981. *Women and Revolution: A Discussion of the Unhappy Marriage of Marxism and Feminism.* Boston: South End Press.

Sawer, Marian. 1996. "Gender, Metaphor, and the State." *The World Upside Down: Feminisms in the Antipodes,* special issue of *Feminist Review* 52 (Spring): 118–143.

Schechter, Susan. 1983. *Women and Male Violence: The Visions and Struggles of the Battered Women's Movement.* Boston: South End Press.

Schneider, Elizabeth M. 2000. *Battered Women and Feminist Lawmaking.* New Haven, CT: Yale University Press.

Schwarz, Roberto. 2001. "City of God." Reviewing Brazilian novel by Paulo Lins. *New Left Review* 12 (November–December). http://www.newleftreview.org/?view=2359.

Seabrook, Jeremy. 2002. "Review of Naila Kabeer, *The Power to Choose: Bangladeshi Women and Labour Market Decisions in London and Dhaka.*" *Race and Class* 43: 78–82.

Sedghi, Hamideh. 2007. *Women and Politics in Iran: Veiling, Unveiling, and Reveiling.* Cambridge, UK: Cambridge University Press.

Semple, Kirk. 2003 "Tiniest of Loans Bring Big Payoff, Aid Group Says." *New York Times,* November 3.

Shih, Shu-mei, Sylvia Marcos, Obioma Nnaemeka, and Marguerite Waller. 2005. "Conversation on 'Feminist Imperialism and the Politics of Difference.'" Pp. 143–162 in *Dialogue and Difference: Feminisms Challenge Globalization,* edited by Marguerite Waller and Sylvia Marcos. New York: Palgrave Macmillan.

Shiva, Vandana. 1989. *Staying Alive: Women, Ecology, and Development.* London: Zed Books.

Shulman, Beth. 2005. *The Betrayal of Work: How Low-Wage Jobs Fail 30 Million Americans.* New York: New Press.

Sicko. 2007. Written, directed, and produced by Michael Moore. Executive produced by Kathleen Glynn, Harvey Weinstein, and Bob Weinstein. Dog Eat Dog Productions.

Silliman, Jael, Marlene Gerber Fried, Loretta Ross, and Elena R. Gutierrez, eds. 2004. *Undivided Rights: Women of Color Organize for Reproductive Justice.* Boston: South End Press.

Sklair, Leslie. 2002. *Globalization: Capitalism and Its Alternatives.* Oxford, UK: Oxford University Press.

Sklar, Kathryn Kish. 1997. *Florence Kelley and the Nation's Work: The Rise of Women's Political Culture.* New Haven, CT: Yale University Press.

Skocpol, Theda. 1992. *Protecting Soldiers and Mothers: The Political Origins of Social Policy in the United States.* Cambridge, MA: Harvard University Press.

Slackman, Michael. 2007. "A Quiet Revolution in Algeria: Gains by Women." *New York Times,* May 26.

Smale, Alison. 2008. "Memo from St. Petersburg: Money Talks at Russian Forum as Business Leaders See Past Hurdles to Investing." *New York Times,* June 9.

Smith, Jackie, Marina Karides, Marc Becker, Dorval Brunelle, Christopher Chase-Dunn, Donatella della Porta, Rosalba Icaza Garza, Jeffrey S. Jris, Lorenzo Mosca, Ellen Reese, Peter (Jay) Smith, and Rolando Vazquez. 2008. *Global Democracy and the World Social Forums.* Boulder, CO: Paradigm Publishers.

Snitow, Ann. 1990. "A Gender Diary." Pp. 9–43 in *Conflicts in Feminism,* edited by Marianne Hirsch and Evelyn Fox Keller. New York: Routledge.

Snyder, Bethany. 2005. "The Welfare of Feminism: Struggle in the Midst of Reform." Pp. 1–21 in *Center on Women and Public Policy Case Study Program.* Hubert Humphrey Institute of Public Affairs, University of Minnesota, Minneapolis. www.hh.umn .edu/img/assets/23793/welfare_case.pdf.

Snyder, Margaret. 2006. "Unlikely Godmother: The UN and the Global Women's Movement." Pp. 24–50 in *Global Feminism: Transnational Women's Activism, Organizing, and Human Rights,* edited by Myra Marx Ferree and Aili Mari Tripp. New York: New York University Press.

Socolovsky, Jerome. 2004. "Spain's New Leader Appoints 8 Women to Cabinet." *Women's e-News,* May 9. http://www.womensenews.org/article.cfm/dyn/aid/1827/context/cover.

Sparr, Pamela, ed. 1994. *Mortgaging Women's Lives: Feminist Critiques of Structural Adjustment.* London: Zed Books.

Spelman, Elizabeth. 1988. *Inessential Woman.* Boston: Beacon Press.

Spivak, Gayatri Chakravorty. 1990. *The Post-colonial Critic: Interviews, Strategies, Dialogues.* New York: Routledge.

———. 1999. *A Critique of Postcolonial Reason: Toward a History of the Vanishing Present.* Cambridge, MA: Harvard University Press.

Spruill, Marjorie. 2008. "Gender and America's Right Turn." Pp. 71–89 in *Rightward Bound: Making America Conservative in the 1970s,* edited by Bruce J. Shulman and Julian E. Zelizer. Cambridge, MA: Harvard University Press.

Srinivasan, Bina. 2004. "Religious Fundamentalism, Community Disintegration, and Violence Against Women: All Issues Are Women's Issues." *Socialism and Democracy* 18, no. 1: 135–149.

Stacey, Judith. 1987. "Sexism by a Subtler Name? Post-industrial Conditions and Post-feminist Consciousness in the Silicon Valley." *Socialist Review* 17, no. 6: 7–28.

———. 1990. *Brave New Families: Stories of Domestic Upheaval in Late Twentieth-Century America.* New York: Basic Books.

———. 2001. "The Empress of Feminist Theory Is Overdressed." *Feminist Theory* 2, no. 1: 99–103.

———. 2006. "Not Acquiescence, but Multilingual Resistance." *WSQ: Women's Studies Quarterly* 34, nos. 1–2: 63–68.

Stein, Rob, and Michael Shear. 2009. "Funding Restored to Groups that Perform Abortions, Other Care." *Washington Post,* January 24. www.washingtonpost.com/wp-dyn/content/article/2009/01/23.

Stephen, Lynn. 1997. *Women and Social Movements in Latin America: Power from Below.* Austin: University of Texas Press.

———. 2007. "'We Are Brown, We Are Short, We Are Fat … We Are the Face of Oaxaca': Women Leaders in the Oaxaca Rebellion." *Socialism and Democracy* 21, no. 2: 97–112.

Stetson, Dorothy McBride, and Amy Mazur. 1995. *Comparative State Feminism.* Thousand Oaks, CA: Sage.

Stevens, Jacob. 2001. "Barring the Doors." *New Left Review* 12 (November–December): 152–159.

Structural Adjustment Participatory Review International Network. 2004. *Structural Adjustment: The SAPRI Report—the Policy Roots of Economic Crisis, Poverty, and Inequality.* London: Zed Books/Third World Network/Books for Change/IBON Foundation.

Sudbury, Julia. 2000. "Building Women's Movement Beyond 'Imperial Feminism.'" *San Francisco Chronicle,* March 27. www.commondreams.org/view/032800–103.htm.

———. 2006. "Rethinking Antiviolence Strategies: Lessons from the Black Women's Movement in Britain." Pp. 13–24 in *Color of Violence: The Incite! Anthology,* edited by Incite! Women of Color Against Violence. Boston: South End Press.

Summers, Lawrence H. 1992. "Investing in *All* the People." Policy Research Working Papers No. 905, Office of the Vice President, World Bank. http://www.worldbank.org.

Susser, Ida. 2009. *AIDS, Sex, and Culture: Global Politics and Survival in Southern Africa.* New York: Wiley/Blackwell.

Susskind, Yifat. 2007. "Promising Democracy, Imposing Theocracy: Gender-Based Violence and the U.S. War on Iraq." MADRE: An International Human Rights Organization. www.madre.org.

Sussman, Gerald. 2006. "The Myths of 'Democracy Assistance': U.S. Political Intervention in Post-Soviet Eastern Europe." *Monthly Review* 58, no. 7: 15–29.

Swarns, Rachel L. 2008. "Blacks Debate Civil Rights Risk in Obama's Rise." *New York Times,* August 25.

Tabb, William K. 1982. *The Long Default: New York City and the Urban Fiscal Crisis.* New York: Monthly Review Press.

———. 2001. *The Amoral Elephant: Globalization and the Struggle for Social Justice in the Twenty-first Century.* New York: Monthly Review Press.

Tait, Vanessa. 2007. "Expanding Labor's Vision: The Challenges of Workfare and Welfare Organizing." Pp. 194–210 in *The Sex of Class: Women Transforming American Labor,* edited by Dorothy Sue Cobble. Ithaca, NY: ILR Press.

Tanzer, Michael. 1995. "Globalizing the Economy: The Influence of the International Monetary Fund and the World Bank." *Monthly Review* 47, no. 4: 1–15.

Tax, Meredith. 2001. *The Rising of Women: Feminist Solidarity and Class Conflict, 1880–1917.* Champaign: University of Illinois Press, 2001.

Thistle, Susan. 2006. *From Marriage to the Market: The Transformation of Women's Lives and Work.* Berkeley and Los Angeles: University of California Press.

Thom, Mary. 1997. *Inside Ms.: 25 Years of the Magazine and the Feminist Movement.* New York: Henry Holt.

Tong, Rosemary. 2008. *Feminist Thought: A More Comprehensive View.* 3rd ed. Boulder, CO: Westview Press.

Tough, Paul. 2008. "A Teachable Moment." *New York Times Magazine,* August 17, 30–37, 46, 50–51.

Tripp, Aili Mari. 2006. "Challenges in Transnational Feminist Mobilization." Pp. 296–312 in *Global Feminism: Transnational Women's Activism, Organizing, and Human Rights,* edited by Myra Marx Ferree and Aili Mari Tripp. New York: New York University Press.

Tronto, Joan C. 1993. *Moral Boundaries: A Political Argument for an Ethic of Care.* New York: Routledge.

Tsikata, Dzodzi. n.d. "Effects of Structural Adjustment on Women and the Poor." *TWN: Third World Network.* http://www.twnside.org.sg/title/adjus-cn.html.

Uchitelle, Louis, and David Leonhardt. 2006. "Men Not Working, and Not Wanting Just Any Job." *New York Times,* July 31.

United Nations Children's Fund. 2006. *The State of the World's Children 2007: Women and Children—the Double Dividend of Gender Equality.* New York: United Nations. www.unicef.org/sowc07/docs/sowc07.pdf.

United Nations Development Programme. 2005. *Arab Human Development Report 2005: Toward the Rise of Women in the Arab World.* New York: United Nations.

United Nations Population Fund. 2006. *State of World Population 2006. A Passage to Hope: Women and International Migration.* www.unfpa.org/upload/lib_pub_file/650_filename-sowp06-en.pdf.

U.S. Census Bureau. 2001. *Statistical Abstract of the United States.* Washington, DC: GPO.

———. 2002. *Statistical Abstract of the United States.* Washington, DC: GPO.

———. 2003. *Statistical Abstract of the United States.* Washington, DC: GPO.

U.S. Department of Labor, Office of Policy Planning and Research. 1965. *The Negro Family: The Case for National Action.* Washington, DC: GPO. http://www.dol.gov/oasam/programs/history/webid-moyniham.htm.

———. 2008. "Usual Weekly Earnings of Wage and Salary Workers: First Quarter 2008." April 17. http://www.bls.gov/news.release/wkyeng.htm.

U.S. Department of State. 2004. "Numbers and Kinds of U.S. Forces Deployed Abroad May Change." http://usinfo.state.gov/utils/printpage.html.

Vance, Carole S., ed. 1984. *Pleasure and Danger: Exploring Female Sexuality.* London: Routledge and Kegan Paul.

Venezuela: A 21st-Century Revolution. 2003. Produced by Global Women's Strike. www .globalwomenstrike.net.

Visvanathan, Nalini, Lynn Duggan, Laurie Nisonoff, and Nan Wiegersma, eds. 1997. *The Women, Gender, and Development Reader.* London: Zed Books.

Vogel, Lise. 1993. *Mothers on the Job: Maternity Policy in the U.S. Workplace.* New Brunswick, NJ: Rutgers University Press.

———. 1995. *Woman Questions: Essays for a Materialist Feminism.* New York: Routledge.

Wagner, Peter. 2002. "Importing Constituents: Prisoners and Political Clout in New York." Prison Policy Initiative Report, April 22. http://www.prisonpolicy.org/ importing/importing.html.

Waldman, Amy. 2003. "Meeting on New Constitution, Afghan Women Find Old Attitudes." *New York Times,* December 16.

Walker, Alice. 1983. *In Search of Our Mothers' Gardens: Womanist Prose.* New York: Harcourt Brace Jovanovich.

———. 1992. *Possessing the Secret of Joy.* New York: Harcourt Brace Jovanovich.

Walker, Alice, and Prathibha Parmar. 1993. *Warrior Marks: Female Genital Mutilation and the Sexual Blinding of Women.* New York: Harcourt Brace.

Walker, Kristen. 2008. "Venezuela's Women's Development Bank—Creating a Caring Economy." *Venezuelanalysis.* http://www.venezualanalysis.com/analysis/3644.

Wallace, Michele. 1979. *Black Macho and the Myth of the Superwoman.* New York: Dial.

"Wanted: A New Regional Agenda for Economic Growth." 2003. *The Economist,* April 24. www.economist.com/world/la/PrinterFriendly.cfm?story_id=17.

Waring, Marilyn. 1999. *Counting for Nothing: What Men Value and What Women Are Worth.* 2nd ed. Toronto: University of Toronto Press.

Warrior Marks. 1993. Produced by Alice Walker. Directed and edited by Prathibha Parmar. Women Make Movies.

Weigand, Kate. 2001. *Red Feminism: American Communism and the Making of Women's Liberation.* Baltimore, MD: Johns Hopkins University Press.

Weinstein, James. 2002 [1976]. "A Job Whose Time Has Come." *In These Times,* 26, no. 6 (February 16), 16.

Weisbrot, Mark. 2006. "'Globalization for Americans Is Really About Income Distribution." Center for Economic and Policy Research, September 2–4. http://www.cepr .net/columns/weisbrot/2006_09_04.htm.

Weisman, Steven R. 2007. "A Battle Fought in the Factories." *New York Times,* December 11.

Weiss, Martin D. 2007. "Financial System in Jeopardy!" *Financial Sense Editorials,* August 13. www.financialsense.com/editorials/weiss2007/0813.html.

Welter, Barbara. 1966. "The Cult of True Womanhood: 1820–1860." *American Quarterly* 18, no. 2, Part 1 (Summer): 151–174.

White House. 2002. *Economic Report of the President.* www.gpoaccess.gov/eop/tables02 .html.

Wichterich, Christa. 2000. *The Globalized Woman: Reports from a Future of Inequality.* London: Zed Books/St. Martin's Press.

————. 2006. "The New 'Smarties' of the World Bank: Competitive Women." Women in Development, Europe, December. http://www.whrnet.org/docs/perspective-smarties–0701.html.

Wickramasinghe, Nira. 2005. "The Idea of Civil Society in the South: Imaginings, Transplants, Designs." *Science and Society* 69: 458–486.

Wise, Tim. 2005. "What's the Matter with White Folks?" *LiP Magazine,* March 21. http://www.lipmagazine.org.

Wolf, Eric R. 1997 [1982]. *Europe and the People Without History.* Berkeley and Los Angeles: University of California Press.

"Womenomics Revisited." 2007. *The Economist,* April 19, 1–3. www.economist.com/finance/PrinterFriendly.cfm?story_id=9038760.

Wood, Ellen Meiksins. 1999. *The Origin of Capitalism.* New York: Monthly Review Press.

Woodward, Susan L. 1995. *Balkan Tragedy: Chaos and Dissolution After the Cold War.* Washington, DC: Brookings Institution Press.

Woolf, Virginia. 1938. *Three Guineas.* New York: Harcourt Brace.

World Bank. 1996. *World Development Report 1996: From Plan to Market.* Oxford, UK: Oxford University Press.

————. 2006. *Gender Equality as Smart Economics: A World Bank Group Gender Action Plan (Fiscal Years 2007–2010).* September. http://siteresources.worldbankorg/INTGENDER/Resources/GAPNov.2/pdf.

World Economic Forum. 2007. "The Global Gender Gap Report 2007." www.wcforum.org/pdf/gendergap/report2007.pdf.

Worldwatch Institute. 2008. "Microloans Pay Off for Planet, Investors." http://us.oneworld.net/article/microloans-pay-off-planet-investors.

Yeatman, Anna. 1990. *Bureaucrats, Technocrats, Femocrats: Essays on the Contemporary Australian State.* Sydney: Allen and Unwin.

Yinger, Nancy V. 2007. "The Feminization of Migration: Limits of the Data." Population Reference Bureau, February. http://www.prb.org/Articles/2007/FeminizationofMigrationLimitsofData.aspx.

Zarembka, Paul, ed. 2006. *The Hidden History of 9-11-2001.* Research in Political Economy Series, vol. 23. Amsterdam: Elsevier/JAI.

Zirin, Dave. 2008. "COINTELPRO Comes to My Town: My First-Hand Experience with Government Spies." http://www.huffingtonpost.com/dave-zirin/cointelpro-comes-to-my-to_b_11390.html.

Zlotnik, Hania. 2003. "The Global Dimensions of Female Migration." Migration Information Source, March 1. http://www.migrationinformation.rg/Feature/display.cfm?ID=109.

Index

❋

About the Author

❋

Hester Eisenstein is a professor of sociology at Queens College and the Graduate Center, City University of New York. Her previous books include *Contemporary Feminist Thought* (1983) and *Inside Agitators: Australian Femocrats and the State* (1996). She has taught at Yale University, Barnard College (Columbia University), and the State University of New York at Buffalo; she also has served as a "femocrat" in the state government of New South Wales, Sydney, Australia.